Grand Crosses of the Court of Honour

Grand Crosses
of the Court of Honour

Concise Scottish Rite Biographical Dictionary

Larissa P. Watkins

Tamera L. Fannin
Editor and Database Consultant

Foreword
by
William Michael Alexander, 33°, Grand Cross
Personal Representative and Secretary, Valley of Seoul Korea
Past Master, Pusan Korea Lodge #1675 AF&AM Grand Lodge of Scotland

Historical Introduction
by
Shane Allen Harshbarger, 33°, Grand Cross
Secretary, Valley of Des Moines, Iowa
Past Master, Malta Lodge #318, AF&AM of Iowa

Thoughts on Masonic Honors
by
S. Brent Morris, 33°, Grand Cross

Former Editor, Scottish Rite Journal and Heredom
Past Master, Patmos-Solomon's Lodge #70, AF&AM of Maryland
Past Master, Quatuor Coronati Lodge #2076, English Constitution

Westphalia Press
Washington, D.C. ● 2022

Westphalia Press
An imprint of Policy Studies Organization
1367 Connecticut Ave NW
Washington, D.C. 20036
info@ipsonet.org

ISBN: 978-1-63723-924-7

Daniel Gutierrez-Sandoval, Executive Director
PSO and Westphalia Press

Updated material and comments on this edition
can be found at the Westphalia Press website:
www.westphaliapress.org

Table of Contents

Foreword

by

Colonel U.S. Army (Retired) ILL. William Michael Alexander, 33°, Grand Cross

The Supreme Council of the Southern Jurisdiction established the Court of Honour on July 10, 1870. The Active Members of the Supreme Council voted (21) twenty-one affirmative and no negative. The vote was announced and attested by Albert G. Mackey, 33°, Grand Secretary, and approved by Sovereign Grand Commander Albert Pike in the official Bulletin of the Supreme Council on the same date—thus began the history of the highest award the Southern Jurisdiction of the Scottish Rite, the Mother Council, can bestow.

On May 9, 1872, 150 years ago to the day that I write this, William Edward Leffingwell of Lyons, Iowa, became the very first recipient of the Grand Cross, and almost three years ago, I was extremely honored to be the first recipient of the Grand Cross from the Valley of Seoul, Korea. As a retired Army officer and currently a museum director and historian of the U.S. Army Museum in Korea, I was aware of the select few military members from the armed services who were recipients of the Grand Cross. My personal favorite or "hero," which, I think, is the correct term to use, is General Harold Keith Johnson, U.S. Army, who served as Chief of Staff of the U.S. Army from 1964-1968.

A true American hero, General Johnson served in World War II, was decorated for bravery, and was a survivor of the Bataan Death March. In the Korean War, he received the Distinguished Service Cross, the second highest decoration for heroism, for his valor and leadership. Upon seeing how the Masons looked out for each during his time as a POW, he was determined to become one. This was accomplished soon after he returned to the United States after WWII. Later in 1965, while serving as the Army Chief of Staff, he served as the active candidate for the 33° Class in Washington D.C. In 1979, he became the Director of Education and Americanism for the Scottish Rite, S. J., and in 1981, was awarded the Grand Cross. General Johnson served the Scottish Rite, S.J., until his death in 1983. He was eulogized by Sovereign Grand Commander Henry C. Clausen in both the 1983 and 1985 Scottish Rite, S.J. *Transactions*.

As a new Mason in my late 20s, the first Scottish Rite brochure I saw had a picture of General Johnson as a Grand Cross. I did not recognize the hat at the time, but I recognized the general who had been Chief of Staff of the Army when I had started JROTC. Because of my interest in the history of the Scottish Rite, I knew that the information about Grand Crosses was spread out among many publications, histories, and transactions of the Scottish Rite, S.J., and I lamented the fact that it was not readily available in one place. I discussed this with several distinguished Scottish Rite Masons but resigned myself to the fact it would not be resolved anytime soon, or so I thought.

Those of us who have the privilege of traveling to the House of the Temple know of the outstanding staff members who keep the flame burning and are true stalwarts and heroes of the day-to-day operations. One though, who stands out is the librarian at the Supreme Council, S.J., Larissa P. Watkins. In the tradition of great librarians before her at the House of the Temple in Washington, D.C.—Harris, Carter, and Baum—Larissa Watkins has been a great steward, faithful to her trust to enable the library to serve as a stellar example of what a library should be. Also, Ms. Watkins' numerous works, including Albert Pike's *String of*

Pearls, are known to most Scottish Rite Masons. It should come as no surprise to discover, working constantly on numerous things at once as she always does, that a comprehensive, correct list with a brief biography of each Grand Cross recipient going back 150 years was one of her pet projects. What you are holding in your hand now is that work. This book is the result of her hard work, and it is the outstanding stories of Scottish Rite Masons who have made a difference, from a president to a king, businessmen, professionals, religious leaders, actors, athletes, members of the armed services, and everyday Masonic Brothers who have left an imprint on their communities. These are their stories and a look at our Great Scottish Rite history.

Please join me as we journey 150 years to the present to see those Brothers who were honored for their service to Freemasonry, the Scottish Rite, our country, and to mankind.

33° Grand Cross

Paengseong

South Korea

May 9, 2022

Historical Introduction

by

Ill. Shane Allen Harshbarger, 33°, Grand Cross

"Before the first day of each regular session each Sovereign Grand Inspector General or Deputy of the Supreme Council may, by sealed letter addressed to the Sovereign Grand Commander, nominate one Inspector General Honorary from his Orient for investiture with the dignity of Grand Cross for signal services and unusual merit, which he shall specify. These letters shall show, on the outside of the envelope, the following words, "Nomination for Grand Cross," without the name of the nominee, and shall be laid, with seals unbroken, before the Sovereign Grand Commander, who shall refer them to a committee consisting of all the members of the Council of Administration present at the session, by whom they shall be opened. The recommendations shall be read, and the committee shall proceed to select, by unanimous consent, the Grand Cross nominees."[1] Thus reads the current *Statutes of the Supreme Council of the Thirty-third Degree* regarding the highest honor available to a Scottish Rite Mason.

The Grand Cross of the Court of Honour was established by our Supreme Council on June 8, 1870.[2] This action created first a Court of Honour in which to house two ranks, the Knight Commander of the Court of Honour and the Grand Cross of the Court of Honour. It was to recognize certain 32° Masters of the Royal Secret for their zeal, devotion, and service to the Scottish Rite. Each Active Member of the Supreme Council was entitled to nominate two Masters of the Royal Secret from his Orient for the Knight Commander of the Court of Honour. From those nominees, three shall be selected by the Supreme Council to receive the Grand Cross.[3]

At the 1872 Supreme Council session, forty-one brethren were elected to receive the Knight Commander of the Court of Honour. From this group, the first to be elected to receive the decoration of Grand Cross was Bro. William E. Leffingwell of Iowa on May 8, 1872, in Louisville, KY.[4] By 1874, Grand Commander Pike had designed the patent and jewels for both the K∴C∴C∴H∴ and the Grand Cross of Honour.[5]

Subsequently, the Supreme Council would modify the Court of Honour to the current system whereby 32° Masters of the Royal Secret are elected to receive the Knight Commander of the Court of Honor and 33° Inspectors General Honorary to receive the Grand Cross.

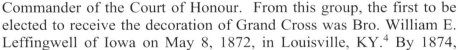

Inspectors-General Honorary prefix the Double Cross in red ink, and sign:

≠ E............... F...................

Insp∴ Gen∴ Honorary.

A Grand Cross Thirty-second Degree of the Court of Honor prefixes the Double Upright Cross, signing thus:

W............... H...................32°

Gr∴ Cross C∴ of Hon∴.

A Knight Commander prefixes a single Upright Cross, and signs:

✝ P............... V...................32°

Kt∴ Comm∴ C∴ of Hon∴

The Official Signatures showing the 32° Grand Cross and 32° KCCH. 1901 Statutes of the Supreme Council

Today, the Grand Cross of the Court of Honour holds the singular place as the highest honor bestowed by the Supreme Council of the Ancient and Accepted Scottish Rite. Each Active Member of the Supreme Council is deemed, *virtute officii sui,* an honorary recipient of the Grand Cross of the Court of Honour.[6] However, they do not receive the Grand Cross jewel or cap. The full honors of the Grand Cross are reserved for those who have been unanimously elected by the Supreme Council. The concept of a Court of Honour was developed by Grand Commander Albert Pike, who had become concerned that the 33° Inspector General Honorary had been given too frequently and without warrant. Therefore, he proposed at the 1870 Supreme Council session in Baltimore, the creation of the Court of Honour, whereby men of merit would be honored.[7] From that select group, after a time, originally one year, the 33° Inspector General Honorary could be conferred upon them. Today, a minimum of forty-four months must elapse between the election to receive the Knight Commander of the Court of Honour and the 33° Inspector General Honorary. There is not a set time that must pass for a 33° Inspector General to be elected to receive the Grand Cross, although the time is often many years or decades for that consideration.

The Grand Cross has always been restricted in number. At its inception, the number to receive the Grand Cross was limited to three per Supreme Council session. Pike decreed that he would only vote to award the Grand Cross of the Court of Honour to men *"for extraordinary services, long-continued labor, and the most faithful and earnest devotion to the Rite."*[8] In reviewing the Grand Cross rolls, one will notice that for many years less than three honorees were approved. The Grand Cross of Honour was often limited to Scottish Rite Masons that were public figures, politicians, or military. The 1990s brought a change in philosophy as more Scottish Rite Masons were recognized for their efforts within Freemasonry by the Supreme Council by being invested with the Grand Cross of the Court of Honour.

The Knight Commander and Grand Cross are unique in Scottish Rite as they are not degrees but ranks and investitures. They are given for outstanding service and actions that have brought honor to the fraternity. Originally, neither honor had an official ceremony of investiture. Oftentimes, the designee was formally presented and invested with his patent and jewel by the Sovereign Grand Commander at the Supreme Council Session and seated in the East.[9]

In 1913, Lt. Grand Commander George Moore, 33° wrote and presided at the first ceremonial investiture for the Knight Commander of the Court of Honour.[10] Then over one-hundred years passed before the Supreme Council approved an investiture ceremony for the Grand Cross. It was written by the Grand Archivist, Arturo De Hoyos, 33° G∴C∴ and approved at the session in 2019.[11]

In the ceremony, the Sovereign Grand Commander tells the designates *"The Grand Cross of the Court of Honour is the highest honor which this, or any Supreme Council, can bestow. It must, of necessity, be conferred sparingly, so as not to diminish the dignity which it represents as the mark of Masonic excellence."*[12]

This book that permanently records and honors those who have received the Grand Cross is a singular and unique record of those who have attained said mark. It remains to be seen what additional names shall be added to this list in future years.

Sincerely and Fraternally,

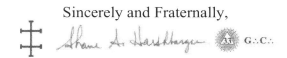

---

[1] Statutes of the Supreme Council, 2019, p. 70.

[2] Transactions of the Supreme Council, 1870, p. 95.

[3] Transactions of the Supreme Council, 1870, p. 254.

[4] Transactions of the Supreme Council, 1872, p. 55.

[5] Transactions of the Supreme Council, 1903, p. 166.

[6] Ritual Monitor and Guide, De Hoyos, 2010, p. 130.

[7] Transactions of the Supreme Council, 1870, p. 17.

[8] Transactions of the Supreme Council, 1872, p. 30.

[9] The Supreme Council, Lobingier, 1931, p. 473.

[10] The Supreme Council, Lobingier, 1931, p. 471.

[11] Transactions of the Supreme Council, 2019, p. 141.

[12] Grand Cross of the Court of Honour, Supreme Council SJ, 2019, p. 10.

Thoughts on Masonic Honors

by

S. Brent Morris, 33°, G.C.

Abraham Lincoln told about a man being tarred, feathered, and ridden out of town on a rail. As he was balancing on the rail with tar dripping off him, he was asked what he thought of the ceremony. The hapless gentlemen replied, "If it weren't for the honor, I wouldn't be doing this."

That may be the incentive for tar and feathers, but it certainly is not the motivation for Masonic recognition. Neither I nor any of the Brethren here this evening—the newly initiated 33rds and we newly decorated Grand Crosses—are in this for recognition. Oh sure, like everyone else we see an award being given and think, "Isn't that nice! Maybe someday I can do something deserving of recognition." And then we get back to doing our work. The prime motivator of Masons is the self-satisfaction of helping others and of doing our jobs well. That's it. Everything else is icing on the cake.

Having now been honored with the Grand Cross, I'm reminded of a caution by Brother Mark Twain: "On the whole, it is better to deserve honors and not have them than to have them and not deserve them." Prior to tonight we had the luxury of thinking we may have been deserving but unrecognized. From now on we will have to worry about having honors and perhaps not deserving them. The best thing for us to do is to get right back to doing what we have been doing, but with a little more dedication and zeal.

Sovereign Grand Commander and members of the Supreme Council, we whom you have honored tonight sincerely thank you for the recognition you have given us and ask only for the opportunity to be of further service to our gentle craft.

Given at the Gala Banquet, 1999 Biennial Session

1872

William Edward Leffingwell
Grand Cross of the Court of Honour at age 50 years, 5 months, and 2 days
Tenure 12 years, 3 months, and 5 days
Nomination by Iowa Scottish Rite Bodies

Born: October 9, 1822 – Died: August 13, 1884
Life span: 61 years, 10 months, and 4 days
Lawyer

Progress in Scottish Rite Masonry:
4°-32°: date, place and by whom Degrees were invested, or communicated, unconfirmed.
32°, KCCH: May 8, 1872.
May 8, 1872, the Sovereign Grand Commander nominated Illustrious Brother William E. Leffingwell as an Honorary Inspector General, the nomination to lie over until the next biennial Session.
Grand Cross of the Court of Honour: May 8, 1872.
May 5, 1874, the nomination of Illustrious Bro. William E. Leffingwell, of Iowa, was withdrawn by the Sovereign Grand Commander.

Scottish Rite Biography:
William Edward Leffingwell, 32°, of Lyons, Iowa elected the Grand Cross of the Court of Honor for distinguished merit and extraordinary services rendered the Order.

Bibliography:
Archive of the Supreme Council, 33°, S.J.
Tableau of the Supreme Council Thirty-third Degree, for the Southern Jurisdiction of the United States, and the Bodies of its Obedience. 1877.

1874

Joseph Thomas Brown
Grand Cross of the Court of Honour at age about 31 years
Tenure about 44 years

Nomination by Sovereign Grand Commander Albert Pike, 33°
Orient of the District of Columbia

Born: 1843 – Died: June 25, 1918
Life span: about 75 years
Banker

Progress in Scottish Rite Masonry:
4°-14°: December 22, 1867, conferred by B.B. French, 33°, SGIG for the Orient of the District of Columbia.
15°-18°: April 19, 1870, conferred by B. B. French, 33°, SGIG for the Orient of the District of Columbia.
19°-32°: May 1, 1870, healed as a Sublime Prince of the Royal Secret by Ill. Benjamin Brown French, 33°, SGIG for the Orient of the District of Columbia by direction of Sovereign Grand Commander Albert Pike, 33°.
33°: May 3, 1870, elected and invested with the Thirty-third Degree of Sovereign Grand Inspector General, but without membership in the Supreme Council.
Grand Cross of the Court of Honour: May 8, 1874.

Scottish Rite Biography:
Brother Joseph Thomas Brown received the Scottish Rite Degrees by SGIG Benjamin B. French beginning in December 1867. He did not, however, complete the Degree process until May 1, 1870. On May 3, 1870, Brown received the Thirty-third Degree by the Supreme Council. On May 20, French appointed Brown his Deputy Inspector General and assisted French in the performance of his duties. Following French's sudden death in August 1870, he prepared a eulogy which was memorialized during the Supreme Council's subsequent Lodge of Sorrow. He succeeded French as the District's Special Deputy of the Supreme Council and participated in the formation of *Mithras* Lodge of Perfection on December 30, 1870. Brother Brown moved to New York in 1873, but continued to attend Supreme Council sessions in Washington, D.C., and on May 8, 1874, was elected by the Supreme Council to receive the Grand Cross.

Bibliography:
Archive of the Supreme Council, 33°, S.J.
Archives of the Orient of the District of Columbia and Archives of the Grand Lodge of the District of Columbia, F.A.A.M.

1874

John William Cook
Grand Cross of the Court of Honour at age about 53 years, 6 months, and 14 days
Tenure 20 years, 10 months, and 2 days
Nomination by Inspector Webber, 33°, Louisville, Orient of Kentucky

Born: August 24, 1820 – Died: March 30, 1895
Life span: about 74 years, 7 months, and 6 days
Jeweler

Progress in Scottish Rite Masonry:
4°-32°: date, place and by whom Degrees were conferred or communicated unconfirmed.
33°, IGH: elected May 2, 1870; coroneted by the Supreme Council, 33°, S.J., May 3, 1870.
KCCH: May 8, 1872.
Grand Cross of the Court of Honour: May 8, 1874.

Scottish Rite Biography:
On May 2, 1870, during the Session of the Supreme Council, Inspector-General Webber nominated John W. Cook, of Louisville, Kentucky to receive the Thirty-Third Degree, and for Honorary Membership; and the vote being taken *viva voce* and being unanimous in favor and he was declared duly elected. On May 3, 1870, Brother Cook was introduced and crowned as Sovereign Grand Inspector-General and Honorary Member of the Supreme Council. On May 8, 1872, during the Session of the Supreme Council, on motion of Inspector Buist, the Supreme Council proceeded to call of the States for the nomination of Honorary Inspectors-General to be invested with the decoration of Knight Commander of the Court of Honour, when the Illustrious John W. Cook, 33°, was elected. On May 8, 1874, during the Session of the Supreme Council, on the nomination of Inspector-General Webber, Illustrious John W. Cook, 33°, was elected to receive the decoration of Grand Cross of the Court of Honor. Based on the Grand Commander's circular-letter of January 10, 1882, Brother Cook participated in communication of the Degrees of the Ancient and Accepted Scottish Rite from 4° to the 32° inclusive, on a few Master Masons.

Bibliography:
Archive of the Supreme Council, 33°, S.J.
Cook, John William. Report. *Transactions.* 1882: 92-93.
In Memoriam. *Transactions.* 1895: 361.

1874

Abraham Ephraim Frankland
Grand Cross of the Court of Honour at age 42 years, 8 months, and 27 days
Tenure 20 years, 11 months, and 25 days
Nomination by Sovereign Grand Commander Albert Pike, 33°, Orient of Tennessee

Born: August 8, 1831 – Died: April 30, 1895
Life span: 63 years, 8 months, and 22 days
Educator

Progress in Scottish Rite Masonry:
4°-32°: date and place unconfirmed, communicated by Sovereign Grand Commander Albert Pike, 33°.
33°, IGH: elected and coroneted September 18, 1868.
KCCH: May 8, 1872.
Deputy: for West Tennessee, c1871 - May 5, 1874.
SGIG: elected and crowned May 5, 1874; resigned and Emeritus October 18, 1880.
Grand Cross of the Court of Honour: May 5, 1874.

Scottish Rite Biography:
Brother Frankland received the Degrees of the Ancient and Accepted Scottish Rite from his warm and steadfast friend and Brother, Albert Pike, and became an indefatigable student of his philosophy. He was elected an Honorary Inspector on September18, 1868; an Active Member of the Supreme Council on May 5, 1874; an Emeritus Member on October 18, 1880; and in all these honorable positions displayed an earnest zeal highly commendable. It was the teaching of the Rite that prompted his action during the terrible ravage of the yellow fever at Memphis. When others fled from the death-striking city he stood fearless and valiant at his post of duty, relieving sorrow, attending to and succoring the sick, burying the dead, and relieving the distressed. Recognizing these faithful and disinterested benevolent deeds, the citizens of Memphis presented him with a beautiful gold medal suitably inscribed, and he received another from the Supreme Council, of which he was an Active Member, for his performance of benevolent Masonic duty.

Bibliography:
Archive of the Supreme Council, 33°, S.J.
In Memoriam. *Transactions*. 1895:9; 343-345.

1874

Robert McCoskry Graham
Grand Cross of the Court of Honour at age 43 years, 7 months, and 9 days
Tenure 13 years, 5 months, and 17 days

Nomination by the Supreme Council, 33°, S.J., USA for Northern Jurisdiction, USA

Born: September 28, 1830 – Died: December 13, 1890
Life span: 60 years, 2 months, and 15 days
Insurance

Progress in Scottish Rite Masonry:
4°-32°: date, place, and by whom Degrees were communicated unconfirmed.
33°, Active Member for the Northern Jurisdiction: 1866.
Representative of this Supreme Council [Southern Jurisdiction] to the Northern Jurisdiction: c1868.
33°, IGH [Southern Jurisdiction]: May 3, 1870, on the Sovereign Grand Commander's recommendation elected to Honorary membership of this Supreme Council, date and place of coronation unconfirmed.
Grand Cross of the Court of Honour: May 7, 1874, Illustrious Brother John M.C. Graham, Representative of this Supreme Council to the Northern Jurisdiction, having been elected by the Supreme Council to receive the decoration of Grand Cross of the Court of Honor, was called before the pedestal and appropriately invested with the decoration by the Sovereign Grand Commander. Illustrious Brother Graham returned his thanks for the honor conferred upon him.

Scottish Rite Biography:
Robert McCoskry Graham, 33°, was an Active Member of the Supreme Council for the Northern Jurisdiction since 1866, and its Deputy for the State of New York since 1878 until 1889; Grand Cross Honorary of our Court of Honour, Emeritus Member of Honor of our Supreme Council, and our Grand Representative near that for the Northern Jurisdiction since 1867. During the last ten years he had regularly been present at our sessions, feeling like one of us, and looked upon by us as one of ourselves, so much so that he sat with us in our confidential sessions, always welcome and beloved by all … Our Supreme Council has lost a true friend and most faithful Representative, whose name shall never be mentioned without honour among us.

Bibliography:
Pike, Albert. *Ex Corde Locutiones. Words from the Heart Spoken of His Dead Brethren.* Washington, D.C.: 1897.
Archive of the Supreme Council, 33°, S.J.
In Memoriam. *Transactions.* 1890: 82.

1874

William Morton Ireland
Grand Cross of the Court of Honour at age 39 years, 11 months, and 23 days
Tenure 11 years, 9 months, and 11 days
Nomination by Sovereign Grand Commander Albert Pike, 33°
Orient of the District of Columbia

Born: May 12, 1834 – Died: December 24, 1892
Life span: 58 years, 7 months, and 11 days
Grand Secretary-General

Progress in Scottish Rite Masonry:
4°-32°: date and place unconfirmed, conferred by the Scottish Rite Bodies of the Northern Jurisdiction.
KCCH: May 8, 1872.
33°, IGH: elected and coroneted May 5, 1874.
Deputy: 1871, appointed Deputy of the Sovereign Grand Commander for the District of Columbia –
resigned 1880.
SGIG: for North Carolina elected and crowned October 18, 1882; [from July 1, 1884, to 1884 the District
of Columbia for jurisdictional purposes annexed to North Carolina]; resigned March 24, 1886.
Grand Cross of the Court of Honour: May 5, 1874.

Scottish Rite Biography:
Brother William Morton Ireland became a Mason in *Union* Lodge, No. 121, Philadelphia, Pennsylvania on
January 10, 1856. He participated in the formation of the Scottish Rite Bodies in the District of Columbia:
Mithras Lodge of Perfection, No. 2; *Kedron* Council of Princes of Jerusalem, No. 1; *Evangelist* Chapter of
Knights Rose Croix, No. 1; *Robert De Bruce* Council of Kadosh, No. 1; *Albert Pike* Consistory, No. 1. He
served as *Mithras* Lodge's first Venerable Master, *Evangelist* Chapter's first Most Eloquent Orator, and
the *Robert De Bruce* Council's first Very Eminent Commander. In the Supreme Council Brother Ireland
was made a KCCH on May 8, 1872; Inspector General Honorary, May 5, 1874; Grand Cross, May 5,
1874; Active Member, elected and crowned, October 18, 1882; became Assistant Grand Auditor in 1874,
and was elected Secretary General, October 18, 1882. Brother Ireland resigned from the Supreme Council
on March 24, 1886.

Bibliography:
Archive of the Supreme Council, 33°, S.J.
Archives of the Orient of the District of Columbia and Archives of the Grand Lodge of the District of
Columbia, F.A.A.M.
In Memoriam. *Transactions.* 1893: 23.

1876

Clement Wells Bennett
Grand Cross of the Court of Honour at age 55 years, 1 month, and 9 days
Tenure 20 years, 4 months, and 17 days
Nomination by the District of Columbia Scottish Rite Bodies

Born: April 21, 1820 – Died: October 17, 1896
Life span: 76 years, 5 months, and 26 days
Lawyer & Claim Agent

Progress in Scottish Rite Masonry:
4°-32°: 1862, communicated by Ill. John L. Lewis, Jr. 33°, Deputy of New Jersey, Northern Jurisdiction.
KCCH: May 6, 1874.
33°, IGH: elected May 6, 1874; coroneted May 7, 1874.
Grand Cross of the Court of Honour: May 30, 1876.

Scottish Rite Biography:
During the year 1845 Brother Bennett was initiated, passed, and raised in Masonic Lodge No. 1078 of Penn Yan, New York. He received the Scottish Rite Degrees, 4° to 32°, in 1862 by John L. Lewis, Jr., 33°, the Deputy of New Jersey, Northern Jurisdiction. Bennett moved to Washington, D.C. and participated in the formation of *Mithras* Lodge of Perfection, No. 2, on December 30, 1870; *Kedron* Council of Princes of Jerusalem, No. 1, on December 30, 1870; *Evangelist* Chapter of Knights Rose Croix, No. 1, on December 7, 1871; *Robert De Bruce* Council of Kadosh, No. 1, on December 11, 1873; *Albert Pike* Consistory, No. 1, on January 6, 1876. On May 6, 1874, Brother Bennett was elected a KCCH, and coroneted Honorary Inspector-General by the Supreme Council, Southern Jurisdiction, the following day, May 7, 1874. Brother Bennett served as Wise Master of *Evangelist* Chapter from 1879-1881 and 1884-1887, Venerable Master of *Albert Pike* Consistory between January 1876-1880 and 1883-1885. Also, he served as trustee for *Robert de Bruce* Council, elected March 10, 1874, and for *Albert Pike* Consistory, elected February 10, 1884.

Bibliography:
Archive of the Supreme Council, 33°, S.J.
Archives of the Orient of the District of Columbia and Archives of the Grand Lodge of the District of Columbia, F.A.A.M.
In Memoriam. *Transactions.* 1897: 200-202.

1876

George Charles Betts
Grand Cross of the Court of Honour at age 36 years, 10 months, and 12 days
Tenure 26 years, 6 months, and 2 days
Nomination by Omaha, Nebraska Scottish Rite Bodies

Born: July 18, 1840 – Died: December 2, 1902
Life span: 61 years, 7 months, and 16 days
Priest

Progress in Scottish Rite Masonry:
4°-32°: date, place and by whom Degrees were conferred or communicated unconfirmed.
33°, IGH: elected May 2, 1870; coroneted by the Supreme Council, 33°, S.J., May 3, 1870.
Grand Cross of the Court of Honour: May 30, 1876.

Scottish Rite Biography:
On May 2, 1870, in the City of Baltimore, at the Masonic Hall, Inspector-General Webber, in behalf of Inspector-General Jordan, nominated George C. Betts, 32°, of Omaha, Nebraska, as a Sovereign Grand Inspector-General, and Honorary Member of the Supreme Council; and the vote being taken *viva voce*, and being unanimous in his favor, he was declared duly elected to receive the Degree and as Honorary Members, as an honorarium. On May 3, 1870, the Senatorial Chamber was thrown open to the Honorary Members of the Supreme Council, seven Brothers, who had been duly elected and prepared, were introduced and crowned as Sovereign Grand Inspectors-General, and Honorary Members of this Supreme Council and among them Ill. George Charles Betts, 33°.

Bibliography:
Archive of the Supreme Council, 33°, S.J.
In Memoriam. *Transactions*.1903: 383.

1876

Robert Farmer Bower
Grand Cross of the Court of Honour at age 53 years, 8 months, and 15 days
Tenure 5 years 11 months, and 11 days
Nomination by Iowa Scottish Rite Bodies

Born: September 15, 1823 – Died: May 19, 1882
Life span: 58 years, 8 months, and 3 days
Merchant

Progress in Scottish Rite Masonry:
4°-32°: date, place and by whom Degrees were invested, or communicated, unconfirmed.
32°, KCCH: May 9, 1872.
33°, IGH: elected May 7, 1868; coroneted September 19, 1868.
SGIG: elected and crowned May 30, 1876; laid down his Craft tools while in Office May 19, 1882.
Grand Cross of the Court of Honour: May 30, 1876.

Scottish Rite Biography:
Brother Bower was invested with the 33° Degree of Honorary Inspector General at St. Louis in September 1868, and crowned Inspector General and Active Member of the Supreme Council on the 30 of May 1876. Of cultivated taste and scholarly habits, he not only devoted his means lavishly to the accumulation of a Masonic and general Library for himself but was a chief founder of the Library of the City, and liberally devoted to its interests his time and money. [Brother Bower was] genial, generous, honourable, always faithful and true.

Bibliography:
Archive of the Supreme Council, 33°, S.J.
In Memoriam. *Transactions*. 1882: 145.

1876

John Sommers Buist
Grand Cross of the Court of Honour at age 36 years, 6 months, and 4 days
Tenure 34 years, 3 months, and 29 days
Nomination by Charleston, South Carolina Scottish Rite Bodies

Born: November 26, 1839 – Died: September 29, 1910
Life span: 70 years, 10 months, and 3 days
Surgeon

Progress in Scottish Rite Masonry:
4°-32°: date unconfirmed, Charleston, South Carolina, communicated by Ill. Albert G. Mackey, 33°, Grand Secretary General.
33°, IGH: elected May 2, 1870; coroneted by the Supreme Council, 33°, S.J., May 3, 1870.
Grand Cross of the Court of Honour: May 30, 1876.

Scottish Rite Biography:
Brother Buist was initiated, passed, and raised in *Washington* Lodge, No. 5, Charleston, South Carolina. He received the Scottish Rite Degrees by communication from Ill. Albert G. Mackey, 33°, Grand Secretary General at Charleston in 1870; served as a Trice Puissant Grand Master of *Delta* Lodge of Perfection, No. 1, Charleston. On May 3, 1870, at Baltimore, Maryland, Brother Buist was coroneted by Ill. Albert Pike, 33°, Sovereign Grand Commander; and six years later elected Grand Cross of the Court of Honour.

Bibliography:
Archive of the Supreme Council, 33°, S.J.
In Memoriam. *Transactions*. 1911: 318.

1876

Stephen Fowler Chadwick
Grand Cross of the Court of Honour at age 51 years, 5 months, and 5 days
Tenure 18 years, 7 months, and 15 days
Nomination by Oregon Scottish Rite Bodies

Born: December 25, 1825 – Died: January 15, 1895
Life span: 69 years and 20 days
Lawyer, Governor of Oregon

Progress in Scottish Rite Masonry:
4°-32°: March 21, 1871, communicated by Ill. John Commingere Ainsworth, 33°, Sovereign Grand
Inspector General for Oregon.
KCCH: May 6, 1874.
33°, IGH: elected May 6, 1874; coroneted 1876.
Grand Cross of the Court of Honour: May 30, 1876.
SGIG: Illustrious Brother Stephen F. Chadwick, 33° was nominated for Active Membership in the
Supreme Council for the State of Oregon, and duly elected May 10, 1878. On the same day was *Resolved*,
that the SGC be authorized to empower Ill. Bros. Ainsworth and McCraken to crown for Active
Membership the Ill. Bro. Chadwick – upon unconfirmed circumstances Ill. Chadwick, 33°, was never
crowned; Idaho was annexed to the Jurisdiction of Oregon May 27, 1878; resigned day unconfirmed.

Scottish Rite Biography:
Brother Chadwick received the three Degrees of Ancient Craft Masonry in *Laurel* Lodge, U.D., Roseburg,
Oregon, in 1856. In 1871, Bro. J. C. Ainsworth communicated to him the Ancient and Accepted Scottish
Rite Degrees from the 4° to 32°, inclusive, and immediately thereafter constituted *Albert Pike* Lodge of
Perfection at Salem, Oregon, Bro. Chadwick being the first Venerable Master. When Ill. Bro. Albert Pike
first visited this Oasis in 1876, he created Bro. Chadweick a 33° Honorary Member for the Southern
Jurisdiction of the United States. He was also a member of Oregon Consistory, Portland, Oregon.

Bibliography:
Archive of the Supreme Council, 33°, S.J.
In Memoriam. Stephen Fowler Chadwick, 33°. *Transactions.* 1895:349.
Robinson, Michael D., and Seth L. Pope. *Seth Pope's Journal of the Oregon Scottish Rite*. Portland:
Michael D. Robinson, 2017.

1876

William Cothran
Grand Cross of the Court of Honour at age 69 years, 5 months, and 29 days
Tenure 4 years, 5 months, and 4 days
Nomination by Mississippi Scottish Rite Bodies

Born: January 1, 1806 – Died: November 4, 1880
Life span: 74 years, 10 months, and 4 days
Judge

Progress in Scottish Rite Masonry:
4°-32°: 1860, communicated by Sovereign Grand Consistory of Sub. Princes of the Royal Secret, 32°, in and for the State for Mississippi.
33°, IGH: elected March 31, 1860; coroneted April 1861.
KCCH: May 8, 1872.
 Deputy: c1871 – laid down his Craft tools while in Office November 4, 1880.
SGIG: May 8, 1872, the Sovereign Grand Commander nominated Ill. Bro.William Cothran, 33°, for the dignity of Active Membership for Mississippi, the nomination to lie over until the next Biennial Session. [Never crowned.]
Grand Cross of the Court of Honour: May 30, 1876.

Scottish Rite Biography:
…All were worthy and estimable men. Bro. Cothran eminently so; but there is little to record of his service to the Rite. His age and judicial duties, and the depressed condition of the people of his State and of Masonry for many years after the close of the war between the States, prevented his working; and the Rite has been let to die out in Mississippi. Brother Cothran was a man of singular purity of character, gentle of manner, of amiable temper, a kindly cheerful man, intelligent, well informed, irreproachable, and greatly beloved.

Bibliography:
Archive of the Supreme Council, 33°, S.J.
In Memoriam. *Official Bulletin*. 1881: 697-698; 1882: 41-47.

Thomas Cripps
Grand Cross of the Court of Honour at age 58 years, 10 months, and 1 day
Tenure 17 years, 5 months, and 17 days
Nomination by New Orleans, Louisiana Scottish Rite Bodies

Born: July 29, 1817 – Died: November 16, 1893
Life span: 76 years, 3 months, and 17 days
Organist and Music Teacher

Progress in Scottish Rite Masonry:
4°-14°: month, day, year, place and by whom Degrees were communicated unconfirmed.
15°-18°: August 9, 1857, conferred by *Pelican* Chapter, No. 11, New Orleans.
19°-30°: August 13, 1857, conferred by *Eagle* Council of Kadosh, No. 6, New Orleans.
31°-32°: August 23, 1857, conferred by Grand Consistory of Louisiana.
33°, IGH: elected May 7, 1870, coroneted by Sovereign Grand Commander Albert Pike, 33°, November 5, 1870.
Grand Organist: May 7, 1870, on the recommendation of the Committee on the Sovereign Grand Commander's Address, Illustrious Brother Thomas Cripps, 32°, of New Orleans, Louisiana was elected to the position of Grand Organist of the Supreme Council.
Grand Cross of the Court of Honour: May 30, 1876.

Scottish Rite Biography:
Brother Thomas Cripps was raised on March 27, 1849, In *Marion* Lodge, No. 4 [afterwards, No. 68], at New Orleans. He received the Scottish Rite Degrees in the Grand Consistory of Louisiana and served in it as Lieutenant Commander. On May 7, 1870, Bro. Cripps was elected 33°, Inspector General Honorary, on the same day coroneted by Sovereign Grand Commander Albert Pike, 33°, and elected to the position of the Grand Organist of the Supreme Council. For that service, at the Session of the Supreme Council in 1872, the special resolution was made, that the Illustrious Brother Thomas Cripps, of New Orleans, for music furnished this Supreme Council, receive our thanks thereof.

Bibliography:
Archive of the Supreme Council, 33°, S.J.
In Memoriam. *Transactions*. 1893: 25.

1876

Robert Wilkinson Furnas
Grand Cross of the Court of Honour at age 52 years and 25 days
Tenure 29 years and 1 day
Nomination by Nebraska Scottish Rite Bodies

Born: May 5, 1824 – Died: June 1, 1905
Life span: 81 years and 22 days
Council of the Territorial Legislature, Public Printer, Governor of Nebraska

Progress in Scottish Rite Masonry:
4°- 32°: March 1867, Washington, D.C., by whom Degrees were communicated unconfirmed.
33°, IGH: elected May 7, 1868; coroneted by Ill. Frederick Webber, 33°, Sovereign Grand Inspector General for Kentucky February 5, 1870.
Deputy Special: May 8, 1872 – c1874.
SGIG: nominated for Active Membership by Ill. Albert Pike, 33°, Sovereign Grand Commander May 8, 1872, but never was elected.
Grand Cross of the Court of Honour: May 30, 1876.

Scottish Rite Biography:
Brother Furnas was initiated, passed, and raised in *Franklin* Lodge, No. 14, Troy, Ohio, April 1852. Received the Scottish Rite Degrees to Thirty-second Degree in Washington, D.C., March 1867, and the Thirty-third Degree at Omaha, February 5, 1870. Never seeking the offices and honor of the Fraternity, yet his eminent fitness and efficient work led to his constant preferment and increasing the debt of the Order to him. Not only by his service but especially by his eminent example, he did much for Freemasonry

Bibliography:
Archive of the Supreme Council, 33°, S.J.
Robert Wilkinson Furnas, 33°. In Memoriam. *Transactions.* 1905: 100; 305; 357-359.

1876

Thomas Elwood Garrett
Grand Cross of the Court of Honour at age 48 years, 2 months, and 4 days
Tenure 29 years and 1 month
Nomination by Missouri Scottish Rite Bodies

Born: March 16, 1828 – Died: June 30, 1905
Life span: 77 years, 3 months, and 14 days
Newspaperman

Progress in Scottish Rite Masonry:
4°-32°: date unconfirmed, communicated gratuitously by Ill. Martin Collins, 33°, by order of Grand Commander Albert Pike, 33°.
33°, IGH: elected May 7, 1868; coroneted August 18, 1868.
Grand Cross of the Court of Honour: May 30, 1876.

Scottish Rite Biography:
In Masonry Brother Thomas Elwood Garreett, 33°, was prominent in all branches. He was a member of the Scottish Rite Bodies in the Valley of St. Louis and was crowned Inspector-General Honorary at a special meeting of the Supreme Council at St. Louis in September 1868. As a critic, scholar and Mason, Bro. Garrett was favorably spoken of wherever known, and that was not confined to his city or State. Bro. Collins, in referring to him, says: "There was not a more enthusiastic Mason in the State of Missouri than Bro. Garrett. He was a Masonic scholar and always ready and willing to assist the brethren."

Bibliography:
Archive of the Supreme Council, 33°, S.J.
In Memoriam. *Transactions*. 1905: 98; 370.

1876

William Leffingwell
Grand Cross of the Court of Honour at age 77 years, 4 months, and 16 days
Tenure 4 months and 3 days
Nomination by Iowa Scottish Rite Bodies

Born: January 4, 1799 – Died: October 3, 1876
Life span: 77 years, 8 months, and 29 days
Lawyer

Progress in Scottish Rite Masonry:
4°-32°: June 16, 1869, communicated by Davenport Scottish Rite Bodies.
33°, IGH: elected and coroneted May 3, 1870.
Grand Cross of the Court of Honour: May 30, 1876.

Scottish Rite Biography:
Brother William Leffingwell became a resident of Iowa, July 4, 1839, and a Mason, September 11, 1848 … And by no one has been surpassed in the zeal, energy, and faithfulness with which he has labored in every department of Masonry. As Master and Secretary of Iowa Lodge … and as a Chief of Scottish Rite Masonry, he has truly been, "in labors abundant" —in energy, unflagging—in intelligent real, unsurpassed. In May 1870, at Baltimore, he was crowned 33°, and as Grand Commander-in-Chief of the Grand Consistory of Iowa, and where else duty called him, he kept faithfully all the promises that he made when crowned.

Bibliography:
Archive of the Supreme Council, 33°, S.J.
In Memoriam. *Official Bulletin.* Vol. III: 363-364; 366-367.

1876

John Lawson Lewis
Grand Cross of the Court of Honour at age 76 years, 1 month, and 26 days
Tenure 9 years, 11 months, and 15 days
Nomination by New Orleans, Louisiana Scottish Rite Bodies

Born: March 26, 1800 – Died: May 15, 1886
Life span: 86 years, 1 month, and 19 days
Major-General

Progress in Scottish Rite Masonry:
4°-32°: date, place and by whom Degrees were communicated unconfirmed.
33°, IGH: February 17, 1855, proclaimed to be Sovereign Grand Inspector General of the 33° Degree and Honorary Member of the Supreme Council at Charleston.
Deputy: February 17, 1855 - October 22, 1884.
Grand Cross of the Court of Honour: elected May 30, 1876; May 6, 1878, *Ex Officio.*
SGIG: elected and transferred to Emeritus, October 22, 1884.

Scottish Rite Biography:
Brother Lewis became an Honorary Member of the Supreme Council for the Southern Jurisdiction of the United States in 1855, and a member of its board of Nine Deputies for Louisiana, having been long connected with other Masonic Bodies in the State and serving Masonry as loyally and zealously as he did his mother land. At its session of October 1884, our Supreme Council elected to Active Membership and thence transferred to the roll of Emeriti.

Bibliography:
Archive of the Supreme Council, 33°, S.J.
In Memoriam. *Transactions*. 1886: Appendix: 91.

1876

Nathaniel Levin
Grand Cross of the Court of Honour at age 60 years, 3 months, and 4 days
Tenure 22 years, 7 months, and 5 days
Nomination by South Carolina Scottish Rite Bodies

Born: February 26, 1816 – Died: January 5, 1899
Life span: 82 years, 10 months, and 10 days
Clerk in the Custom House

Progress in Scottish Rite Masonry:
4°-14°: March 12, 1868, communicated by Ill. Albert G. Mackey, 33°, Grand Secretary General.
15°-18°: June 24, 1870, communicated by Ill. Albert G. Mackey, 33°, Grand Secretary General.
19°-30°: July 17, 1870, communicated by Ill. Albert G. Mackey, 33°, Grand Secretary General.
31°-32°: September 30, 1870.
32°, KCCH: May 30, 1872.
33°, IGH: elected and coroneted by the Supreme Council, 33°, S.J., May 5, 1874.
Grand Cross of the Court of Honour: May 30, 1876.
SGIG: elected and crowned October 16, 1888; laid down his Craft tools while in Office January 5, 1899.

Scottish Rite Biography:
Brother Levin was initiated an Apprentice Mason in *Solomon* Lodge, No. 11, in Charleston, South Carolina, on the 10th day of May 1841; passed June 12, 1841, and raised to the Degree of Master Mason on the 7th day of July 1841. He was made a 14° Mason on the 12th day of March 1868; an 18° on June 24, 1870; a 30° on July 17, 1870, and 32° on the 30th of September 1870; all the Degrees from the 4° to the 32° being conferred by our late Bro. Albert G. Mackey, 33°, the Dean of the Supreme Council, and at that time its Secretary-General. He was elected Knight Commander of the Court of Honour, May 30, 1876; coroneted 33° Honorary by the Supreme Council in Washington, D.C., on the 5th day of May 1874, and crowned Active Member and Inspector-General for the State of South Carolina by the Supreme Council for the State of South Carolina on the 16th day of October 1888, at Washington, D.C.

Bibliography:
Archive of the Supreme Council, 33°, S.J.
In Memoriam. *Transactions.* 1899: 496-497; 511-513.

1876

William Napoleon Loker
Grand Cross of the Court of Honour at age 58 years and 5 months
Tenure 11 years, 7 months, and I day
Nomination by St. Louis, Missouri

Born: December 31, 1817 – Died: December 31, 1895
Life span: 78 years
Banker

Progress in Scottish Rite Masonry:
4°-32°: date, place and by whom Degrees were communicated unconfirmed.
33°, IGH: elected April 18, 1866; coroneted by the Supreme Council, 33°, S.J., April 20, 1866.
Grand Cross of the Court of Honour: May 30, 1876.

Scottish Rite Biography:
When Brother Locker received the Scottish Rite Degrees is unconfirmed. More likely the Degrees were communicated to him by Ill. Anthony O'Sullivan, 33°, Inspector General Honorary for the Orient of Missouri. Brother Loker was present at a Session of the Supreme Council for 1866, where he was elected and on April 20, 1866, coroneted a 33°, Inspector General Honorary. On April 21, 1866, at the solicitation of Brother Sullivan, Brother Loker was appointed Special Deputy Inspector to assist Brother Sullivan in propagating the Rite in the State of Missouri. He was present on the following Session of the Supreme Council and appointed to the Committee on Lodge of Sorrow. On May 30, 1876, Ill. William Napoleon Loker received the Scottish Rite's highest honor, the Grand Cross of the Court of Honour.

Bibliography:
Archive of the Supreme Council, 33°, S.J.
Photo courtesy of Missouri History Museum Photograph and Prints Collection.

1876

Edwin Balridge MacGrotty

Grand Cross of the Court of Honour at age 47 years and 7 months
Tenure 22 years, 8 months, and 11 days
Nomination by the District of Columbia Scottish Rite Bodies

Born: July 31, 1828 – Died: March 11, 1899
Life span: 70 years, 7 months, and 10 days
U.S. Treasury Department Clerk

Progress in Scottish Rite Masonry:
4°-14°: March 5, 1872, conferred by *Mithras* Lodge of Perfection, No. 1, Washington, D.C.
15°-18°: May 1873, communicated by Bro. W. M. Ireland, 32°,
19°-30°: October 1873, communicated by Bro. W. M. Ireland, 32°.
31°-32°: March 5, 1874, communicated by Bro. W. M. Ireland, 32°, Special Deputy of the Grand
Commander Albert Pike, 33°.
KCCH: May 6, 1874.
Grand Cross of the Court of Honour: May 30, 1876.
33°, IGH: elected October 2, 1882; no indication regarding coronation.

Scottish Rite Biography:
Brother MacGrotty was made a Master Mason in *La Fayette* Lodge, No. 19, in Washington D.C., on July
21, 1864. He received the 4°-14° Degrees in March 5, 1872, in *Mithras* Lodge and the remainder by Bro.
William M. Ireland, 32°, the Special Deputy of the Grand Commander, Albert Pike, 33°. MacGrotty
participated in the formation of the *Robert De Bruce* Council of Kadosh, No. 1 and *Albert Pike* Consistory,
No. 1. He served as Venerable Master of *Mithras* Lodge in 1875-1876, and its Secretary in 1882; Wise
Master of *Evangelist* Chapter in 1882-1884. Brother Bennett was elected a Knight Commander of the
Court of Honour, May 6, 1874, a Grand Cross of the Court of Honour, May 30, 1876, and coroneted
Honorary Inspector-General, October 20, 1882. He was for many sessions of the Supreme Council elected
as its Assistant Secretary. His work for the Supreme Council was such that it might be called
extraordinary … the beautiful chromo-lithographic plates of the clothing and jewels of each Degree and of
the many beautiful drawings of the *Liturgies.*

Bibliography:
Archive of the Supreme Council, 33°
Archives of the Orient of the District of Columbia and Archives of the Grand Lodge of the District of
Columbia, F.A.A.M.
In Memoriam. *Transactions.* 1899: 345-347; 524.

1876

Angel Martin
Grand Cross of the Court of Honour at age 83 years, 5 months, and 6 days
Tenure 3 months and 3 days
Nomination by New Orleans, Louisiana Scottish Rite Bodies

Born: December 24, 1792 – Died: September 3, 1876
Life span: 83 years, 8 months, and 9 days
Merchant

Progress in Scottish Rite Masonry:
4°-32°: date, place and by whom Degrees were conferred, or communicated unconfirmed.
33°, IGH: elected and coroneted in February 1858.
Grand Cross of the Court of Honour: May 30, 1876.

Scottish Rite Biography:
Brother Angel Martin was initiated in *St. John's Lodge* at Gibraltar, Louisiana, in November 1832. Since 1839 he had resided in New Orleans and was many years Most Worshipful Master and Commander of *Los Amigos del Orden* Chapter of Rose Croix and Council of Kadosh. He was distinguished for his zeal in the service of the Ancient and Accepted Rite—a worthy, good, true, honorable man, of stalwart frame and a large generous heart—a frank, cordial, friendly man, whom, having once met him, one always wished to meet again. Crowned 33° in February 1858, and chosen Grand Cross in 1876, he deserved both honours.

Bibliography:
Archive of the Supreme Council, 33°, S.J.
Official Bulletin. Vol. III: 363.

1876

Richard Joseph Nunn
Grand Cross of the Court of Honour at age 44 years, 5 months, and 17 days
Tenure 34 years and 29 days
Nomination by Georgia Scottish Rite Bodies

Born: December 13, 1831 – Died: June 29, 1910
Life span: 78 years, 6 months, and 16 days
Physician

Progress in Scottish Rite Masonry:
4°-32°: 1865, communicated by Ill. William Spencer Rockwell, 33°, SGIG for Georgia.
33°, IGH: elected November 17, 1865; coroneted by Ill. William Spencer Rockwell, 33°, SGIG for Georgia 1865.
Deputy: May 9, 1868 - October 16, 1888.
Grand Cross of the Court of Honour: May 30, 1876.
SGIG: elected and crowned October 16, 1888; laid down his Craft tools while in Office June 29, 1910.

Scottish Rite Biography:
Brother Nunn was initiated, passed, and raised as a Master Mason in *Zerubabel* Lodge, No. 15, Savannah, in 1852. He received the Degrees of our Rite by communication from Bro. W. S. Rockwell at Savannah, in 1865. On the 17th day of November of that year he was elected to the 33° Honorary by the Supreme Council, and this Degree was later communicated to him by Bro∴ Rockwell. On October 16, 1888, Illustrious Nunn was elected to Active Membership in the Council, and on the same day was crowned with that honor. In 1897 he was elected Grand Almoner of the Supreme Council, which office he filled until the first day of November 1907, when he was appointed Treasurer-General of the Supreme Council by the Grand Commander. The latter position he held until the first day of June 1908, when he was promoted by the Grand Commander to the office of Grand Minister of State of the Supreme Council, which appointment was confirmed by the Council in October last. In the science and philosophy of Freemasonry Brother Nunn shone with great brilliancy. The writer doubts if, among all the vast membership of the Scottish Rite in the Unites States, there was one who was more profoundly learned in its philosophy and dogma … it might be truly said that when his light went out our Supreme Council lost its best scholar, its profoundest philosopher, its most earnest student, its raciest speaker and its most cultured member.

Bibliography:
Archive of the Supreme Council, 33°, S.J.
In Memoriam. *Transactions.* 1911: 268-273.

1876

Harvey Allen Olney
Grand Cross of the Court of Honour at age 42 years, 1 month, and 16 days
Tenure unconfirmed
Nomination by Virginia Scottish Rite Bodies

Born: July 16, 1842 – Died: date unconfirmed
Life span: unconfirmed
Mining Engineer

Progress in Scottish Rite Masonry:
4°-14°: September 1874, communicated by Ill. John Robin McDaniel, 33°, SGIG for Virginia.
15°-18°: January 1875, communicated by Ill. John Robin McDaniel, 33°, SGIG for Virginia.
19°-30°: February 1875, communicated by Ill. John Robin McDaniel, 33°, SGIG for Virginia.
31°-32°: March 1875, communicated by Ill. John Robin McDaniel, 33°, SGIG for Virginia.
KCCH: May 6, 1874
33°, IGH: elected May 7, 1874; coroneted by Ill. John Robin McDaniel, 33°, SGIG for Virginia in June 1877.
Grand Cross of the Court of Honour: May 30, 1876.

Scottish Rite Biography:
Brother Olney was initiate in June 1869 in *St. George* Lodge, No. 32, at Liverpool, England, passed September 1869, and raised in May 1870. The Scottish Rite Degrees he received in the United Stated of America, at Lynchburg, Virginia, by communication, by Ill. John Robin McDaniel, 33°, SGIG for Virginia. He received a rank and decoration of a Knight Commander of the Court of Honour in 1874 and on the same Session of the Supreme Council was elected 33°, IGH. And on the following Session Ill. Harvey Allen Olney was elected the Grand Cross of the Court of Honour. Bro. Olney served at Lynchburg Scottish Rite Bodies as Venerable Master of the Lodge of Perfection, Wise Master of the Chapter of Rose Croix, and Commander of Lynchburg Consistory.

Bibliography:
Archive of the Supreme Council, 33°, S.J.

1876

William Lewis Page
Grand Cross of the Court of Honour at age 52 years, 5 months, and 24 days
Tenure 13 years and 1 day
Nomination by Lynchburg, Virginia Scottish Rite Bodies

Born: December 6, 1824 – Died: May 31, 1890
Life span: 65 years, 5 months, and 25 days
Merchant

Progress in Scottish Rite Masonry:
4°-32°: date unconfirmed, invested at Lynchburg by the Grand Consistory of Virginia.
33°, IGH: elected May 2, 1870; coroneted by the Supreme Council, 33°, S.J., May 3, 1870.
Grand Cross of the Court of Honour: May 30, 1876.

Scottish Rite Biography:
Brother Page received the Scottish Rite Degrees from the Grand Consistory of Virginia and later on served as a Grand Treasurer of the Grand Consistory. On May 2, 1870, in the City of Baltimore, at the Masonic Hall, Inspector-General McDaniel was nominated to receive the Thirty-third Degree as an honorarium, and for Honorary Membership … William L. Page, 32°, of Lynchburg, Virginia … and the vote being taken *viva voce*, and being unanimous in his favor, he was declared duly elected to receive the Degree and as Honorary Members, as an honorarium. On May 3, 1870, the Senatorial Chamber was thrown open to the Honorary Members of the Supreme Council, seven Brothers, who had been duly elected and prepared, were introduced and crowned as Sovereign Grand Inspectors-General, and Honorary Members of this Supreme Council and among them Brother Page. On May 30, 1876, Ill. William Lewis Page, 33°, received the Grand Cross of the Court of Honour.

Bibliography:
Archive of the Supreme Council, 33°, S.J.

1876

Benjamin Perley Poore
Grand Cross of the Court of Honour at age 55 years, 6 months, and 28 days
Tenure 10 years, 11 months, and 29 days
Nomination by the District of Columbia Scottish Rite Bodies

Born: November 2, 1820 – Died: May 29, 1887
Life span: 66 years, 6 months, and 27 days
Journalist, Clerk of the Senate Committee on Printing

Progress in Scottish Rite Masonry:
4°-32°: c1850[th] conferred or communicated in Paris, France.
33°, IGH: elected and coroneted March 31, 1860.
KCCH: May 8, 1872.
Grand Cross of the Court of Honour: May 30, 1876.

Scottish Rite Biography:
Brother Benjamin Perley Poore received the first three masonic degrees at *Mt. Vernon* Lodge No. 22, in Athens, Georgia. He later relocated to Germany to serve as Secretary to the American Minister to Germany. During his time abroad, he received the Scottish Rite degrees, 4° to 32°, in Paris, France. He returned, worked as a journalist in Washington, D.C., and was later appointed clerk to the Senate Committee on Printing, a position he held until his death on May 29, 1887. Brother Poore participated in the formation of District of Columbia's Grand Consistory and *Osiris* Lodge of Perfection on June 22, 1860, and *Mithras* Lodge of Perfection on December 16, 1870. *Mithras* Lodge of Perfection elected Poore their first Grand Orator and later, on March 3, 1885, as a Life Member. The Supreme Council elected and coroneted Poore a 33°, IGH in 1860 and the Grand Cross of the Court of Honour in 1876.

Bibliography:
Pike, Albert. *Ex Corde Locutiones. Words from the Heart Spoken of His Dead Brethren.* Washington, D.C.: 1897.
Archive of the Supreme Council, 33°, S.J.
Archives of the Orient of the District of Columbia and Archives of the Grand Lodge of the District of Columbia, F.A.A.M.

1876

John Lonsdale Roper
Grand Cross of the Court of Honour at age 40 years, 5 months, and 22 days
Tenure 45 years and 23 days
Nomination of Ill. Thomas H. Caswell, 33°, Sovereign Grand Inspector-General for
California
Nomination by Virginia Scottish Rite Bodies

Born: October 9, 1835 – Died: June 23, 1921
Life span: 85 years, 8 months, and 13 days
Lumber Businessman

Progress in Scottish Rite Masonry:
4°-32°: 1875 invested by communication from Illustrious John Robin McDaniel, 33°.
33°, IGH: nominated May 29, 1876, elected and coroneted May 30, 1876.
Grand Cross of the Court of Honour: May 31, 1876.
Deputy: Deputy and Legate for Virginia and North Carolina May 27, 1878 - October 20, 1880.
SGIG: elected and coroneted October 20, 1880; resigned and Emeritus, October 18, 1886.

Scottish Rite Biography:
Brother Roper was made a Mason in January 1862, receiving Degrees on the same date, in *Clarion* Lodge, No. 277, at Clarion, Pennsylvania, from which he demitted to affiliate, about 1868, with *Atlantic* Lodge, No. 2, at Norfolk. Bro. Roper received the Scottish Rite Degrees, Fourth to Thirty-second, by communication from Inspector McDaniel in 1875, and was elected an Honorary Member of the Supreme Council the following year. In 1878 he was appointed its Deputy in Virginia and North Carolina. He attended the Sessions of 1882 and 1884, served on the Committees on Finance, Correspondence, Subordinate Bodies, etc., but resigned in 1886 and was transferred to the Emeritus List.

Bibliography:
In Memoriam. *Transactions.* 1921: 180-181.
Archive of the Supreme Council, 33°, S.J.

1876

Ezekiel Salomon
Grand Cross of the Court of Honour at age 60 years, 6 months, and 4 days
Tenure 6 years, 4 months, and 16 days
Nomination by New Orleans, Louisiana Scottish Rite Bodies

Born: November 26, 1815 – Died: October 16, 1882
Life span: 66 years, 11 months, and 10 days
Deputy Collector of Customs

Progress in Scottish Rite Masonry:
4°-32°: date, place and by whom Degrees were conferred, or communicated unconfirmed.
33°, IGH: elected and coroneted February 17, 1857.
Grand Cross of the Court of Honour: May 30, 1876.

Scottish Rite Biography:
Brother Ezekiel Salomon, 33°, since 1857, once of Louisiana, but for several years before his death residing in New York, was for some years the Grand Representative of the Supreme Council of Belgium near our Supreme Council. I knew him in Louisiana for some years as a loyal Mason and upright man, energetic and enterprising, a man of intelligence and mark among his fellows. [Albert Pike.]

Bibliography:
Archive of the Supreme Council, 33°, S.J.
Pike, Albert. Allocution. *Transactions*.1884: 6-7.
In Memoriam. *Transactions*.1886: 97.

1876

Robert Mark Smith
Grand Cross of the Court of Honour at age 50 years, 4 months, and 17 days
Tenure 2 years, 8 months, and 1 day
Nomination by Georgia Scottish Rite Bodies

Born: January 13, 1826 – Died: February 1, 1879
Life span: 53 years and 18 days
Physician

Progress in Scottish Rite Masonry:
4°-32°: date, place, and by whom Degrees were conferred, or communicated, unconfirmed.
KCCH: May 8, 1872.
33°, IGH: elected May 6, 1874; coroneted by the Supreme Council, 33°, S.J., May 7, 1874.
Grand Cross of the Court of Honour: May 30, 1876.

Scottish Rite Biography:
Brother Robert Mark Smith, M.D., joined the *Mount Vernon* Lodge, No. 22, on March 1, 1850. He was a bright member of the Scottish Rite and enjoyed the distinction of being a Thirty-third Degree Mason. The high honor was conferred upon him in 1876. As Deputy of the Inspector General for Georgia, he rendered valuable service to the Rite. In his profession, in private life, in official position he was ever the true gentleman—faithful, honorable, considerate, unselfish, and loyal in all duties of his life.

Bibliography:
Archive of the Supreme Council, 33°, S.J.
In Memoriam. *Transactions*. 1880: 55.
Memoirs of Georgia. Atlanta: The Southern Historical Association, 1895.

1876

Joshua Otis Stanton
Grand Cross of the Court of Honour at age 38 years, 7 months, and 8 days
Tenure 14 years, 11 months, and 10 days
Nomination by the District of Columbia Scottish Rite Bodies

Born: October 22, 1837 – Died: April 10, 1891
Life span: 53 years, 5 months, and 18 days
Physician

Progress in Scottish Rite Masonry:
4°-14°: December 20, 1868, communicated by Ill. Benjamin Brown French, 33°, SGIG for the District of Columbia.
15°-32°: December 27, 1868, communicated by Ill. Benjamin Brown French, 33°, SGIG for the District of Columbia.
KCCH: May 7, 1874.
Grand Cross of the Court of Honour: May 30, 1876 [no indication about nomination and election in the *Transactions* for 1876.]

Scottish Rite Biography:
Brother Stanton received the first three masonic degrees in *Pentalpha* Lodge, No. 23, in Washington, D.C. SGIG French personally conferred the 4°-32° upon Stanton in December 1868. On December 16, 1870, Stanton participated in the formation of *Mithras* Lodge of Perfection No. 2; on December 30, 1870, *Kedron* Council of Princes of Jerusalem, No. 1; on December 7, 1871, *Evangelist* Chapter of Knights Rose Croix, No. 1; on December 11, 1873, *Robert De Bruce* Council of Kadosh, No. 1; and on January 6, 1876, *Albert Pike* Consistory No. 1. He served as *Evangelist* Chapter's first *Most Wise Master* from 1872-1875 and 1878.

Bibliography:
Archive of the Supreme Council, 33°, S. J.
Archives of the Orient of the District of Columbia and Archives of the Grand Lodge of the District of Columbia, F.A.A.M.

1876

Isaac Sutvene Titus
Grand Cross of the Court of Honour at age 48 years, 7 months, and 16 days
Tenure 15 years, 11 months, and 22 days
Nomination by San Francisco, California Scottish Rite Bodies

Born: October 14, 1827 – Died: April 22, 1892
Life span: 64 years, 5 months, and 8 days
Physician

Progress in Scottish Rite Masonry:
4°-32°: October 17, 1867, communicated at San Francisco by Ill. Ebenezer Hamilton Shaw, 33°, Sovereign Grand Inspector General for California.
33°, IGH: elected September 17, 1868; coroneted by the Supreme Council, 33°, S.J. September 18, 1868.
Grand Cross of the Court of Honour: May 30, 1876.

Scottish Rite Biography:
Brother Titus was initiated on August 9, 1851, passed on December 20, 1851, and raised to the Sublime Degree of Master Mason on January 31, 1852, in Cedar Lodge, No. 11, in town of Tipton, Iowa. In the Ancient and Accepted Scottish Rite Brother Titus received the Degrees by communication at San Francisco in October 1867, from the Ill. Ebenezer H. Shaw, 33°, SGIG in California, up to and including the 32°, and was coroneted an Honorary SGIG by the Supreme Council at St. Louis, on September 18, 1868, the Sovereign Grand Commander Albert Pike, 33°, presiding. On the instituting and formation at Placerville of *Kilwining* Lodge of Perfection, No. 5, Ill. Bro. Titus was elected Thrice Puissant Grand Master for 1867, 1868, 1869, and again in 1871. Of *Libanus* Council of Princes of Jerusalem, No. 3, he was elected Most Illustrious Tarshatha for the years 1867 to 1873, and of St. Paul's Chapter of Knights of Rose Croix, No. 3, Most Wise Master for the same years. In all the above-named Bodies of the Rite, much active work was performed for a long period. On May 30, 1876, Ill. Isaac Sutvene Titus was elected Grand Cross of the Court of Honour, the first Brother to receive the same in California

Bibliography:
Archive of the Supreme Council, 33°, S.J.
The Trestle Board. c1892.

1878

Only nominations for and no election of the Honour of Grand Cross

1880

Elisha Ingraham Baily
Grand Cross of the Court of Honour at age 55 years, 11 months, and 7 days
Tenure 27 years, 5 months, and 2 days
Nomination by Oregon Scottish Rite Bodies

Born: November 14, 1824 – Died: March 23, 1908
Life span: 84 years, 4 months, and 9 days
U.S. Army Surgeon

Progress in Scottish Rite Masonry:
4°-32°: January 1870, communicated by Ill. Benjamin B. French, 33°, Sovereign Grand Inspector General for the District of Colombia with assistance of Ill. Albert Pike, 33°, Sovereign Grand Commander.
KCCH: May 7, 1878.
33°, IGH: elected May 7, 1878; coroneted at Portland by Ill. John McCracken, 33°, on December 27, 1878.
The said Brother is adjudged to be worthy of the dignity of Grand Cross of the Court of Honour and is entitled to wear the Jewel of the same: October 21, 1880.

Scottish Rite Biography:
As official Director in the U.S. Army, Brother Baily was assigned to the Department of Columbia and stationed at Portland in 1874, affiliating with *Portland* Lodge, No. 55. He received the Scottish Rite Degrees by communication from Ill. Benjamin B. French, 33°, Sovereign Grand Inspector General for the District of Colombia with assistance of Ill. Albert Pike, 33°, Sovereign Grand Commander. On the Session of the Supreme Council of 1878, Brother Baily was elected to receive the Knight Commander of the Court of Honour as well as a 33°, Inspector General Honorary, and on December 27 of the same year was coroneted by Ill. John McCracken, 33°, Sovereign Grand Inspector General for Oregon. On October 21, 1880, the highest honor was bestowed upon Ill. Elisha Ingraham Baily, 33°, he was elected the Grand Cross of the Court of Honour.

Bibliography:
Archive of the Supreme Council, 33°, S.J.
Robinson, Michael D., and Seth L. Pope. *Seth Pope's Journal of the Oregon Scottish Rite*. Portland: Michael D. Robinson, 2017.

1880

Stephen Henry Beasley
Grand Cross of the Court of Honour at age 46 years, 10 months, and 6 days
Tenure 29 years, 5 months, and 24 days
Nomination by Alabama Scottish Rite Bodies

Born: January 15, 1834 – Died: April 15, 1910
Life span: 76 years and 3 months
Insurance Agent

Progress in Scottish Rite Masonry:
4°-14°: date, place and by whom Degrees were communicated unconfirmed.
15°-32°: September 20, 1877, communicated by Ill. Frederick Webber, 33°, Sovereign Grand Inspector General for Kentucky.
KCCH: May 6, 1878.
33°, IGH: elected May 6, 1878; coroneted May 7, 1878.
Deputy: May 1878 – resigned, date unconfirmed.
The said Brother is adjudged to be worthy of the dignity of Grand Cross of the Court of Honour and is entitled to wear the Jewel of the same: October 21, 1880.

Scottish Rite Biography:
The State of Alabama for years showed no progress in the Rite … Bro. Beasley has planted anew and cultivated, and wheat beautifies the land. Earnestly, faithfully he labors. Last spring Bros. Pike, Batchelor and Ireland went to his support, and found him, like the Scottish Highlander, "ready, aye ready." He has done his duty and deserves well of the Rite.

Bibliography:
Archive of the Supreme Council, 33°, S.J.
Note. *Transactions*. 1882: 37.

1880

Charles T. Brown
Grand Cross of the Court of Honour at age unconfirmed
Tenure unconfirmed
Nomination by San Francisco, California Scottish Rite Bodies

Born: unconfirmed – Died: unconfirmed

Progress in Scottish Rite Masonry:
4°-32°: date, place, and by whom Degrees were communicated unconfirmed.
The said Brother is adjudged to be worthy of the dignity of Grand Cross of the Court of Honour and is entitled to wear the Jewel of the same: October 21, 1880.

Scottish Rite Biography:
Little-known about Brother Brown, more likely, that the Scottish Rite Degrees were communicated to him at San Francisco by Ill. Ebenezer Hamilton Shaw, 33°, Sovereign Grand Inspector General for California. However, the *Transactions* of the Supreme Council, 33, S.J., indicated, that Ill. Charles T. Brown, 33°, was elected the Grand Cross of the Court of Honour on October 21, 1880.

1880

Edward Addison Craighill
Grand Cross of the Court of Honour at age 40 years, 11 months, and 19 days
Tenure 42 years, 2 months, and 11 days
Nomination by Lynchburg, Virginia Scottish Rite Bodies

Born: November 2, 1840 – Died: January 2, 1923
Life span: 82 years and 2 months
Physician

Progress in Scottish Rite Masonry:
4°-14°: March 1864, conferred by *Albert Pike* Lodge of Perfection, Lynchburg.
15°-18°: March 1864, conferred by Rose Croix Chapter, Lynchburg.
19°-30°: March 1864, conferred by Council of Kadosh, Lynchburg.
31°-32°: March 1864, conferred by Grand Consistory, Lynchburg.
KCCH: May 30, 1876.
33°, IGH: elected May 30, 1876; coroneted at Lynchburg, VA, by Ill. John Robinson McDaniel, 33°, February 24, 1877.
The said Brother is adjudged to be worthy of the dignity of Grand Cross of the Court of Honour and is entitled to wear the Jewel of the same: October 21, 1880.

Scottish Rite Biography:
Brother Craighill was raised in November 1863 in *Marshall* Lodge, No. 39, Lynchburg, Virginia. On next year he received the Scottish Rite Degrees from Grand Consistory of Lynchburg; on May 30, 1876, was elected KCCH, and 33° Inspector General Honorary, but coroneted at Lynchburg on February 24, 1877, by Ill. John Robinson McDaniel, 33°, Sovereign Grand Inspector General for Virginia. On October 21, 1880, Ill. Edward Addison Craighill, 33°, was selected for investiture with the dignity of the Grand Cross of the Court of Honour

Bibliography:
Archive of the Supreme Council, 33°, S.J.

1880

John Fox Damon
Grand Cross of the Court of Honour at age 53 years, 8 months, and 4 days
Tenure 22 years, 2 months, and 20 days
Nomination by Washington Scottish Rite Bodies

Born: February 17, 1827 – Died: January 11, 1904.
Life span: 76 years, 11 months, and 24 days
Minister

Progress in Scottish Rite Masonry:
4°-32°: September 9, 1876, communicated by Ill. James Smyth Lawson, 33°, Sovereign Grand Inspector General for Washington Territory.
KCCH: May 7, 1878.
The said Brother is adjudged to be worthy of the dignity of Grand Cross of the Court of Honour and is entitled to wear the Jewel of the same: October 21, 1880.
33°, IGH: elected October 18, 1882; no indication regarding coronation.

Scottish Rite Biography:
Brother Damon was a Master Mason in *Salem* Lodge, No. 4, Salem, Oregon. He received the Scottish Rite Degrees by communication from Ill. James Smyth Lawson, 33°, Sovereign Grand Inspector General for Washington Territory on September 9, 1876. On the Session of the Supreme Council, 33°, S.J. for 1878, Brother Damon was nominated to receive the dignity of Knight Commander of the Court of Honour and was duly elected. On the following Session on October 21, 1880, he was duly elected to the dignity of Grand Cross of the Court of Honour. And on the Session for 1882, John Fox Damon, 32°, Grand Cross, was elected to receive a 33°, Inspector General Honorary, but there is no trace in the historical records when and by whom he was coroneted.

Bibliography:
Archive of the Supreme Council, 33°, S.J.

1880

John Owen Dominis
Grand Cross of the Court of Honour at age 48 years, 7 months, and 11 days
Tenure 10 years, 10 months, and 7 days
Orient of Hawaii

Born: March 10, 1832 – Died: August 28, 1891
Life span: 58 years, 5 months, and 17 days
Governor of Hawaii

Progress in Scottish Rite Masonry:
4°-32°: summer, 1874, communicated by Bro. Pitkin Cowles Wright, 32°, KCCH.
KCCH: May 31, 1876.
33°, IGH: elected May 31, 1876; no indication regarding coronation.
Deputy: September-December 1874 - laid down his Craft tools while in Office August 28, 1891.
The said Brother is adjudged to be worthy of the dignity of Grand Cross of the Court of Honour and is entitled to wear the Jewel of the same: October 21, 1880.

Scottish Rite Biography:
Brother John Owen Dominis was a brother-in-law of the King of Hawaii and his participation in Masonry was similar to that of the royal family of Masons. He petitioned Lodge *le Progress de l'Oceanie*, April 30, 1858, and by August15 had moved through the three Degrees and been raised a Master Mason. The Scottish Rite history of Dominis also parallels that of Kalakaua. He was elected Venerable Master of the *Kamehameha* Lodge of Perfection, July 16, 1874, and Venerable Almoner of *Nuuanu* Chapter of Rose Croix, September 12. Shortly after, Brother Dominis was appointed Deputy of the Supreme Council for the Kingdom of Hawaii by Sovereign Grand Commander Albert Pike, 33°, and served as such until his death in 1891. He was the first Thirty-third Degree Mason coroneted in Hawaii. The Supreme Council on October 21, 1880, elected Ill. John Owen Dominis, 33°, the Grand Cross of the Court of Honour.

Bibliography:
Archive of the Supreme Council, 33°, S.J.
In Memoriam. *Transactions*. 1892: 51.
The New Age. August 1968.

1880

Rockey Preston Earhart
Grand Cross of the Court of Honour at age 44 years, 3 months, and 28 days
Tenure 12 years, 6 months, and 20 days
Nomination by Oregon Scottish Rite Bodies

Born: June 23, 1836 – Died: May 11, 1892
Life span: 55 years, 10 months, and 18 days
Lawyer

Progress in Scottish Rite Masonry:
4°- 32°: January 1870, communicated by Ill. Benjamin B. French, 33°, Sovereign Grand Inspector General for the District of Columbia with assistance of Ill. Albert Pike, 33°, Sovereign Grand Commander.
KCCH: May 7, 1878.
33°, IGH: elected May 7, 1878, coroneted at Portland by Ill. John McCracken, 33°, on December 27, 1878.
The said Brother is adjudged to be worthy of the dignity of Grand Cross of the Court of Honour and is entitled to wear the Jewel of the same: October 21, 1880.
Deputy: date unconfirmed - July 1883.
SGIG: elected October 18, 1882; crowned July 1883; resigned July 4, 1890; Emeritus October 21, 1890.

Scottish Rite Biography:
Brother Earhart was raised to the Sublime Degree in *Salem* Lodge, No. 4, in Salem. The Scottish Rite Degrees from 4° to 32° were communicated to him in January 1870, by Ill. Benjamin B. French, 33°, Sovereign Grand Inspector General for the District of Columbia with assistance of Ill. Albert Pike, 33°, Sovereign Grand Commander. Brother Earhart was invested as a Knight Commander of the Court of Honour on May 7, 1878. On the same day the Supreme Council, 33°, S.J. had elected him a 33°, Inspector General Honorary, and Ill. John McCracken, 33°, crooned him at Portland on December 27, 1878. Ill. Rockey Preston Earhart, 33°, received the highest Scottish Rite honor, the Grand Cross of the Court of Honour on October 21, 1880, and faithfully served his Orient as a Deputy of the Supreme Council and from July 1883 to July 1890 as Sovereign Grand Inspector General for the Orient of Oregon.

Bibliography:
Archive of the Supreme Council, 33°, S.J.
In Memoriam. *Transactions.* 1892: 44.
Robinson, Michael D., and Seth L. Pope. *Seth Pope's Journal of the Oregon Scottish Rite*. Portland: Michael D. Robinson, 2017.

1880

Josiah Essex
Grand Cross of the Court of Honour at age 78 years, 1 month, and 24 days
Tenure 2 years, 7 months, and 1 day
Nomination by the District of Columbia Scottish Rite Bodies

Born: August 27, 1802 – Died: May 22, 1883
Life span: 80 years, 8 months, and 25 days
Carpenter Builder of the Naval Observatory

Progress in Scottish Rite Masonry:
4°-32°: date, place, and by whom Degrees were conferred or communicated unconfirmed.
KCCH: May 7, 1878.
33°, IGH: elected October 19, 1880; coroneted October 20, 1880.
The said Brother is adjudged to be worthy of the dignity of Grand Cross of the Court of Honour and is entitled to wear the Jewel of the same: October 21, 1880.

Scottish Rite Biography:
Josiah Essex was a member of *Federal* Lodge No. 1, of Washington, D.C., and served as their Master in 1856. While his record in the District of Columbia Scottish Rite Bodies is scant, Essex had close interactions with Sovereign Grand Inspector General Benjamin B. French, Gustavus A. Schwarzman, and others who established the District's Grand Consistory and *Osiris* Lodge of Perfection on June 22, 1860.

Bibliography:
Archive of the Supreme Council, 33°, S.J.
Archives of the Orient of the District of Columbia and Archives of the Grand Lodge of the District of Columbia, F.A.A.M.

James Bennet Gibbs
Grand Cross of the Court of Honour at age about 69 years and 3 months
Tenure 3 years, 8 months, and 18 days
Nomination by the District of Columbia Scottish Rite Bodies

Born: July 1811 – Died: June 3, 1884
Life span: about 72 years and 11 months
Dentist

Progress in Scottish Rite Masonry:
4°-18°: April 19, 1870, communicated by SGIG Benjamin B. French, 33°, at French's residence.
19°-32°: May 1, 1870, place unconfirmed, communicated by SGIG Benjamin B. French, 33°.
KCCH: May 6, 1874.
33°, IGH: elected October 19, 1880; coroneted by the Supreme Council, 33°, S.J., October 20, 1880.
The said Brother is adjudged to be worthy of the dignity of Grand Cross of the Court of Honour and is entitled to wear the Jewel of the same: October 21, 1880.

Scottish Rite Biography:
Brother James Bennet Gibbs was a member of *Potomac* Lodge, No. 5. On December 16, 1870, he participated in the formation of *Mithras* Lodge of Perfection No. 2; on December 30, 1870, *Kedron* Council of Princes of Jerusalem, No. 1; on December 7, 1871, *Evangelist* Chapter of Knights Rose Croix, No. 1; on December 11, 1873, *Robert De Bruce* Council of Kadosh, No. 1; and on January 6, 1876, *Albert Pike* Consistory No. 1. On May 21, 1878, *Mithras* Lodge of Perfection voted to elect Brother Gibbs an honorary life member. While never serving as the head of any Scottish Rite Body, Gibbs did serve in various positions and committees including: *Mirthas'* first Senior Grand Warden, *Evangelist* Chapter's first Junior Warden, and *Albert Pike* Consistory's first Almoner.

Bibliography:
Archive of the Supreme Council, 33°, S.J.
Archives of the Orient of the District of Columbia and Archives of the Grand Lodge of the District of Columbia, F.A.A.M.

1880

Ferdinand James Samuel Gorgas
Grand Cross of the Court of Honour at age 45 years, 2 months, and 24 days
Tenure 1 year about
Nomination by Maryland Scottish Rite Bodies

Born: July 27, 1835 – Died: April 8, 1914
Life span: 79 years, 8 months, and 11 days
Dentist

Progress in Scottish Rite Masonry:
4°-32°: date unconfirmed, conferred by the *Maryland* Grand Consistory.
KCCH: May 6, 1874.
33°, IGH: May 3, 1876, nominated by Sovereign Grand Commander Albert Pike, 33°; the said nomination to lie over until the next Session; elected May 10, 1878.
The said Brother is adjudged to be worthy of the dignity of Grand Cross of the Court of Honour and is entitled to wear the Jewel of the same: October 21, 1880.

Scottish Rite Biography:
Brother Gorgas received the Symbolic Degrees in *St. John* Lodge, at Carlisle, Pennsylvania. Upon taking up his residence in Baltimore about 1857, he affiliated with *Concordia* Lodge No. 13, at Baltimore. He demitted from *Concordia* Lodge in 1871 and was a Charter member and first Master of *Oriental* Lodge, No. 158. The Scottish Rite Degrees Brother Gorgas received from the Grand Consistory of Maryland. On May 6, 1874, he was elected Knight Commander of the Court of Honour. On May 3, 1876, the Grand Commander nominated Ferdinand J. S. Gorgas for the 33° and Honorary Membership in the Supreme Council, the said nomination to lie over until the next Session, when on May 10, 1878, he was duly elected. On the following Session of the Supreme Council, Brother Gorgas was elected the Grand Cross of the Court of Honour. But in 1881 he withdrew therefrom and affiliated with the Body known as the Cerneau Supreme Council of which he became the presiding officer.

Bibliography:
Archive of the Supreme Council, 33°, S.J.
Proceedings of the Royal Arch Masons in Maryland. 1897: 189.

1880

Lawrence Nichols Greenleaf
Grand Cross of the Court of Honour at age 42 years and 15 days
Tenure 42 years and 3 days
Nomination by Colorado Scottish Rite Bodies

Born: October 4, 1838 – Died: October 25, 1922
Life span: 84 years and 20 days
Editor and Publisher

Progress in Scottish Rite Masonry:
4°-32°: on the 18th of February, 1877, I administrated the Oath of Allegiance to our Supreme Council to Ill. Bro. Laurence N. Greenleaf, 32°, who had originally received the Degrees of the Rite in the Northern Jurisdiction, and granted him a Diploma certifying the same. Albert G. Mackey, 33°.
KCCH: May 7, 1878.
33°, IGH: elected October 19, 1880; coroneted by the Supreme Council, 33°, October 20, 1880.
Deputy: October 7, 1878 – resigned c1915.
The said Brother is adjudged to be worthy of the dignity of Grand Cross of the Court of Honour and is entitled to wear the Jewel of the same: October 21, 1880.

Scottish Rite Biography:
Brother Greenleaf was a Master Mason in *Columbian* Lodge, A.F and A.M., at Boston, Massachusetts. On November 21, 1863, he affiliated with *Denver* Lodge, No. 5, A.F. and A.M., at Denver, Colorado. Brother Greenleaf received the Degrees of the Ancient and Accepted Scottish Rite from Albert G. Mackey. He initiated the movement for and was the principal factor in the organization of the several Bodies of this Rite in Denver; was a charter member of each of them and had been the presiding officer of the *Delta* Lodge of Perfection, No. 1, from 1877 to 1888, *Mackey* Chapter of Rose Croix, No. 1, from 1877 to 1888, *Colorado* Consistory, No.1, from 1889 to 1892. Albert Pike, Grand Commander of the Scottish Rite, recognizing the great worth and abilities of Brother Greenleaf, in 1878 appointed him Deputy for Colorado, which position he filled for many years. On October 19, 1880, he received the 33° Degree of this Rite.

Bibliography:
Archive of the Supreme Council, 33°, S.J.
In Memoriam. *Transactions.* 1923: 297.

1880

Frederick Greenwood
Grand Cross of the Court of Honour at age 43 years, 3 months, and 6 days
Tenure 39 years, 3 months 2 days
Nomination by Richmond, Virginia Scottish Rite Bodies

Born: July 15, 1837 – Died: January 23, 1920
Life span: 82 years, 6 months, and 8 days
Merchant

Progress in Scottish Rite Masonry:
4°-14°: date unconfirmed, invested by *Libertas* Lodge of Perfection, Richmond.
15°-18°: date unconfirmed, invested by *Pelican* Chapter of Rose Croix, Richmond.
19°-30°: date unconfirmed, invested by *St. Omar* Council of Kadosh, Richmond.
31°-32°: date unconfirmed, invested by *Dalcho* Consistory, Richmond.
KCCH: May 6, 1878.
33°, IGH: elected May 6, 1878; coroneted by the Supreme Council, 33°, S.J., May 7, 1878.
May 8, 1878, appointed on the Committee "On the Dead."
The said Brother is adjudged to be worthy of the dignity of Grand Cross of the Court of Honour and is entitled to wear the Jewel of the same: October 21, 1880.

Scottish Rite Biography:
McDaniel Lodge of Perfection, No. 3, in the Valley of Norfolk, seems to be awakening from its lethargy. Last May a meeting of the brethren was called and resulted in their reorganization by electing a Venerable Master and a full corps of officers. This summer months coming on, they were completed to call off owning to the extreme heat, but the outlook, I understand, from Bro. Fred Greenwood, 33°, Hon., whom I made my Deputy, to reorganize this Lodge, is very good. He is taking a very active interest in its revival, and I hope ere another year rolls around to be able to report it on its feet again and in its former vigor.

Bibliography:
Archive of the Supreme Council, 33°, S.J.
Report of Bro. John F. Mayer, 33°, Sovereign Grand Inspector General for Virginia. *Transactiosn.* 1901: 233.

1880

Edwin Gilbert Hall
Grand Cross of the Court of Honour at age 51 years, 11 months, and 7 days
Tenure 39 years, 8 months, and 5 days
Nomination by Kentucky Scottish Rite Bodies

Born: November 14, 1829 – Died: June 26, 1920
Life span: 90 years, 7 months, and 12 days
Manufacturer

Progress in Scottish Rite Masonry:
4°-14°: 1872, invested by *Union* Lodge, No. 3, Louisville.
15°-18°: 1872, invested by *Pelican* Chapter of Rose Croix, No. 1, Louisville.
19°-31°: 1872, invested by *Kilwinning* Council of Kadosh, Louisville.
32°-33°: 1872, invested by Grand Consistory of Kentucky, Louisville.
KCCH: May 30, 1876.
33°, IGH: elected May 6, 1878; coroneted by Sovereign Grand Commander Albert Pike, 33°, May 7, 1878.
The said Brother is adjudged to be worthy of the dignity of Grand Cross of the Court of Honour and is entitled to wear the Jewel of the same: October 21, 1880.

Scottish Rite Biography:
Brother Hall was made an Entered Apprentice Mason in January 1852, was passed in February and raised in April, all in *Jerusalem* Lodge, No. 9, at Henderson . . . Brother Hall was a member of all the Scottish Rite Bodies in Louisville, having received the Degrees 4° to 32° there, and has served in various offices including the Grand Commander of the Grand Consistory of Kentucky. He received the rank and decoration of a Knight Commander of the Court of Honour in 1876, elected 33°, Inspector General Honorary on May 6, 1878, and coroneted by Sovereign Grand Commander Albert Pike, 33°, on May 7, 1878. Ill. Edwin Gilbert Hall, 33°, received the highest honor of the Supreme Council, the Grand Cross of the Court of Honour, on October 21, 1880.

Bibliography:
Archive of the Supreme Council, 33°, S.J.
In Memoriam. *Transactions.* 1921: 200-201.

1880

James Rudolph Hayden
Grand Cross of the Court of Honour at age 43 years, 7 months, and 29 days
Tenure 22 years, 1 month, and 7 days
Nomination by Washington Scottish Rite Bodies

Born: February 22, 1837 – Died: November 14, 1902
Life span: 64 years, 8 months, and 21 days
Banker

Progress in Scottish Rite Masonry:
4°-18°: March 18, 1872, communicated by Bro. Edwin A. Sherman, 32°, Special Deputy.
19°-30°: March 19, 1872, communicated by Bro. Edwin A. Sherman, 32°, Special Deputy.
31°-32°: March 20, 1872, communicated by Bro. Edwin A. Sherman, 32°, Special Deputy.
KCCH: May 6, 1878.
33°, IGH: elected May 6, 1878; coroneted by Ill. James S. Lawson, 33°, SGIG, November 16, 1879
The said Brother is adjudged to be worthy of the dignity of Grand Cross of the Court of Honour and is entitled to wear the Jewel of the same: October 21, 1880.
Deputy: November 27, 1880 – July 8, 1883.
SGIG: elected October 18, 1882; crowned by Ill. Albert Pike, 33°, Sovereign Grand Commander July 8, 1883; laid down his Craft tools while in Office November 14, 1902.

Scottish Rite Biography:
Brother Hayden was made a Master Mason in *Blair* Lodge, No. 393, Chicago, Illinois, August 26, 1869; received the Degree of the AASR up to and including the 32°, in March 1872, at Olympia. Was made KCCH May 6, 1878; was coroneted Hon∴ Inspector-General 33°, November 16, 1879, and on July 8, 1883, was crowned an Active Member of the Supreme Council by Grand Commander Albert Pike, at Portland, Oregon. He filled at different times nearly all the stations from the lowest to the highest in these Bodies. In the Supreme Council Ill. Hayden filled the stations of First Grand Equerry and Grand Standard-Bearer.

Bibliography:
Archive of the Supreme Council, 33°, S.J.
In Memoriam. *Transactions.* 1903: 84; 304-305; 332-334.

1880

John Frazier Head
Grand Cross of the Court of Honour at age 59 years, 9 months, and 12 days
Tenure 27 years, 3 months, and 14 days
Nomination by Kentucky Scottish Rite Bodies

Born: January 9, 1821 – Died: February 5, 1908
Life span: 87 years and 26 days
United States Army Officer and Surgeon

Progress in Scottish Rite Masonry:
4°-14°: October 27, 1863, *Gibulum* Lodge of Perfection, Cincinnati.
15°-18°: March 2, 1864, *Cincinnati* Chapter of Rose Croix, Cincinnati.
19°-30°: March 9, 1864, *Ohio* Council, Cincinnati.
31°-32°: March 9, 1864, *Ohio* Consistory, Cincinnati.
KCCH: May 30, 1876.
33°, IGH: May 30, 1876; coroneted by Sovereign Grand Commander Albert Pike, 33°, June 2, 1876.
The said Brother is adjudged to be worthy of the dignity of Grand Cross of the Court of Honour and is entitled to wear the Jewel of the same: October 21, 1880.

Scottish Rite Biography:
Brother Head was raised to the Sublime Degree on July 2, 1846, in *St. John's* Lodge, No. 1, at Boston, Massachusetts. He joined the Scottish Rite in Cincinnati, Ohio, the Supreme Council, 33°, of the Northern Masonic Jurisdiction. Bro. Head joined the Scottish Rite of the Southern Masonic Jurisdiction and served as a Venerable Master of *Carmel* Lodge of Perfection at St. Paul, Minnesota, from its organization in March 1873 to February 1876. On the Session of the Supreme Council, 33°, S.J. of 1876, he was nominated by the Sovereign Grand Commander Albert Pike, 33°, for election as a Knight Commander of the Court of Honour and 33°, Inspector General Honorary, and on June 2, 1876, was invested with the dignity of Honorary Membership by SGC Albert Pike, 33°. Ill. John Fraizer Head, 33°, was awarded the Grand Cross of the Court of Honour October 21, 1880.

Bibliography:
Archive of the Supreme Council, 33°, S.J.

1880

George John Hobe
Grand Cross of the Court of Honour at age 55 years, 2 months, and 13 days
Tenure 20 years and 8 months
Nomination by San Francisco, California Scottish Rite Bodies

Born: August 8, 1825 – Died: July 21, 1900
Life span: 74 years, 11 months, and 13 days
Bookkeeper

Progress in Scottish Rite Masonry:
4°-32°: July 8, 1868, communicated at San Francisco by Ill. Ebenezer Hamilton Shaw, 33°, Sovereign Grand Inspector General for California.
KCCH: May 8, 1872.
33°, IGH: elected May 30, 1876; coroneted by Sovereign Grand Commander Albert Pike, 33°, on July 26, 1876.
The said Brother is adjudged to be worthy of the dignity of Grand Cross of the Court of Honour and is entitled to wear the Jewel of the same: October 21, 1880.

Scottish Rite Biography:
Brother Hobe was initiated on May 20, 1852, passed May 23, 1852, and raised to the Sublime Degree of Master Mason on June 24, 1852, in *California* Lodge, No. 1, at San Francisco. The Scottish Rite Degrees Brother Hobe received by communication at San Francisco on October 8, 1867, from Ill. Ebenezer H. Shaw, 33°, SGIG in California. On May 8, 1872, he was elected Knight Commander of the Court of Honour, and at the Session of the Supreme Council, 33°, on May 30, 1876, was elected 33°, Inspector General Honorary. The coronation ceremony was performed at San Francisco by Sovereign Grand Commander Albert Pike, 33°, on July 26, 1876. Brother Hobe served as Venerable Master of *Yerba Buena* Lodge of Perfection, No. 6, as well as its Secretary also, Secretary of *Yerba Buena* Chapter of Rose Croix, No. 4, Recorder of *Godfrey de St. Omar* Council of Kadosh, No. 4, and Grand Registrar of Grand Consistory of California. On October 21, 1880, Ill. George John Hobe, 33°, was elected The Grand Cross of the Court of Honour.

Bibliography:
Archive of the Supreme Council, 33º, S.J.
In Memoriam. *Transactions*. 1901: 343.

1880

King David Kalakaula
Grand Cross of the Court of Honour at age 44 years, 11 months, and 5 days
Tenure 10 years, 2 months, and 29 days
Orient of Hawaii

Born: November 16, 1836 – Died: January 20, 1891
Life span: 55 years, 2 months, and 4 days
King of the Hawaiian Islands

Progress in Scottish Rite Masonry:
4°-32°: June 1874, Honolulu, communicated by Ill. Pitkin Cowels Wright, 33°, General Deputy and Legate: for Sandwich Islands [Hawaii] and the Islands of Japan.
KCCH: May 31, 1976.
33°, IGH: elected May 31, 1876; coroneted July 14, 1878.
The said Brother is adjudged to be worthy of the dignity of Grand Cross of the Court of Honour and is entitled to wear the Jewel of the same: October 21, 1880.

Scottish Rite Biography:
Brother King David Kalakaula's Blue Lodge was *Le Progress de l'Oceanie*, No. 124, and he was initiated an Entered Apprentice, March 25, 1859, a Fellow-Craft, May 4, and Master Mason, July 28. The Scottish Rite proved to be a great Masonic field for Kalakaula's interest. He was created a member of *Kamehameha* Lodge of Perfection, July 16, 1874, and installed as Most Wise Master of Nuuanu Chapter of Rose Croix, on September 12. He served in this capacity through 1879. In the *Alexander Liholiho* Council of Kadosh he was elected Chancellor, July 12, 1875. The signal honor of Knight Commander of the Court of Honour came to him by way of election, May 31, 1876. The honors continued in this Rite, when he was elected to an Inspector General Honorary, and coroneted on July 14, 1878. A little later, October 21, 1880, he was awarded the Grand Cross of the Court of Honour.

Bibliography:
Archive of the Supreme Council, 33°, S.J.
In Memoriam. *Transactions*. 1892. Appendix: 49.
The New Age. August 1968.

1880

John Hazlehurts Bonneval Latrobe
Grand Cross of the Court of Honour at age 77 years, 5 months, and 17 days
Tenure 10 years, 10 months, and 28 days
Nomination by Maryland Scottish Rite Bodies

Born: May 4, 1803 – Died: September 19, 1891
Life span: 88 years, 4 months, and 15 days
Lawyer

Progress in Scottish Rite Masonry:
4°-32°: It is appearing that Bro. John H. B. Latrobe, of Baltimore, belonged, many years ago, to a Body, or Bodies of the High Degrees, working, but illegal, under the illegitimate Sovereign Grand Consistory or so-called Supreme Council existing in New York, founded by Joseph Cerneau, and he claiming to have received there the 33°, the Sovereign Grand Commander Albert Pike, 33°, healed him to the 32nd Degree in 1872.
KCCH: May 6, 1874.
33°, IGH: May 30, 1976, Bro. Latrobe, by Inspector Cunningham, asking to be healed in the 33d Degree, doth unanimously consent that he be healed by receiving the Degree anew in due form, upon the customary terms, and taking the oath of allegiance; coroneted the Supreme Council, 33°, S.J., May 7, 1878.
The said Brother is adjudged to be worthy of the dignity of Grand Cross of the Court of Honour and is entitled to wear the Jewel of the same: October 21, 1880.

Scottish Rite Biography:
Brother Latrobe was initiated, passed, and raised in 1825 in *Wilder* Lodge, No. 77, at Baltimore. He received the Scottish Rite Degrees in the illegitimate Sovereign Grand Consistory or co-called Supreme Council existing founded by Joseph Cerneau in New York. In 1872 the Sovereign Grand Commander Albert Pike, 33°, healed him to the 32nd Degree. Brother Latrobe received the rank and decoration of a Knight Commander of the Court of Honour on May 6, 1874. On May 7, 1878, he was invested with the Thirty-third Degree of the Ancient and Accepted Scottish Rite and the dignity of Honorary Membership in the Supreme Council. Ill. John Hazlehurts Bonneval Latrobe, 33°, received the Scottish Rite's highest honor, the Grand Cross on October 21, 1880.

Bibliography:
Archive of the Supreme Council, 33°, S.J.

1880

Charles Erastus Laughton
Grand Cross of the Court of Honour at age 34 years, 4 months, and 17 days
Tenure 14 years, 4 months, and 25 days
Nomination by Nevada Scottish Rite Bodies

Born: June 4, 1846 – Died: March 16, 1895
Life span: 48 years, 9 months, and 12 days
Attorney
First Lieutenant Governor of Washington and Fifth Lieutenant Governor of
Nevada

Progress in Scottish Rite Masonry:
4°-32°: date, place, and by whom Degrees were invested, or communicated unconfirmed.
KCCH: May 7, 1978.
33°, IGH: elected May 7, 1878; date of coronation unconfirmed.
Deputy: c1880 – resigned, date unconfirmed.
The said Brother is adjudged to be worthy of the dignity of Grand Cross of the Court of Honour and is entitled to wear the Jewel of the same: October 21, 1880.

Scottish Rite Biography:
From the Report of the Deputy for Nevada: "Carson, Nev., May 20th, 1880. My Dear General: At last my correspondence, aided by the efforts of Ill. Bro. Henley, have borne fruit, and it affords me pleasure to enclose herewith a draft … for eleven hundred and twenty-five dollars, as the result of conferring the Degrees upon twelve of the best citizens of Eureka, who proposed early next fall, organizing a Lodge of Perfection, and possibly a Chapter of Rose Croix there, if matters can be arranged satisfactorily with you. The gentleman to whom I communicated the Degrees in Eureka, together with several other 32nd who were made by Bro. Caswell several years ago, are very anxious to study the Degrees, and very earnestly petitioned me to appoint there a special deputy, whose jurisdiction would cover Eureka and White Pine Counties … I told them that I would address you on the subject, and I had no doubt you would kindly accede to their wishes. Fraternally yours, Chas. E. Laughton.

Bibliography:
Laughton, Charles E. Report of the Deputy for Nevada. *Transactions*. 1880: 88-90.

1880

Orville Gilbert Miller
Grand Cross of the Court of Honour at age 48 years, 10 months, and 4 days
Tenure 12 years, 6 months, and 9 days
Nomination by Minnesota Scottish Rite Bodies

Born: January 17, 1832 – Died: May 30, 1893
Life span: 61 years, 4 months, and 13 days
Printer

Progress in Scottish Rite Masonry:
4°-32°: February 1869, at St. Paul, communicated by Ill. Azariah Theodore Crane Pierson, 33°, Sovereign Grand Inspector General for Minnesota.
KCCH: May 31, 1876.
33°, IGH: elected and coroneted by the Supreme Council, 33°, S.J., May 7, 1878.
The said Brother is adjudged to be worthy of the dignity of Grand Cross of the Court of Honour and is entitled to wear the Jewel of the same: October 21, 1880.

Scottish Rite Biography:
Brother Miller initiated on July 2, 1858, in *Pacific* Lodge, No. 10, at St. Paul, passed on July 23, and raised to the Sublime Degree on August 27, 1858. The Scottish Rite Degrees from 4° to 32° were invested to him by communication by Ill. Azariah Theodore Crane Pierson, 33°, Sovereign Grand Inspector General for Minnesota in February 1869, at St. Paul. Brother Miller served his Valley as a Presiding Officer for all five Bodies – Lodge of Perfection, Council of Princes of Jerusalem, Chapter of Rose Croix, Council of Kadosh, and Consistory. He received the rank and decoration of a Knight Commander of the Court of Honour on May 31, 1876, elected and coroneted a 33°, Inspector General Honorary on May 7, 1878, and received the highest honor of the Supreme Council, 33°, S.J., the Grand Cross of the Court of Honour on October 21, 1880.

Bibliography:
Archive of the Supreme Council, 33°, S.J.
In Memoriam. *Transactions*. 1893: 26.

1880

Luther Hamilton Pike
Grand Cross of the Court of Honour at age 42 years, 2 months, and 11 days
Tenure 14 years, 2 months, and 18 days
Nomination by the District of Columbia Scottish Rite Bodies

Born: August 10, 1838 – Died: January 9, 1895
Life span: 56 years, 4 months, and 29 days
Lawyer

Progress in Scottish Rite Masonry:
4°-32°: date unconfirmed, conferred by Little Rock Scottish Rite Bodies, Arkansas.
KCCH: May 6, 1874.
33°, IGH: elected and coroneted by the Supreme Council, 33°, May 30, 1876.
The said Brother is adjudged to be worthy of the dignity of Grand Cross of the Court of Honour and is entitled to wear the Jewel of the same: October 21, 1880.

Scottish Rite Biography:
Brother Luther Pike, Albert Pike's son, likely received the Scottish Rite Degrees in Little Rock, Arkansas. He later moved to Washington, D.C. to join his father's law practice; submitted his petition for affiliation to *Mithras* Lodge of Perfection, D.C., on August 1, 1871, and was elected the same night. Luther was an active Scottish Rite Mason serving on various committees. He also participated in the formation of *Kedron* Council of Princes of Jerusalem, No. 1, and *Evangelist* Chapter of Knights Rose Croix, No. 1, on December 7, 1871; *Robert De Bruce* Council of Kadosh, No. 1, on December 11, 1873; *Albert Pike* Consistory No. 1, on January 6, 1876. Brother Pike served as *Evangelist* Chapter's second Wise Master from 1875 to 1878. Luther oversaw his father's Scottish Rite funeral services, which included a request to *Robert De Bruce* Council to perform an honor guard over Albert Pike's remains and a midnight Kadosh funeral service.

Bibliography:
Archive of the Supreme Council, 33°, S.J.
Archives of the Orient of the District of Columbia and Archives of the Grand Lodge of the District of Columbia, F.A.A.M.
In Memoriam. *Transactions*. 1895: 375.

1880

Irving Washington Pratt
Grand Cross of the Court of Honour at age 42 years, 7 months, and 4 days
Tenure 27 years, 8 months, and 20 days
Nomination by Oregon Scottish Rite Bodies

Born: March 17, 1838 – Died: July 11, 1908
Life span: 70 years, 3 months, and 24 days
Teacher, Superintendent of the City Schools

Progress in Scottish Rite Masonry:
4°-18°: April 1871, communicated by the Scottish Rite Bodies in Portland
19°-32°: April 30, 1872, communicated by Ill. John C. Ainsworth, 33°, SGIG for Oregon.
KCCH: May 7, 1878.
33°, IGH: elected May 7, 1878; coroneted at Portland by Ill. John McCracken, 33°, on December 27, 1878.
The said Brother is adjudged to be worthy of the dignity of Grand Cross of the Court of Honour and is entitled to wear the Jewel of the same: October 21, 1880.
Deputy: July 4, 1890 – October 21, 1892.
SGIG: elected and crowned October 21, 1892; laid down his Craft tools while in Office, July 11, 1908.

Scottish Rite Biography:
Brother Pratt was initiated an Entered Apprentice, September 5, 1865, passed to the Degree of Fellow Craft, November 4, 1865, and raised to the Degree of Master Mason, December 14, 1865, all in *Pilot Hill* Lodge, No. 160, at Pilot Hill, California. Brother Pratt received the Degrees of the Ancient and Accepted Scottish Rite, up to and including the Thirty-second Degree, in Portland, in 1872; was coroneted Honorary Inspector General of the Supreme Council, December 27, 1878, and was crowned an Active Member, October 21, 1892. Illustrious Pratt presided over all Subordinate Bodies of the Scottish Rite in Portland and filled all the offices of the Supreme Council below that of Grand Master of Ceremonies.

Bibliography:
Archive of the Supreme Council, 33°, S.J.
In Memoriam. *Transactions.* 1909: 290-294.
Robinson, Michael D. and Seth L. Pope. *Seth Pope's Journal of the Oregon Scottish Rite*. Portland: Michael D. Robinson, 2017.

1880

William Reinecke
Grand Cross of the Court of Honour at age 38 years, 9 months, and 28 days
Tenure 20 years, 9 months, and 27 days
Nomination by Kentucky Scottish Rite Bodies

Born: January 23, 1842 – Died: August 18, 1901
Life span: 59 years, 6 months, and 25 days
Lawyer

Progress in Scottish Rite Masonry:
4°-14°: January 20, 1873, invested by *Union* Lodge of Perfection, Louisville.
15°-18°: February 6, 1873, invested by *Pelican* Chapter of Rose Croix, No.1, Louisville.
19°-30°: February 12, 1873, invested by *Kilwinning* Council of Kadosh, Louisville
31°-32°: February 13, 1873, invested by Grand Consistory of Kentucky, Louisville.
KCCH: May 30, 1876.
33°, IGH: elected May 6, 1878; coroneted by the Supreme Council, 33°, S.J., May 7, 1878.
The said Brother is adjudged to be worthy of the dignity of Grand Cross of the Court of Honour and is entitled to wear the Jewel of the same: October 21, 1880.

Scottish Rite Biography:
Brother Reinecke was raised to the Sublime Degrees in *Excelsior* Lodge, No. 258, Louisville, Kentucky, and a 32°, Master of the Royal Secret in the Grand Consistory of Kentucky. Brother Reinecke served his Orient as a Venerable Master of the *Union* Lodge of Perfection, No. 3, and as a Grand Master of the Grand Consistory. He was invested with the rank and decoration of a Knight Commander of the Court of Honour in 1876, and on the following year coronated an Inspector General Honorary. On October 21, 1880, Ill. William Reinecke, 33°, received the highest honor of the Supreme Council, the Grand Cross of the Court of Honour.

Bibliography:
Archive of the Supreme Council, 33°, S.J.
In Memoriam. *Transactions.* 1901: 345.

1880

William Thomas Reynolds
Grand Cross of the Court of Honour at age 53 years, 6 months, and 7 days
Tenure 28 years, 1 month, and 6 days
Nomination by San Francisco, California Scottish Rite Bodies

Born: September 1, 1822 – Died: July 6, 1900
Life span: 77 years, 1 month, and 25 days
Stockbroker

Progress in Scottish Rite Masonry:
4°-32°: January 1868, communicated at San Francisco by Ill. Ebenezer Hamilton Shaw, 33°, Sovereign
Grand Inspector General for California.
KCCH: May 8, 1872.
33°, IGH: elected May 30, 1876; coroneted by Sovereign Grand Commander Albert Pike, 33°, on July 26,
1876.
**The said Brother is adjudged to be worthy of the dignity of Grand Cross of the Court of Honour and
is entitled to wear the Jewel of the same: October 21, 1880.**

Scottish Rite Biography:
Brother Reynolds was initiated, passed, and raised in *Metropolitan* Lodge, No. 273, at New York. The
Scottish Rite Degrees Brother Reynolds received by communication at San Francisco on January 1868,
from Ill. Ebenezer H. Shaw, 33°, SGIG in California. Brother Reynolds served as a Grand Commander of
the Grand Consistory of California from 1870 to 1872; was elected a Knight Commander of the Court of
Honour on May 8, 1872, and Inspector General Honorary on May 30, 1876. The coronation ceremony was
performed at San Francisco by Sovereign Grand Commander Albert Pike, 33°, on July 26, 1876. On
October 21, 1880, Ill. William Thomas Reynolds was elected Grand Cross of the Court of Honour.

Bibliography:
Archive of the Supreme Council, 33°, S.J.
In Memoriam. *Transactions.* 1901: 343.

William Ryan
Grand Cross of the Court of Honour at age 52 years and 7 days
Tenure 24 years and 27 days
Nomination by Kentucky Scottish Rite Bodies

Born: October 28, 1828 – Died: November 18, 1904
Life span: 76 years and 20 days
Insurance Agent

Progress in Scottish Rite Masonry:
4°-32°: July 11, 1866, conferred by the Grand Consistory of Kentucky.
KCCH: May 30, 1876.
33°, IGH: elected May 6, 1878; coroneted June 18, 1878.
The said Brother is adjudged to be worthy of the dignity of Grand Cross of the Court of Honour and is entitled to wear the Jewel of the same: October 21, 1880.

Scottish Rite Biography:
Brother Ryan received the Degrees of the Blue Lodge in *Cedar* Rapids, Iowa, in 1863. Early in his Masonic Career his zeal for the Order induced him to investigate the Ancient and Accepted Scottish Rite, receiving the 32° in the Grand Consistory of Kentucky, July 11, 1866. The Supreme Council recognizing his zeal and energy in behalf of the Rite, elected him Knight Commander in 1876, and further by electing him to receive the Degree of Inspector-General, 33° Honorary, which honor was conferred June 18, 1878. Ill. Ryan was Grand Master of the Grand Consistory of Kentucky from 1884 to 1887.

Bibliography:
Archive of the Supreme Council, 33°, S.J.
In Memoriam. *Transactions*. 1905: 95; 299; 350-352.

1880

Buren Robinson Sherman
Grand Cross of the Court of Honour at age 44 years, 4 months, and 23 days
Tenure 24 years and 20 days
Nomination by Iowa Scottish Rite Bodies

Born: May 28, 1836 – Died: November 11, 1904
Life span: 68 years, 5 months, and 12 days
Lawyer

Progress in Scottish Rite Masonry:
4°-14°: February 27, 1872, invested by *Iowa* Lodge of Perfection, No. 1, Lyons.
15°-18°: February 28, 1872, invested by *Delphi* Chapter of Rose Croix, No. 1, Lyons.
19°-30°: February 29, 1872, invested by *Hugh de Payens* Council of Kadosh, No. 1, Lyons.
31°-32°: March 1, 1872, invested by *De Molay* Consistory, No. 1, Lyons.
KCCH: May 7, 1878.
33°, IGH: elected May 7, 1878; coroneted September 23, 1878.
The said Brother is adjudged to be worthy of the dignity of Grand Cross of the Court of Honour and is entitled to wear the Jewel of the same: October 21, 1880.
SGIG: elected October 22, 1882; crowned by Illustrious Albert Pike, 33°, Sovereign Grand Commander, January 13, 1883; laid down his Craft tools while in Office November 11, 1904.

Scottish Rite Biography:
Brother Sherman was initiated, passed, and raised in his Lodge, at Vinton during the month of October 1861. Received the Scottish Rite Degrees up to and including the 32°, in 1872 in the Bodies of the Rite at Lyons, Iowa. He was made Knight Commander of the Court of Honour May 6, 1878; was coroneted Honorary Inspector General September 23, 1878; and was crowned Active Member of the Supreme Council by General Albert Pike, Grand Commander, January 13, 1883. Illustrious Sherman lived upon a plane of exalted citizenship, and throughout a long and somewhat eventful life, bore a spotless name and character.

Bibliography:
Archive of the Supreme Council, 33°, S.J.
In Memoriam. *Transactions.* 1905: 274-275; 315-317.

1880

William Reynolds Singleton
Grand Cross of the Court of Honour at age 62 years, 11 months, and 27 days
Tenure 20 years, 4 months, and 2 days
Nomination by the District of Columbia Scottish Rite Bodies

Born: October 24, 1818 – Died: February 23, 1901
Life span: 82 years, 3 months, and 29 days
Civil Engineer

Progress in Scottish Rite Masonry:
4°-5°, July 18, 1871; 6°-9°, July 27, 1871; 10°-12°, August 1, 1871; 13°, August 2, 1871; 14°: August 15, 1871; conferred by *Mithras* Lodge of Perfection, Washington, D.C.
15°-16°: March 26, 1872, communicated by W. M. Ireland, 32°, by dispensation from GC Albert Pike, 33°.
17°-18°: March 27, 1872, communicated by W. M. Ireland, 32°, by dispensation from GC Albert Pike, 33°.
19°-30°: date, place and by whom Degrees were conferred, or communicated unconfirmed.
31°-32°: September 24, 1874, conferred by *Albert Pike* Consistory, Washington, D.C.
KCCH: May 30, 1876.
33°, IGH: elected May 6, 1878; coroneted by the Supreme Council, 33°, May 7, 1878.
Grand Tiler: May 10, 1878 – February 23, 1901.
The said Brother is adjudged to be worthy of the dignity of Grand Cross of the Court of Honour and is entitled to wear the Jewel of the same: October 21, 1880.

Scottish Rite Biography:
Brother Singleton was made a Master Mason in *Naphtail* Lodge, No. 25, St. Louis, Missouri and became an affiliated member of *Osiris* Lodge No. 23, Washington, D.C. He submitted his petition for the Scottish Rite Degrees to *Mithras* Lodge of Perfection on June 6, 1871, and received the 32° in 1874. He received the KCCH on May 28, 1876, coroneted Honorary Inspector General May 7, 1878, and elected Grand Cross October 21, 1880. Ill. Singleton, 33°, served on various committees and officer positions including Senior Warden of *Mithras* Lodge of Perfection, Orator of *Evangelist* Chapter of Rose Croix, Orator of *Robert de Bruce* Council of Kadosh, and Registrar of *Albert Pike* Consistory. Brother Singleton was appointed Grand Tiler of the Supreme Council by Grand Commander Albert Pike, 33°, in 1878, which station he filled for life.

Bibliography:
Archive of the Supreme Council, 33°, S.J.
Archives of the Orient of the District of Columbia and Archives of the Grand Lodge of the District of Columbia, F.A.A.M.
In Memoriam. *Transactions*. 1901: 313; 330-332.

1880

Charles Thomas Sisco
Grand Cross of the Court of Honour at age 42 years, 9 months, and 28 days
Nomination by Maryland Scottish Rite Bodies

Born: December 23, 1837 – Died: c1912
Life span: about 75 years

Progress in Scottish Rite Masonry:
4°-32°: February 26, 1870, communicated by Bro. Henry Bell, Deputy of Ill. Thomas Augustus Cunningham, 33°, Sovereign Grand Inspector General for Maryland.
33°, IGH: May 3, 1976, nominated by Sovereign Grand Commander Albert Pike, 33°, the said nomination to lie over until the next Session; elected May 10, 1878; coroneted October 19, 1880.
The said Brother is adjudged to be worthy of the dignity of Grand Cross of the Court of Honour and is entitled to wear the Jewel of the same: October 21, 1880.

Scottish Rite Biography:
Brother Sisco was raised to the sublime Degree on February 16, 1860, in *Centre* Lodge, No. 108, at Baltimore. He received the Scottish Rite Degrees by communication from Henry Bell, Deputy of Ill. Thomas Augustus Cunningham, 33°, Sovereign Grand Inspector General for Maryland on February 26, 1870. On the Session of the Supreme Council, 33°, S.J., for 1876, Sovereign Grand Commander Albert Pike, 33°, nominated Brother Sisco for the 33°, and Honorary Membership in the Supreme Council, the said nomination to lie over until the next Session. On the following Session Sovereign Grand Commander Albert Pike, 33°, reaffirmed nomination, and Brother Sisco was elected 33°, Inspector General Honorary on May 10, 1878. On the following Session for 1880, Ill. Charles Thomas Sisco, 33°, was elected a Grand Cross of the Court of Honour.

Bibliography:
Archive of the Supreme Council, 33°, S.J.

1880

Charles Schaeffer Streeper
Grand Cross of the Court of Honour at age 42 years, 11 months, and 26 days
Tenure 29 years, 4 months, and 13 days
Nomination by Davenport, Iowa Scottish Rite Bodies

Born: October 25, 1837 – Died: March 4, 1910
Life span: 72 years, 4 months, and 9 days

Progress in Scottish Rite Masonry:
4°-32°: date, place and by whom Degrees were conferred, or communicated, unconfirmed.
KCCH: May 6, 1874.
33°, IGH: elected May 7, 1878; coroneted September 23, 1878.
The said Brother is adjudged to be worthy of the dignity of Grand Cross of the Court of Honour and is entitled to wear the Jewel of the same: October 21, 1880.

Scottish Rite Biography:
No data exist in the Archive of the Supreme Council about Ill. Charles Schaeffer Streeper, 33, GC, besides his name, which was listed in the *Transactions* of the Supreme Council, 33°, S.J., among other Brothers, receiving honorary titles in 1874, 1878, and 1880.

Bibliography:
Archive of the Supreme Council, 33°, S.J.

1880

John Fitzhenry Townshead
Grand Cross of the Court of Honour at age 69 years, 9 months, and 20 days
Tenure 12 years, 3 months, and 11 days
Supreme Council, 33°, for Ireland

Born: January 1, 1811 – Died: February 2, 1893
Life span: 82 years, 1 month, and 1 day
Sovereign Grand Commander of the Supreme Council, 33°, for Ireland

Progress in Scottish Rite Masonry:
4°-32°: date, place and by whom Degrees were invested or communicated unconfirmed.
33°, IGH: date, place and by whom Degree was invested unconfirmed.
Sovereign Grand Commander of the Supreme Council, 33°, for Ireland: 1874-1893.
The said Brother is adjudged to be worthy of the dignity of Grand Cross of the Court of Honour and is entitled to wear the Jewel of the same: October 21, 1880.

Scottish Rite Biography:
Brother John Fitzhenry Townshead had a membership of the Supreme Council, 33°, for Ireland nearly forty years duration, during the latter half of which period he had presided in it as Sovereign Grand Commander. He was indeed one of the burning and shining lights in every Degree. His dignity and fine presence bespoke the true gentleman born; his courtesy and patience, his excellent judgment and common sense, all contributed to fit him to be a commander of men. His thorough knowledge of our symbolism, acquired in a school which will never be surpassed. His style of speaking was chaste and cultivated, showing without effort the refinement and purity of the fountain from which it flowed.

Bibliography:
Archive of the Supreme Council, 33°, S.J.
Chatterton, Hedges Eyer, 33°, Lieutenant Commander of the Supreme Council, 33°, for Ireland. In Memoriam. *Transactions.* 1903: 30-32.

1880

Kephart Delwar Walker
Grand Cross of the Court of Honour at age 43 years, 8 months, and 7 days
Tenure 38 years, 11 months, and 20 days
Nomination by West Virginia Scottish Rite Bodies

Born: February 14, 1838 – Died: September 11, 1919
Life span: 83 years, 6 months, and 27 days
Railroad Conductor

Progress in Scottish Rite Masonry:
4°-14°: December 10, 1875, communicated at Wheeling by Ill. Odell S. Long, 33°, Sovereign Grand Inspector for West Virginia.
15°-18°: May 13, 1876, communicated at Wheeling by Ill. Albert G. Mackey, 33°, General Secretary of the Supreme Council, 33°, S.J.
19°-32°: July 18, 1876, communicated at Wheeling by Ill. Odell S. Long, 33°, Sovereign Grand Inspector for West Virginia.
KCCH: May 6, 1878.
33°, IGH: elected May 6, 1878; coroneted by the Supreme Council, 33°, S.J., May 7, 1878.
The said Brother is adjudged to be worthy of the dignity of Grand Cross of the Court of Honour and is entitled to wear the Jewel of the same: October 21, 1880.

Scottish Rite Biography:
Brother Kephart was initiated an Entered Apprentice on April 6, 1870, passed to the Degree of Fellow Craft April 18, and raised to the Sublime Degree of Master Mason on May 3, 1870, in *Fairmount* Lodge, No. 9, at Fairmount, West Virginia. On May 6, 1878, Sovereign Grand Commander Albert Pike, 33°, nominated Brother Kephart for Knight Commander of the Court of Honour, and he was elected, immediately after he was nominated for the 33° as an honorarium, and elected. On October 21, 1880, Ill. Kephart Delwar Walker, 33°, received the highest honor of the Supreme Council, the Grand Cross of the Court of Honour.

Bibliography:
Archive of the Supreme Council, 33°, S.J.
In Memoriam. *Transactions.* 1919: 292-293.

1882

No nominations for and no election

of the Honour of Grand Cross

1884

Joseph Knight Ashby
Grand Cross of the Court of Honour at age 57 years, and 10 days
Tenure 20 years, 7 months, and 8 days
Nomination by Fort Worth, Texas Scottish Rite Bodies

Born: October 13, 1827 – Died: June 1, 1905
Life span: 77 years, 7 months, and 18 days
Saddler Business

Progress in Scottish Rite Masonry:
4°-14°: June 15, 1881, communicated by Sovereign Grand Commander Albert Pike, 33°.
15°-30°: June 16, 1881, communicated by Sovereign Grand Commander Albert Pike, 33°.
31°-32°: June 17, 1881, communicated by Sovereign Grand Commander Albert Pike, 33°.
32°, KCCH: October 18, 1882.
33°, IGH: elected October 23, 1884; coroneted by the Supreme Council, 33°, S.J., October 24, 1884.
Grand Cross of the Court of Honour: October 23, 1884.

Scottish Rite Biography:
Brother Joseph Knight Ashby raised December 7, 1878, in *Fort Worth* Lodge, No. 48, made Perfect Elu, June 15, 1881, by Ill. Brother Albert Pike; made Knight Rose Croix, June 16, 1881, by Ill. Brother Albert Pike; made Knight Kadosh, June 16, 1881, by Ill. Brother Albert Pike; made 32°, June 17, 1881, by Ill. Brother Albert Pike; elected Knight Commander of the of the Court of Honor, October, 1882; elected Grand Cross of the Court of Honour, October 23, 1884; coroneted Inspector-General Honorary, October 23, 1884, by the Supreme Council at Washington, D.C. Brother Ashby devoted most of his time to Scottish Rite Masonry, doing a good deal of work, and finally succeeded in instituting a Consistory in Fort Worth.

Bibliography:
Archive of the Supreme Council, 33°, S.J.
In Memoriam. *Transactions*. 1905: 102; 293; 343-344.

1884

William Oscar Roome
Grand Cross of the Court of Honour at age 45 years, 2 months, and 14 days
Tenure 37 years, 3 months, and 10 days
Nomination by the District of Columbia Scottish Rite Bodies

Born: August 9, 1839 – Died: February 3, 1922
Life span: 82 years, 5 months, and 24 days
Clerk

Progress in Scottish Rite Masonry:
4°-14°: October1, 1878, conferred by *Mithras* Lodge of Perfection, Washington, D.C.
15°-18°: November 5, 1878, conferred by *Evangelist* Chapter of Rose Croix, Washington, D.C.
19°-30°: date unconfirmed, conferred by *Robert de Bruce* Council of Kadosh, Washington, D.C.
31°-32°: February 14, 1882, conferred by *Albert Pike* Consistory, Washington, D.C.
KCCH: October 18, 1882.
33°, IGH: elected October 23, 1884; coroneted October 24, 1884.
Grand Cross of the Court of Honour: October 23, 1884.

Scottish Rite Biography:
Brother Roome received his masonic degrees in *Greenwich* Lodge, No. 467, New York. He submitted his petition for the Scottish Rite Degrees to *Mithras* Lodge of Perfection on August 8, 1878. On June 22, 1881, he was elected as one of Albert G. Mackey's Pallbearers, representing the *Robert De Bruce* Council of Kadosh. He served as Venerable Master of Mithras Lodge of Perfection, (1883-1895), Wise Master of *Evangelist* Chapter (1890-1894, 1897-1899), and Venerable Master of *Albert Pike* Consistory (1899-1900). Roome served as Chairman of the building committee that acquired the DC SR cathedral on 1007 G Street, N.W. and president of the building's board of trustees. Roome later married Lilian Pike, Albert Pike's daughter, around 1903.

Bibliography:
Archive of the Supreme Council, 33°, S.J.
Archives of the Orient of the District of Columbia and Archives of the Grand Lodge of the District of Columbia, F.A.A.M.
In Memoriam. *Transactions.* 1923: 312-313.

1886

No nominations for and no election
of the Honour of Grand Cross

1888

Rudolph Gunner
Grand Cross as an Honorary Member of the Court of Honour at age 54 years, 10 months, and 3 days
Tenure 22 years, 10 months, and 6 days
Nomination by Dallas, Texas Scottish Rite Bodies

Born: December 15, 1833 – Died: August 24, 1911
Life span: 77 years, 8 months, and 9 days
Bookseller

Progress in Scottish Rite Masonry:
4°-32°: date unconfirmed, invested by the Supreme Council, 33°, of Mexico.
33°, IGH: June 20, 1866, coroneted by the Supreme Council, 33°, of Mexico.
October 18, 1888, affiliated with Dallas Scottish Rite Bodies.
Grand Cross of the Court of Honour: October 18, 1888.

Scottish Rite Biography:
Brother Gunner was made a Mason in the country of Mexico in 1864 and was coroneted 33° Honorary in 1866. He was speaker for two years there, and while occupying this high station was compelled to speak Spanish, French and German to the Brethren. He came to Texas and immediately received the Southern Jurisdiction Diploma, sighed by General Albert Pike. He succeeded Col. John C. McCoy as Deputy of the Inspector General for North Texas, and during his incumbency in office conferred the Degrees on several of those who are now among our most prominent members of Dallas Consistory. His Masonic record shows many years of activity and usefulness in the Fraternity, and in all these relations and responsibilities he fully met the expectations of his Brethren and heard their well-earned words of commendation.

Bibliography:
Archive of the Supreme Council, 33°, S.J.
In Memoriam. *Transactions.* 1911: 339.

1890

Alexander Hollenbeck Holt
Grand Cross of the Court of Honour at age 52 years, 11 months, and 12 days
Tenure 24 years, 1 month, and 9 days
Nomination by the District of Columbia Scottish Rite Bodies

Born: September 9, 1838 – Died: January 14, 1918
Life span: 79 years, 4 months, and 5 days
Colonel

Progress in Scottish Rite Masonry:
4°-14°: December 28, 1866, conferred by *Monmouth* Lodge of Perfection No. 3, of Monmouth, Illinois.
15°-18°: December 28, 1866, conferred by *Monmouth* Council of Princes of Jerusalem and *Monmouth* Chapter of Rose Croix, of Monmouth, Illinois.
19°-30°: December 29, 1866, conferred by *Monmouth* Council of Kadosh, Monmouth, Illinois.
31°-32°: December 29, 1866, conferred by *Monmouth* Consistory, Monmouth, Illinois.
KCCH: October 20, 1886.
Grand Cross of the Court of Honour: October 22, 1890.
33°, IGH: elected October 21, 1897; coroneted October 22, 1897; demitted December 1, 1914.

Scottish Rite Biography:
Brother Alexander Hollenbeck Holt, originally from *Monmouth* Lodge of Perfection No. 3, of Monmouth, Illinois, submitted his petition for affiliation to *Mirthas* Lodge of Perfection on February 5, 1877, and was elected to membership on April 11, 1877. Brother Holt served as Venerable Master of *Albert Pike* Consistory between 1889-1895 and secretary of the Board of Trustees, *Mirthas* Lodge of Perfection, *Robert De Bruce* Council of Kadosh, and *Evanglist* Chapter Rose Croix throughout his tenure in the DC Scottish Rite. On December 26, 1894, Grand Commander Philip C. Tucker appointed Holt Deputy Inspector General in the absence of John Mills Browne. Holt dropped from the membership rolls of *Mitrhas* Lodge of Perfection on December 1, 1914. Brother Holt deserved well of the Order: and the Supreme Council, well informed of this, desires to bear witness to it unto all the Brethren of the Obedience, and to that end has selected him from among all the Master Masons of the Royal Secret to be invested with the dignity of Grand Cross of the Court of Honour, with all the rights and privileges belonging to the same.

Bibliography:
Pike, Albert. Investiture with the jewel of The Grand Cross of the Court of Honour. *Transactions.* 1890: 55.
Archive of the Supreme Council, 33°, S.J.
Archives of the Orient of the District of Columbia and Archives of the Grand Lodge of the District of Columbia, F.A.A.M.

1892

Harry Pryor Collins
Grand Cross of the Court of Honour at age 39 years, 4 months, and 23 days
Tenure 14 years, 7 months, and 3 days
Nomination by Des Moines, Iowa Scottish Rite Bodies

Born: May 29, 1853 – Died: May 25, 1907
Life span: 53 years, 11 months, and 26 days
Commercial Officer

Progress in Scottish Rite Masonry:
4°- 14°: April 7, 1886, invested by *Van Rensselaer* Lodge of Perfection, Chicago.
15°- 18°: April 7, 1886, invested by *Gourgas* Chapter of Rose Croix, Chicago.
19°- 32°: April 9, 1886, invested by *Oriental* Consistory, Chicago.
March 1, 1900, affiliated with Des Moines Scottish Rite Bodies, Iowa.
KCCH: October 19, 1892.
Grand Cross of the Court of Honour: October 22, 1892.
33°, IGH: elected October 18, 1893; coroneted by Ill. John H. Cowles, 33°, Grand Secretary General November 9, 1899.

Scottish Rite Biography:
Brother Frank Prior Collins was made a Master Mason in *Pioneer* Lodge No. 22, A.F. & A.M., Des Moines, April 30, 1881. Received Consistory Degrees in Orient Consistory in Chicago, Illinois. Was a charter member of the Scottish Rite Bodies of Des Moines, Iowa, and the first Wise Master of *Emanuel* Chapter, Knights Rose Croix., and served as Lieutenant Commander of Des Moines Consistory. Elected Knight Commander of the Court of Honor October 19, 1892. Was voted the Grand Cross of Honor by the Supreme Council October 22, 1892. Elected to 33° by the Supreme Council October 18, 1893.

Bibliography:
Archive of the Supreme Council, 33°, S.J.
In Memoriam. *Transactions*. 1907: 150; 334.

1892

Daniel Emerson Cummings
Grand Cross of the Court of Honour at age 39 years, 8 months, and 4 days
Tenure unconfirmed
Nomination by South Dakota Scottish Rite Bodies

Born: February 18, 1853 – Died: unconfirmed
Life span: unconfirmed
Locomotive Engineer

Progress in Scottish Rite Masonry:
4°-14°: February 5, 1885, communicated at Lincoln, Nebraska by Ill. Robert Carrel Jordan, 33°, SGIG.
15°-18°: February 6, 1885, communicated at Lincoln, Nebraska by Ill. Robert Carrel Jordan, 33°, SGIG.
19°-30°: February 7, 1885, communicated at Lincoln, Nebraska by Ill. Robert Carrel Jordan, 33°, SGIG.
31°-32°: February 8, 1885, communicated at Lincoln, Nebraska by Ill. Robert Carrel Jordan, 33°, SGIG.
32°, KCCH: October 19, 1892.
33°, IGH: elected October 18, 1893; coroneted by the Supreme Council, 33°, S.J., October 19, 1893.
Grand Cross of the Court of Honour: October 22, 1892.

Scottish Rite Biography:
Brother Cummings was initiated on July 20, 1881, passed on September 5, and raised to the Sublime Degree on October 3, 1881, in *Plattsmouth* Lodge No. 6, at Plattsmouth, Nebraska. He received the Scottish Rite Degrees by communication by Ill. Robert Carrel Jordan, 33°, Sovereign Grand Inspector General for Nebraska and became a Master of the Royal Secret on February 8, 1885. Later on, he joined the Scottish Rite Bodies in South Dakota, and on May 23 was appointed Deputy of Ill. Rufus Eberle Fleming, 33°, Sovereign Grand Inspector General for South Dakota. Brother Cummings was invested as a Knight Commander of the Court of Honour on October 19, 1892, and on the same session received the highest honor of the Supreme Council, 33°, S.J., the Grand Cross of the Court of Honour. On the following Session on October 19, 1893, Brother Daniel Emerson Cummings, 32°, KCCH, GC, was elected and coroneted as 33°, Inspector General Honorary.

Bibliography:
Archive of the Supreme Council, 33°, S.J.

1892

William Schuyler Moses
Grand Cross of the Court of Honour at age 65 years, 2 months, and 14 days
Tenure 20 years, 1 month, and 17 days
Nomination by San Francisco, California Scottish Rite Bodies

Born: August 8, 1827 – Died: December 9, 1912
Life span: 85 years, 4 months, and 1 day
Millwright

Progress in Scottish Rite Masonry:
4°-32°: June 1864, communicated by Ill. Ebenezer H. Shaw, 33°, Sovereign Grand Inspector General for California.
32°, KCCH: October 20, 1886.
33°, IGH: elected October 18, 1905; no indication regarding coronation.
Grand Cross of the Court of Honour: October 22, 1892.

Scottish Rite Biography:
William Schuyler Moses was one of the most interesting and picturesque Masons of the great State of California. He was one of the last links, connecting the early history of Masonry with the present. Tall, majestic, patriarchal in appearance, kind of heart, gentle of manner, uttering none but words of kindness; a mind replete with anecdote and story; to be seen night after night at the Masonic gatherings. He was made a Mason in *Valley* Lodge, at Rochester, New York, receiving the Master's Degree on March 12, 1849. He received the Degrees of the Scottish Rite in June 1864, by communication, from Brother Ebenezer H. Shaw, 33°, Sovereign Grand Inspector General in California … his best work was in Scottish Rite, his nature seeming to respond with enthusiastic fervor to the beautiful truths expressed in its ritual. He was selected for the first and most important position in all the co-ordinate Bodies and served them faithfully. He was the Almoner of all the Bodies. The Supreme Council, recognizing his devotion to the true principles of Masonry, and especially of the Scottish Rite, honored him with the Grand Cross of the Court of Honour.

Bibliography:
Archive of the Supreme Council, 33°, S.J.
In Memoriam. *Transactions*. 1913: 201.

1893

No nominations for and no election

of the Honour of Grand Cross

1895

Trevanion W. Hugo
Grand Cross of the Court of Honour at age 46 years, 8 months, and 2 days
Tenure 27 years, 4 months, and 1 day
Nomination by Minneapolis, Minnesota Scottish Rite Bodies

Born: July 24, 1848 – Died: February 27, 1923
Life span: 75 years, 7 months, and 2 days
Engineer

Progress in Scottish Rite Masonry:
4°-14°: April 6, 1887, invested by *Excelsior* Lodge of Perfection, No. 2, Minneapolis.
15°-18°: April 7, 1887, invested by *St. Vincent de Paul* Chapter of Rose Croix, No. 2 Minneapolis.
19°-30°: April 8, 1887, invested by *Alfred Elisha Ames* Council of Kadosh, No. 2, Minneapolis.
31°-32°: December 4, 1887, invested by *Minneapolis* Consistory, No. 2, Minneapolis.
32°, KCCH: October 22, 1890.
33°, IGH: elected October 22, 1890; coroneted by Ill. Albert Pike, 33°, SGC October 22, 1890.
Grand Cross Court of the Court of Honour: October 26, 1895.
Deputy: May 21, 1912 – October 25, 1913.
SGIG: elected October 24, 1913; crowned October 25, 1913; laid down his Craft tools while in Office February 27, 1923.

Scottish Rite Biography:
Brother Hugo was a Master Mason in *Minden* Lodge No. 235 in Minden, Ontario, and affiliated with *Palestine* Lodge No. 79 in Duluth on December 3, 1888. Illustrious Brother Hugo received the Scottish Rite Degrees in the Minneapolis Scottish Rite Bodies in 1887, and demitted to the Duluth Bodies on March 7, 1889, as a Charter Member. He became the first Venerable Master of *North Star* Lodge of Perfection, first Wise Master of *A.T.C. Pierson* Chapter of Rose Croix, first Commander of *Zenith* Council of Kadosh, and first Venerable Master of the *Duluth* Consistory, serving continuously as the Head of all four bodies until 1912. The knowledge thus acquired inspired his special activity in the prosecution of the educational program of the Scottish Rite Supreme Council. Brother Hugo raised the funds to purchase and install a handsome organ in The Scottish Rite Cathedral. He founded the Infant Welfare Bureau under the sponsorship of the Scottish Rite Bodies of Duluth and guided its growth into an instrumentality of great achievement.

Bibliography:
Archive of the Supreme Council, 33°, S.J.
In Memoriam. *Transactions.* 1923: 89; 177; 282-283.

1895

Ernest Bertrand Hussey
Grand Cross of the Court of Honour at age 30 years, 10 months, and 16 days
Tenure 43 years, 2 months, and 3 days
Nomination by Washington Scottish Rite Bodies

Born: January 10, 1865 – Died: December 27, 1938
Life span: 72 years, 11 months, and 16 days
Engineer

Progress in Scottish Rite Masonry:
4°-30°: date, place and by whom Degrees were communicated unconfirmed.
31°-32°: December 23, 1887, invested by Massachusetts Consistory, Boston.
KCCH: October 23, 1895.
Grand Cross of the Court of Honor: October 26, 1895.
33°, IGH: elected October 19, 1897, coroneted October 23, 1898.
Deputy: January 21, 1903, for Washington and Alaska – October 24, 1903.
SGIG: elected and crowned October 24, 1903; demitted May 20, 1920.

Scottish Rite Biography:
Brother Hussey received the Scottish Rite Degrees in the Scottish Rite Bodies at Boston, Massachusetts. He moved to the East Coast and in 1894 affiliated with the Scottish Rite Bodies at Seattle. On the following year in October 1895, Brother Hussey was elected to both Courts of Honour – Knight Commander of the Court of Honour and the Grand Cross of the Court of Honour. On the following Session of the Supreme Council, Brother Hussey was elected 33°, IGH, and coroneted on October 23, 1898. On January 21, 1903, Ill. Ernest Bertrand Hussey, 33°, was appointed Deputy of the Supreme Council for the Orient of Washington and Alaska, elected and crowned Sovereign Grand Inspector General on October 24, 1903, and served in this position 17 years, 3 months, and 29 days. Demitted by request May 20, 1938.

Bibliography:
Archive of the Supreme Council, 33°, S.J.

1895

Philip S. Malcolm
Grand Cross of the Court of Honour at age 47 years, 11 months, and 26 days
Tenure 33 years, 3 months, and 5 days
Nomination by Oregon Scottish Rite Bodies

Born: October 30, 1847 – Died: February 1, 1929
Life span: 81 years, 3 months, and 1 day
Engineer

Progress in Scottish Rite Masonry:
4°-30: date unconfirmed, 1876, Panama.
31°-32°: March 7, 1883, communicated by Illustrious Rockey Preston Earhart, 33°, Sovereign Grand Inspector General for Oregon.
32°, KCCH: October 22, 1890.
33°, IGH: elected October 22, 1890; coroneted February 14, 1891.
Grand Cross Court of the Court of Honour: October 26, 1895.
Deputy: November 17, 1908 – October 21, 1911.
SGIG: elected October 19, 1911; crowned October 21, 1911; laid down his Craft tools while in Office, February 1, 1929.

Scottish Rite Biography:
Brother Malcolm was passed and raised in *Sodus* Lodge, No. 392, New York State. He received the Scottish Rite Degrees, up to and including the 30°, in 1876 in Panama, under the authority of the Grand Orient of the Unites States of Columbia. The 32° was conferred upon him in Portland, Oregon, in 1883. He was elected a KCCH and an Inspector General Honorary October 22, 1890, and coroneted 33° Honorary on February 14, 1891. He was also one of the few members of the Supreme Council that ever received the distinguished honor of the Grand Cross of the Court of Honour, this occurring at the Supreme Council session October 26, 1895, and he was elected and crowned an Active Member of the Supreme Council in October 1911. Brother Malcolm held several offices in the Supreme Council. He was the Representative of the Supreme Council of the Netherlands, and of the Grand Lodge of Norway near our Supreme Council.

Bibliography:
Archive of the Supreme Council, 33°, S.J.
In Memoriam. *Transactions*. 1929: 306-310.
Robinson, Michael D., and Seth L. Pope. *Seth Pope's Journal of the Oregon Scottish Rite*. Portland: Michael D. Robinson, 2017.

1897

Albert Brewer Guptill
Grand Cross of the Court of Honour at age 43 years, 4 months, and 25 days
Tenure 34 years, 2 months, and 9 days
Nomination by North Dakota Scottish Rite Bodies

Born: May 26, 1854 – Died: January 1, 1931
Life span: 76 years, 7 months, and 5 days
Lawyer and Writer

Progress in Scottish Rite Masonry:
4°-14°: May 30, 1883, at Fargo, communicated by Ill. Robert Carrel Jordan, 33°, SGIG for Nebraska.
15°-18°: May 31, 1883, at Fargo, communicated by Ill. Robert Carrel Jordan, 33°, SGIG for Nebraska.
19°-30°: June 1, 1883, at Fargo, communicated by Ill. Robert Carrel Jordan, 33°, SGIG for Nebraska.
31°-32°: June 2, 1883, at Fargo, communicated by Ill. Robert Carrel Jordan, 33°, SGIG for Nebraska.
KCCH: October 17, 1888.
33°, IGH: elected October 18, 1892; coroneted by Ill. Rufus Eberle Fleming, 33°, SGIG for North Dakota on December 30, 1895.
Grand Cross of the Court of Honour: October 21, 1897.

Scottish Rite Biography:
Brother Guptill was initiated on October 3, 1876, in *Hermon* Lodge, No. 41, at Zumbrota, Minnesota, passed on October 18, and raised on October 24 in the same year. He was one of the ten Brothers, who formed the class to whom the Scottish Rite Degrees from 4° to 32° were communicated by Ill. Robert Carrel Jordan, 33°, SGIG for Nebraska in 1883 at Fargo. Brother Guptill became a Charter member of the Fargo Scottish Rite Bodies, and since that time has been an active worker in them, serving as a Master of Ceremonies to all four Bodies. He was elected Knight Commander of the Court of Honour in 1888; coroneted 33°, Inspector General Honorary in 1895, and on the following year Ill. Albert Brewer Guptill was elected the Grand Cross of the Court of Honour.

Bibliography:
Archive of the Supreme Council, 33°, S.J.
In Memoriam. *Transactions.* 1933: 284-285.

Elliot Lang
Grand Cross of the Court of Honour at age 39 years, 2 months, and 21 days
Tenure 26 years, 7 months, and 8 days
Nomination by Memphis, Tennessee Scottish Rite Bodies

Born: July 30, 1858 – Died: May 29, 1924
Life span: 65 years, 9 months, and 29 days
Businessman

Progress in Scottish Rite Masonry:
4°-14°: May 17, 1892, invested by *Mizpah* Lodge of Perfection, No. 5, Memphis.
15°-18°: June 1892, invested by *Calvary* Chapter of Rose Croix, No. 1, Memphis.
19°-32°: July 1892, communicated by Ill. Pitkin Cowels Wright, 33°, Deputy for Tennessee. 32°.
KCCH: October 19, 1897.
33°, IGH: elected October 22, 1901; coroneted October 3, 1903.
Grand Cross of the Court of Honour: October 21, 1897.

Scottish Rite Biography:
Brother Land was initiated on February 29, 1892, passed on March 18, 1892, and raised on April 16, 1892, in *DeSoto* Lodge, 299, At Memphis, Tennessee. Without delay, on the following month May 17, 1892, he received the Scottish Rite Degrees from 4° to 14° from *Mizpah* Lodge of Perfection, No. 5, at Memphis. The Degrees 15° to 18° were invested to him by *Calvary* Chapter of Rose Croix, No. 1, Memphis. And the Degrees of the Council of Kadosh and Consistory were communicated to him by Ill. Pitkin Cowels Wright, 33°, Deputy for Tennessee. Brother Lang served in Memphis Valley as Venerable Master of *Mizpah* Lodge of Perfection and Wise Master of *Calvary* Chapter of Rose Croix. In October 1897, Brother Elliot Lang was elected to both Courts of Honour – Knight Commander of the Court of Honour and the Grand Cross of the Court of Honour.

Bibliography:
Archive of the Supreme Council, 33°, S.J.
In Memoriam. *Transactions*. 1925: 274-275.

1899

Edwin Allen Sherman
Grand Cross of the Court of Honour at age 70 years, 1 month, and 25 days
Tenure 14 years, 4 months, and 27 days
Nomination by Oakland, California Scottish Rite Bodies

Born: August 25, 1829 – Died: March 17, 1914
Life span: 84 years, 6 months, and 20 days
Editor

Progress in Scottish Rite Masonry:
4°-14°: May 1868, invested by *Palestine* Lodge of Perfection, No. 3, Sacramento.
15°-32°: date, place and by whom Degrees were communicated unconfirmed.
32°, KCCH: October 23, 1884.
33°, IGH: elected October 23, 1884; coroneted October 20, 1885.
Special Deputy for all the Territories: fall 1871 – May 11, 1872.
Grand Cross of the Court of Honour: October 20, 1899.

Scottish Rite Biography:
Brother Sherman was made a Mason in June 1854, in *Columbia* Lodge, Boston; he received the Perfection Degrees in *Palestine* Lodge, No. 3, Sacramento, California, in May 1868, and the other Degrees later on by communication. He was elected Knight Commander of the Court of Honour in October 1884, and coroneted 33°, October 20, 1885, and for extraordinary and valuable services to the Rite was elected and received the Grand Cross of the Court of Honour in October 1899. His Masonic Life marked by vitalized activity, for he served in nearly all the offices of the Scottish Rite. Illustrious Sherman was a patriotic citizen, a soldier, a prolific writer of Masonic treaties and an editor of note.

Bibliography:
Archive of the Supreme Council, 33°, S.J.
In Memoriam. *Transactions*. 1915: 281-282.

1901

No nominations for and no election

of the Honour of Grand Cross

1903

No nominations for and no election
of the Honour of Grand Cross

1905

No nominations for and no election

of the Honour of Grand Cross

1907

Benjamin Bentley Allen
Grand Cross of the Court of Honour at age 52 years, 4 months, and 19 days
Tenure 2 years, 8 months, and 19 days
Nomination by Nashville, Tennessee Scottish Rite Bodies

June 5, 1855 – Died: July 13, 1910
Life span: 55 years, 1 month, and 8 days
Capitalist

Progress in Scottish Rite Masonry:
4°-32°: November 7, 1904, communicated by Ill. George F. Moore, 33°, Sovereign Grand Inspector General for Alabama.
32°, KCCH: October 24, 1907.
33°, IGH: elected October 20, 1909; crowned by the Supreme Council, 33°, S.J., October 22, 1909.
Grand Cross of the Court of Honour: October 24, 1907.

Scottish Rite Biography:
Benjamin Bentley Allan was a member of *Cumberland* Lodge, No. 1, of Nashville, in which Lodge he received his first three Degrees of Masonry. He received the Scottish Rite Degrees at Nashville by communication in November 1904; was elected Knight Commander of the Court of Honor October 24, 1907, and the same day was elected Grand Cross by the Supreme Council for meritorious and conspicuous services to the Rite. On October 20, 1909, was elected 33° Honorary, and was coroneted by the Supreme Council October 22, of the same year. He was a great student of Freemasonry and especially of the Ancient and Accepted Scottish Rite. From the date of the founding of the Bodies of the Rite at Nashville in September 1905, he was Director of the work therein, and to him more than any other one Brother is due the marvelous success achieved by the Bodies in the Valley of Nashville.

Bibliography:
Archive of the Supreme Council, 33°, S.J.
In Memoriam. *Transactions.* 1911: 310.

1907

William Harris Laird
Grand Cross of the Court of Honour at age 74 years
Tenure 2 years, 3 months, and 10 days
Nomination by Winona, Minnesota Scottish Rite Bodies

Born: October 24, 1833 – Died: February 4, 1910
Life span: 76 years, 3 months, and 10 days
Businessman

Progress in Scottish Rite Masonry:
4°-14°: October 12, 1896, invested by *Excelsior* Lodge of Perfection, Minneapolis.
15°-18°: October 13, 1896, invested by *St. Vincent de Paul* Chapter of Rose Croix, Minneapolis.
19°-30°: October 14, 1896, invested by *Alfred Elisha Ames* Council of Kadosh, Minneapolis.
31°-32°: October 15, 1896, invested by *Minneapolis* Consistory, Minneapolis.
32°, KCCH: October 19, 1899.
33°, IGH: elected October 22, 1901; coroneted by the Supreme Council, 33°, S.J., October 25, 1901
Grand Cross of the Court of Honour: October 24, 1907.

Scottish Rite Biography:
Brother Laird was initiated on April 2, 1895, in *Winona* Lodge, No. 18, at Winona, passed on April 16, and raised on May 13, 1895. On the following year Brother Laird was invested with the Scottish Rite Degrees by Minneapolis Bodies. He received the rank and decoration of Knight Commander of the Court of Honour in 1899, and on the next Session of the Supreme Council was elected and coroneted 33°, Inspector General Honorary. Ill. William Harris Laird, 33° was elected the Grand Cross of the Court of Honour on October 24, 1907.

Bibliography:
Archive of the Supreme Council, 33°, S.J.

1909

Hyman Wallace Witcover
Grand Cross of the Court of Honour at age 38 years, 3 months, and 6 days
Tenure 26 years 11 months, and 10 days
Nomination by Savannah, Georgia Scottish Rite Bodies

Born: July 16, 1871 – Died: October 1, 1936
Life span: 65 years, 2 months, and 15 days
Architect

Progress in Scottish Rite Masonry:
4°-14°: c1901, invested by *Alpha* Lodge of Perfection, No. 1, Savannah.
15°-18°: c1901, invested by *Temple* Chapter of Rose Croix, No. 1, Savannah.
19°-30°: c1901, invested by *Gethsemane* Council of Knights of Kadosh, No. 1, Savannah.
31°-32°: c1901, invested by *Benzabee* Consistory, No. 1, Savannah.
32°, KCCH: October 18, 1905.
33°, IGH: elected October 24, 1907; coroneted by the Supreme Council, 33°, S.J., October 25, 1907.
Grand Cross of the Court of Honour: October 22, 1909.
Deputy: for Savannah April 8, 1911 – October 21, 1911.
SGIG: elected and crowned October 21, 1911; laid down his Craft tools while in Office October 1, 1936.

Scottish Rite Biography:
Brother Witcover was a Master Mason in *Ancient Landmark* Lodge, No. 231.He received the Degree of the AASR in Savannah, Georgia, and all in the year 1901. He was given the rank and decoration of KCCH, October 19, 1905, was elected to the Grand Cross of the Court of Honour October 22, 1909, and was coroneted a 33° Inspector General, Honorary, October 23, 1907. In 1910 Illustrious Witcover was appointed Deputy in the Orient of Georgia, and was crowned an Active Member, October 21, 1911 … Illustrious Witcover served on several Committees of the Supreme Council. He was holding the office of First Grand Equerry when he was elected Secretary General in which capacity, he served from October 1923, until he resigned on June 30, 1934.

Bibliography:
Archive of the Supreme Council, 33°, S.J.
In Memoriam. *Transactions.* 1937: 280-286.

1911

William Abial Scott
Grand Cross of the Court of Honour at age 55 years, 10 months, and 12 days
Tenure 6 years, 2 months, and 11 days
Nomination by Fargo, North Dakota Scottish Rite Bodies

Born: December 8, 1856 – Died: December 31, 1917
Life span: 61 years and 22 days
President of the Pioneer Insurance Company

Progress in Scottish Rite Masonry:
4°-14°: May 8, 1889, invested by *Enoch* Lodge of Perfection, No. 2, Fargo.
15°-18°: March 28, 1890, invested by P*elican* Chapter of Rose Croix, No. 2, Fargo.
19°-30°: March 28, 1890, invested by *Fargo* Council of Kadosh, No. 1, Fargo.
31°-32°: March 28, 1890, invested by *Dakota* Consistory, No. 1, Fargo.
32°, KCCH: October 18, 1893.
33°, IGH: elected October 23, 1895; coroneted by Ill. Rufus Eberle Fleming, 33°, Sovereign Grand Inspector General for North Dakota on December 18, 1895.
Deputy: November 5, 1905 – resigned c1907.
Grand Cross of the Court of Honour: October 20, 1911.

Scottish Rite Biography:
Brother Scott was initiated on August 5, 1881, in *Lafayette* Lodge, No. 16, at Manhattan, in the State of Kansas, passed on October 21 of the same year, and raised on May 18, 1882. Brother Scott was made a Master of the Royal Secret in the Valley of Fargo on March 28, 1890, and served as a Venerable Master of *Enoch* Lodge of Perfection, No. 2, from 1892 to 1897. He received the rank and decoration of a Knight Commander of the Court of Honour in 1893; he was elected a 33°, Inspector General Honorary in October 1895, and coroneted by Ill. Rufus Eberle Fleming, 33°, Sovereign Grand Inspector General for North Dakota on December 18, 1895, and participated to build the Masonic Temple in Fargo. For a short period of time Brother Scott served as Deputy of the Supreme Council, 33, S.J., for North Dakota. On October 20, 1911, Ill. William Abial Scott, 33°, received the Scottish Rite's highest honour, the Grand Cross of the Court of Honour.

Bibliography:
Archive of the Supreme Council, 33°, S.J.
In Memoriam. *Transactions*. 1919: 288-289.

1913

George Kopmeier
Grand Cross of the Court of Honour at age 58 years, 6 months, and 20 days
Tenure 13 years, 9 months, and 25 days
Nomination by Kentucky Scottish Rite Bodies

Born: March 4, 1855 – Died: August 19, 1927
Life span: 72 years, 6 months, and 15 days
Bookkeeper

Progress in Scottish Rite Masonry:
4°-14°: February 28, 1880, invested by *Union* Lodge of Perfection, Louisville.
15°-18°: March 10, 1880, invested by *Pelican* Chapter of Rose Croix, No. 1, Louisville.
19°-30°: April 3, 1880, invested by *Kilwinning* Council of Kadosh, Louisville.
31°-32°: April 3, 1880, by Grand Consistory of Kentucky.
KCCH: October 17, 1888.
33°, IGH: elected October 22, 1890; coroneted by Ill. Frederick Webber, 33°, Sovereign Grand Inspector General for Kentucky on May 25, 1891.
Grand Cross of the Court of Honour: October 24, 1913.

Scottish Rite Biography:
Brother Kopmeier was initiated on October 19, 1877, passed on November 7, 1877, and raised on December 5, 1877, in *Preston* Lodge, No. 218, at Louisville. In 1880, Brother Kopmier joined the Scottish Rite and received the 4°-32°, which were invested by the Grand Consistory of Kentucky. He was a Presiding Officer in the Scottish Rite of Kentucky continuously from 1883 to 1918, and served as a Wise Master of Pelican Chapter of Rose Croix, a Commander of the *Killwining* Council of Kadosh, and a Grand Master of the Grand Consistory of Kentucky. He received his KCCH on October 17, 1888, elected as a 33°, IGH on October 22, 1890, and was coroneted on May 25, 1891, by Ill. Frederick Webber, 33°, Sovereign Grand Inspector General for Kentucky. On October 24, 1913, Ill. George Kopmeier was honored with the title of Grand Cross of the Court of Honour.

Bibliography:
Archive of the Supreme Council, 33°, S.J.
In Memoriam. *Transactions*. 1929: 336-337.

1915

No nominations for and no election

of the Honour of Grand Cross

1917

George L. Schoonover
Grand Cross of the Court of Honour at age 37 years, 8 months, and 13 days
Tenure unconfirmed
Nomination by Iowa Scottish Rite Bodies

Born: February 7, 1880 – Died: September 3, 1961
Life span: 81 years, 6 months, and 26 days
Banker

Progress in Scottish Rite Masonry:
4°-30°: date, place and by whom Degrees were invested unconfirmed.
31°-32°: May 17, 1907, communicated by Ill. Lavren Chase Eastman, 33°, from Clinton Scottish Rite Bodies.
32°, KCCH: October 21, 1909.
33°, IGH: elected October 20, 1915; coroneted by Ill. H. C. Alverson, 33°, SGIG for Iowa November 13, 1915.
Grand Cross of the Court of Honour: October 20, 1917.

Scottish Rite Biography:
Brother Schoonover received his Master Mason's Degree in Anamosa Lodge, No. 46, Anamosa, on August 23, 1901, and immediately became actively interested in the Fraternity; he continued his pursuit of truth and soon became an enthusiastic member and worker in *DeMolay* Consistory, No. 1, Clinton. Brother Schoonover was active in 15°, 16°, 30° and 31° Degrees from1908 to 1918. He was a fine ritualist and a very effective worker. His work in conferring the Degrees in the Consistory has attracted much attention. On October 21, 1909, he was elected Knight Commander of the Court of Honour, and an Honorary 33° was conferred upon him at Des Moines, on November 13, 1915; and on October 20, 1917, Brother Schoonover was elected the Grand Cross of the Court of Honour. On May 17, 1920, at a special Session of the Supreme Council at Colorado Springs, Colorado, Ill. George L. Sshoonover, 33°, as a Chaiman of the Executive Committee of the Masonic Service Association was welcomed, and he addressed the Supreme Council regarding the plans and work of this newly established Masonic Association.

Bibliography:
Archive of the Supreme Council, 33°, S.J.
Grand Lodge of Iowa. *Proceedings*. 1919.Supreme Council, 33°, S.J. *Proceedings*:1921: 6.

1919

Oscar Julian Hoberg
Grand Cross of the Court of Honour at age 53 years, 10 months, and 5 days
Tenure 28 years, 4 months, and 25 days
Nomination by Sioux City, Iowa Scottish Rite Bodies

Born: December 19, 1865 – Died: March 20, 1948
Life span: 82 years, 3 months, and 1 day
Jeweler

Progress in Scottish Rite Masonry:
4°-14°: April 21, 1903, invested by *Des Moines* Lodge, No. 3, Des Moines.
15°-18°: April 22, 1903, invested by *Des Moines* Chapter, No. 3, Des Moines.
19°-30°: April 23, 1903, invested by *Des Moines* Council, No. 3, Des Moines.
31°-32°: April 24, 1903, invested by *Des Moines* Consistory, No. 3, Des Moines.
32°, KCCH: October 24, 1907.
33°, IGH: elected October 20, 1909; coroneted by the Supreme Council, 33°, S.J., October 22, 1909.
Grand Cross of the Court of Honour: October 25, 1919.

Scottish Rite Biography:
Brother Hoberg was raised in *Landmark* Lodge, No. 103, at Sioux City on April 16, 1888. The Scottish Rite Degrees were invested to Brother Hoberg by the Des Moines Scottish Rite Bodies. Later Brother Hoberg became a Charter member for a newly established Valley of Sioux City. He was the best known of the Charter members because he was acting as Chairman of the arrangement Committee for the first Reunion; became the first Wise Master of *Boaz* Chapter of Rose Croix, No. 5; served as Director of Work, and as Deputy to the Sovereign Grand Inspector General. Brother Hoberg was invested as a Knight Commander of the Court of Honor in October 1907, and during the following Session in October 1909 coroneted a 33°, IGH. His long record, his busy record, his indomitable energy, and his leadership of the Scottish Rite, in Sioux City particularly, caused the Supreme Council to confer on Ill. Oscar Julian Hoberg, 33°, its unusual honor, the Grand Cross of the Court of Honour, which it did on October 25, 1919.

Bibliography:
Archive of the Supreme Council, 33°, S.J.
In Memoriam. *Transactions*. 1949: 304-305.
The New Age. May 1948.

1919

Henry Wallenstein
Grand Cross of the Court of Honour at age 63 years, 6 months, and 6 days
Tenure 17 years and 4 days
Nomination by Wichita, Kansas Scottish Rite Bodies

Born: March 19, 1855 – Died: November 29, 1936
Life span: 81 years, 8 months, and 9 days
Merchant

Progress in Scottish Rite Masonry:
4°- 30°: date, place and by whom Degrees were communicated unconfirmed.
31°-32°: February 25, 1892, communicated by Ill. Jeremiah G. Smith, 33°, Member of the Scottish Rite Valley, Wichita.
KCCH: October 23, 1895.
33°, IGH: elected October 19, 1897; coroneted by Ill. Rufus Eberle Fleming, 33°, SGIG for Dakota Territory.
Deputy: for Wichita June 24, 1910; Deputy for Kansas October 25, 1913; last appointment as Deputy for Kansas December 16, 1915 – c1916-1917.
Grand Cross of the Court of Honour: October 25, 1919.

Scottish Rite Biography:
The Degree of the Sublime Prince of the Royal Secret were communicated to Bro. Wallenstein by Ill. Rufus Eberle Fleming, 33°, Sovereign Grand Inspector General for Dakota Territory. Since that day, February 25, 1892, Scottish Rite Masonry became 'his very life, his work, his religion, his zeal, and the paramount rising to paragon heights for his much-loved *Wichita* Consistory, No. 4, Wichita, his ambition, his pride his hope. The Scottish Rite Brothers recognize in Henry Wallenstein lofty conception of duty, his indefatigable and tireless interest, in season and out, to the welfare of the Scottish Rite everywhere, and in the Valley of Wichita, Orient of Kansas particular." On October 23, 1895, Bro. Wallenstein was elected Knight Commander of the Court of Honour, on the following Session of the Supreme Council was elected 33°, IGH; and on October 25, 1919, Ill. Henry Wallenstein, 33°, was elected to the highest honor, the Grand Cross of the Court of Honour.

Bibliography:
Archive of the Supreme Council, 33°, S.J.
In Memoriam. *Transactions.* 1937: 352-353.
The Wichita Eagle. July 3, 1910.

1921

Louis Gaylord Clarke
Grand Cross of the Court of Honour at age 66 years, 3 months, and 11 days
Tenure 22 years, 1 month, and 14 days
Nomination by Oregon Scottish Rite Bodies

Born: July 31, 1855 – Died: December 4, 1943
Life span: 88 years, 4 months, and 4 days
Attorney-at-Law

Progress in Scottish Rite Masonry:
4°-30°: date, place and by whom Degrees were communicated unconfirmed.
31°-32°: March 15, 1883, communicated by Ill. Irving W. Pratt, 33°, SGIG for Oregon.
32°, KCCH: October 19, 1892.
33°, IGH: elected October 18, 1893; coroneted January 27, 1894.
Deputy: February 21, 1929 – October 26, 1929.
SGIG: elected October 25, 1929; crowned October 26, 1929; retired and Emeritus, October 24, 1941.
Grand Cross of the Court of Honour: October 20, 1921.

Scottish Rite Biography:
Brother Clarke became a Master Mason June 18, 1880, in *Portland* Lodge, No. 55. He received the Degrees of the Lodge of Perfection of the Ancient and Accepted Scottish Rite in 1883, and in the Consistory that same year; and then was invested with the rank and decoration of Knight Commander of the Court of Honour, October 19, 1892. He was coroneted Inspector General Honorary, January 27, 1894. He served both as Preceptor of *Multnomah* Council of Knights Kadosh for six years, 1904-10, and Master of Kadosh, Oregon Consistory, from November 1, 1908, to 1929, twenty-one years, which is a great honor. Because of his rare efficiency and devotion, he was elected Grand Cross of the Court of Honour, October 20, 1921; and on February 21, 1929, he was appointed the Deputy of the Supreme Council in the Orient of Oregon; and then in the fall of that year he was crowned an Inspector General Active Member, October 26, 1929.   Illustrious Clarke has held several offices in the Supreme Council, served on several of the committees, and was always faithful and devoted and showed efficiency and ability in every position that he held.

Bibliography:
Archive of the Supreme Council, 33°, S.J.
In Memoriam. *Transactions.* 1945: 258-262.

1921

Frank Bacon Ladd
Grand Cross of the Court of Honour at age 63 years and 1 month
Tenure 5 months and 24 days
Nomination by San Francisco, California Scottish Rite Bodies

Born: September 20, 1858 – Died: April 14, 1922
Life span: 63 years, 5 months, and 24 days
Clerk

Progress in Scottish Rite Masonry:
4°-14°: May 22, 1896, invested by *Yerba Buena* Lodge of Perfection, No. 1, San Francisco.
15°-18°: 1896, invested by *Yerba Buena* Chapter of Rose Croix, No. 1, San Francisco.
19°-30°: December 18, 1896, invested by *Godfrey de St. Omer* Council of Kadosh, No. 1, San Francisco.
31°-32°: January 14, 1897, invested by *San Francisco* Consistory, No. 1, San Francisco.
KCCH: October 19, 1899.
33°, IGH: elected October 22, 1901; coroneted December 28, 1901.
Grand Cross of the Court of Honour: October 20, 1921.

Scottish Rite Biography:
Brother Ladd was initiated, passed, and raised in *Oriental* Lodge, No. 144, at San Francisco, in 1892. The Scottish Rite Degrees were invested to Brother Ladd by San Francisco Bodies. Shortly after he became one of the prime movers in the formation of California Bodies; he was a Charter Member and First Venerable Master of all four newly established Lodges of Perfection in the Orient of California. Brother Ladd was a Vice-President, and then President of a Board of Directors of the Albert Pike Memorial Temple Association. Brother Ladd was Director of Degree Work. His proficiency and knowledge of the Scottish Rite Ritual was phenomenal, and he had taken part in practically every Degree presented. On October 20, 1921, the Supreme Council elected Ill. Frank Bacon Ladd, 33°, the Grand Cross of the Court of Honour.

Bibliography:
Archive of the Supreme Council, 33°, S.J.
In Memoriam. *Transactions.* 1923: 304-305.

1923

Richard Henry Hanna
Grand Cross of the Court of Honour at age 42 years, 2 months, and 19 days
Tenure 22 years, 9 months, and 28 days
Nomination by New Mexico Scottish Rite Bodies

Born: July 31, 1878 – Died: August 17, 1946
Life span: 68 years and 17 days
Lawyer

Progress in Scottish Rite Masonry:
4°-32°: September 22, 1908, received by communication from Ill. Harper Samuel Cunningham, 33°, Sovereign Grand Inspector General for Oklahoma Territory.
KCCH: October 19, 1911.
33°, IGH: elected October 22, 1913; coroneted by the Supreme Council, 33°, S. J., October 24, 1913.
Deputy: April 8, 1911 – resigned c1925.
Grand Cross of the Court of Honour: October 19, 1923.

Scottish Rite Biography:
Illustrious Brother Richard Henry Hanna, Thirty-third Degree, Grand Cross of the Court of Honour for many years was Deputy of the Supreme Council in New Mexico, where his service to our Order richly earned the honor conferred upon him. He was also Past Grand Master of the Grand Lodge of New Mexico and in many ways exemplified the best in the teachings of the Masonic Fraternity.

Bibliography:
Archive of the Supreme Council, 33°, S. J.
In Memoriam. *Transactions.* 1947: 193-194.

1923

Thomas Burchinal Miller

Grand Cross of the Court of Honour at age 61 years, 6 months, and 23 days
Tenure 9 years and 2 days
Nomination by Helena, Montana Scottish Rite Bodies

Born: March 26, 1862 – Died: October 21, 1932
Life span: 70 years, 6 months, and 25 days
Insurance Agent

Progress in Scottish Rite Masonry:
4°-14°: March 21, 1910, invested by *King Solomon* Lodge of Perfection, No. 5, Butte.
15°-18°: March 22, 1910, invested by *Butte* Chapter of Rose Croix, No. 3, Butte.
19°-30°: March 23, 1910, invested by *Butte* Council of Kadosh, No. 2, Butte.
31°-32°: March 24, 1910, invested by *Butte* Consistory, No. 2, Butte.
32°, KCCH: October 19, 1911.
33°, IGH: elected October 22, 1913; coroneted by the Supreme Council, 33°, S.J., October 24, 1913.
Grand Cross of the Court of Honour: October 19, 1923.

Scottish Rite Biography:
Brother Miller was initiated on June 15, 1883, in *Benevolence* Lodge, No. 145, at Mason City, Iowa, passed August 24, and raised October 12, 1883, later on affiliated with *Helena* Lodge, No. 3, Helena, Montana, and became a Scottish Rite Member in the Valley of Butte in March 1910. Ill. Erasmus T. Carr, 33°, Sovereign Grand Inspector General for Montana appointed Bro. Miller as his Deputy to carry on the work in the organization of the Bodies of the Scottish Rite in Helena. Brother Miller served as Venerable Master of *Helena* Lodge of Perfection, Master of Kadosh of *Helena* Consistory, and Member of the Board of Trustees. He was invested with the rank and decoration of Knight Commander of the Court of Honour in 1911, coroneted a 33°, Inspector General Honorary in 1913, and received the Grand Cross Court of Honour in 1923.

Bibliography:
Archive of the Supreme Council, 33°, S.J.
In Memoriam. *Transactions*. 1933: 196-197.

1923

Charles Alfred Nesbitt
Grand Cross of the Court of Honour at age 70 years, 6 months, and 23 days
Tenure 5 years, 3 months, and 12 days
Nomination by Richmond, Virginia Scottish Rite Bodies

Born: March 26, 1852 – Died: January 31, 1929
Life span: 76 years, 10 months, and 5 days
Clerk

Progress in Scottish Rite Masonry:
4°-14°: date, place and whom Degrees were conferred, or communicated unconfirmed.
15°-32°: March 22, 1883; place and by whom Degrees were conferred or communicated unconfirmed.
32°, KCCH: October 23, 1884.
33°, IGH: elected October 20, 1886; coroneted by the Supreme Council, 33°, S.J., October 21, 1886.
Grand Cross of the Court of Honour: October 19, 1923.

Scottish Rite Biography:
Brother Nesbit was initiated on May 12, 1874, in *St. John* Lodge, No. 36, at Richmond, Virginia. He received the Degrees of the Lodge of Perfection on December 18, 1878, at Richmond, by communication from Sovereign Grand Commander Albert Pike, 33°. The remaining Scottish Rite Degrees he received on March 22, 1883, at Norfolk by communication from Ill. John Lonsdale Roper, 33°, SGIG for Virginia. Brother Nesbit was Venerable Master of *John L. Roper* Lodge of Perfection, No. 5, and Master of Ceremonies of *Pelican* Chapter of Rose Croix, No. 2. On October 23, 1884, he was elected Knight Commander of the Court of Honour, two years later he became 33°, Inspector General Honorary. Ill. Nesbit, 33° was honored with the title of the Grand Cross of the Court of Honour on October 19, 1923.

Bibliography:
Archive of the Supreme Council, 33°, S.J.
In Memoriam. *Transactions*. 1931: 356-357.

1925

Edwin Carmi Hopkins
Grand Cross of the Court of Honour at age 76 years, 1 month, and 20 days
Tenure 8 years, 11 months, and 15 days
Nomination by Sacramento, California Scottish Rite Bodies

Born: August 31, 1849 – Died: October 5, 1934
Life span: 85 years, 1 month, and 5 days
Merchant

Progress in Scottish Rite Masonry:
4°-18°: April 25, 1895, communicated by Ill. William Frank Pierce, 33°, Sovereign Grand Inspector General for California.
19°-32°: April 26 and 27, 1895; communicated by Ill. William Frank Pierce, 33°, Sovereign Grand Inspector General for California.
32°, KCCH: October 19, 1899.
33°, IGH: elected October 17, 1911; coroneted February 22, 1912.
Grand Cross of the Court of Honour: October 20, 1925.

Scottish Rite Biography:
Brother Hopkins was Master Mason in Sacramento Lodge, No. 40, Sacramento. He received the Scottish Rite Degrees by communication by Ill. William Frank Pierce, 33°, Sovereign Grand Inspector General for California. He was elected KCCH on October 19, 1899, and coroneted 33°, IGH on February 22, 1912. Brother Hopkins has been a very important worker in the rite continuously since he became a member of it, and the most deserving of the honour of the Grand Cross Court of Honour, which he received on October 20, 1925. His hands actively assisted here in the foundation of the Rite. His zeal nursed it in its infancy and guided it in its strength. His devotion to its ideals as an inspiring model to its thousands of members.

Bibliography:
Archive of the Supreme Council, 33°, S.J.
In Memoriam. *Transactions*. 1935: 290-291.

1925

Charles Sumner Lobingier
Grand Cross of the Court of Honour at age 59 years, 6 months, and 10 days
Tenure 30 years, 6 months, and 8 days
Nomination by Manila, Philippines Islands Scottish Rite Bodies

Born: April 30, 1866 – Died: April 28, 1956
Life span: 89 years, 11 months, and 27 days
Attorney at Law

Progress in Scottish Rite Masonry:
4°-14°: April 26, 1898, invested by *Mount Moriah* Lodge of Perfection, No. 1, Omaha.
15°-18°: March 7, 1899, invested by *Semper Fidelis* Chapter of Rose Croix, No. 1, Omaha.
19°-30°: March 16, 1899, invested by *St. Andrew* Council of Kadosh, No. 1, Omaha.
31°-32°: March 17, 1899, invested by *Nebraska* Consistory, No. 1, Omaha.
32°, KCCH: October 22, 1901.
33°, IGH: elected October 22, 1901; coroneted by the Supreme Council, 33°, S.J., October 24, 1901.
Deputy for Philippine Islands: December 1910 – c1921.
Deputy for China: c1921– c1925.
Grand Cross of the Court of Honour: October 20, 1925.

Scottish Rite Biography:
I have the honor to report that the past two years have witnessed the steady gain of our Rite in this Archipelago; in fact, its formal establishment and growth have practically all occurred within that period. On September 15, 1909, acting then as the Deputy of the Sovereign Grand Inspector General of California and Arizona, and assisted by members of the Scottish Rite Lyceum of the Philippines I conferred (for the first time, so far as is known in these islands) the 4° upon a candidate who had been elected by *Washington* Lodge of Perfection of Seattle. The Scottish Rite Lyceum has been organized on December 29, 1907, of Scottish Rite Masons residing in the Philippines, and in my first Commission from the Inspector General of California, I was authorized to confer or communicate the Scottish Rite Degrees upon candidates to be selected by the Lyceum. ... in March 1910, a petition for Letters Temporary for a Lodge of Perfection was signed by more than thirty Perfect Elu, all of whom except myself had received the degrees in Manila...

Bibliography:
Archive of the Supreme Council, 33°, S.J.
In Memoriam. *Transactions*: 1957: 428-429.

1925

Robert Edward Simpson
Grand Cross of the Court of Honour at age 56 years
Tenure 12 years, 4 months, and 16 days
Nomination by Charlotte, North Carolina Scottish Rite Bodies

Born: October 20, 1869 – Died: March 6, 1938
Life span: 68 years, 4 months, and 16 days
General Manager Southern Railway System

Progress in Scottish Rite Masonry:
4°-14°: April 19, 1901, invested by *Alpha* Lodge of Perfection, No. 1, Asheville, North Carolina.
15°-18°: February 22, 1911, invested by *Calvary* Chapter, No. 1, Memphis.
19°-30°: February 22, 1911, invested by *Cypress* Council of Kadosh, No. 1, Memphis.
31°-32°: February 23, 1911, invested by *Tennessee* Consistory, No. 1, Memphis.
32°, KCCH: October 22, 1913.
33°, IGH: elected October 16, 1917; coroneted by the Supreme Council, 33°, S.J., October 19, 1917.
December 1922, affiliated with Charlotte Scottish Rite Bodies, Charlotte.
Grand Cross of the Court of Honour: October 20, 1925.

Scottish Rite Biography:
Brother Simpson was made a Mason in *Joppa* Lodge, No. 401, at Old Fort, North Carolina, in 1892, being initiated January 9, passed January 29, and raised February 13. The Scottish Rite Degrees of the Lodge of Perfection he received in *Alpha* Lodge of Perfection, No. 1, Asheville, North Carolina. The rest of the Degrees were invested by Memphis Bodies, Tennessee. Brother Simpson invested his spending service in extending the Rite in the Valley of Memphis, devoting his time and energy without compensation. In 1913 he was elected a Knight Commander of the Court of Honour, and in 1917 an Honorary Member of the Supreme Council. In December 1922, Ill. Robert Edward Simpson, 33°, affiliated with Charlotte Scottish Rite Bodies, Charlotte, and in 1925 he received the title the Grand Cross of the Court of Honour.

Bibliography:
Archive of the Supreme Council, 33°, S.J.
In Memoriam. *Transactions.* 1939: 282-283.
Scottish Rite News Bureau. March 1938.

1927

Tomas E. Ramos
Honorary Grand Cross of the Court of Honour at age unconfirmed
Nomination by Sovereign Grand Commander John H. Cowles, 33°

Born: unconfirmed – Died: unconfirmed
Sovereign Grand Commander of the Supreme Council, 33° of Mexico

Progress in Scottish Rite Masonry:
4°-32°: date, place and by whom Degree were communicated unconfirmed.
33°, IGH: date, place, and by whom crowned unconfirmed.
Sovereign Grand Commander of the Supreme Council, 33° of Mexico: April 27, 1926 – April 27, 1928.
Emeriti Member of Honour of the Supreme Council, 33°, SJ, USA: October 18, 1927.
Honorary Grand Cross of the Court of Honour: October 18, 1927.

Scottish Rite Biography:
No data about Ill. Thomas E. Ramos, 33°, in the Archive of the Supreme Council, 33°, S.J. His name is listed in the *Transactions* of the Supreme Council, 33°, S.J., as a recipient of the Grand Cross of the Court of Honour.

Bibliography:
Boletin Supremo Consejo del REAyA para la Jurisdiccion Masonica de los EE UU Mexicanos. 1927.

1927

George William Vallery

Grand Cross of the Court of Honour at age 65 years, 8 months, and 24 days
Tenure 6 years, 2 months, and 11 days
Nomination by Denver, Colorado Scottish Rite Bodies

Born: January 24, 1862 – Died: December 29, 1933
Life span: 71 years, 11 months, and 5 days
Railroad Agent

Progress in Scottish Rite Masonry:
4°-32°: 1894, invested by *Denver* Scottish Rite Bodies, Denver.
32°, KCCH: October 21, 1909.
33°, IGH: elected October 17, 1911; coroneted November 11, 1911.
Grand Cross of the Court of Honour: October 18, 1927.

Scottish Rite Biography:
Brother Vallery was made a Mason in *Oriental* Lodge 87 in Denver on June 28, 1893. He received the 32° of the Ancient and Accepted Scottish Rite in Denver in January of 1894. At the Biennial Session of the Supreme Council in Washington, D.C., October 1909, he was elected a Knight Commander of the Court of Honor, and two years later the Thirty-third Degree was conferred upon him. On October 27, 1927, Ill. George William Vallery received the highest honor, the Grand Cross of the Court of Honour.

Bibliography:
Archive of the Supreme Council, 33°, S.J.
In Memoriam. *Transactions*. 1936: 318-319.
The New Age. February 1934.

1927

Alfred Frederick Webster
Grand Cross of the Court of Honour at age 61 years and 24 days
Tenure 10 years, 6 months, and 19 days
Canada, nomination by Sovereign Grand Commander John H. Cowles, 33°

Born: November 12, 1866 – Died: May 7, 1938
Life span: 71 years, 5 months and 25 days
Sovereign Grand Commander of the Supreme Council, 33°, of Canada

Progress in Scottish Rite Masonry:
4°-32°: date unconfirmed, conferred by Toronto Scottish Rite Bodies, Canada.
33°, IGH: coroneted October 26, 1905.
SGIG: crowned October 29, 1914.
Grand Master of Ceremonies: November 20, 1918 – October 26, 1922.
Lieutenant Grand Commander: October 26, 1922 – October 8, 1925.
Sovereign Grand Commander: October 8, 1925 – October 3, 1934.
Emeriti Member of Honour of the Supreme Council, 33°, S.J., USA: October 18, 1927.
Honorary Grand Cross of the Court of Honour: October 18, 1927.

Scottish Rite Biography:
Brother Webster was made a Master Mason in *Ashlar* Lodge, No. 247, in Toronto. He was a diligent student of the *Morals and Dogma* of the Scottish Rite for many years. He early became a leader of the Lodge of Perfection and the Chapter of Rose Croix in Toronto, thence, step by step attained great influence not only in the local Bodies, but in the Supreme Council, first, as an Honorary Member, next, as an Active Member, and, finally, as M.P. Sovereign Grand Commander, which exalted office he held for nine years with honor to himself and great benefit to our Institution. During his long tenure of this high and important office, he travelled extensively in Europe and the United States, and was known and recognized throughout the Masonic world as an outstanding figure in Scottish Rite Masonry. He was an Emeritus Member of Honour of the Supreme Council, 33°, of the Southern Jurisdiction of the United States of America, the Northern Jurisdiction of the United States of America, and of the Supreme Council, 33°, of England and Wales.

Bibliography:
Archive of the Supreme Council, 33°, S.J.
In Memoriam. *Proceedings*. 1938: 68-70.

1929

No nominations for and no election

of the Honour of Grand Cross

1931

No nominations for and no election
of the Honour of Grand Cross

1933

Thomas Archer Goodman
Grand Cross of the Court of Honour at age 62 years, 11 months, and 22 days
Tenure 3 years, 11 months, and 29 days
Nomination by St. Louis, Missouri Scottish Rite Bodies

Born: September 25, 1871 – Died: September 16, 1936
Life span: 64 years, 11 months, and 21 days
Publisher

Progress in Scottish Rite Masonry:
4°-14°: date unconfirmed, invested by *St. Louis* Lodge of Perfection, No. 1. St. Louis.
15°-18°: date unconfirmed, invested by *St. Louis* Chapter of Rose Croix, No. 1, St. Louis.
19°-30°: date unconfirmed, invested by *Missouri* Council of Kadosh, No. 1, St. Louis.
31°-32°: May 21, 1910, invested by *Missouri* Consistory, No. 1, St. Louis.
32°, KCCH: October 22, 1913.
33°, IGH: elected October 21, 1919; coroneted by the Supreme Council, 33°, S.J., October 24, 1919.
Grand Cross of the Court of Honour: October 17, 1933.

Scottish Rite Biography:
Since Brother Goodman received the Scottish Rite Degrees, he has been an important factor in the life and success of the Scottish Rite in the Valley of St. Louis. Following the Reunion at which he received the Degrees, he immediately threw himself into the work of building up the Scottish Rite membership in St. Louis, which at that time numbered only 1583. In November 1913, Bro. Goodman created the "3,000 Membership Committee," of which he was made a Chairman, in the Valley of St. Louis. Four years later a new goal has been reached and it was changed to the "10,000 Membership Committee" whose aspiration was nearly realized in May 1930, when the actual membership of the Lodge of Perfection was 9,522. This most remarkable growth was due primarily to Ill. Thomas Archer Goodman, 33° indomitable energy and efforts.

Bibliography:
Archive of the Supreme Council, 33°, S.J.
In Memoriam. *Transactions.* 1937: 310-311.

1933

Wallace McCamant
Grand Cross of the Court of Honour at age 66 years and 25 days
Tenure 11 years and 2 months
Nomination by Portland, Oregon Scottish Rite Bodies

Born: September 22, 1867 – Died: December 17, 1944
Life span: 76 years, 2 months, and 25 days
Judge

Progress in Scottish Rite Masonry:
4°-14°: May 6, 1902, invested by *Oregon* Lodge of Perfection, Portland.
15°-18°: January 16, 1903, invested by *Ainsworth* Chapter of Rose Croix, Portland.
19°-30°: May 30, 1903, invested by *Multnomah* Council of Kadosh, Portland.
31°-32°: June 9, 1903, invested by *Oregon* Consistory, Portland.
32°, KCCH: October 24, 1907.
33°, IGH: elected October 17, 1911; coroneted January 24, 1912.
Grand Cross of the Court of Honour: October 17, 1933.

Scottish Rite Biography:
Brother McCamant was raised a Master Mason in *Willamette* Lodge, No. 2 in Portland on February 17, 1902. He attended the Scottish Rite Reunion in June of 1903 and was a member of the 1st Cathedral Class to receive their Degrees in the new Scottish Rite Temple at Lownsdale. He received the Scottish Rite Degrees in Portland, 4°- 14° May 6, 1902, 18° January 16, 1903, 30° May 30, 1903, and the 32° with the 1st Cathedral Class on June 9, 1903. He served as Wise Master of *Ainsworth* Chapter Rose Croix No. 1 and was Master of the 18° from 1903 to 1936. Brother McCamant was elected KCCH on October 24, 1907, and elected 33°, IGH on October 17, 1911. Ill. Wallace McCamant received the Grand Cross of the Court of Honor on October 17, 1933, the third member in the Orient of Oregon to be awarded that honor.

Bibliography:
Archive of the Supreme Council, 33°, S.J.
In Memoriam. *Transactions.* 1945: 312-313.
The New Age. February – March 1945.
Archive of the Orient of Oregon.

1935

William Rhodes Hervey
Grand Cross of the Court of Honour at age 65 years, 6 months, and 26 days
Tenure 17 years, 3 months, and 9 days
Nomination by Los Angeles, California Scottish Rite Bodies

Born: March 26, 1870 – Died: February 1, 1953
Life span: 82 years, 10 months, and 5 days
Lawyer

Progress in Scottish Rite Masonry:
4°-14°: 1900, invested by *King Solomon* Lodge of Perfection, No. 3, Los Angeles.
15°-18°: 1900, invested by *Robert Bruce* Chapter of Rose Croix, No. 3, Los Angeles.
19°-30°: 1900, invested by *Hugh de Payens* Council of Kadosh, No. 3, Los Angeles.
31°-32°: November 2, 1900, invested by *Los Angeles* Consistory, No. 3, Los Angeles.
32°, KCCH: October 20, 1903.
33°, IGH: elected October 18, 1905; coroneted May 30, 1906.
Grand Cross of the Court of Honour: October 22, 1935.
Deputy: c1942-1943 – October 22, 1943.
SGIG: elected October 21, 1943; crowned October 22, 1943; laid down his Craft tools while in Office
February 1, 1953.

Scottish Rite Biography:
Brother Hervey was raised in *Pentalpha* Lodge, No. 202, in Los Angeles, in 1895. During the year 1900,
Brother Hervey received the Degrees of the Scottish Rite in the Scottish Rite Bodies at Los Angeles. He
was elected a KCCH by the Supreme Council, on October 20, 1903, and was coroneted a 33° IGH, on June
2, 1906. Illustrious Hervey was one of the very few Scottish Rite Masons ever to have conferred upon him
the Grand Cross of the Court of Honour. Brother Hervey served as Master of his Lodge of Perfection and
Chancellor of his Consistory from 1904 to 1952, and it was largely through his efforts, in cooperation with
Ill∴ Brother Perry W. Weidner, that the Scottish Rite Temple was constructed in the city of Los Angeles.
He served as Deputy of the SGIG in California and later on an Active Member of the Supreme Council.

Bibliography:
Archive of the Supreme Council, 33°, S.J.
In Memoriam. William Rhodes Hervey, 33°, *The New Age*, March 1953: 190.

1935

Isaac Thomas Woodson
Grand Cross of the Court of Honour at age 62 years, 10 months, and 8 days
Tenure 3 years, 8 months, and 20 days
Nomination by Louisville, Kentucky Scottish Rite Bodies

Born: December 16, 1872 – Died: July 12, 1939
Life span: 66 years, 6 months, and 26 days
Monument Manufacturer

Progress in Scottish Rite Masonry:
4°-18°: date, place and by whom Degrees were invested, unconfirmed.
19°-30°: November 17, 1922, invested by *Kilwinning* Council of Kadosh, Louisville.
31°-32°: November 18, 1922, invested by Grand Consistory of Kentucky, Louisville.
32°, KCCH: October 20, 1925.
33°, IGH: elected October 22, 1929, coroneted October 25, 1929.
Grand Cross of the Court of Honour: October 22, 1935.

Scottish Rite Biography:
Brother Woodson was originally a member of *Louisville* Lodge, No. 400, at Louisville, KY. He petitioned May 17, 1897, was made an Entered Apprentice in that Lodge on July 19, 1897; passed to the Fellowcraft Degree on November 15, 1897; and raised to the sublime Degree of Master Mason on December 17, 1897. Later, Brother Woodson affiliated with *Daylight* Lodge, No. 760 and became a Scottish Rite Mason in the Grand Consistory of Kentucky. Brother Woods became a loyal and useful member of Louisville Valley; served as a Grand Master of the Grand Consistory of Kentucky and was a good ritualist. Ill. Isaac Thomas Woodson in October 1929 received the 33°, IGH, and in October 1935, was elected a Grand Cross of the Court of Honour, by the Supreme Council, being one of the few who have attained that honor.

Bibliography:
Archive of the Supreme Council, 33°, S.J.
In Memoriam. *Transactions.* 1941: 374-375.
Prominent Kentucky Mason… *The New Age.* August 1939.

1937

James Monroe Clift
Grand Cross of the Court of Honour at age 70 years, 11 months, and 21 days
Tenure 16 years, 11 months, and 27 days
Nomination by Richmond, Virginia Scottish Rite Bodies

Born: September 28, 1867 – Died: October 16, 1954
Life span: 86 years, 11 months, and 18 days
Telephone Operator

Progress in Scottish Rite Masonry:
4°-14°: January 4, 1892, invested by *Libertas* Lodge of Perfection, No. 5, Richmond.
15°-18°: date unconfirmed, invested by *Pelican* Chapter of Rose Croix, No. 2, Richmond.
19°-30°: date unconfirmed, invested by *St. Omar* Council of Kadosh, No. 1, Richmond.
31°-32°: April 12, 1894, invested by *Dalcho* Consistory, No. 1, Richmond.
32°, KCCH: October 19, 1899.
33°, IGH: elected October 22, 1901; coroneted by the Supreme Council, 33°, S.J., October 25, 1901.
Grand Cross of the Court of Honour: October 19, 1937.

Scottish Rite Biography:
Brother Clift received the first Scottish Rite Degrees from 4° to 14° from *Libertas* Lodge of Perfection, No. 5, at Richmond, and became a Sublime Prince of the Royal Secret on April 12, 1894. Five years later, he received a rank and decoration of Knight Commander of the Court of Honour; on October 25, 1901, coroneted 33°, Inspector General Honorary by the Supreme Council; and on October 19, 1937, was elected the Grand Cross of the Court of Honour.

Bibliography:
Archive of the Supreme Council, 33°, S.J.
In Memoriam. *Transactions.* 1955: 312-313.

1937

Theodore Wilson McCullough
Grand Cross of the Court of Honour at age 75 years, 11 months, and 23 days
Tenure 1 month, and 19 days
Nomination by Omaha, Nebraska Scottish Rite Bodies

Born: September 26, 1861 – Died: December 8, 1937
Life span: 76 years, 2 months, and 12 days
Editor

Progress in Scottish Rite Masonry:
4°-14°: September 20, 1915, invested by *Mt. Moriah* Lodge of Perfection, No. 1, Omaha.
15°-18°: October 18, 1915, invested by *Semper Fidelis* Chapter of Rose Croix, No. 1, Omaha.
19°-30°: December 1915, invested by *St. Andrews* Council of Kadosh, No. 1, Omaha.
31°-32°: December 1915, invested by *Nebraska* Consistory, No. 1, Omaha.
32°, KCCH: October 21, 1919.
33°, IGH: elected October 18, 1921; coroneted by Ill. Frank Cargill Patton, 33°, Sovereign Grand Inspector General for Nebraska December 3, 1921.
Grand Cross of the Court of Honour: October 19, 1937.

Scottish Rite Biography:
Brother McCullogh was raised to the sublime Degree of a Master Mason June 29, 1914, in *Capitol* Lodge, No. 3, Omaha; received the 14th Degree of the Scottish Rite, September 20, 1915, in Mt. Moria Lodge of Perfection; the 18th Degree in *Semper Fidelis* Chapter of Rose Croix, October 18, 1915; the 30th Degree in *St. Andrews* Council of Kadosh, and the 32nd Degree, Prince of the Royal Secret, in *Nebraska* Consistory in December 1915. He was honored the Supreme Council as a Knight Commander of the Court of Honour on October 19; and was coroneted 33°, Inspector General Honorary on December 3, 1921, by Ill. Frank Cargill Patton, SGIG in Nebraska. He was further honored by being elected a Grand Cross of the Court of Honour on October 19, 1937. The decoration of the Grand Cross was pinned on Ill. Theodore Wilson McCullough personally by the Sovereign Grand Commander, John H. Cowles, 33°.

Bibliography:
Archive of the Supreme Council, 33°, S.J.
In Memoriam. *Transactions*. 1939: 268-269.

1939

Haslett Platt Burke
Grand Cross of the Court of Honour at age 65 years, 5 months, and 19 days
Tenure 17 years, 11 months, and 17 days
Nomination by Colorado Scottish Rite Bodies

Born: April 28, 1874 – Died: October 4, 1957
Life span: 83 years, 5 months, and 9 days
State Supreme Court Judge

Progress in Scottish Rite Masonry:
4°-14°: October 29, 1905, invested by *Delta* Lodge of Perfection, No. 1, Denver.
15°-18°: October 29, 1905, invested by *Mackey* Chapter of Rose Croix, No. 1, Denver.
19°-30°: October 31, 1905, invested by *Denver* Council of Kadosh, No. 1, Denver.
31°-32°: November 2, 1905, invested by *Colorado* Consistory, No. 1, Denver.
32°, KCCH: October 21, 1909.
33°, IGH: February 3, 1914.
Grand Cross of the Court of Honour: October 17, 1939.
Deputy: January 1, 1940 – October 24, 1941.
SGIG: elected October 23, 1941; crowned by the Supreme Council, 33°, October 24, 1941; laid down his Craft tools while in Office October 4, 1957.

Scottish Rite Biography:
Brother Burke was a Master Mason in *Sterling* Lodge No. 54. In 1905 he received the Degrees of the AASR. In 1909 he received the rank and decoration of a KCCH. In 1914 he became a 33°, Inspector General Honorary and in 1939 Illustrious Burke received the Grand Cross. In 1941 Illustrious Burke was elected Sovereign Grand Inspector General for Colorado, in 1955 he was elected Lieutenant Grand Commander of the Supreme Council, 33°, S.J. Illustrious Burke was a tower of strength in the administration of the affairs of the Supreme Council, particularly in his work on the Committee on Education, and on Jurisprudence and Legislation.

Bibliography:
Archive of the Supreme Council, 33°, S.J.
In Memoriam. *Transactions.* 1957: 370-379.

1941

William Burchard Roberts
Grand Cross of the Court of Honour at age 66 years, 5 months, and 2 days
Tenure 15 years, 6 months, and 17 days
Nomination by Minneapolis, Minnesota Scottish Rite Bodies

Born: May 19, 1875 – Died: May 8, 1957
Life span: 81 years, 11 months, and 16 days
Surgeon

Progress in Scottish Rite Masonry:
4°-14°: December 5, 1916, invested by *Excelsior* Lodge, No. 2, Minneapolis.
15°-18°: March 29, 1917, invested St. *Vincent De Paul* Chapter of Rose Croix, No. 2, Minneapolis.
19°-30°: April 11, 1917, invested by *Alfred Elisha Ames* Council of Kadosh, No. 2, Minneapolis.
31°-32°: April 12, 1917, invested by *Minneapolis* Consistory, No. 2, Minneapolis.
32°, KCCH: October 18, 1921.
33°, IGH: elected October 20, 1925; coroneted by the Supreme Council, 33°, S.J.
October 23, 1925.
Deputy: May 29, 1944 – October 19, 1945.
Grand Cross of the Court of Honour: October 21, 1941.
SGIG: elected October 18, 1945, crowned October 19, 1945; laid down his Craft tools while in Office May 8, 1957.

Scottish Rite Biography:
Brother Roberts Masonic activities began September 9, 1916, when he was raised as a Master Mason in *Minneapolis* Lodge, No. 19. Between December 1916 and April 1917, Brother Roberts received the Degrees of the Scottish Rite in the Minneapolis Bodies. In 1918 he served in the Official Line of the Consistory, becoming Venerable Master of Kadosh from 1925 to 1927. Regular attendance at the weekly meetings of the Scottish Rite Bodies made him an influential member of the groups, which conducted the business of the Rite. On October 18, 1921, he received the rank and decoration of KCCH, and on October 23,1925, he was coroneted SGIG Honorary. His labors for the good of the Rite brought him further honors and on October 21, 1941, he was elected a Grand Cross of the Court of Honor. In 1944 Brother Roberts was appointed Deputy of the Supreme Council of Minnesota, and in October 1945, was crowned an Active Member of the Supreme Council and became SGIG in Minnesota. He served in this capacity faithfully and well.

Bibliography:
Archive of the Supreme Council, 33°, S.J.
In Memoriam. *Transactions.* 1957: 356-361.

1941

Emmett Dolphin Tumlin
Grand Cross of the Court of Honour at age 69 years, 6 months, and 1 day
Tenure 3 years, 7 months, and 8 days
Nomination by Wheeling, West Virginia Scottish Rite Bodies

Born: April 20, 1872 – Died: May 29, 1945
Life span: 73 years, 1 month, and 9 days
Barrister

Progress in Scottish Rite Masonry:
4°-30°: date, place and by whom Degrees were communicated, unconfirmed.
31°-32°: April 16, 1908, invested by H. Byron Baguley, 32°, KCCH.
32°, KCCH: October 18, 1921.
33°, IGH: elected October 18, 1927; coroneted by the Supreme Council, 33º, S.J., October 21, 1927.
Deputy: December 18, 1929 – c1941.
Grand Cross of the Court of Honour: October 21, 1941.

Scottish Rite Biography:
Brother Tumlin was a most enthusiastic, as well as a most valued Scottish Rite Mason. He was the first Venerable Master of *Morgantown* Lodge of Perfection at Morgantown and was most successful, and then he organized and got a Charter for the Rose Croix Chapter there and was its first Wise Master. After returning from these offices, he was appointed Deputy of the Supreme Council in the Orient of West Virginia, the duties of which office he performed valiantly and efficiently for a number of years. Ill. Emmett Dolphin Tumlin, 33°, received the Scottish Rite's highest honor, the Grand Cross of the Court of Honour on October 21, 1941.

Bibliography:
Archive of the Supreme Council, 33º, S.J.
In Memoriam. *Transactions*. 1947: 428-429.
The New Age. July 1945.

1943

No nominations for and no election

of the Honour of Grand Cross

1945

Frank Centennial Ruppel
Grand Cross of the Court of Honour at age 69 years, 4 months, and 26 days
Tenure 2 years, 3 months, and 25 days
Nomination by San Francisco, California Scottish Rite Bodies

Born: May 20, 1876 – Died: February 9, 1948
Life span: 71 years, 7 months, and 19 days
Businessman

Progress in Scottish Rite Masonry:
4°-14°: January 8, 1913, invested by *California* Lodge of Perfection, No. 10, San Francisco.
15°-18°: January 8, 1913, invested by *California* Chapter of Rose Croix, No. 10, San Francisco.
19°-30°: January 8, 1913, invested by *California* Council of Kadosh, No. 7, San Francisco.
31°-32°: January 8, 1913, invested by *California* Consistory, No. 5, San Francisco.
32°, KCCH: October 16, 1917.
33°, IGH: elected October 16, 1923; coroneted by Ill. William Parker Filmer, 33°, Sovereign Grand Inspector General for California December 15, 1923.
Grand Cross of the Court of Honour: October 16, 1945.

Scottish Rite Biography:
Brother Ruppel was a Master Mason in *Richmond* Lodge, No. 375, San Francisco, California. Brother Ruppel received the Degrees of the Scottish Rite in the California Bodies, and in due time served as a Venerable Master of *California* Lodge of Perfection. He was one of the most active and zealous workers in California Bodies. Especially, he was a very active Degree worker – taking prominent and effective parts and acting as orator for the communication of many of the Degrees. Brother Ruppel received the rank and decoration of KCCH in 1917; coroneted 33°, IGH in 1923; and elected a Grand Cross of the Court of Honour on October 16, 1945.

Bibliography:
Archive of the Supreme Council, 33°, S.J.
In Memoriam. *Transactions.* 1949: 331.
Frank C. Ruppel, 33°, G.C. *The New Age.* March 1948.

1947

No nominations for and no election

of the Honour of Grand Cross

1949

No nominations for and no election
of the Honour of Grand Cross

1951

No nominations for and no election of the Honour of Grand Cross

1953

Charles Bailey Newcomb
Grand Cross of the Court of Honour at age 66 years, 1 month, and 6 days
Tenure 12 years, 1 month, and 29 days
Nomination by Wilmington, North Carolina Scottish Rite Bodies

Born: September 15, 1887 – Died: December 20, 1965
Life span: 78 years, 3 months, and 5 days
Accountant

Progress in Scottish Rite Masonry:
4°-14°: July 2, 1909, invested by *Johnston Blakely* Lodge of Perfection, Wilmington.
15°-18°: January 18, 1912, invested by *Cape Fear* Chapter of Rose Croix, Wilmington.
19°-30°: November 13, 1912, invested by *Charlotte* Council of Kadosh, Charlotte.
31°-32°: November 14, 1912, invested by *Charlotte* Consistory, Charlotte.
32°, KCCH: October 20, 1915.
33°, IGH: elected October 16, 1923; coroneted by the Supreme Council, 33°, S.J., October 19, 1923.
Grand Cross of the Court of Honour: October 21, 1953.

Scottish Rite Biography:
Brother Newcomb was a Master in *St. John's* Lodge, No. 1, Wilmington. Brother Newcomb received the Degrees of the Ancient and Accepted Scottish Rite from 4° to 18° in the Bodies of Wilmington and the reminder in the Bodies of Charlotte, later demitting from the Charlotte Bodies to become a charter member of the Bodies at Wilmington. Elected Secretary of the Wilmington Scottish Rite Bodies in 1915, he served in that capacity until his death. For more than 30 years Brother Newcomb has been an outstanding leader in organizing and directing the work of the Scottish Rite Bodies. His influence for better and more accurate work in the Degrees of the Rite and the customs of the Rite have given to the Rite throughout the State a tone of dignity and proficiency. In 1953 he was selected for Investiture with the dignity of Grand Cross of Honour for his long, faithful, and efficient service to the Fraternity.

Bibliography:
Archive of the Supreme Council, 33°, S.J.
In Memoriam. *Transactions*. 1967: 388.
The New Age, February 1966.

1955

Frank Sherman Land
Grand Cross of the Court of Honour at age 65 years, 4 months, and 3 days
Tenure 4 years and 20 days
Nomination by Kansas City, Missouri Scottish Rite Bodies

Born: June 21, 1890 – Died: November 8, 1959
Life span: 69 years, 4 months, and 17 days
Founder and Secretary General of The International Supreme Council Order of DeMolay

Progress in Scottish Rite Masonry:
4°-14°: November 11, 1912, invested by *Adoniram* Lodge of Perfection, Kansas City.
15°-18°: November 12, 1912, invested by *Areiopagus* Chapter of Rose Croix, Kansas City.
19°-30°: November 13, 1912, invested by *De Molay* Council of Kadosh, Kansas City.
31°-32°: November 14, 1912, invested by *Western Missouri* Consistory, Kansas City.
32°, KCCH: October 21, 1919.
33°, IGH: elected October 20, 1925; coroneted by the Supreme Council, 33°, S.J., October 23, 1925.
Grand Cross of the Court of Honour: October 18, 1955.

Scottish Rite Biography:
Brother Land was initiated an Entered Apprentice in *Ivanhoe* Lodge, No. 446, Kansas City, Missouri, on May 25, 1912, passed to the Degree of Fellowcraft June 17, 1912, and raised to the sublime Degree of Master Mason on June 29, 1912. Brother Frank became a 32nd Degree member of the Ancient and Accepted Scottish Rite of Freemasonry in the November Class of 1912 at Kansas City, Missouri. His interest was so great that he immediately started to work in the various Degrees and committees in Scottish Rite Masonry, including the position of the Secretary of the Scottish Rite Employment Bureau. In 1919, Brother Land founded the Order of DeMolay and was invested with the rank and decoration of a Knight Commander of the Court of Honour. On October 23, 1925, he was coroneted 33°, Inspector General Honorary. Ill. Frank Sherman Land was elected the Grand Cross of the Court of Honour on October 18, 1955.

Bibliography:
Archive of the Supreme Council, 33°, S.J.
In Memoriam. *Transactions.* 1961: 395.

Renah F. Camalier
Grand Cross of the Court of Honour at age 67 years and 14 days
Tenure 20 years, 7 months, and 22 days
Nomination by Washington, District of Columbia Scottish Rite Bodies

Born: October 8, 1890 – Died: June 14, 1978
Life span: 87 years, 8 months, and 6 days
Lawyer

Progress in Scottish Rite Masonry:
4°-14°: May 20, 1935, invested by *Mithras* Lodge of Perfection, Washington, D.C.
15°-18°: May 21, 1935, invested by *Evangelist* Chapter of Rose Croix, Washington, D.C.
19°-30°: May 24, 1935, invested by *Robert de Bruce* Council of Kadosh, Washington, D.C.
31°-32°: May 25, 1935, invested by *Albert Pike* Consistory, Washington, D.C.
32°, KCCH: October 18, 1949.
33°, IGH: elected October 20, 1953; coroneted October 23, 1953.
Deputy: January 30, 1962 – retired, 1977, Emeritus October 19, 1977.
Grand Cross of the Court of Honour: October 22, 1957.

Scottish Rite Biography:
Brother Camalier was a Master of *Benjamin B. French* Lodge, No. 15, F.A.&A.M. A member of the District of Columbia Scottish Rite Bodies, he was honored with the rank and decoration of Knight Commander of the Court of Honour in 1949, Coroneted an Inspector General Honorary of the Thirty-third Degree in 1953 and in 1957 was selected for Investiture with the dignity of the Grand Cross of Honor. In 1973 he was presented with the Certificate of Appreciation and Meritorious Service Award of the Supreme Council. Illustrious Camalier served as Deputy of the Supreme Council in the District of Columbia from January 30, 1962 – October 19, 1977. He was then elected an Emeritus Member of Honor of the Supreme Council. While serving as Grand Master of the District of Columbia, Brother Camalier was designated by President Truman to handle distribution of 102 Fraternal Stones removed from the foundation of the White House during renovation.

Bibliography:
Archive of the Supreme Council, 33°, S.J.
In Memoriam. *Transactions.* 1979: 152-154; 264.

1959

Robert Bernard Anderson
Grand Cross of the Court of Honour at age 49 years, 3 months, and 16 days
Tenure 29 years, 9 months, and 24 days
Nomination by Dallas, Texas Scottish Rite Bodies

Born: June 4, 1910 – Died: August 14, 1989
Life span: 79 years, 2 month, and 10 days
Lawyer
Secretary of the Navy; Secretary of the Treasury

Progress in Scottish Rite Masonry:
4°-14°: March 25, 1942, invested by *Dallas* Lodge of Perfection, Dallas.
15°-18°: March 25, 1942, invested by *Dallas* Chapter of Rose Croix, Dallas.
19°-30°: March 25, 1942, invested by *Dallas* Council of Kadosh, Dallas.
31°-32°: March 26, 1942, invested by *Dallas* Consistory, Dallas.
32°, KCCH: October 21, 1947.
33°, IGH: elected October 20, 1959; coroneted by the Supreme Council, 33°, S.J., October 23, 1953.
Grand Cross of the Court of Honour: October 20, 1959.

Scottish Rite Biography:
Brother Anderson was a Master Mason in *Vernon* Lodge, No. 655, Vernon, Texas, and received the Scottish Rite Degrees in Dallas Scottish Rite Bodies in 1942. On October 21, 1947, he was invested with the rank and decoration of a Knight Commander of the Court of Honour, and on October 20, 1953, was elected a 33°, Inspector General Honorary, and on October 23, 1953, was coroneted by the Supreme Council. Ill. Robert Bernard Anderson received the Grand Cross of the Court of Honour on October 20, 1959.

Bibliography:
Archive of the Supreme Council, 33°, S.J.

1961

Charles Galloway Calhoun
Grand Cross of the Court of Honour at age 67 years, 1 month, and 25 days
Tenure 5 months and 29 days
Nomination by Dallas, Texas Scottish Rite Bodies

Born: August 22, 1894 – Died: April 16, 1962
Life span: 67 years, 7 months, and 24 days
Attorney

Progress in Scottish Rite Masonry:
4°-14°: April 7, 1919, invested by *Dallas* Lodge of Perfection, Dallas.
15°-18°: April 8, 1919, invested by *Lone Star* Chapter of Rose Croix, Dallas.
19°-30°: April 9, 1919, invested by *Dallas* Council of Kadosh, Dallas.
31°-32°: April 10, 1919, invested by *Dallas* Consistory, Dallas.
32°, KCCH: October 19, 1937.
33°, IGH: elected October 21, 1941; coroneted by the Supreme Council, 33°, S.J., October 24, 1941.
Grand Cross of the Court of Honour: October 17, 1961.

Scottish Rite Biography:
Brother Calhoun was member of *St. John's* Lodge, No. 53, of Tyler, wherein he was made a Master Mason on August 18, 1916. He received the Scottish Rite Degrees in April 1919 and became a KCCH on October 19, 1937. Brother Calhoun was coroneted an Inspector General Honorary of the Thirty-third Degree in 1941, and in 1961 was selected for investiture with the dignity of Grand Cross of the Court of Honour. Throughout his busy life Brother Calhoun was always ready to give freely of his time and talents to Masonry.

Bibliography:
Archive of the Supreme Council, 33°, S.J.
In Memoriam. *Transactions.* 1963: 325.
The New Age, June 1962: 33.

1963

Harry Flood Byrd
Grand Cross of the Court of Honour at age 76 years, 4 months, and 12 days
Tenure 2 years, 11 months, and 2 days
Nomination by Alexandria, Virginia Scottish Rite Bodies

Born: June 10, 1887 – Died: October 20, 1966
Life span: 79 years, 4 months, and 10 days
Governor of Virginia and Senator

Progress in Scottish Rite Masonry:
4°-14°: October 15, 1929, invested by *Washington Memorial* Lodge of Perfection, Alexandria.
15°-18°: October 16, 1929, invested by *Randolph* Chapter of Rose Croix, Alexandria.
19°-30°: October 17, 1929, invested by *Lafayette* Council of Kadosh, Alexandria.
31°-32°: October 18, 1929, invested by *Virginia* Consistory, Alexandria.
32°, KCCH: October 17, 1939.
33°, IGH: elected October 19, 1943; coroneted by the Supreme Council, 33°, S.J., October 22, 1943.
Grand Cross of the Court of Honour: October 22, 1963.

Scottish Rite Biography:
Brother Byrd was a Master Mason in *Winchester Hiram* Lodge, No. 21, at Winchester and the Alexandria Scottish Rite Bodies. He was coroneted an Inspector General Honorary of the Thirty-third Degree in 1943, and in 1963 was invested by the Supreme Council with its highest honor, the dignity of the Grand Cross of the Court of Honour. The Supreme Council's highest honor was presented to Ill. Harry Flood Byrd, 33°, by Sovereign Grand Commander Luther A. Smith, 33°, at the House of the Temple, Washington, D.C., on March 20, 1964.

Bibliography:
Archive of the Supreme Council, 33°, S.J.
In Memoriam. *Transactions*. 1967: 360.
The New Age, January 1967.
Image courtesy of https://encyclopediavirginia.org/entries/byrd-harry-flood-jr-1914-2013/

Otto Ernest Passman
Grand Cross of the Court of Honour at age 63 years, 3 months, and 25 days
Tenure 24 years, 9 months, and 21 days
Nomination by Monroe, Louisiana Scottish Rite Bodies

Born: June 27, 1900 – Died: August 13, 1988
Life span: 88 years, 1 month, and 16 days
U.S. Congressman

Progress in Scottish Rite Masonry:
4°-14°: date unconfirmed, invested by *L. C. Allen* Lodge of Perfection, Shreveport.
15°-18°: date unconfirmed, invested by *Eureka* Chapter of Rose Croix, Shreveport.
19°-30°: date unconfirmed, invested by *Caddo* Council of Kadosh, Shreveport.
31°-32°: May 7, 1936, invested by *Shreveport* Consistory, Shreveport.
32°, KCCH: October 20, 1959.
33°, IGH: elected October 20, 1959; coroneted by the Supreme Council, 33°, S.J., October 23, 1959.
Grand Cross of the Court of Honour: October 22, 1963.

Scottish Rite Biography:
In 1932 Brother Passman took his Degree in *Graham Surghnor* Lodge, No. 383, at Monroe, Louisiana. The philosophy of Freemasonry had a profound influence upon Otto Passman's life. In recognition of his illustrious record, he received on succeeding days, in October of 1959, the distinction of being made a Knight Commander of the Court of Honor and becoming a recipient of the Scottish Rite's 33rd Degree. Brother Passman received the Council's Grand Cross of the Court of Honour during a special ceremony in the Executive Chamber where, during the Biennial Session of the Supreme Council on October 1963, he was elected to this great honor. The Supreme Council's highest honor was presented to Ill. Otto E. Passman, 33°, by Sovereign Grand Commander Luther A. Smith, 33°, at the House of the Temple, Washington, D.C., on March 20, 1964.

Bibliography:
Archive of the Supreme Council, 33°, S.J.
In Memoriam. *Transactions.* 1989: 161-162.

1965

Richard Hiller Amberg
Grand Cross of the Court of Honour at age 53 years, 4 months, and 14 days
Tenure 1 year, 11 months, and 14 days
Nomination by St. Louis, Missouri Scottish Rite Bodies

Born: June 5, 1912 – Died: September 3, 1967
Life span: 55 years, 2 months, and 28 days
Publisher

Progress in Scottish Rite Masonry:
4°-32°: date unconfirmed, invested by *Syracuse* Scottish Rite Bodies, Northern Masonic Jurisdiction.
November 16, 1956, affiliated with *St. Louis* Scottish Rite Bodies, Missouri.
32°, KCCH: October 22, 1957.
33°, IGH: elected October 17, 1961; coroneted by the Supreme Council, 33°, S.J., October 20, 1961.
Grand Cross of the Court of Honour: October 19, 1965.

Scottish Rite Biography:
Brother Amberg was a member of *Oil City* Lodge, No. 710, of Oil City, Pennsylvania, and the Scottish Rite Bodies in St. Louis, Missouri. Brother Amberg was a member of the Speakers Bureau of the St. Louis Scottish Rite Bodies and served as Chairman of the Grand Commander's Advisory Committee on Education. He was honored with the rank and decoration of Knight Commander of the Court of Honour in 1957, coroneted an Inspector General Honorary of the Thirty-third Degree in 1961, and in 1965 he was selected for investiture with the dignity of Grand Cross of the Court of Honour.

Bibliography:
Archive of the Supreme Council, 33°, S.J.
In Memoriam. *Transactions*. 1967: 341.
The New Age, November 1967.

1965

John Edgar Hoover
Grand Cross of the Court of Honour at age 70 years, 10 months, and 18 days
Tenure 6 years, 6 months, and 13 days
Nomination by Washington, District of Columbia Scottish Rite Bodies

Born: January 1, 1895 – Died: May 2, 1972
Life span: 77 years, 5 months, and 1 day
First Director of the Federal Bureau of Investigation of the United States

Progress in Scottish Rite Masonry:
4°-14°: December 6, 1954, invested by *Mithras* Lodge of Perfection, Washington, D.C.
15°-18°: December 6, 1954, invested by *Evangelist* Chapter of Rose Croix, Washington, D.C.
19°-30°: December 6, 1954, invested by *Robert de Bruce* Council of Kadosh, Washington, D.C.
31°-32°: December 6, 1954, invested by *Albert Pike* Consistory, Washington, D.C.
32°, KCCH: October 18, 1955.
33°, IGH: elected October 18, 1955; coroneted by the Supreme Council, 33°, S.J., October 21, 1955.
Grand Cross of the Court of Honour: October 19, 1965.

Scottish Rite Biography:
Brother Hoover joined *Federal* Lodge, No. 1, Washington, D.C. and received the first three degrees between September and November 1920. Illustrious Brother Hoover was coroneted an Inspector General Honorary of the Thirty-third Degree in 1955, and in 1965 he was invested with the dignity of the Grand Cross of Honour. His awards from his Country and from countless other sources attested the universal personal and professional esteem in which he was held.

Bibliography:
Archive of the Supreme Council, 33°, S.J.
Archives of the Orient of the District of Columbia and Archives of the Grand Lodge of the District of Columbia, F.A.A.M.
In Memoriam. *Transactions.* 1973: 153.

1967

James David Carter
Grand Cross of the Court of Honour at age 60 years, 9 months, and 6 days
Tenure 26 years, 11 months, and 26 days
Nomination by Waco, Texas Scottish Rite Bodies

Born: January 27, 1907 – Died: September 29, 1994
Life span: 87 years, 8 months, and 2 days
Librarian and Historian of the Supreme Council

Progress in Scottish Rite Masonry:
4°-32°: October 1948, by whom Degrees were invested unconfirmed.
32°, KCCH: October 22, 1957.
33°, IGH: elected October 22, 1963; coroneted by the Supreme Council, 33°, S.J., October 25, 1963.
Grand Cross of the Court of Honour: October 3, 1967.

Scottish Rite Biography:
Brother Carter was a Master Mason in *Bee House* Lodge, No. 550 of Evant, Texas. A member of the Waco, Texas, Scottish Rite Bodies since 1959, Ill. Carter excelled in Degree work and was a leading member on various membership, Reunions, and publicity committees. In addition, he was Orator of the Waco Lodge of Perfection and Chapter of Rose Croix as well as Director of the Scottish Rite Foundation of Texas. In recognition of these accomplishments, he was elected a KCCH in 1957 and received the Thirty-third Degree in 1963. In that same year, following the passing of Ill. Ray Barker Harris, Librarian-historian of The Supreme Council, Sovereign Grand Commander Luther A. Smith appointed Ill. Carter to this high post. Within four years, Dr. Carter produced the first volume of his three-volume study, *The History of the Supreme Council, 33°, U.S.A.* To this fundamental accomplishment must be added innumerable articles in *The New Age* magazine, and many, many other popular and scholarly Masonic publications. In recognition of these many accomplishments, he was elected to Scottish Rite Freemasonry's highest honor, the Grand Cross, in 1967.

Bibliography:
Archive of the Supreme Council, 33°, S.J.
In Memoriam. *Transactions.* 1995: 216-217.

1967

Horace Winslow McCurdy
Grand Cross of the Court of Honour at age 68 years, 2 months, and 3 days
Tenure 22 years, 1 month and 10 days
Nomination by Seattle, Washington Scottish Rite Bodies

Born: July 30, 1899 – Died: November 13, 1989
Life span: 90 years, 3 months, and 23 days
Shipbuilder

Progress in Scottish Rite Masonry:
4°-14°: October 4, 1932, invested by *Washington* Lodge of Perfection, Seattle.
15°-18°: November 1, 1932, invested by *Washington* Chapter of Rose Croix, Seattle.
19°-30°: November 9, 1932, invested by *Washington* Council of Kadosh, Seattle.
31°-32°: December 13, 1932, invested by *Lawson* Consistory, Seattle.
32°, KCCH: October 16, 1945.
33°, IGH: elected October 18, 1949; coroneted by the Supreme Council, 33°, S.J., October 21, 1949.
Grand Cross of the Court of Honour: October 3, 1967.

Scottish Rite Biography:
Brother McCurdy was a member of *George Washington* Lodge No. 251, F&AM, of Seattle, Washington, and a member of the Scottish Rite Bodies of that city. He was coroneted an Inspector General Honorary in 1949 and was selected for investiture with the dignity of the Grand Cross of the Court of Honour in 1967. Considering his many contributions to America and Freemasonry, the Seattle Brethren held a Masonic memorial service in the Seattle Scottish Rite Temple … it is appropriate to honor this great American and Mason who built bridges, ships and aircraft that became synonymous with quality.

Bibliography:
Archive of the Supreme Council, 33°, S.J.
In Memoriam. *Transactions.* 1991: 176-177.

1969

Christian Frederick Kleinknecht
Grand Cross of the Court of Honour at age 80 years, 5 months, and 21 days
Tenure 9 months and 25 days
Nomination by Washington, District of Columbia Scottish Rite Bodies

Born: April 25, 1889 – Died: August 11, 1970
Life span: 81 years, 3 months, and 26 days
Acting Secretary General of the Supreme Council, 33°, SJ

Progress in Scottish Rite Masonry:
4°-14°: April 12, 1921, invested by *Mithras* Lodge of Perfection, Washington, D.C.
15°-18°: April 13, 1921, invested by *Evangelist* Chapter of Rose Croix, Washington, D.C.
19°-30°: April 14, 1921, invested by *Robert de Bruce* Council of Kadosh, Washington, D.C.
31°-32°: April 15, 1921, invested by *Albert Pike* Consistory, Washington, D.C.
32°, KCCH: October 20, 1931.
33°, IGH: elected October 17, 1933; coroneted October 20, 1933.
Grand Cross of the Court of Honour: October 16, 1969.

Scottish Rite Biography:
Brother Christian Frederick Kleinknecht was a Master Mason in *Silver Spring* Lodge, No. 215, and was a member of both York and Scottish Rites, received every honor given by The Supreme Council, the last near the end of his incomparable career, investiture of the Grand Cross enjoyed by a select group never reaching as many as the numbers of months of the Apostles. Every tribute paid to him dwells upon his profound knowledge of Masonic teaching and procedure. He had at his fingertips the vast fund of Masonic lore in the archives of the Temple, and could find in an incredibly short time the correct answer to questions propounded to him, often astonishing a seeker by instantly giving the solution of the problem. He served the Supreme Council for 14 years as Acting Secretary General. The late Ill. John H. Cowles, 33°, who, before his election as Sovereign Grand Commander filled the office of the Grand Secretary General, said on several occasions – "Chis was a much better Secretary General that I ever was." – A remarkable tribute and expressed with utmost sincerity.

Bibliography:
Archive of the Supreme Council, 33°, S.J.
In Memoriam. *Transactions.* 1971: 203-205.

1969

Lyman Louis Lemnitzer
Grand Cross of the Court of Honour at age 70 years, 1 month, and 24 days
Tenure 19 years and 26 days
Nomination by Tokyo, Japan and Korea Scottish Rite Bodies

Born: August 29, 1899 – Died: November 12, 1988
Life span: 89 years, 2 months, and 13 days
U. S. General

Progress in Scottish Rite Masonry:
4°-14°: November 2, 1955, invested by *Tokyo* Lodge Perfection, Tokyo.
15°-18°: November 3, 1955, invested by *Tokyo* Chapter of Rose Croix, Tokyo.
19°-30°: November 4, 1955, invested by *Tokyo* Council of Kadosh, Tokyo.
31°-32°: November 5, 1955, invested by *Tokyo* Consistory, Tokyo.
32°, KCCH: October 20, 1959.
33°, IGH: elected October 20, 1959; coroneted by the Supreme Council, 33°, S.J., October 23, 1959.
Grand Cross of the Court of Honour: October 16, 1969.

Scottish Rite Biography:
Brother Lemnitzer was a member of *St. Paul* Lodge, Middleton, Rhode Island, and of the Tokyo Scottish Rite Bodies. He was coroneted 33° in 1959 and awarded the Grand Cross of the Court of Honour by our Supreme Council in 1969. In peace and war, our Brother exemplified the highest ideals of Masonry and of military service.

Bibliography:
Archive of the Supreme Council, 33°, S.J.
In Memoriam. *Transactions.* 1989: 163-164.

1969

Robert Burnham Watts
Grand Cross of the Court of Honour at age 68 years, 5 months, and 18 days
Tenure 12 years, 7 months, and 7 days
Nomination by San Diego, California Scottish Rite Bodies

Born: May 28, 1901 – Died: May 23, 1982
Life span: 80 years, 11 months, and 25 days
Director of Education and Americanism of the Supreme Council, 33°, S.J., USA

Progress in Scottish Rite Masonry:
4°-14°: September 26, 1951, invested by *San Diego* Lodge of Perfection, San Diego.
15°-18°: September 26, 1951, invested by *San Diego* Chapter of Rose Croix, San Diego.
19°-30°: September 26, 1951, invested by *San Diego* Council of Kadosh, San Diego.
31°-32°: September 26, 1951, invested by *San Diego* Consitory, San Diego.
32°, KCCH: October 22, 1957.
33°, IGH: elected October 17, 1961; coroneted October 20, 1961.
Grand Cross of the Court of Honour: October 16, 1969.

Scottish Rite Biography:
Brother Watts was Master Mason in *Teaneck* Lodge, No. 274. As a member of the San Diego Scottish Rite Bodies, Brother Watts was invested with the Rank and Decoration of Knight Commander of the Court of Honour in 1957, coroneted 33° Inspector General Honorary in 1961, and invested with the Grand Cross of the Court of Honour in 1969. Ill. Dr. Robert B. Watts, 33°, GC, was Grand Chaplain, Director of Education and Americanism, and one of the brightest stars of our Supreme Council.

Bibliography:
Archive of the Supreme Council, 33°, S.J.
In Memoriam. *Transactions.* 1983: 196-197.

1971

Bruce Cooper Clarke
Grand Cross of the Court of Honour at age 70 years, 5 months, and 18 days
Tenure 16 years, 5 months, and 3 days
Nomination by Dallas, Texas Scottish Rite Bodies

Born: April 29, 1901 – Died: March 17, 1988
Life span: 86 years, 11 months, and 18 days
General

Progress in Scottish Rite Masonry:
4°-14°: April 21, 1952, invested by *Dallas* Lodge of Perfection, Dallas.
15°-18°: April 22, 1952, invested by *Lone Star* Chapter of Rose Croix, Dallas.
19°-30°: April 23, 1952, invested by *Dallas* Council of Kadosh, Dallas.
31°-32°: April 24, 1952, invested by *Dallas* Consistory, Dallas.
32°, KCCH: October 22, 1957.
33°, IGH: elected October 22, 1963; coroneted by the Supreme Council, 33°, S.J., October 25, 1963
Grand Cross of the Court of Honour: October 14, 1971.

Scottish Rite Biography:
Brother Clark was a Master Mason of *West Point* Lodge in Highland Falls, New York, and of the Dallas Scottish Rite Bodies. In 1957 he received the KCCH and was coroneted with the 33° in 1963. In addition, on October 14, 1971, he received the Grand Cross of the Court of Honour in recognition of his many services to the Craft and America.

Bibliography:
Archive of the Supreme Council, 33°, S.J.
In Memoriam. *Transactions.* 1989: 158-159.
The New Age, August 1988: 37-38.

1971

Wilbur Daigh Mills
Grand Cross of the Court of Honour at age 62 years and 5 months
Tenure 20 years, 6 months, and 8 days
Nomination by Little Rock, Arkansas Scottish Rite Bodies

Born: May 24, 1909 – Died: May 2, 1992
Life span: 82 years, 11 months, and 8 days
U.S. Congressman

Progress in Scottish Rite Masonry:
4°-14°: November 7, 1938, invested by *Little Rock* Lodge of Perfection, Little Rock.
15°-18°: November 8, 1938, invested by *Little Rock* Chapter of Rose Croix, Little Rock.
19°-30°: November 9, 1938, invested by *Little Rock* Council of Kadosh, Little Rock.
31°-32°: November 9, 1938, invested by *Little Rock* Consistory, Little Rock.
32°, KCCH: October 22, 1957.
33°, IGH: elected October 22, 1963; coroneted by Ill. Joshua K. Shepherd, 33°, Sovereign Grand Inspector General for Arkansas November 30, 1963.
Grand Cross of the Court of Honour: October 24, 1971.

Scottish Rite Biography:
A member of *Kensett* Lodge, No. 674 of Kensett, Arkansas, Brother Mills was made a Thirty-second Degree Mason in Little Rock, Arkansas, Scottish Rite Bodies and was active in the Rite when able to spare time from his pressing legislative obligations. For his many services to Freemasonry and America, he was honored by our Order with the rank and decoration of Knight Commander of the Court of Honour in 1957, the dignity of Inspector General Honorary in 1963, and the Grand Cross in 1971.

Bibliography:
Archive of the Supreme Council, 33°, S.J.
In Memoriam. *Transactions.* 1993: 222-223.

1971

Joseph David Waggonner, Jr.
Grand Cross of the Court of Honour at age 53 years, 1 month, and 7 days
Tenure 35 years, 11 months, and 24 days
Nomination by Shreveport, Louisiana Scottish Rite Bodies

Born: September 7, 1918 – Died: October 8, 2007
Life span: 89 years, 1 month, and 1 day
U.S. Congressman

Progress in Scottish Rite Masonry:
4°-14°: April 15, 1961, invested by *Shreveport* Lodge of Perfection, Shreveport.
15°-18°: date unconfirmed, invested by *Shreveport* Chapter of Rose Croix, Shreveport.
19°-30°: date unconfirmed, invested by *Shreveport* Council of Kadosh, Shreveport.
31°-32°: date unconfirmed, invested by *Shreveport* Consistory, Shreveport.
32°, KCCH: October 19, 1965.
33°, IGH: elected October 3, 1967, coroneted by the Supreme Council, 33°, S.J., October 6, 1967.
Grand Cross of the Court of Honour: October 14, 1971.

Scottish Rite Biography:
Brother Waggoner was a member of *Plain Dealing* Lodge, No. 237, received the Scottish Rite Degrees in 1961 in the Valley of Shreveport, and the rank and decoration of a Knight Commander Court of Honour in 1965. In 1967 he was coroneted an Inspector General Honorary and was elected a Grand Cross of the Court of Honour in 1971.

Bibliography:
Archive of the Supreme Council, 33°, S.J.
In Memoriam. *Transactions*. 2009: 250.

1973

Samuel James Ervin, Jr.
Grand Cross of the Court of Honour at age 76 years, 11 months, and 14 days
Tenure 11 years, 6 months, and 12 days
Nomination by Charlotte, North Carolina Scottish Rite Bodies

Born: September 27, 1896 – Died: April 23, 1985
Life span: 88 years, 7 months, and 26 days
U. S. Senator

Progress in Scottish Rite Masonry:
4°-14°: November 14, 1922, invested by *Charlotte* Lodge of Perfection, Charlotte.
15°-18°: November 14, 1922, invested by *Mecklenburg* Chapter of Rose Croix, Charlotte.
19°-30°: November 14, 1922, invested by *Charlotte* Council of Kadosh, Charlotte.
31°-32°: November 14, 1922, invested by *Carolina* Consistory, Charlotte.
32°, KCCH: October 22, 1963.
33°, IGH: elected October 22, 1963; coroneted by the Supreme Council, 33°, S.J., October 25, 1963.
Grand Cross of the Court of Honour: October 11, 1973.

Scottish Rite Biography:
Brother Ervin was a Master Mason in *Catawba Valley* Lodge, No. 217, in Morgantown, having been initiated February 2, 1922, passed February 16, 1922, and raised February 23, 1922. Brother Ervin became a member of the Charlotte Scottish Rite Bodies in the same year in November. In 1963 he received both honors – the Knight Commander of the Court of Honour and a 33°, Inspector General Honorary. Ill. Samuel James Ervin, Jr. 33°, received our Supreme Council's highest honor – the Grand Cross of the Court of Honour – in 1973. On many occasions in many ways Brother Ervin served the Craft well.

Bibliography:
Archive of the Supreme Council, 33°, S.J.
In Memoriam. *Transactions.* 1885: 156-157.
Grand Lodge of North Carolina. *Sam J. Ervin, Jr.: The Man and the Mason.* 1985.

1973

Raymond Wiley Miller
Grand Cross of the Court of Honour at age 78 years, 8 months, and 20 days
Tenure 14 years, 4 months, and 7 days
Nomination by Salt Lake City, Utah Scottish Rite Bodies

Born: January 21, 1895 – Died: February 18, 1988
Life span: 92 years, 11 months, and 27 days
Businessman

Progress in Scottish Rite Masonry:
4°-14°: October 17, 1942, invested by *Jordan* Lodge of Perfection, Salt Lake City.
15°-18°: October 18, 1942, invested by *James Lowe* Chapter of Rose Croix, Salt Lake City.
19°-30°: October 19, 1942, invested by *Salt Lake* Council of Kadosh, Salt Lake City.
31°-32°: October 19, 1942, invested by *Utah* Consistory, Salt Lake City.
32°, KCCH: October 17, 1961.
33°, IGH: elected October 22, 1963; coroneted by the Supreme Council, 33°, S.J., October 25, 1963.
Grand Cross of the Court of Honour: October 11, 1973.

Scottish Rite Biography:
One of the most highly respected contributors to *The New Age* magazine, Brother Miller received his early Degrees in Velley Lodge in Linden, California, was a member of the Scottish Rite Bodies of Salt Lake City, was decorated with KCCH in 1961, and coroneted 33° in 1963. He was awarded the Grand Cross of the Court of Honour by our Supreme Council in 1973. Brother Miller was an author of numerous works in agriculture, public relations, and business, but it was as writer of his monthly *The New Age* articles that he was so widely recognized by his Masonic peers. For more than 16 years these timely and inclusive works were eagerly anticipated by the several hundred thousand members of the Rite, and others who were his readers.

Bibliography:
Archive of the Supreme Council, 33°, S.J.
In Memoriam. *Transactions*. 1989: 159.

1973

Aemil Pouler
Grand Cross of the Court of Honour at age 57 years, 5 months, and 21 days
Tenure 35 years, 11 months, and 16 days
Nomination by Charleston, South Carolina Scottish Rite Bodies

Born: April 20, 1916 – Died: September 27, 2009
Life span: 93 years, 5 months, and 7 days
Managing Editor of *The New Age*

Progress in Scottish Rite Masonry:
4°-14°: October 3, 1944, invested by *Greenville* Lodge of Perfection, Greenville.
15°-18°: October 24, 1944, invested by *Buist* Chapter of Rose Croix, Greenville.
19°-30°: October 25, 1944, invested by *Bethlehem* Council of Kadosh, Greenville.
31°-32°: October 26, 1944, invested by *Dalcho* Consistory, Greenville.
32°, KCCH: October 17, 1961.
33°, IGH: elected October 19, 1965; coroneted the Supreme Council, 33°, S.J., October 22, 1965.
Grand Cross of the Court of Honour: October 11, 1973.

Scottish Rite Biography:
Brother Pouler was a member of *Recovery* Lodge, No. 31 in Greenville and joined the Greenville Scottish Rite Bodies in 1944. By 1961 he was in Washington, D.C., working on the staff of *The New Age* magazine (former name of *The Scottish Rite Journal*). In 1979, he became Managing Editor and continued in that position until 1986, when he became Grand Archivist. Brother Pouler was a member of the Society of Indexers, England, and the Society of American Archivists and put these skills to great use indexing the *Transactions* from 1857, *The New Age* from 1904, *History of the Supreme Council, 33°, 1801-1861* and *1891-1921*, various Supreme Council Publications, and organizing the Supreme Council archives. While he was editor, *The New Age* received several Freedoms Foundations awards. Ill. Pouler received the KCCH in 1961, the 33° in 1965, the Grand Cross in 1973.

Bibliography:
Archive of the Supreme Council, 33°, S.J.
In Memoriam. *Transactions.* 2009: 261.

1975

Montague Graham Clark, Jr.
Grand Cross of the Court of Honour at age 65 years, 7 months, and 21 days
Tenure 25 years, 5 months, and 29 days
Nomination by Joplin, Missouri Scottish Rite Bodies

Born: February 25, 1909 – Died: March 15, 2001
Life span: 91 years, 11 months, and 20 days
President School of the Ozarks

Progress in Scottish Rite Masonry:
4°-14°: April 26, 1957, invested by *Joplin* Lodge of Perfection, Joplin.
15°-18°: April 27, 1957, invested by *Joplin* Chapter of Rose Croix, Joplin.
19°-30°: May 3, 1957, invested by *Joplin* Council of Kadosh, Joplin.
31°-32°: May 4, 1957, invested by *Joplin* Consistory, Joplin.
32°, KCCH: October 22, 1969.
33°, IGH: elected October 20, 1969; coroneted by Ill. Walter C. Ploeser, 33°, Sovereign Grand Inspector General for Missouri December 7, 1969.
Grand Cross of the Court of Honour: October 16, 1975.

Scottish Rite Biography:
Raised a Master Mason in *Morningside* Lodge, No. 245, Atlanta, Georgia, in May 1946, Ill. Clark joined Branson Lodge, No. 387 at Branson, Missouri, joined the Valley of Joplin on May 4, 1957. Dr. Clark was invested a KCCH on October 16, 1963; coroneted a 33°, IGH on December 6, 1969; and granted the Grand Cross of the Supreme Council on October 16, 1975. In May 1996, Dr. Clark was given a Life Achievement Award by the Scottish Rite Foundation of Missouri.

Bibliography:
Archive of the Supreme Council, 33°, S.J.
In Memoriam. *Transactions.* 2001: 262.

1975

Gerald Rudolph Ford
Grand Cross of the Court of Honour at age 62 years, 3 months, and 2 days
Tenure 31 years, 2 months, and 10 days
Nomination by the Supreme Council, 33°, S.J., USA for Northern Jurisdiction, USA

Born: July 14, 1913 – Died: December 26, 2006
Life span: 93 years, 5 months, and 12 days
U.S.A. President

Progress in Scottish Rite Masonry:
4°-14°: October 1, 1957, received from *Grand Rapids* Lodge of Perfection, Grand Rapids.
15°-16°: October 1, 1957, received from *Grand Rapids* Council of Princes of Jerusalem, Grand Rapids.
17°-18°: October 1, 1957, received from *Grand Rapids* Chapter of Rose Croix, Grand Rapids.
19°-32°: October 1, 1957, received from *Grand Rapids* Consistory, Grand Rapids.
33°: conferred September 26, 1962.
Grand Cross of the Court of Honour: October 16, 1975.

Scottish Rite Biography:
Brother Ford was Initiated in *Malta* Lodge No. 465, in Grand Rapids, Michigan on September 30, 1949. *Columbia* Lodge No. 3, of the District of Columbia, conferred the Degrees of Fellowcraft and Master Mason on Brother Ford as a courtesy to *Malta* Lodge on May 18, 1951. Brother Ford's father, Gerald R. Sr., a 33rd Degree Mason presented him the lambskin apron. Brother Ford received the Scottish Rite degrees in the Valley of Grand Rapids in 1957, and was made a Sovereign Grand Inspector General, 33°, and Honorary Member, Supreme Council, 33°, N.J. at the Academy of Music in Philadelphia, on September 26, 1962, for which he served as Exemplar (Representative) for his Class. While in office, on October 16, 1975, the Grand Cross of the Court of Honour the Thirty-eighth President of the United States of America Gerald Rudolph Ford was elected by the Supreme Council, 33°, S.J. to receive the Scottish Rite's highest honor,

Bibliography:
Brother Gerald Ford, 33rd degree Mason of the Shrine | Aftermath News (wordpress.com)

1975

John Lewis Hall
Grand Cross of the Court of Honour at age 71 years, 2 months, and 20 days
Tenure 9 years
Nomination by Tallahassee, Florida Scottish Rite Bodies

Born: July 26, 1904 – Died: October 16, 1984
Life span: 80 years, 2 months, and 2 days
Attorney

Progress in Scottish Rite Masonry:
4°-14°: October 30, 1945, invested by *Orient* Lodge of Perfection, Jacksonville.
15°-18°: November 2, 1945, invested by *Jacksonville* Chapter of Rose Croix, Jacksonville.
19°-30°: November 8, 1945, invested by *McLean* Council of Kadosh, Jacksonville.
31°-32°: November 9, 1945, invested by *Florida* Consistory, Jacksonville.
August 7, 1958, affiliated with Tallahassee Scottish Rite Bodies, Florida.
32°, KCCH: October 22, 1963.
33°, IGH: elected October 20, 1969; coroneted by the Supreme Council, 33°, October 23, 1969.
Grand Cross of the Court of Honour: October 16, 1975.

Scottish Rite Biography:
Brother Hall was raised to the sublime Degree of Master Mason in *Jackson* Lodge, No. 1, Tallahassee, in 1943. Two years later, in October – November 1945, he joined the Scottish Rite Bodies in Jacksonville and was invested with the Scottish Rite Degrees by *Orient* Lodge of Perfection, *Jacksonville* Chapter of Rose Croix, *McLean* Council of Kadosh and *Florida* Consistory, and became a Master of the Royal Secret on November 9, 1945. Since that year, Brother Hall has given unselfishly of his time to any cause to advance Masonry in Florida and the nation, including the Chairman position of the Legal Advisory Committee to the Sovereign Grand Inspector General of Florida. On October 22, 1963, Brother Hall was elected Knight Commander of the Court of Honour; on October 23, 1969, coroneted 33°, Inspector General Honorary. On October 16, 1975, Ill. John Lewis Hall, 33°, received the highest recognition of the Supreme Council, 33°, the Grand Cross of the Court of Honour.

Bibliography:
Archive of the Supreme Council, 33°, S.J.
In Memoriam. *Transactions*. 1985: 228.

1977

Robert Carlyle Byrd
Grand Cross of the Court of Honour at age 59 years, 10 months, and 23 days
Tenure 32 years, 8 months, and 15 days
Nomination by Charleston, West Virginia Scottish Rite Bodies

Born: November 20, 1917 – Died: June 28, 2010
Life span: 92 years, 7 months, and 8 days
U. S. Senator

Progress in Scottish Rite Masonry:
4°-14°: April 21, 1958, invested by *Odell Squier Long* Lodge of Perfection, Charleston.
15°-18°: April 22, 1958, invested by *Charleston* Chapter of Rose Croix, Charleston.
19°-30°: April 23, 1958, invested by *John C. Riheldaffer* Council of Kadosh, Charleston.
31°-32°: April 24, 1958, invested by *John W. Morris* Consistory, Charleston.
32°, KCCH: October 3, 1967.
33°, IGH: elected and coroneted by the Supreme Council, 33°, S.J., October 3, 1967
Grand Cross of the Court of Honour: October 13, 1977.

Scottish Rite Biography:
Ill. Brother Byrd was a member at the *Mountain* Lodge, No. 156, in Coal City, West Virginia, was invested with the rank and decoration of the Knight Commander of the Court of Honour, coroneted a 33° Inspector General Honorary in 1967, and received the Grand Cross of the Court of Honour in 1977.

Bibliography:
Archive of the Supreme Council, 33°, S.J.
In Memoriam. *Transactions.* 2011: 237.

1977

John Jacob Rhodes
Grand Cross of the Court of Honour at age 60 years, 11 months, and 25 days
Tenure 25 years, 10 months, and 11 days
Nomination by Phoenix, Arizona Scottish Rite Bodies

Born: September 18, 1916 – Died: August 24, 2003
Life span: 86 years, 11 months, and 6 days
U.S. Congressman

Progress in Scottish Rite Masonry:
4°-14°: November 11, 1954, invested by *Phoenix* Lodge of Perfection, Phoenix.
15°-18°: November 12, 1954, invested by *Phoenix* Chapter of Rose Croix, Phoenix.
19°-30°: November 13, 1954, invested by *Phoenix* Council of Kadosh, Phoenix.
31°-32°: November 13, 1954, invested by *Phoenix* Consistory, Phoenix.
32°, KCCH: October 17, 1961.
33°, IGH: elected October 17, 1961; coroneted by the Supreme Council, 33°, S.J., October 20, 1961.
Grand Cross of the Court of Honour: October 13, 1977.

Scottish Rite Biography:
Brother Rhodes was raised in *Oriental* Lodge, No. 20, Mesa, Arizona, in 1950, and became a 32° Scottish Rite Mason in the Valley of Phoenix in 1954. Honored with the 33° in 1961 and the Grand Cross in 1977. In remembering Illustrious John J. Rhodes, 33°, Grand Cross, one is reminded of the great statue on the Greek island of Rhodes, one of the seven wonders of the ancient world. The towering Colossus of Rhodes served as a warning light for ancient mariners approaching the coast. Similarly, Ill. Rhodes provided light to this world.

Bibliography:
Archive of the Supreme Council, 33°, S.J.
In Memoriam. *Transactions*. 2005: 263.

Allan Shivers
Grand Cross of the Court of Honour at age 70 years, and 8 days
Tenure 7 years, 3 months, and 1 day
Nomination by Austin, Texas Scottish Rite Bodies

Born: October 5, 1907 – Died: January 14, 1985
Life span: 77 years, 3 months, and 9 days
Governor of Texas

Progress in Scottish Rite Masonry:
4°-14°: April 21, 1952, invested by *Fidelity* Lodge of Perfection, Austin.
15°-18°: April 22, 1952, invested by *Philip C. Tucker* Chapter of Rose Croix, Austin.
19°-30°: April 23, 1952, invested by *James D. Richardson* Council of Kadosh, Austin.
31°-32°: April 24, 1952, invested by *Austin* Consistory, Austin.
32°, KCCH: October 18, 1955.
33°, IGH: elected October 20, 1959; coroneted by Ill. Robert L. Lockwood, 33°, Sovereign Grand Inspector General for Texas November 28, 1959.
Grand Cross of the Court of Honour: October 13, 1977.

Scottish Rite Biography:
Brother Shivers was raised in *Magnolia* Lodge in Woodville, Texas. He received the Scottish Rite Degrees in 1952, Knight Commander of the Court of Honour in 1955, and was coroneted Inspector General Honorary in 1959. He was chairman of the Inspector General's Advisory Conference in Austin, chairman of the Board of Trustees of the Texas Scottish Rite Hospital for Crippled Children, and chairman of the Texas Scottish Rite Foundation. In 1977, our Supreme Council bestowed on Brother Shivers its highest award, the Grand Cross of the Court of Honour.

Bibliography:
Archive of the Supreme Council, 33°, S.J.
In Memoriam. *Transactions.* 1987: 164-165.

1979

Wiley Odell May
Grand Cross of the Court of Honour at age 73 years, 10 months, and 13 days
Tenure 12 years and 26 days
Nomination by Memphis, Tennessee Scottish Rite Bodies

Born: December 28, 1905 – Died: November 7, 1991
Life span: 85 years, 11 months, and 9 days
Businessman

Progress in Scottish Rite Masonry:
4°-14°: May 18, 1930, invested by *John Chester* Lodge of Perfection, Memphis.
15°-18°: May 19, 1930, invested by *Calvary* Chapter of Rose Croix, Memphis.
19°-30°: May 19, 1930, invested by *Cyprus* Council of Kadosh, Memphis.
31°-32°: May 20, 1930, invested by *Tennessee* Consistory, Memphis.
32°, KCCH: October 19, 1943.
33°, IGH: elected October 18, 1949; coroneted by the Supreme Council, 33°, S.J., October 21, 1949.
Grand Cross of the Court of Honour: October 11, 1979.

Scottish Rite Biography:
Brother May was a Master Mason of the *O. K. Houck* Lodge, No. 707, served for many years as Venerable Master in his Scottish Rite Bodies. By virtue of his active involvement in and many contributions to the Scottish Rite Fraternity, he was recognized in 1979 as one of the top members of Scottish Rite in the world – at the Supreme Council Session in Washington he was awarded the Grand Cross of the Court of Honour.

Bibliography:
Archive of the Supreme Council, 33°, S.J.
In Memoriam. *Transactions.* 1993: 221.

1981

Andrew Burke
Grand Cross of the Court of Honour at age 90 years, 7 months, and 9 days
Tenure 3 years, 9 months, and 3 days
Nomination by San Francisco, California Scottish Rite Bodies

Born: March 9, 1890 – Died: July 19, 1985
Life span: 95 years, 3 months, and 10 days
Social Service

Progress in Scottish Rite Masonry:
4°-14°: January 21, 1919, invested by *Guthrie* Lodge of Perfection, Guthrie.
15°-18°: January 22, 1919, invested by *Guthrie* Chapter of Rose Croix, Guthrie.
19°-30°: January 23, 1919, invested by *DeSonnac* Council of Kadosh, Guthrie.
31°-32°: January 23, 1919, invested by *Oklahoma* Consistory, Guthrie.
32°, KCCH: October 20, 1931.
33°, IGH: elected October 19, 1943; coroneted by Ill. William Rhodes Hervey, 33°, Sovereign Grand Inspector General for California January 15, 1944.
Grand Cross of the Court of Honour: October 16, 1981.

Scottish Rite Biography:
It was in *Lawton* Lodge, Oklahoma, that Brother Burke was Raised in 1919, moving within the year to San Francisco where he was Charter Junior Warden of *Justice* Lodge. Brother Burke was an active participant and dynamic ritualist in the principal roles of the Degrees of the Rite. He held a long tenure in the roll of Sovereign Grand Commander in the investiture ceremonies for Knight Commander of the Court of Honour for the Valleys of Northern California. His unselfish devotion to our Fraternity and his outstanding leadership resulted in his receiving the Grand Cross of the Court of Honour, awarded by the Supreme Council in 1981.

Bibliography:
Archive of the Supreme Council, 33°, S.J.
In Memoriam. *Transactions.* 1987: 165-166.

1981

Harold Keith Johnson
Grand Cross of the Court of Honour at age 68 years, 7 months, and 24 days
Tenure 1 year, 11 months, and 10 days
Nomination by Aberdeen, South Dakota Scottish Rite Bodies

Born: February 22, 1912 – Died: September 24, 1983
Life span: 71 years, 7 months, and 2 days
U.S. Army General

Progress in Scottish Rite Masonry:
4°-14°: February 9, 1946, invested by *James C. Batchelor* Lodge of Perfection, Aberdeen.
15°-18°: February 9, 1946, invested by *Aberdeen* Chapter of Rose Croix, Aberdeen.
19°-30°: February 9, 1946, invested by *Albert Pike* Council of Kadosh, Aberdeen.
31°-32°: February 9, 1946, invested by *South Dakota* Consistory, Aberdeen.
32°, KCCH: October 19, 1965.
33°, IGH: elected October 19, 1965; coroneted by the Supreme Council, 33°, S.J., October 22, 1965.
Grand Cross of the Court of Honour: October 16, 1981.

Scottish Rite Biography:
Brother Johnson was a Master Mason in *Crescent* Lodge, No. 11, and a member of the Aberdeen, South Dakota Scottish Rite Bodies. In 1979, Brother Johnson was appointed Director of Education and Americanism in our Supreme Council, and his leadership gave renewed energy to this essential program of the Rite. He was coroneted a 33° Inspector General Honorary in 1981 and invested with the Grand Cross of the Court of Honour in 1981.

Bibliography:
Archive of the Supreme Council, 33°, S.J.
In Memoriam. *Transactions*. 1983: 193-194.

1981

Wood Wilson Lovell
Grand Cross of the Court of Honour at age 65 years, 9 months, and 12 days
Tenure 25 years, 8 months, and 22 days
Nomination by Atlanta, Georgia Scottish Rite Bodies

Born: January 4, 1916 – Died: July 13, 2007
Life span: 91 years, 6 months, and 9 days
Surgeon-in-Chief, Scottish Rite Hospital for Crippled Children

Progress in Scottish Rite Masonry:
4°-14°: October 13, 1949, invested by *Hermes* Lodge of Perfection, Atlanta.
15°-18°: November 9, 1949, invested by *White Eagle* Chapter of Rose Croix, Atlanta.
19°-30°: November 10, 1949, invested by *Binah* Council of Kadosh, Atlanta.
31°-32°: November 11, 1949, invested by *Atlanta* Consistory, Atlanta.
32°, KCCH: October 3, 1967.
33°, IGH: elected October 18, 1971; coroneted by the Supreme Council, 33°, S.J., October 21, 1971.
Grand Cross of the Court of Honour: October 16, 1981.

Scottish Rite Biography:
Ill. Lovell joined *Morningside* Lodge, No. 295, Atlanta, Georgia, and then the Scottish Rite in October 1949. He received the rank and decoration of a KCCH in October 1967, the 33°, Inspector General Honorary, in October 1971, and the Grand Cross of the Court of Honour in October 1981. Bro. Lovell volunteered for duty during World War II and served as a Captain of the U.S. Army Medical Corps. After leaving the army, Bro. Lovell did a residency in orthopedics and then had a two-year fellowship at the Scottish Rite Children's Hospital in Decatur, Georgia. In 1965, he became Medical Director for the hospital. He retired seventeen years later, and left a legacy of thousands of children whose bodies have been restored either directly or indirectly through his efforts.

Bibliography:
Archive of the Supreme Council, 33°, S.J.
In Memoriam. *Transactions*. 2007: 247.

1983

Melvin Guy Hall
Grand Cross of the Court of Honour at age 69 years, 1 month, and 10 days
Tenure 22 years, 11 months, and 23 days
Nomination by St. Louis, Missouri Scottish Rite Bodies

Born: September 4, 1914 – Died: October 9, 2006
Life span: 92 years, 1 month, and 4 days
Banker

Progress in Scottish Rite Masonry:
4°-14°: September 14, 1965, invested by *St. Louis* Lodge of Perfection, St. Louis.
15°-18°: September 14, 1965, invested by *St. Louis* Chapter of Rose Croix, St. Louis.
19°-30°: date unconfirmed, invested by *St. Louis* Council of Kadosh, St. Louis.
31°-32°: date unconfirmed, invested by *St. Louis* Consistory, St. Louis.
32°, KCCH: October 18, 1971.
33°, IGH: elected October 20, 1975; coroneted by Ill. Walter C. Ploeser, 33°, Sovereign Grand Inspector General for Missouri, December 13, 1975.
Grand Cross of the Court of Honour: October 14, 1983.

Scottish Rite Biography:
A member of *Webster Groves* Lodge, No. 84, Webster Groves, Missouri, Brother Hall joined the Scottish Rite in St. Louis in 1951, receiving the rank and decoration of the Knight Commander of the Court of Honour in 1971, the 33° in 1975, and the Scottish Rite's highest honor, the Grand Cross, in 1983. He served as president, treasurer, and chairman of the investment committee of the Scottish Rite Foundation of Missouri, and chairman of the St. Louis Scottish Rite Residence Foundation.

Bibliography:
Archive of the Supreme Council, 33°, S.J.
In Memoriam. *Transaction.* 2007: 244.

1983

Carl William Hopp
Grand Cross of the Court of Honour at age 78 years, 7 months, and 25 days
Tenure 3 years, 3 months, and 1 day
Nomination by Portland, Oregon Scottish Rite Bodies

Born: February 19, 1905 – Died: January 15, 1987
Life span: 81 years, 11 months, and 26 days
Businessman

Progress in Scottish Rite Masonry:
4°-14°: October 29, 1930, invested by *Oregon* Lodge of Perfection, Portland.
15°-18°: October 30, 1930, invested by *Ainsworth* Chapter of Rose Croix, Portland.
19°-30°: October 30, 1930, invested by *Multnomah* Council of Kadosh, Portland.
31°-32°: October 31, 1930, invested by *Oregon* Consistory, Portland.
32°, KCCH: October 18, 1943.
33°, IGH: elected October 21, 1947; coroneted by Sovereign Grand Commander John H. Cowles, 33°, November 29, 1947.
Grand Cross of the Court of Honour: October 14, 1983.

Scottish Rite Biography:
Brother Hopp was barely 21 when, in 1926, he became a Master Mason in *Albert Pike* Lodge. The historical and philosophical aspects of the Scottish Rite had such appeal for him that he became deeply involved and held many responsible offices in the Rite during his over 50 years of membership. In 1943 he received the rank and decoration of Knight Commander of the Court of Honour. He would be one of the youngest men in Oregon ever to receive the 33° when he was coroneted as Inspector General Honorary in 1947. Brother Hopp was president of the Scottish Rite Educational Foundation for Oregon.

Bibliography:
Archive of the Supreme Council, 33°, S.J.
In Memoriam. *Transactions.* 1987: 166-167.

1983

John Everett Houser
Grand Cross of the Court of Honour at age 81 years, 11 months, and 9 days
Tenure 4 years and 26 days
Nomination by Long Beach, California Scottish Rite Bodies

Born: September 5, 1902 – Died: November 10, 1987
Life span: 85 years, 2 months, and 5 days
Attorney

Progress in Scottish Rite Masonry:
4°-14°: May 17, 1950, invested by *Long Beach* Lodge of Perfection, Long Beach.
15°-18°: May 18, 1950, invested by *Long Beach* Chapter of Rose Croix, Long Beach.
19°-30°: May 19, 1950, invested by *Long Beach* Council of Kadosh, Long Beach.
31°-32°: May 19, 1950, invested by *Long Beach* Consistory, Long Beach.
32°, KCCH: October 18, 1955.
33°, IGH: elected October 20, 1959; coroneted by Ill. Henry C. Clausen, 33°, Sovereign Grand Inspector General for California December 19, 1959.
Grand Cross of the Court of Honour: October 14, 1983.

Scottish Rite Biography:
Brother Houser's Masonic career began in 1942, when he was raised in *Seaside* Lodge in Long Beach, where he was later to serve as Master. Brother Houser's dedication to the Scottish Rite resulted in his designation as KCCH in 1955, coronation as 33° in 1959, and recipient of The Supreme Council's highest award – the Grand Cross of the Court of Honour – in 1983. He was Chairman of his Valley's Advisory Conference for 24 years and served as a President of their Temple Association. His life was a reflection of his belief in the Masonic and Biblical tenet of brotherly love.

Bibliography:
Archive of the Supreme Council, 33°, S.J.
In Memoriam. *Transactions*. 1989: 156.

1985

Henry Agnew Bubb
Grand Cross of the Court of Honour at age 78 years, 6 months, and 24 days
Tenure 3 years, 2 months, and 17 days
Nomination by Topeka, Kansas Scottish Rite Bodies

Born: March 26, 1907 – Died: January 10, 1989
Life span: 82 years, 9 months, and 14 days
Businessman

Progress in Scottish Rite Masonry:
4°-14°: October 8, 1946, invested by *Oriental* Lodge of Perfection, Topeka.
15°-18°: October 15, 1946, invested by *Unity* Chapter of Rose Croix, Topeka.
19°-30°: October 29, 1946, invested by *Godfrey de St. Omar* Council of Kadosh, Topeka.
31°-32°: November 5, 1946, invested by *Topeka* Consistory, Topeka.
32°, KCCH: October 19, 1965.
33°, IGH: elected October 20, 1969; coroneted by the Supreme Council, 33°, S.J., October 23, 1969.
Grand Cross of the Court of Honour: October 18, 1985.

Scottish Rite Biography:
Brother Budd became a Mason in *Siloam* Lodge, No. 225, Tecumseh, Kansas. He joined the Scottish Rite in 1946 in the Valley in Topeka, received the rank and decoration of a Knight Commander of the Court of Honour in 1965; elected and coroneted 33°, Inspector General Honorary in 1969, and awarded the Grand Cross of the Court of Honour on October 18, 1985. Brother Bubb's Masonic contributions were far reaching. He was Chairman of the Valley of Topeka. The inspiration of this great life remains as a model for all Masons.

Bibliography:
Archive of the Supreme Council, 33°, S.J.
In Memoriam. *Transactions.* 1989: 166.

1985

Manley Palmer Hall
Grand Cross of the Court of Honour at age 84 years, 7 months, and 2 days
Tenure 4 years, 10 months, and 6 days
Nomination by San Francisco, California Scottish Rite Bodies

Born: March 18, 1901 – Died: August 29, 1990
Life span: 89 years, 5 months, and 11 days
Philosopher

Progress in Scottish Rite Masonry:
4°-30°: date unconfirmed, invested by *San Francisco* Scottish Rite Bodies, San Francisco.
31°-32°: December 2, 1955, by *San Francisco* Consistory, San Francisco.
32°, KCCH: October 17, 1961.
33°, IGH: elected October 15, 1973; coroneted by Ill. Henry C. Clausen,33°, Sovereign Grand Inspector General for California December 15, 1973.
Grand Cross of the Court of Honour: October 18, 1985.

Scottish Rite Biography:
A member of the Scottish Rite Bodies in the Valley of San Francisco, Brother Hall was made a Mason in *San Francisco's Jewe*l Lodge, No. 374, and received the Scottish Rite's highest honor, the Grand Cross, in 1985 because of his exceptional contributions to Freemasonry, the Scottish Rite, and the public good. Like Grand Commander Albert Pike before him, Brother Hall didn't teach a new doctrine but was an ambassador of an ageless tradition of wisdom that enriches us to this day. His piety, wisdom, warmth, and humility have touched the lives of millions in America and around the globe. The world is a far better place because of Manley Palmer Hall, and we are better persons for having known him and his work.

Bibliography:
Archive of the Supreme Council, 33°, S.J.
In Memoriam. *Transactions.* 1991: 177-178.

1985

Joseph Sidney Lewis
Grand Cross of the Court of Honour at age 86 years, 5 months, and 15 days
Tenure 10 years, 6 months, and 25 days
Nomination by Guthrie, Oklahoma Scottish Rite Bodies

Born: April 6, 1899 – Died: May 18, 1996
Life span: 97 years, 1 month, and 12 days
Attorney

Progress in Scottish Rite Masonry:
4°-14°: April 19, 1921, invested by *Guthrie* Lodge of Perfection, No. 1, Guthrie.
15°-18°: April 20, 1921, invested by *Guthrie* Chapter of Rose Croix, No. 1, Guthrie.
19°-30°: April 20, 1921, invested by *DeSonnac* Council of Kadosh, No. 1, Guthrie.
31°-32°: April 21, 1921, invested by *Oklahoma* Consistory, No. 1, Guthrie.
32°, KCCH: October 21, 1947.
33°, IGH: elected October 17, 1951; coroneted by the Supreme Council, 33°, S.J., October 19, 1951
Grand Cross of the Court of Honour: October 18, 1985.

Scottish Rite Biography:
To Ill. Joseph S. Lewis, 33°, GC., Freemason's greatest strength was its ability to unite men strong in mind, spirit, and character. He was that kind of man himself. He craved the friendships and connections made possible to great men only through the Fraternity. Brother Joe was a Master Mason in Oklahoma City Lodge, No. 36, and he was a joiner. He wanted to help and was glad to offer his service. He belonged to two Symbolic Lodges, six Scottish Rite Valleys, &c. Always the expressive master of ceremonies, when he was recognized by his Supreme Council for his 75 years of service to the Rite at a reception held in his honor in Guthrie, Oklahoma, on April 28, 1996, Brother Lewis entertained the crowd with a couple of his favorite jokes. It was a meeting. It was important. He was in charge. There was work to be done and fellowship to share. That was Ill. Joseph S. Lewis.

Bibliography:
Archive of the Supreme Council, 33°, S.J.
In Memoriam. *Transactions.* 1997: 205-206.

1987

Norman Vincent Peale
Grand Cross of the Court of Honour at age 89 years, 4 months, and 16 days
Tenure 5 years, 2 months, and 8 days
Nomination by the Supreme Council, 33°, S.J., USA for Northern Jurisdiction, USA

Born: May 31, 1898 – Died: December 24, 1993
Life span: 95 years, 6 months, and 24 days
Minister

Progress in Scottish Rite Masonry:
4°-14°: December 1, 1927, received from *New York City* Lodge of Perfection, New York
15°-16°: January 1, 1928, received from *New York City* Council of Princes of Jerusalem, New York.
17°-18°: January 1, 1928, received from *New York City* Chapter of Rose Croix, New York.
19°-32°: February 11, 1928, received from *New York City* Consistory, New York.
33°: conferred September 23, 1959.
Grand Cross of the Court of Honour: October 16, 1987.

Scottish Rite Biography:
Dr. Peale had been a dedicated Mason and outspoken proponent of Freemasonry since his raising nearly 70 years ago in *Midwood* Lodge, No. 1062, Brooklyn, New York. Coroneted a Thirty-third Degree Mason in the Northern Masonic Jurisdiction, he was honored with the Grand Cross by the Southern Jurisdiction, and his portrait was placed in the Temple Architects Hall of Honor at the House of the Temple in Washington, D.C., on November 29, 1992. This portrait recognizes Dr. Peale's world-acclaimed contributions to humanity as a minister and author. More specifically, however, it pays tribute to his special relationship with the Scottish Rite of Freemasonry, Southern Jurisdiction. For instance, he contributed articles to the *Scottish Rite Journal* and delivered a dynamic sermon during the Vesper Service at the opening of the 1989 biennial Session of our Supreme Council.

Bibliography:
In Memoriam. *Transactions.*1995: 213-214.

1987

William Donald Schaefer
Grand Cross of the Court of Honour at age 65 years, 11 months, and 14 days
Tenure 23 years, 6 months, and 2 days
Nomination by Baltimore, Maryland Scottish Rite Bodies

Born: November 2, 1921 – Died: April 18, 2011
Life span: 89 years, 5 months, and 16 days
Governor of Maryland

Progress in Scottish Rite Masonry:
4°-14°: November 10, 1973, invested by *Albert Pike* Lodge of Perfection, Baltimore.
15°-18°: November 10, 1973, invested by *Albert Pike* Chapter of Rose Croix, Baltimore.
19°-30°: November 10, 1973, invested by *Albert Pike* Council of Kadosh, Baltimore.
31°-32°: November 10, 1973, invested by *Albert Pike* Consistory, Baltimore.
32°, KCCH: October 17, 1977.
33°, IGH: elected October 19, 1981; coroneted by Ill. John Winfred Donaldson, 33°, Sovereign Grand Inspector General for Maryland November 7, 1981.
Grand Cross of the Court of Honour: October 16, 1987.

Scottish Rite Biography:
Brother Schaefer was raised a Master Mason in *Mystic Circle* Lodge, No. 109, Baltimore, became a 32° Master of the Royal Secret in 1973, received the rank and decoration of a Knight Commander of the Court of Honour in 1977, was coroneted an Inspector General Honorary in 1981, and received the Grand Cross of the Court of Honour in 1987.

Bibliography:
Archive of the Supreme Council, 33°, S.J.
In Memoriam. *Transactions.* 2011: 241.

1987

William Henry Stafford, Jr.
Grand Cross of the Court of Honour at age 56 years, 5 months, and 5 days
Tenure present
Nomination by Tallahassee, Florida Scottish Rite Bodies

Born: May 11, 1931 – present
Senior Judge of the United States District Court for the Northern District of Florida

Progress in Scottish Rite Masonry:

4°-14°: October 14, 1964, invested by *Pensacola* Lodge of Perfection, Pensacola.

15°-18°: October 15, 1964, invested by *Pensacola* Chapter of Rose Croix, Pensacola.

19°-30°: October 29, 1964, invested by *Pensacola* Council of Kadosh, Pensacola.

31°-32°: October 29, 1964, invested by *Pensacola* Consistory, Pensacola.

32°, KCCH: October 20, 1975.

33°, IGH: elected October 15, 1979; coroneted by Ill. William Mercer Hollis, 33°, Sovereign Grand Inspector General for Florida December 8, 1979.

Grand Cross of the Court of Honour: October 16, 1987.

Scottish Rite Biography:

Brother Stafford is a Master Mason in *Escambia* Lodge, No. 15, Pensacola. In 1964, he joined the Scottish Rite Bodies of the Valley of Pensacola and became a Master of the Royal Secret on October 14, 1964. Brother Stafford was invested as a Knight Commander of the Court of Honour in 1975, elected by the Supreme Council 33°, S.J., Inspector General Honorary, 33°, on October 15, 1979, and coroneted by Ill. William Mercer Hollis, 33°, Sovereign Grand Inspector General for Florida December 8, 1979. Ill. William Henry Stafford, Jr., 33°, received the Scottish Rite's highest honor, the Grand Cross on October 16, 1987.

Bibliography:

Archive of the Supreme Council, 33º, S.J.

1987

James Strom Thurmond
Grand Cross of the Court of Honour at age 85 years, 10 months, and 11 days
Tenure 15 years, 8 months, and 10 days
Nomination by Columbia, South Carolina Scottish Rite Bodies

Born: December 5, 1902 – Died: June 26, 2003
Life span: 100 years, 7 months, and 21 days
U.S. Senator

Progress in Scottish Rite Masonry:
4°-14°: April 13, 1948, invested by *Aleph* Lodge of Perfection, Columbia.
15°-18°: April 14, 1948, invested by *Will Chester Plant* Chapter of Rose Croix, Columbia.
19°-30°: April 15, 1948, invested by *Barron* Council of Kadosh, Columbia.
31°-32°: April 16, 1948, invested by *Columbia* Consistory, Columbia.
32°, KCCH: October 3, 1967.
33°, IGH: elected October 20, 1969; coroneted by the Supreme Council, 33°, S.J., October 23, 1969.
Grand Cross of the Court of Honour: October 16, 1987.

Scottish Rite Biography:
Raised a Master Mason in *Concordia* Lodge, No. 50, Edgefield, S.C. in 1925, Bro. Thurmond was invested with the 32°, Valley of Columbia, in 1948 (transferring his membership in the Lodge of Perfection from Columbia to Aiken in 1971; received the KCCH in 1967; was coroneted a 33° in 1969; and elected a Grand Cross, the Scottish Rite's highest honor, in 1987. He was proud of his membership in Masonry and the Scottish Rite, and on many occasions evidenced his genuine interest in and support of their great principles.

Bibliography:
In Memoriam. *Transactions*. 2003: 213.
Archive of the Supreme Council, 33°, S.J.

1987

Graves Hampton Trumbo
Grand Cross of the Court of Honour at age 73 years, 8 months, and 2 days
Tenure 7 years, 5 months, and 14 days
Nomination by Charleston, West Virginia Scottish Rite Bodies

Born: January 14, 1913 – Died: March 30, 1995
Life span: 82 years, 2 months, and 16 days
Businessman

Progress in Scottish Rite Masonry:
4°-14°: November 3, 1947, invested by *Odel Squier Long* Lodge of Perfection, Charleston.
15°-18°: November 4, 1947, invested by *Charleston* Chapter of Rose Croix, Charleston.
19°-30°: November 5, 1947, invested by *John C. Riheldaffer* Council of Kadosh, Charleston.
31°-32°: November 6, 1947, invested by *John W. Morris* Consistory, Charleston.
32°, KCCH: October 22, 1963.
33°, IGH: elected October 20, 1969; coroneted Supreme Council, 33°, S.J., October 23, 1969.
Grand Cross of the Court of Honour: October 16, 1987.

Scottish Rite Biography:
In 1947, Brother Trumbo petitioned *Kanawha* Lodge, No. 20 and the Scottish Rite of Charleston. Known by his co-workers and friends for his sincere handshake, warm smile, and wise council, Ill. Trumbo was an active Scottish Rite ritualist and a dynamic chairman of the entertainment and membership Committees. During his tenure in these offices, the Charleston Scottish Rite Bodies experienced their greatest growth. His enthusiasm continued during his nearly eight years tenure as Secretary, Recorder, and Registrar of the Charleston Bodies. In recognition to many services to our Rite, he was invested with the rank and decoration of KCCH in 1963 and coroneted an Inspector General Honorary in 1969. His election, on October 16, 1987, to receive the Grand Cross, the Scottish Rite's highest honor, was well deserved and long expected, for he had dedicated a lifetime to serving Freemasonry, the Scottish Rite, many other Masonic organizations, his community, and Church.

Bibliography:
Archive of the Supreme Council, 33°.
In Memoriam. *Transactions.* 1995: 215-216.

1989

Gene Autry
Grand Cross of the Court of Honour at age 81 years, 11 months, and 15 days
Tenure 8 years, 11 months, and 19 days
Nomination by Long Beach, California Scottish Rite Bodies

Born: September 29, 1907 – Died: October 2, 1998
Life span: 91 years and 4 days
Actor and Radio Entertainer

Progress in Scottish Rite Masonry:
4°-14°: March 31, 1938, invested by *Long Beach* Lodge of Perfection, Long Beach.
15°-18°: March 31, 1938, invested by *Long Beach* Chapter of Rose Croix, Long Beach.
19°-30°: April 1, 1938, invested by *Long Beach* Council of Kadosh, Long Beach.
31°-32°: April 2, 1938, invested by *Long Beach* Consistory, Long Beach.
32°, KCCH: October 15, 1979.
33°, IGH: elected October 17, 1983; coroneted by Ill. Henry C. Clausen, 33°, Sovereign Grand Inspector General for California December 17, 1983.
Grand Cross of the Court of Honour: October 13, 1989.

Scottish Rite Biography:
Made a Master Mason in *Catoosa* Lodge, No. 185, Catoosa, Oklahoma, on August 29, 1929, Bro. Autry supported Masonry throughout his career, became a Life Member of his Home Lodge, and was raised a 32° Scottish Rite Mason in the Valley of Long Beach, California, in 1938. During a 1990 interview with *Business Journal*, he commented that his phenomenal success in life was due in great measure to the moral teachings of Freemasonry, and he stated, "The world would be a better place if all men were Masons." In recognition of his service to America and the Craft, he was honored as a KCCH in 1979, a 33°, IGH in 1983, and Grand Cross in 1989. His example as a Brother will remain fresh in the hearts of Freemasons forever.

Bibliography:
Archive of the Supreme Council, 33°, S.J.
In Memoriam. *Transactions.* 1999: 209-210.

1989

Martin Dale Carlin
Grand Cross of the Court of Honour at age 73 years, 11 months, and 24 days
Tenure 16 years and 17 days
Nomination by Washington, District of Columbia Scottish Rite Bodies

Born: September 19, 1916 – Died: October 30, 2005.
Life span: 88 years, 11 months, and 11 days
Accountant

Progress in Scottish Rite Masonry:
4°-14°: October 14, 1952, invested by *Mithras* Lodge of Perfection, Washington, D.C.
15°-18°: October 28, 1952, invested by *Evangelist* Chapter of Rose Croix, Washington, D.C.
19°-30°: November 25, 1952, invested by *Robert de Bruce* Council of Kadosh, Washington, D.C.
31°-32°: December 9, 1952, invested by *Albert Pike* Consistory, Washington, D.C.
32°, KCCH: October 19, 1965.
33°, IGH: elected October 20, 1975; coroneted by the Supreme Council, 33°, S.J., October 23, 1975.
Grand Cross of the Court of Honour: October 13, 1989.

Scottish Rite Biography:
Brother Martin Dale Carlin received the first three Masonic Degrees in *Federal* Lodge, No. 1 in 1951 and later transferred his membership to *Albert Pike* Lodge, No. 33. He received his Scottish Rite Degrees in 1952 and served as the Commander of *Robert de Bruce* Council in 1981. He also served as Chairman of the Scottish Rite Audit Committee for a number of years and portrayed the Benedict Arnold role in the DCSR's production of the "Traitor" Degree. In 1987, Brother Carlin was appointed Project Manager to construct the Scottish Rite Center for Childhood Language Disorders, Valley of Washington, Orient of the District of Columbia. In 1988, he was elected to serve as Secretary of the Scottish Rite Bodies and the District's Scottish Rite Foundation, which he performed until his retirement on June 1, 1995.

Bibliography:
Archive of the Supreme Council, 33°, S.J.
Archives of the Orient of the District of Columbia and Archives of the Grand Lodge of the District of Columbia, F.A.A.M.

1989

James Harold Doolittle
Grand Cross of the Court of Honour at age 92 years, 9 months, and 29 days
Tenure 3 years, 11 months, and 14 days
Nomination by San Diego, California Scottish Rite Bodies

Born: December 14, 1896 – Died: September 27, 1993
Life span: 96 years, 9 months, and 13 days
U.S. Lt. General, Aviation Pioneer

Progress in Scottish Rite Masonry:
4°-14°: December 11, 1918, invested by *Constans* Lodge of Perfection, No. 8, San Diego.
15°-18°: December 12, 1918, invested by *Constans* Chapter of Rose Croix, No. 5, San Diego.
19°-30°: December 13, 1918, invested by *San Diego* Council of Kadosh, No. 6, San Diego.
31°-32°: December 14, 1918, invested by *San Diego* Consistory, No. 6, San Diego.
32°, KCCH: October 19, 1943.
33°, IGH: elected October 16, 1945; date of coronation unconfirmed.
Grand Cross of the Court of Honour: October 13, 1989.

Scottish Rite Biography:
Brother Doolittle became a Master Mason on August 16, 1918, in *Hollenbeck* Lodge, No. 319, Los Angeles, California, and Master of the Royal Secret in the San Diego Consistory on December 14, 1918. He received the Thirty-third Degree Honorary in 1945 and the Grand Cross of the Court of Honour in 1989. In 1991, as a gift of the Scottish Rite Masons of California, his portrait was received in the Temple Architects Hall of Honor in the House of the Temple in Washington, DC. In recognition of their distinguished Brother, the California Scottish Rite Valleys will each name a 1993 Reunion class the "Jimmy Doolittle Class."

Bibliography:
Archive of the Supreme Council, 33°, S.J.
In Memoriam. *Transactions.* 1993: 225-226.

1989

Forrest DeLoss Haggard
Grand Cross of the Court of Honour at age 63 years, 5 months, and 21 days
Tenure 17 years, 8 months, and 27 days
Nomination by Kansas City, Kansas Scottish Rite Bodies

Born: April 21, 1925 – Died: August 10, 2007
Life span: 82 years, 3 months, and 19 days
Minister

Progress in Scottish Rite Masonry:
4°-14°: April 21, 1947, invested by *Albert Pike* Lodge of Perfection, McAlester.
15°-18°: April 22, 1947, invested by *South McAlester* Chapter of Rose Croix, McAlester.
19°-30°: April 22, 1947, invested by *Tuskahoma* Council of Kadosh, McAlester.
31°-32°: April 22, 1947, invested by *Indian* Consistory, McAlester.
32°, KCCH: October 17, 1961.
33°, IGH: elected October 19, 1965; coroneted by Ill. Claud F. Young, 33°, Sovereign Grand Inspector General for Kansas December 4, 1965.
Grand Cross of the Court of Honour: October 13, 1989.

Scottish Rite Biography:
On September 27, 1946, a twenty-one-year-old minister was raised in *Kiefer* Lodge, No. 488, Keifer, Oklahoma. After being raised in *Kiefer* Lodge, he joined the *Indian* Consistory (now the Valley of McAlester, Oklahoma) of the Scottish Rite on April 22, 1947. Soon thereafter he moved to Kansas. Ill. Haggard was appointed Personal Representative of the SGIG in Kansas for Northeast Kansas in 1990, serving until 2000. A Charter Member of the Scottish Rite Research Society, he served the Society as President from 1955 until 2002. Invested with the KCCH in 1961 and coroneted a 33° in 1965, Ill. Haggard was elected by the Supreme Council, 33°, to receive the Grand Cross of the Court of Honour, the highest recognition given by the Scottish Rite, S.J., in 1989. Ill. Forrest D. Haggard's life was illuminated by remarkable service to God, his church, and Freemasonry.

Biography:
Archive of the Supreme Council, 33°, S.J.
In Memoriam. *Transactions*. 2007: 248.

1989

Chester Earl McCarty
Grand Cross of the Court of Honour at age 3 years, 9 months, and 13 days
Tenure 9 years, 5 months, and 22 days
Nomination by Portland, Oregon Scottish Rite Bodies

Born: December 31, 1905 – Died: April 5, 1999
Life span: 93 years, 3 months, and 5 days
U.S. Army Major-General

Progress in Scottish Rite Masonry:
4°-14°: May 22, 1930, invested by *Oregon* Lodge of Perfection, Portland.
15°-18°: May 23, 1930, invested by *Ainsworth* Chapter of Rose Croix, Portland.
19°-30°: May 23, 1930, invested by *Multnomah* Council of Kadosh, Portland.
31°-32°: May 24, 1930, invested by *Oregon* Consistory, Portland.
32°, KCCH: October 15, 1979.
33°, IGH: elected October 17, 1983; coroneted by Ill. David O. Johnson, 33°, Sovereign Grand Inspector General for Oregon November 5, 1983.
Grand Cross of the Court of Honour: October 13, 1989.

Scottish Rite Biography:
General McCarty was a member Portland Oregon's *Friendship* Lodge, No. 160, and Scottish Rite Bodies, becoming a 32° Master of Royal Secret in 1930. In recognizing his many services to Freemasonry and America, he was invested with the KCCH in 1979, and elected a 33°, IGH in 1983. In 1989 he received the Grand Cross, the highest honor awarded by the Supreme Council. In the passing of General Chester E. McCarty, 33°, GC, America and Freemasonry lost a soldier of freedom and a Freemason of world renown.

Bibliography:
Archive of the Supreme Council, 33°, S.J.
In Memoriam. *Transactions.* 1999: 214-215.

1991

Clarence Leroy Bartholic
Grand Cross of the Court of Honour at age 90 years, 7 months, and 2 days
Tenure 7 years, 2 months, and 13 days
Nomination by Denver, Colorado Scottish Rite Bodies

Born: March 16, 1901 – Died: December 31, 1998
Life span: 96 years, 9 months, and 15 days
Attorney

Progress in Scottish Rite Masonry:
4°-14°: April 27, 1936, invested by *Centennial* Lodge of Perfection, Denver.
15°-18°: April 28, 1936, invested by *Sangre de Cristo* Chapter of Rose Croix, Denver.
19°-30°: April 29, 1936, invested by *Pike's Peak* Council of Kadosh, Denver.
31°-32°: April 30, 1936, invested by *Rocky Mountain* Consistory, Denver.
32°, KCCH: October 16, 1945.
33°, IGH: elected October 17, 1951; coroneted by Ill. Haslett Platt Burke, 33°, Sovereign Grand Inspector General for Colorado December 18, 1951.
Grand Cross of the Court of Honour: October 18, 1991.

Scottish Rite Biography:
Brother Bartholic's Masonic life was one of service. He served his Lodge, *Highlands*, No. 86. He served the Scottish Rite as both Wise Master of Rose Croix and Master of Kadosh, subsequently becoming the Personal Representative of *Rocky Mountain* Consistory and then Orient Personal Representative for Colorado. He was elected Inspector General Honorary in 1951 and a Grand Cross in 1991. Clarence was one of the attorneys that drafted the original article for the first-ever Scottish Rite Foundation, which started the Scottish Rite's involvement in the treatment of children's language disorders. The name of Ill. Clarence Leroy Bartholic, 33°, Grand Cross, splendid with the luster of his great deeds and philanthropies, will live forever on the pages of history and the rolls of fame.

Bibliography:
Archive of the Supreme Council, 33°, S.J.
In Memoriam. *Transactions.* 1999: 210-211.

1991

Ernest Efrem Borgnine
Grand Cross of the Court of Honour at age 73 years, 9 months, and 24 days
Tenure 20 years, 8 months, and 20 days
Nomination by Los Angeles/Long Beach, California Scottish Rite Bodies

Born: January 24, 1917 – Died: July 8, 2012
Life span: 95 years, 5 months, and 14 days
American Actor

Progress in Scottish Rite Masonry:
4°-14°: March 13, 1964, invested by *Los Angeles* Lodge of Perfection, Los Angeles.
15°-18°: March 14, 1964, invested by *Los Angeles* Chapter of Rose Croix, Los Angeles.
19°-30°: March 14, 1964, invested by *Los Angeles* Council of Kadosh, Los Angeles.
31°-32°: March 14, 1964, invested by *Los Angeles* Consistory, Los Angeles.
32°, KCCH: October 15, 1979.
33°, IGH: elected October 17, 1983; coroneted by Ill. Henry C. Clausen, 33°, Sovereign Grand Inspector General for California December 17, 1983.
Grand Cross of the Court of Honour: October 18, 1991.

Scottish Rite Biography:
Ill. Brother Borgnine was initiated into the Masonic fraternity on May 2, 1949, in *Abingdon* Lodge, No. 48, Abingdon, Virginia. He became a Master of the Royal Secret in the Valley of Los Angeles on March 14, 1964, was invested with the rank and decoration of a Knight Commander of the Court of Honour in 1979; coroneted an Inspector General Honorary in 1983. At the Supreme Council Biennial Session of 1991, he was elected to receive the Grand Cross of the Court of Honour. Bro. Ernest became a plural member of the Valley of Long Beach in 1967. The Long Beach Scottish Rite Theatre was dedicated to Bro. Borgnine on May 7, 2011. Ill. Borgnine was the Honorary Chairman of the Scottish Rite's national philanthropy program, RiteCare.

Bibliography:
Archive of the Supreme Council, 33°, S.J.
In Memoriam. *Transactions*. 2013: 186.

1991

Curtis LeRoy Carlson
Grand Cross of the Court of Honour at age 77 years, 3 months, and 10 days
Tenure 7 years, 4 months, and 1 day
Nomination by Minneapolis, Minnesota Scottish Rite Bodies

Born: July 9, 1914 – Died: February 19, 1999
Life span: 84 years, 7 months, and 10 days
Merchant

Progress in Scottish Rite Masonry:
4°-14°: February 27, 1947, invested by *Minneapolis* Lodge of Perfection, Minneapolis.
15°-18°: March 20, 1947, invested by *Minneapolis* Chapter of Rose Croix, Minneapolis.
19°-30°: May 15, 1947, invested by *Minneapolis* Council of Kadosh, Minneapolis.
31°-32°: May 29, 1947, invested by *Minneapolis* Consistory, Minneapolis.
32°, KCCH: October 17, 1983.
33°, IGH: elected October 19, 1987; coroneted by Ill. Louis K. Thompson, 33°, Sovereign Grand Inspector General for Minnesota on December 12, 1987.
Grand Cross of the Court of Honour: October 18, 1991.

Scottish Rite Biography:
Brother Carlson became a Master Mason in *Cataract* Lodge, No. 2, Richfield, Minnesota in 1946; a 32° Scottish Rite Mason in 1947, Valley of Minneapolis; a KCCH in 1983; a 33°, IGH in 1987; and a Grand Cross in 1991. Crediting Masonry as one of the underlying reasons for his success, Ill. Carlson wrote: "Being a Mason has contributed to my leadership skills, my self-esteem, and my understanding of the collaborative experience. It instills the sense of individual responsibility, crucial for a healthy organization such as our beloved Craft. Fraternal experience benefits our families, our communities, and our nation."

Bibliography:
Archive of the Supreme Council, 33°, S.J.
In Memoriam. *Transactions.* 1999: 11-212.

1991

Walter Scott Downs
Grand Cross of the Court of Honour at age 63 years, 8 months, and 24 days
Tenure 24 years and 8 days
Nomination by Alexandria, Virginia Scottish Rite Bodies

Born: January 24, 1928 – Died: October 26, 2015
Life span: 87 years, 10 months, and 2 days
Secretary of the Valley

Progress in Scottish Rite Masonry:
4°-14°: April 26, 1958, invested by *Washington Memorial* Lodge of Perfection, Alexandria.
15°-18°: April 28, 1958, invested by *Randolph* Chapter of Rose Croix, Alexandria.
19°-30°: May 5, 1958, invested by *Lafayette* Council of Kadosh, Alexandria.
31°-32°: May 6, 1958, invested by *Virginia* Consistory, Alexandria.
32°, KCCH: October 15, 1973.
33°, IGH: elected by October 15, 1979; coroneted by Ill. Charles E. Webber, 33°, Sovereign Grand Inspector General for Virginia November 10, 1979.
Grand Cross of the Court of Honour: October 18, 1991.

Scottish Rite Biography:
Brother Walter began his Masonic life in 1957 when raised a Master Mason in *Henry Knox Field* Lodge, No. 349. He subsequently became a member of the Alexandria Scottish Rite Bodies in 1959. Elected to receive the Knight Commander of the Court of Honour in 1973, he was coroneted as a 33° Inspector General Honorary in 1979. In 1983 Ill. Downs became a Secretary of the Alexandria Scottish Rite Bodies, holding that office for the next 27 years. In 1991, Ill. Downs was awarded the Grand Cross of the Court of Honour.

Bibliography:
Archive of the Supreme Council, 33°, S.J.
In Memoriam. *Transactions*. 2017: 105.

1991

John Paul Hammerschmidt
Grand Cross of the Court of Honour at age 69 years, 5 months, and 14 days
Tenure 23 years, 5 months, and 13 days
Nomination by Ft. Smith, Arkansas Scottish Rite Bodies

Born: May 4, 1922 – Died: April 1, 2015
Life span: 92 years, 11 months, and 27 days
U.S. Congressman

Progress in Scottish Rite Masonry:
4°-14°: May 5, 1947, invested by *Little Rock* Lodge of Perfection, Little Rock.
15°-18°: May 6, 1947, invested by *Little Rock* Chapter of Rose Croix, Little Rock.
19°-30°: May 7, 1947, invested by *Little Rock* Council of Kadosh, Little Rock.
31°-32°: May 7, 1947, invested by *Little Rock* Consistory, Little Rock.
32°, KCCH: October 17, 1977.
33°, IGH: elected October 19, 1987; coroneted by Ill. Aaron B. Pierce, 33°, Sovereign Grand Inspector General for Arkansas December 12, 1987.
Grand Cross of the Court of Honour: October 18, 1991.

Scottish Rite Biography:
Brother Hammerschmidt was a Master Mason of *Boone* Lodge, No. 314, in Harrison, Arkansas, and the Scottish Rite Bodies of Fort Smith, Arkansas. He was elected a Knight Commander of the Court of Honour in 1977; elected 33°, Inspector General Honoray by the Supreme Council, 33°, S.J., on October 19, 1987, and coroneted by Ill. Aaron B. Pierce, 33°, Sovereign Grand Inspector General for Arkansas December 12, 1987. Ill. John Paul Hammerschmidt, 33°, was awarded the Grand Cross of the Court of Honour on October 18, 1991.

Bibliography:
Archive of the Supreme Council, 33°, S.J.
In Memoriam. *Transactions.* 2015: 151.

1991

Abner Vernon McCall
Grand Cross of the Court of Honour at age 76 years, 4 months, and 10 days
Tenure 3 years, 7 months, and 23 days
Nomination by Waco, Texas Scottish Rite Bodies

Born: June 8, 1915 – Died: June 11, 1995
Life span: 80 years and 3 days
Dean of Baylor Law School

Progress in Scottish Rite Masonry:
4°-14°: October 22, 1956, invested by *Fidelity* Lodge of Perfection, Austin.
15°-18°: October 23, 1956, invested by *Philip C. Tacker* Chapter of Rose Croix, Austin.
19°-30°: October 24, 1956, invested by *James D. Richardson* Council of Kadosh, Austin.
31°-32°: October 25, 1956, invested by *Austin* Consistory, Austin.
February 4, 1958, affiliated with Waco, Texas Scottish Rite Bodies.
32°, KCCH: October 17, 1961.
33°, IGH: elected October 19, 1965; coroneted by Ill. Robert Lee Lockwood, 33°, Sovereign Grand
Inspector General for Texas December 11, 1965.
Grand Cross of the Court of Honour: October 18, 1991.

Scottish Rite Biography:
Ill. McCall was raised a Master Mason in *Baylor* Lodge, No. 1235, Waco, Texas, and was a member of the
Waco Scottish Rite Bodies since 1958, serving as the first Master of Waco Consistory, and working in the
22°. For his many services to our Order, he was elected KCCH in 1961, a 33°, IGH in 1965, and a Grand
Cross in 1991. During the 1992-93 "study" of Freemasonry by the SBC, he defended the Craft in a *Scottish
Rite Journal* article (February 1993) saying: "In thousands of meetings of Freemasons and Baptists
stretching back sixty years, I have seen nothing that made my belief and work in the Fraternity of
Freemasons incompatible with my belief and work as a member of Southern Baptist Church."

Bibliography:
Archive of the Supreme Council, 33°, S.J.
In Memoriam. *Transactions.* 1995: 212-213.

1991

William Henson Moore, III
Grand Cross of the Court of Honour at age 52 years, 11 months, and 16 days
Tenure present
Nomination by Baton Rouge, Louisiana Scottish Rite Bodies

Born: October 4, 1939 – present
U.S. Congressman

Progress in Scottish Rite Masonry:
4°-14°: October 11, 1975, invested by *Baton Rouge* Lodge of Perfection, Baton Rouge.
15°-18°: October 12, 1975, invested by *Baton Rouge* Chapter of Rose Croix, Baton Rouge.
19°-30°: November 1, 1975, invested by *Baton Rouge* Council of Kadosh, Baton Rouge.
31°-32°: November 2, 1975, invested by *Baton Rouge* Consistory, Baton Rouge.
32°, KCCH: October 19, 1981.
33°, IGH: elected October 16, 1989; coroneted by Ill. Dietrich Walter Jessen, 33°, Sovereign Grand Inspector General for Louisiana November 11, 1989.
Grand Cross of the Court of Honour: October 18, 1991.

Scottish Rite Biography:
Brother Moore is a Master Mason in *Trinity Union* Lodge, No. 372, at Baton Rouge. In 1975 he joined the Scottish Rite Bodies of the Valley of Baton Rouge and became a 32°, Master of the Royal Secret on November 2, 1975. Brother Moore was invested as a Knight Commander of the Court of Honour in 1981, elected 33°, Inspector General Honorary on October 16, 1989, and coroneted by Ill. Dietrich Walter Jessen, 33°, Sovereign Grand Inspector General for Louisiana November 11, 1989. Ill. William Henson Moore, III, 33°, was elected by the Supreme Council to receive the Grand Cross of the Court of Honour on October 18, 1991.

Bibliography:
Archive of the Supreme Council, 33°, S.J.

1991

Herman Nickerson, Jr.
Grand Cross of the Court of Honour at age 78 years, 2 months, and 18 days
Tenure 9 years, 2 months, and 9 days
Nomination by New Bern, North Carolina Scottish Rite Bodies

Born: July 30, 1913 – Died: December 27, 2000
Life span: 87 years, 4 months, and 27 days
U.S. Marine Corps General

Progress in Scottish Rite Masonry:
4°-14°: May 17, 1965, invested by *California* Lodge of Perfection, San Francisco.
15°-18°: May 18, 1965, invested by *California* Chapter of Rose Croix, San Francisco.
19°-30°: May 19, 1965, invested by *California* Council of Kadosh, San Francisco.
31°-32°: May 21, 1965, invested by *California* Consistory, San Francisco.
32°, KCCH: October 19, 1965.
33°, IGH: elected October 19, 1965; coroneted by Ill. Henry C. Clausen, 33°, Sovereign Grand Inspector General for California December 18, 1965.
September 10, 1979, affiliated with New Bern Scottish Rite Bodies.
Grand Cross of the Court of Honour: October 18, 1991.

Scottish Rite Biography:
General Nickerson was a member of *Barstow* Lodge, No. 682, California, and the Scottish Rite Bodies of New Bern, North Carolina. In recognition of his many services to Freemasonry and America, he was elected an Inspector General Honorary, 33°, in 1965, and recognized with the Scottish Rite's highest honor, the Grand Cross, in 1991. An ardent advocate of the Supreme Council's Americanism and Education Program, General Nickerson often spoke to Freemasons and to the general public on the subject of patriotism, family, and character. He was also a frequent contributor of articles to the *Scottish Rite Journal* (then *The New Age Magazine*).

Bibliography:
Archive of the Supreme Council, 33°, S.J.
In Memoriam. *Transactions.* 2001: 259.

1991

Carl Julian Sanders
Grand Cross of the Court of Honour at age 79 years, 5 months, and 4 days
Tenure 15 years, 4 months, and 19 days
Nomination by Dothan, Alabama Scottish Rite Bodies

Born: 1912, May 14 – Died: March 7, 2007
Life span: 94 years, 9 months, and 23 days
Bishop of the United Methodist Church

Progress in Scottish Rite Masonry:
4°-14°: November 21, 1976, invested by *Birmingham* Lodge of Perfection, Birmingham.
15°-18°: November 21, 1976, invested by *Birmingham* Chapter of Rose Croix, Birmingham.
19°-30°: November 21, 1976, invested by *Birmingham* Council of Kadosh, Birmingham.
31°-32°: November 21, 1976, invested by *Birmingham* Consistory, Birmingham.
32°, KCCH: October 17, 1983.
33°, IGH: elected October 19; coroneted by Ill. James R. Rogers, 33°, Sovereign Grand Inspector General for Alabama December 12, 1987.
Grand Cross of the Court of Honour: October 18, 1991.

Scottish Rite Biography:
Ill. Sanders became a Mason in 1937 and 32° Master of the Royal Secret in 1976. He received the rank and decoration of a KCCH in 1983, was coroneted a 33° Inspector General Honorary in 1987, and received the highest honor of the Supreme Council, the Grand Cross of the Court of Honour, in 1991. The Supreme Council elected him Grand Chaplain in 1989, which position he held until 1999. He was honored as a Supreme Temple Architect in 1991 and his portrait hangs in the Hall of Honor in the House of the Temple in Washington, D.C.

Bibliography:
Archive of the Supreme Council, 33°, S.J.
In Memoriam. *Transactions.* 2007: 245.

1991

Fred Delbert Schwengel
Grand Cross of the Court of Honour at age 84 years, 4 months, and 20 days
Nomination by Davenport, Iowa Scottish Rite Bodies

Born: May 28, 1907 – Died: April 1, 1993
Life span: 85 years, 11 months, and 4 days
U.S. Congressman
President U.S. Capitol Historical Society

Progress in Scottish Rite Masonry:
4°-14°: May 7, 1940, invested by *Adoniram* Lodge of Perfection, Davenport.
15°-18°: May 8, 1940, invested by *Saint John's* Chapter of Rose Croix, Davenport.
19°-30°: May 9, 1940, invested by *Coeur de Leon* Council of Kadosh, Davenport.
31°-32°: May 10, 1940, invested by *Zarephath* Consistory, Davenport.
32°, KCCH: October 18, 1949.
33°, IGH: elected October 22, 1963; coroneted by the Supreme Council, 33°, S.J., October 25, 1963.
Grand Cross of the Court of Honour: October 18, 1991.

Scottish Rite Biography:
With the passing of Ill. Fred Delbert Schwengel, 33°, Grand Cross, American Freemasonry lost one of its true stalwarts, a man who tirelessly labored to bring Masonic principles to bear on all levels of public life and policy … He was one of the most ardent defenders on Capitol Hill of the Scottish Rite principle of church/state separation. He was a leading force in developing art projects, such as the 1993 painting of "George Washington Laying of the Cornerstone of the U.S. Capitol" for The Supreme Council as a commemoration of the bicentennial of this significant Masonic Occasion. A member of the Davenport, Iowa, Scottish Rite, who presided as an officer of all the Bodies. In recognition of these many services, he was invested with the Rank and Decoration of KCCH in 1949, conferred with the 33° in 1964, and bestowed the Scottish Rite's highest honor, the Grand Cross, in 1991.

Bibliography:
Archive of the Supreme Council, 33°, S.J.
In Memoriam. *Transactions.* 1993: 219-220.

1991

Elvio Sciubba
Grand Cross of the Court of Honour at age unconfirmed
Tenure unconfirmed
Nomination by the Supreme Council, 33°, SJ, USA

Born: unconfirmed – Died: January 28, 2001
Life span: unconfirmed
Sovereign Grand Commander of the Supreme Council, 33°, for Italy

Progress in Scottish Rite Masonry:
4°-33°: date, place, and by whom Degrees were invested unconfirmed.
Sovereign Grand Commander of the Supreme Council, 33°, for Italy: 1989 – 1991.
Grand Cross of the Court of Honour: October 18, 1991.

Scottish Rite Biography:
Ill. Elvio Sciubba, 33°, GC, as Grand Representative of our Supreme Council near their, was a strong friend of the Southern Jurisdiction and a constant champion of worldwide Masonic unity and progress. For over 30 years Ill. Sciubba was a stabilizing figure in the Grand Lodge of Italy, and, as Sovereign Grand Commander from 1989 to 1991, he was a catalyst holding the Supreme Council of Italy together during some very perilous times, such as the Italian P-2 Lodge controversy. His thoughtful counsel and advice enabled the Grand Masters of North America to deal with this situation and accomplished an appropriate closure. Regarding the Scottish Rite, he single-handedly translated *A Bridge to Light* into the Italian language and for many years headed a distinguished Masonic publication *L'Incontro delle genti*, which features articles, many of them about the Rite, translated simultaneously into Italian, English, German, and Spanish. Following the Cold War, Ill. Sciubba was instrumental in the re-establishment of the Scottish Rite in the emerging democracies of Eastern European, especially Czechoslovakia, Yugoslavia, and Hungary. Designated an Honorary Member of this Supreme Council in recognition of his many services to the Southern Jurisdiction, he was elected in 1991 to the Scottish Rite's highest honor, the Grand Cross.

Bibliography:
Archive of the Supreme Council, 33°, S.J.
In Memoriam. *Transactions.* 2001: 261.

1991

Alan Kooi Simpson
Grand Cross of the Court of Honour at age 60 years, 1 month, and 16 days
Tenure present
Nomination by Sheridan, Wyoming Scottish Rite Bodies

Born: September 2, 1931 – Present
U.S. Senator

Progress in Scottish Rite Masonry:

4°-14°: April 25, 1961, invested by *Sheridan* Lodge of Perfection, Sheridan.

15°-18°: April 26, 1961, invested by *Sheridan* Chapter of Rose Croix, Sheridan.

19°-30°: April 27, 1961, invested by *Sheridan* Council of Kadosh, Sheridan.

31°-32°: April 28, 1961, invested by *Sheridan* Consistory, Sheridan.

32°, KCCH: October 15, 1979.

33°, IGH: elected October 21, 1985; coroneted by Ill. Jack E. Nixon, 33°, Sovereign Grand Inspector General for Wyoming November 9, 1985.

Grand Cross of the Court of Honour: October 18, 1991.

Scottish Rite Biography:

Brother Simpson was raised to the Sublime Degree in *Shoshone* Lodge, No. 21, at Cody. He became a member of the Scottish Rite Bodies in the Valley of Sheridan in 1961; was invested as a Knight Commander of the Court of Honour on October 15, 1979; elected by the Supreme Council an Inspector General Honorary, 33° and coroneted by Ill. Jack E. Nixon, 33°, Sovereign Grand Inspector General for Wyoming November 9, 1985. Ill. Alan Kooi Simpson, 33° received the highest honor of the Supreme Council, the Grand Cross of the Court of Honour on October 18, 1991.

Bibliography:

Archive of the Supreme Council, 33°, S. J.

1991

William Gene Sizemore
Grand Cross of the Court of Honour at age 63 years, 10 months, and 16 days
Tenure – present
Nomination by Jacksonville, Florida and Washington, D.C. Scottish Rite Bodies

Born: August 4, 1927 – present
U.S. Navy Rear Admiral

Progress in Scottish Rite Masonry:
4°-14°: November 9, 1955, invested by *San Jose* Lodge of Perfection, San Jose.
15°-18°: November 10, 1955, invested by *San Jose* Chapter of Rose Croix, San Jose.
19°-30°: November 11, 1955, invested by *San Jose* Council of Kadosh, San Jose.
31°-32°: November 12, 1955, invested by *San Jose* Consistory, San Jose.
December 4, 1970, affiliated with Jacksonville Scottish Bodies, Florida.
32°, KCCH: October 17, 1977.
33°, IGH: elected October 15, 1979; coroneted by Ill. William Mercer Hollis, 33°, Sovereign Grand Inspector General for Florida December 8, 1979.
January 14, 1986, dual membership in Washington, D.C. Scottish Rite Bodies.
Grand Cross of the Court of Honour: October 18, 1991.

Scottish Rite Biography:
Brother Gene was raised a Master Mason in 1948 in *Edwin Dobbins* Lodge, No. 164, Lawrenceville, Illinois. He received the rank and decoration of a Knight Commander of the Court of Honour in 1977, was coroneted an Inspector General Honorary in 1980, and received the Grand Cross of the Court of Honour in 1989. Ill. Gene first served the Supreme Council as Director of Education and Americanism in 1983 and then on July 19, 1989, became Assistant Grand Secretary General. The position title later changed to Grand Executive Director. At our 2013 Session, the Supreme Council, 33°, SJ created Ill. Sizemore a Past Sovereign Grand Commander *honoris causa*, the first such creation in the 212-year history of the Southern Jurisdiction. This was a fitting tribute to a Brother whose entire career has been in service to others.

Bibliography:
Archive of the Supreme Council, 33°, S.J.
Morris, S. Brent, 33°, Grand Cross. A Lifetime of Service … *Transactions.* 2013: 15-16.

1991

Samuel Arch Thompson
Grand Cross of the Court of Honour at age 90 years and 2 days
Tenure 10 years, 7 months, and 20 days
Nomination by McAlester, Oklahoma Scottish Rite Bodies

Born: September 16, 1901 – Died: June 8, 2002
Life span: 100 years, 8 months, and 22 days
Principal

Progress in Scottish Rite Masonry:
4°-14°: May 28, 1956, invested by *Albert Pike* Lodge of Perfection, McAlester.
15°-18°: May 28, 1956, invested by *South McAlester* Chapter of Rose Croix, McAlester.
19°-30°: May 29, 1956, invested by *Tuskahoma* Council of Kadosh, McAlester.
31°-32°: May 30, 1956, invested by *Indian* Consistory, McAlester.
32°, KCCH: October 17, 1961.
33°, IGH: elected October 20, 1975; coroneted by Ill. Charles P. Rosenberg, 33°, Sovereign Grand
Inspector General for Oklahoma November 29, 1975.
Grand Cross of the Court of Honour: October 18, 1991.

Scottish Rite Biography:
In 1953, Brother Thompson began his illustrious Masonic career by petitioning *South McAlester* Lodge,
No. 96, McAlester, Oklahoma. He received the Scottish Rite Degrees in May 1956 and was honored with
the KCCH in 1961, the Thirty-third Degree in 1975, and the Grand Cross in 1991. Active in all phases of
the Scottish Rite work, he served as Venerable Master of the Lodge of Perfection and held positions in
several Degrees and on the Membership, Fellowship and Americanism Committees. Upon the formation of
the McAlester Charitable and Educational Foundation in 1960, he became Chairman of the Scholarship
Committee, which awarded approximately $1.4 million in scholarships to over 3,000 deserving
undergraduate, graduate, and blind students.

Bibliography:
Archive of the Supreme Council, 33°, S.J.
In Memoriam. *Transactions*. 2003: 212.

Kenneth E. Waddell
Grand Cross of the Court of Honour at age 62 years, 4 months, and 18 days
Tenure 5 years, 1 month, and 8 days
Nomination by Joplin, Missouri Scottish Rite Bodies

Born: May 31, 1929 – Died: November 26, 1996
Life span: 67 years, 5 months, and 26 days
Obstetrician

Progress in Scottish Rite Masonry:
4°-14°: October 16, 1964, invested by *Joplin* Lodge of Perfection, Joplin.
15°-18°: October 17, 1964, invested by *Joplin* Chapter of Rose Croix, Joplin.
19°-30°: October 23, 1964, invested by *Joplin* Council of Kadosh, Joplin.
31°-32°: October 24, 1964, invested by *Joplin* Consistory, Joplin.
32°, KCCH: October 20, 1969.
33°, IGH: elected October 15, 1973; coroneted by Ill. Walter Christian Ploeser, 33°, Sovereign Grand Inspector General December 8, 1973.
Deputy: May 3, 1988 – resigned, 1989.
Grand Cross of the Court of Honour: October 18, 1991.

Scottish Rite Biography:
Brother Waddell was a Master Mason of *Grandfield* Lodge, No. 378, Oklahoma. After joining the Scottish Rite, Valley of Joplin, in 1964, he served as President of the Metropolitan Scottish Rite Club of Springfield in 1968 and as Master of Kadosh of the Scottish Rite Consistory, Valley of Joplin, in 1973. For his many services to our Order, he was invested a KCCH, in 1969; coroneted a 33°, IGH, in 1973; appointed Deputy of the Supreme Council for Missouri in 1988; appointed Orient Personal Representative in 1989; and awarded the Grand Cross in 1991. In May 1996, Ill.·. Waddell received the Life Achievement Award from the Scottish Rite Foundation of Missouri in recognition of his guidance during the development and expansion of the Orient's Childhood Language Disorders Program.

Bibliography:
Archive of the Supreme Council, 33°, S.J.
In Memoriam. *Transactions.* 1997: 207-208.

1991

Eugene Allen Wright
Grand Cross of the Court of Honour at age 78 years, 7 months, and 25 days
Tenure 10 years, 11 months, and 15 days
Nomination by Seattle, Washington Scottish Rite Bodies

Born: February 23, 1913 – Died: September 3, 2002
Life span: 89 years, 8 months, and 10 days
Senior Judge of the United States Court of Appeals for the Ninth Circuit, Washington

Progress in Scottish Rite Masonry:
4°-14°: November 11, 1953, invested by *Seattle* Lodge of Perfection, Seattle.
15°-18°: November 12, 1953, invested by *Seattle* Chapter of Rose Croix, Seattle.
19°-30°: November 14, 1953, invested by *Seattle* Council of Kadosh, Seattle.
31°-32°: November 14, 1953, invested by *Seattle* Consistory, Seattle.
32°, KCCH: October 20, 1975.
33°, IGH: elected October 15, 1979; coroneted by Ill. John D. Blankinship, 33°, Sovereign Grand Inspector General for Washington November 10, 1979.
Grand Cross of the Court of Honour: October 18, 1991.

Scottish Rite Biography:
A Master Mason in *St. John's* Lodge, No. 9, Judge Wright joined the Scottish Rite Bodies of Seattle in 1953, was invested with the KCCH in 1975, coroneted a 33°, IGH in 1979, and elected to our Order's highest honor, the Grand Cross, in 1991.

Bibliography:
Archive of the Supreme Council, 33°, S.J.
In Memoriam. *Transactions.* 2003: 214.

1993

Quinn Henderson Becker

Grand Cross of the Court of Honour at age 63 years, 4 months, and 4 days
Tenure 28 years, 4 months, and 4 days
Nomination by Shreveport, Louisiana Scottish Rite Bodies

Born: June 11, 1930 – March 13, 2022
Life span: 91 years, 9 months, and 2 days
Surgeon General, United States Army; Chief of Staff, Veterans Administration Medical
Center

Progress in Scottish Rite Masonry:
4°-14°: October 10, 1959, invested by *Shreveport* Lodge of Perfection, Shreveport.
15°-18°: October 11, 1959, invested by *Shreveport* Chapter of Rose Croix, Shreveport.
19°-30°: October 17, 1959, invested by *Shreveport* Council of Kadosh, Shreveport.
31°-32°: October 18, 1959, invested by *Shreveport* Consistory, Shreveport.
32°, KCCH: October 19, 1987.
33°, IGH: elected October 16, 1989; coroneted by Ill. Dietrich Walter Jessen, 33°, Sovereign Grand
Inspector General for Louisiana November 11, 1989.
Grand Cross of the Court of Honour: October 15, 1993.

Scottish Rite Biography:
Brother Becker was raised to the Sublime Degree in *Western Star* Lodge, No. 24, at Monroe. In 1959 he
received the Scottish Rite Degrees from the Bodies of the Valley of Shreveport. On April 4, 1983, Brother
Beker affiliated with the Scottish Rite Bodies of the Valley of Monroe. He elected to receive the Knight
Commander of the Court of Honour on October 19, 1987, and on the following Session of the Supreme
Council on October 16, 1989, was elected a 33°, Inspector General Honorary. Brother Becker was
coroneted by Ill. Dietrich Walter Jessen, 33°, Sovereign Grand Inspector General for Louisiana on
November 11, 1989. On October 15, 1993, Ill. Quinn Henderson Becker, 33°, was awarded the Grand
Cross of the Court of Honour.

Bibliography:
Archive of the Supreme Council, 33°, S.J.

1993

John William Boettjer
Grand Cross of the Court of Honour at age 57 years, 7 months and 26 days
Tenure present
Nomination by Alexandria, Virginia Scottish Rite Bodies

Born: February 18, 1936 – present
Life span: present
Editor of *The Scottish Rite Journal*

Progress in Scottish Rite Masonry:
4°-14°: September 12, 1989, invested by *Alexandria* Lodge of Perfection, Alexandria.
15°-18°: September 12, 1989, invested by *Alexandria* Chapter of Rose Croix, Alexandria.
19°-30°: September 12, 1989, invested by *Alexandria* Council of Kadosh, Alexandria.
31°-32°: September 12, 1989, invested by *Alexandria* Consistory, Alexandria.
32°, KCCH: October 16, 1989.
33°, IGH: elected October 21, 1991; coroneted by the Supreme Council, 33°, S.J., October 22, 1991.
Grand Cross of the Court of Honour: October 15, 1993.

Scottish Rite Biography:
Brother John William Boettjer is Master Mason in *Cypress* Lodge, No. 295, Naples, Florida. On April 1, 1989, Dr. Boettjer, formerly a Colonel and Professor of English, assumed the editor's chair of *The New Age* after having been associated with the magazine informally as a free-lance writer for many years. Based on his advice the magazine changed its title to *The Scottish Rite Journal*. Dr. Boettjer virtually transformed *The Journal* through his professional expertise and creative ability, making it a very attractive and readable magazine. Nor is the end in sight as he continues to refine and improve each issue during his career as a Managing Editor. His experiences, as well as his long association with The Supreme Council allowed Brother Boettjer to contribute to the Supreme Council truly outstanding service, which was recognized and reflected Ill. John William Boettjer, 33°, remarkable progress in Scottish Rite Masonry.

Bibliography:
Archive of the Supreme Council, 33°, S.J.
Allocutions. *Transactions*. 1989: 49 and 1991: 67.

1993

Robert Joseph Dole
Grand Cross of the Court of Honour at age 69 years, 9 months, and 23 days
Tenure 28 years, 1 month, and 20 days
Nomination by Scottish Rite Bodies of Kansas

Born: July 22, 1923 – December 5, 2021
Life span: 98 years, 4 months, and 13 days
Lawyer, U. S. Congressman; Minority Leader of the U.S. Senate

Progress in Scottish Rite Masonry:
4°-14°: December 10, 1966, invested by *Salina* Lodge of Perfection, Salina, Kansas.
15°-18°: December 10, 1966, invested by *Salina* Chapter of Rose Croix, Salina, Kansas.
19°-30°: December 10, 1966, invested by *Salina* Council of Kadosh, Salina, Kansas.
31°-32°: December 10, 1966, invested by *Salina* Consistory, Salina, Kansas.
32°, KCCH: October 18, 1971.
33°, IGH: elected October 20, 1975; coroneted by Ill. William Earl Montgomery, 33°, Sovereign Grand Inspector General for Kansas November 15, 1975.
Grand Cross of the Court of Honour: October 15, 1993.

Scottish Rite Biography:
Brother Dole was initiated, passed, and raised in *Russel* Lodge, No. 177, Russell Kansas. In 1966 he joined the Scottish Rite Bodies of Salina, Kansas, and received the rank and decoration of a Knight Commander of the Court of Honour in 1971. In 1975 he was elected 33°, Inspector General Honorary and coroneted by Ill. William Earl Montgomery, 33°, Sovereign Grand Inspector General for Kansas on November 15, 1975, and awarded the Grand Cross of the Court of Honour on October 15, 1993. The portrait of Ill. Robert Joseph Dole, 33°, GC, U.S. Congressman and Senator from Kansas, Humanitarian and Philanthropist was donated to the House of the Temple by the Orient of Kansas and is on display in the Hall of Honor among the most outstanding Scottish Rite Brethren.

Bibliography:
Archive of the Supreme Council, 33°, S.J.

1993

Willard Holt Erwin, Jr.
Grand Cross of the Court of Honour at age 78 years, 11 months, and 5 days
Tenure 7 months, and 6 days
Nomination by West Virginia Scottish Rite Bodies

Born: November 10, 1914 – Died: May 21, 1994
Life span: 79 years, 6 months, and 11 days
Accountant; Public Service Award Honoree

Progress in Scottish Rite Masonry:
4°-14°: October 23, 1939, invested by *Odell S. Long* Lodge of Perfection, Charleston.
15°-18°: October 24, 1939, invested by *Charleston* Chapter of Rose Croix, Charleston.
19°-30°: October 25, 1939, invested by *John C. Riheldaffer* Council of Kadosh, Charleston.
31°-32°: October 26, 1939, invested by *John W. Morris* Consistory, Charleston.
32°, KCCH: October 18, 1949.
33°, IGH: elected October 3, 1967; coroneted Supreme Council, 33°, S.J., October 6, 1967.
Grand Cross of the Court of Honour: October 15, 1993.

Scottish Rite Biography:
Ill. Erwin was raised in *Charleston* Lodge, No. 153 in 1939 and became a member of the Scottish Rite Bodies of Charleston the same year, serving as Venerable Master, 1954-55, and Master of Kadosh, 1980-81. In recognition of his many services to the Order, he was elected KCCH in 1949 and 33° Inspector General Honorary in 1967. For several years recently he was a member of the Advisory Board of the Scottish Rite Language Center.

Bibliography:
Archive of the Supreme Council, 33°, S.J.
In Memoriam. *Transactions.* 1995: 218-219.

Marvin Edward Fowler
Grand Cross of the Court of Honour at age 89 years and 3 days
Tenure 8 years, 1 month, and 26 days
Nomination by Washington, District of Columbia Scottish Rite Bodies

Born: October 12, 1904 – Died: December 11, 2001
Life span: 97 years, 1 month, and 30 days
Scientist
Provincial Grand Master of Royal Order of Scotland for U.S.A. for 44 years

Progress in Scottish Rite Masonry:
4°-14°: March 1, 1932, invested by *Mithras* Lodge of Perfection, Washington, D.C.
15°-18°: March 22, 1932, invested by *Evangelist* Chapter of Rose Croix, Washington, D.C.
19°-30°: March 22, 1932, invested by *Robert de Bruce* Council of Kadosh, Washington, D.C.
31°-32°: May 10, 1932, invested by *Albert Pike* Consistory, Washington, D.C.
32°, KCCH: October 19, 1937.
33°, IGH: elected October 19, 1943; coroneted the Supreme Council, 33°, S.J., October 22, 1943.
Grand Cross of the Court of Honour: October 15, 1993.

Scottish Rite Biography:
After affiliation from a *Missouri* Lodge to *LaFayette-Dupont* Lodge, No. 19, Brother Fowler became a 32° Mason in the District of Columbia in 1932, ultimately serving as the presiding officer of all four coordinate Bodies of the Scottish Rite: *Mithras* Lodge of Perfection, 1946; Evangelist Chapter Rose Croix, 1940; *Robert De Bruce* Council of Knights Kadosh, 1943; *Albert Pike* Consistory, 1945. As a result of his effort, he was invested a KCCH in 1937, coroneted a 33°, IGH in 1943, and elected a Grand Cross in 1993. Ill. Marvin E. Fowler's affable spirit, intense dedication, and fraternal excellence will be long remembered and deeply missed.

Bibliography:
Archive of the Supreme Council, 33°, S.J.
Archives of the Orient of the District of Columbia and Archives of the Grand Lodge of the District of Columbia, F.A.A.M.
In Memoriam. *Transactions.* 2003: 207.

Burl Icle Ives
Grand Cross of the Court of Honour at age 84 years, 4 months, and 1 day
Tenure 1 year, 5 months, and 29 days
Nomination by Santa Barbara, California and Bellingham, Washington Scottish Rite Bodies

Born: June 14, 1909 – Died: April 14, 1995
Life span: 85 years and 10 months
Actor, Singer

Progress in Scottish Rite Masonry:
4°-14°: May 21, 1977, invested by *Santa Barbara* Lodge of Perfection, Santa Barbara.
15°-18°: May 21, 1977, invested by *Santa Barbara* Chapter of Rose Croix, Santa Barbara.
19°-30°: May 21, 1977, invested by *Santa Barbara* Council of Kadosh, Santa Barbara.
31°-32°: May 21, 1977, invested by *Santa Barbara* Consistory, Santa Barbara.
32°, KCCH: October 21, 1985.
33°, IGH: elected October 19, 1987; coroneted by the Supreme Council, 33°, S.J., October 21, 1987.
Grand Cross of the Court of Honour: October 15, 1993.

Scottish Rite Biography:
After moving to California, Brother Ives became a member of *Magnolia* (now *Magnolia-La Cumbre*) Lodge, No. 242, the Scottish Rite Bodies of Santa Barbara, California, in 1977, becoming a dual member in the Bellingham, Washington, Scottish Rite Bodies in 1990. In recognition of his many services to our Order, he was invested with the KCCH in 1985, coroneted a 33° Inspector General Honorary in 1987, and elected a Grand Cross of the Court of Honour in 1993. When Bro. Ives became a full-time entertainer, he often performed for charities, including the Scottish Rite. Ill. Burl Icle Ives, 33°, GC, will never age but remain forever a dedicated Brother and great American.

Bibliography:
Archive of the Supreme Council, 33°, S.J.
In Memoriam. *Transactions.* 1995: 211-212.

1993

Samuel Augustus Nunn
Grand Cross of the Court of Honour at age 55 years, 1 month, and 7 days
Tenure present
Nomination by Macon, Scottish Rite Bodies of Georgia

Born: September 8, 1938 – present
Senator, Chairman of the Senate Committee on Armed Services

Progress in Scottish Rite Masonry:
4°-14°: October 10, 1980, invested by *Macon* Lodge of Perfection, Macon, Georgia.
15°-18°: October 11, 1980, invested by *Macon* Chapter of Rose Croix, Macon, Georgia.
19°-30°: October 11, 1980, invested by *Macon* Council of Kadosh, Macon, Georgia.
31°-32°: October 11, 1980, invested by *Macon* Consistory, Macon, Georgia.
32°, KCCH: October 21, 1985.
33°, IGH: elected October 19, 1987; coroneted by the Supreme Council, 33°, S.J., October 21, 1987.
Grand Cross of the Court of Honour: October 15, 1993.

Scottish Rite Biography:
The Hall of Honor portrait of Ill. Samuel Augustus Nunn, 33°, G.C., Ranking Member of the Senate's Armed Services Committee, was dedicated during the 1995 Biennial Session of the Supreme Council. Brother Nunn is proud of his lifelong ties to Freemasonry and is active in the Craft. In 1991, for instance, he participated in the Biennial Session of the Supreme Council, and in 1994, he spoke to the Conference of the Grand Masters. His Address titled "Perspectives of America in 1994" was presented as an article in the July 1994 Scottish Rite Journal. Senator Nunn's portrait was made possible by donations from two sources. The first was the Scottish Rite Foundation of Georgia. The second source was the fundraising activity of Ill. Thomas T. Irvin, 33°. Brother Nunn's portrait is entered into the Temple Architects Hall of Honor as a permanent recognition of his outstanding services to America and Freemasonry.

Bibliography:
Archive of the Supreme Council, 33°, S.J.
Hall of Honor Portraits. *Transactions.* 1995: 39-40.

1993

Charles Robert Richey
Grand Cross of the Court of Honour at age 69 years, 10 months, and 29 days
Tenure 3 years, 5 months, and 4 days
Nomination by Washington, District of Columbia Scottish Rite Bodies and Columbus,
Scottish Rite Bodies of Ohio

Born: October 16, 1923 – Died: March 19, 1997
Life span: 74 years, 5 months, and 3 days
Federal Judge in the United States District Court for the District of Columbia,
Advisor in the preparation of the Code of Conduct for United States Judges

Progress in Scottish Rite Masonry:
4°-32°: November 1, 1949, invested by Columbus, Ohio, Scottish Rite Bodies.
4°-32°: February 10, 1993, affiliated with Washington, D.C., Scottish Rite Bodies.
32°, KCCH: October 18, 1993.
33°, IGH: elected October 18, 1993; coroneted the Supreme Council, 33°, S.J., October 19, 1993.
Grand Cross of the Court of Honour: October 15, 1993.

Scottish Rite Biography:
Raised a Mason in *Hiram* Lodge, No. 18, Delaware, Ohio, Brother Richey was a member of the Columbus, Ohio, Scottish Rite Bodies, attaining the rank of 33°, IGH in the Northern Masonic Jurisdiction, before affiliating as a dual member with the Washington, D.C., Scottish Rite Bodies and receiving the Southern Jurisdiction's highest honor, the Grand Cross, in 1993. As a public advocate of our Craft, Chuck Richey heard Masonry's strong voice of reason and responded to its inspiration with his own unparalleled defense of the Fraternity. Given facts, it was entirely appropriate that he earned Scottish Rite Freemasonry's 33° from both the Northern and Southern Jurisdiction, an accomplishment few men have ever attained.

Bibliography:
Archive of the Supreme Council, 33°, S.J.
In Memoriam. *Transactions.* 1999: 204-205.

1995

Thomas Miller Boles
Grand Cross of the Court of Honour at age 68 years, 6 months, and 2 days
Tenure 23 years, 11 months, and 26 days
Nomination by Santa Ana, California Scottish Rite Bodies

Born: March 5, 1927 – Died: September 3, 2019
Life span: 92 years, 5 months, and 28 days
Director of Development for the Supreme Council, 33°

Progress in Scottish Rite Masonry:
4°-14°: July 18, 1980, invested by *Santa Ana* Lodge of Perfection, Santa Ana.
15°-18°: July 19, 1980, invested by *Santa Ana* Chapter of Rose Croix, Santa Ana.
19°-30°: July 19, 1980, invested by *Santa Ana* Council of Kadosh, Santa Ana.
31°-32°: July 19, 1980, invested by *Santa Ana* Consistory, Santa Ana.
32°, KCCH: October 21, 1985.
33°, IGH: elected October 21, 1991; coroneted by the Supreme Council, 33°, S.J., October 22, 1991.
Grand Cross of the Court of Honour: October 7, 1995.

Scottish Rite Biography:
Brother Thomas Miller Boles was raised in *William D. Stephens* Lodge, No. 698, Los Angeles. He was invested with the Scottish Rite Degrees by Santa Ana Scottish Rite Bodies on July 1880; elected 32°, KCCH, on October 21, 1985, and coroneted 33°, IGH, on October 21, 1991. Ill. Boles, 33°, started to work for the Supreme Council as the Foundation's Director of Development. It was an unpaid volunteer position, and Brother Tom often gave 60 hours a week to answer inquiries and follow up with people who contacted him. Shortly he became instrumental in shaping the Gift Annuities program to early fine results and was appointed Director of Development of the Supreme Council. Tom's enthusiasm was inexhaustible and his knowledge in the area of financial planning was always up to date. Without Ill. Boles, 33°, the Development Program would either be of very different character or even nonexistent.

Bibliography:
Archive of the Supreme Council, 33°, S.J.
Allocution. 1995.

1995

Donald Ben Constine
Grand Cross of the Court of Honour at age 70 years, 7 months, and 28 days
Tenure 21 years, 5 months, and 8 days
Nomination by San Francisco, California Scottish Rite Bodies

Born: February 9, 1925 – Died: March 15, 2017
Life span: 92 years, 1 month and 6 days
Judge

Progress in Scottish Rite Masonry:
4°-14°: October 15, 1954, invested by *San Francisco* Lodge of Perfection, San Francisco.
15°-18°: October 15, 1954, invested by *San Francisco* Chapter of Rose Croix, San Francisco.
19°-30°: November 12, 1954, invested by *San Francisco* Council of Kadosh, San Francisco.
31°-32°: December 3, 1954, invested by *San Francisco* Consistory, San Francisco.
32°, KCCH: October 20, 1959.
33°, IGH: elected October 15, 1973; coroneted by Sovereign Grand Commander Henry C. Clausen, 33°, December 15, 1973.
Grand Cross of the Court of Honour: October 7, 1995.

Scottish Rite Biography:
Brother Donald, a fourth generation Mason, was a member of *Pacific Starr King* Lodge, No. 136. He received the Scottish Rite Degrees in 1954 from the Valley of San Francisco, California, was invested as a Knight Commander of the Court of Honour in 1959, coroneted as Inspector General Honorary, 33°, in 1973, and elected by the Supreme Council to receive the Grand Cross of the Court of Honour on October 7, 1995. Brother Constine's skill and experience as arbitration mediator learned years as Judge were critical, when in 1991 the two Valleys in San Francisco consolidated. Ill. Constine was Chairman of the Consolidation Committee and following consolidation, was appointed the first Personal Representative of the consolidated San Francisco Valley.

Bibliography:
Archive of the Supreme Council, 33°, S.J.
In Memoriam. Transactions. 2017: 113.

1995

Robert Lionel Dillard, Jr.
Grand Cross of the Court of Honour at age 82 years, and 8 days
Tenure 5 years, 1 month, and 23 days
Nomination by Dallas, Texas Scottish Rite Bodies

Born: September 30, 1913 – Died: November 30, 2000
Life span: 87 years and 2 months
Attorney

Progress in Scottish Rite Masonry:
4°-14°: November 8, 1942, invested by *Dallas* Lodge of Perfection, Dallas.
15°-18°: April 24, 1944, invested by *Lone Star* Chapter of Rose Croix, Dallas.
19°-30°: April 24, 1944, invested by, *Dallas* Council of Kadosh, Dallas.
31°-32°: April 25, 1944, invested by *Dallas* Consistory, Dallas.
32°, KCCH: October 18, 1949.
33°, IGH: elected October 20, 1953; coroneted by the Supreme Council, 33°., S.J., October 23, 1953.
Grand Cross of the Court of Honour: October 7, 1995.

Scottish Rite Biography:
Ill. Robert Lionel Dillard, Jr., 33°, made a Master Mason in *Dallas* Lodge, No. 760 in 1938. Having received the Scottish Rite Degrees in Dallas Consistory in 1944, he was designated a KCCH in 1949, coroneted a 33° in 1953, and honored as a Grand Cross in 1995. He served as Wise Master of *Dallas* Chapter of Rose Croix, Venerable Master of *Dallas* Lodge of Perfection, and as Degree Master of the 31° for 25 years. In 1992, his original oil portrait was received into the Scottish Rite Hall of Honor. Ill. Dillard was especially dedicated to the Texas Scottish Rite Hospital for Children in Dallas. Famous for his boundless energy, enthusiasm, and perseverance, Ill. Robert Lionel Dillard, Jr., 33°, Grand Cross, has established a lifelong record of excellence which will stand forever.

Bibliography:
Archive of the Supreme Council, 33°, S.J.
In Memoriam. *Transactions.* 2001: 258.

1995

Rex Richard Hutchens
Grand Cross of the Court of Honour at age 53 years and 22 days
Tenure present
Nomination by Tucson, Arizona Scottish Rite Bodies

Born: November 29, 1942 – present
Anthropologist, PhD

Progress in Scottish Rite Masonry:

4°-14°: November 4, 1982, invested by *Tucson* Lodge of Perfection, Tucson, Arizona.

15°-18°: November 5, 1982, invested by *Tucson* Chapter of Rose Croix, Tucson, Arizona.

19°-30°: November 6, 1982, invested by *Tucson* Council of Kadosh, Tucson, Arizona.

31°-32°: November 8, 1982, invested by *Tucson* Consistory, Tucson, Arizona.

32°, KCCH: October 19, 1987.

33°, IGH: elected October 16, 1989; coroneted by the Supreme Council, 33°, S.J., October 18, 1989.

Grand Cross of the Court of Honour: October 7, 1995.

Scottish Rite Biography:

Brother Hutchens was raised to the Sublime Degree in *Epes Randolph* Lodge, No. 32, at Tucson. He was made a Master of the Royal Secret on November 8, 1982, in the Valley of Tucson. Since that date Brother Hutchens' intellectual investment and activity in the Scottish Rite are countless. He received the rank and decoration of a Knight Commander of the Court of Honour in 1987, was coroneted a 33°, Inspector General Honorary in 1989, and received the highest honor of the Supreme Council, the Grand Cross of the Court of Honour in 1995. In 1997, Dr. Rex R. Hutchens, 33°, GC, like Pike before him, was able to accept the Supreme Council's charge to revise the Ritual. Ill. Hutchens comes to the task well prepared. His earlier publications – *A Bridge to Light*; a *Glossary of "Morals and Dogma"*; *The Bible in Albert Pike's "Morals and Dogma"*; and *Pillars of Wisdom, The Writing of Albert Pike* – have proved this scholarly ability and Masonic insight, which allow Ill. Hutchens to assume this monumental and historical labor. Brother Hutchens served his Valley as Commander of Tucson Council of Kadosh and Personal Representative in the Valley of Tucson. Now Ill. Rex Richard Hutchens, 33°, GC, is a Deputy of the Supreme Council, 33°, S.J. for the Orient of Arizona.

Bibliography:
Archive of the Supreme Council, 33°, S.J.
Allocution. *Transactions*. 1997: 45.

1995

Paul Eddie Manners
Grand Cross of the Court of Honour at age 77 years, 9 months, and 9 days
Tenure 16 years, 10 months, and 21 days
Nomination by Atlanta, Georgia Scottish Rite Bodies

Born: December 28, 1918 – August 28, 2012
Life span: 94 years and 8 months
Banker

Progress in Scottish Rite Masonry:
4°-14°: May 31, 1980, invested by *Atlanta* Lodge of Perfection, Atlanta.
15°-18°: May 31, 1980, invested by *Atlanta* Chapter of Rose Croix, Atlanta.
19°-30°: May 31, 1980, invested by *Atlanta* Council of Kadosh, Atlanta.
31°-32°: May 31, 1980, invested by *Atlanta* Consistory, Atlanta.
32°, KCCH: October 17, 1983.
33°, IGH: elected October 19, 1987; coroneted by Ill. Thomas Shean Perry, 33°, Sovereign Grand Inspector General for Georgia December 12, 1987.
Grand Cross of the Court of Honour: October 7, 1995.

Scottish Rite Biography:
Brother Paul was raised to the Sublime Degree of a Master Mason in *Gate City* Lodge, No. 2, in Atlanta, Georgia on November 13, 1979. He became a Master of the Royal Secret in the Valley of Atlanta on May 31, 1980, was invested with the rank and decoration of a Knight Commander of the Court of Honour in 1983, was coroneted an Inspector General Honorary in 1987, and elected to receive the Grand Cross of the Court of Honour on October 7, 1995. Ill. Paul's greatest joy in the Masonic and business career came when he served for many years as a Trustee of the Scottish Rite Hospital for Crippled Children, Inc., now Children's Healthcare of Atlanta. Through his vision, relentless energy, skill as a planner, and gift for forging strong personal relationships, Brother Manners raised a small children's hospital to the heights of pediatric medical care.

Bibliography:
Archive of the Supreme Council, 33°, S.J.
In Memoriam. *Transactions.* 2013: 188.

1997

Norman Lawrence Crosby
Grand Cross of the Court of Honour at age 69 years, 11 months, and 28 days
Tenure 23 years and 24 days
Nomination by Long Beach, California Scottish Rite Bodies

Born: September 15, 1927 – Died: November 7, 2020
Life span: 93 years, 1 month, and 22 days
American Comedian

Progress in Scottish Rite Masonry:
4°-14°: December 1, 1982, invested by *Long Beach* Lodge of Perfection, Long Beach.
15°-18°: December 1, 1982, invested by *Long Beach* Chapter of Rose Croix, Long Beach.
19°-30°: December 1, 1982, invested by *Long Beach* Council of Kadosh, Long Beach.
31°-32°: December 1, 1982, invested by *Long Beach* Consistory, Long Beach.
32°, KCCH: October 21, 1985.
33°, IGH: elected October 19, 1987; coroneted by Ill. Douglas Lemons, 33°, Sovereign Grand Inspector General for California December 19, 1987.
Grand Cross of the Court of Honour: October 3, 1997.

Scottish Rite Biography:
Brother Crosby was raised a Master Mason in *Euclid* Lodge in Weymouth, Massachusetts, and made a Master of the Royal Secret on December 1, 1982, in the Valley of Long Beach, California. On October 21, 1985, he was elected a Knight Commander of the Court of Honour, and on the following year on December 19, 1987, was coroneted a 33°, Inspector General Honorary by Ill. Douglas Lemons, 33°, Sovereign Grand Inspector General for California. On October 13, 1997, the Supreme Council. 33°, S.J. elected Ill. Norman Lawrence Crosby, 33°, a Grand Cross of the Court of Honour. The first "Celebration of the Craft" web event premiered in the House of the Temple on Saturday, May 19, 2012. The six hours broadcast hosted by Ill. Norm Crosby, 33°, Grand Cross, an entertainment industry veteran, not only successfully supported the Rebuilding the Temple Campaign and Valley, but also allowed for an opportunity to celebrate the Scottish Rite and Freemasonry.

Bibliography:
Archive of the Supreme Council, 33°, S.J.

1997

Chester Trent Lott
Grand Cross of the Court of Honour at age 43 years, 11 months, and 24 days
Nomination by Gulfport, Mississippi Scottish Rite Bodies

Born: October 9, 1941 – present
U. S. Congressman

Progress in Scottish Rite Masonry:

4°-14°: October 18, 1975, invested by *Gulfport* Lodge of Perfection, Gulfport.

15°-18°: October 18, 1975, invested by *Gulfport* Chapter of Rose Croix, Gulfport.

19°-30°: October 18, 1975, invested by *Gulfport* Council of Kadosh, Gulfport.

31°-32°: October 23, 1976, invested by *Gulfport* Consistory, Gulfport.

32°, KCCH: October 17, 1983.

33°, IGH: elected October 19, 1987; coroneted by Ill. Paul Gilbert Alexander, 33°, Sovereign Grand Inspector General for Mississippi, December 12, 1987,

Grand Cross of the Court of Honour: October 3, 1997.

Scottish Rite Biography:

During his years in the U.S. House of Representatives, Chester Trent Lott advanced in Masonry; he had petitioned, been accepted, and was initiated an Entered Apprentice in *Pascagoula* Lodge, No. 419, on September 18, 1967. However, the busy schedule of a congressional aid and freshman House member made advancement a challenge. Nonetheless, he was finally passed to the Degree of Fellowcraft on August 23, 1975, and raised a Master Mason on August 29, 1975. That October Brother Lott took most of the Scottish Rite Degrees in the Valley of Gulfport but didn't receive his 32nd Degree until October 23, 1976. He subsequently received the KCCH in 1983, and was coroneted a 33°, Inspector General Honorary on December 12, 1987. Since becoming Senate Majority Leader in June 1996, one additional Masonic honor came to Chester Trent Lott. On October 3, 1997, he was elected to receive the Grand Cross, the highest honor the Scottish Rite Southern Jurisdiction can bestow.

Bibliography:

Archive of the Supreme Council, 33°, S.J.

Tribe, Ivan M. Illustrious Trent Lott, 33°, Grand Cross: Contemporary Senate Leader. *The Scottish Rite Journal*, August 1999.

1997

Sidney Sanders McMath
Grand Cross of the Court of Honour at age 84 years, 7 months, and 19 days
Tenure 6 years and 1 day
Nomination by Little Rock, Arkansas Scottish Rite Bodies

Born: June 14, 1912 – Died: October 4, 2003
Life span: 91 years, 3 months, and 20 days
Attorney/Governor

Progress in Scottish Rite Masonry:
4°-14°: May 2, 1949, invested by *Little Rock* Lodge of Perfection, Little Rock.
15°-18°: May 3, 1949, invested by *Little Rock* Chapter of Rose Croix, Little Rock.
19°-30°: May 3, 1949, invested by *Little Rock* Council of Kadosh, Little Rock.
31°-32°: May 4, 1949, invested by *Little Rock* Consistory, Little Rock.
32°, KCCH: October 19, 1987.
33°, IGH: elected October 21, 1991; coroneted by Ill. Aaron Pierce, 33°, Sovereign Grand Inspector General for Arkansas December 7, 1991.
Grand Cross of the Court of Honour: October 3, 1997.

Scottish Rite Biography:
Brother McMath was a Master Mason of *Sumpter* Lodge, No. 419, became a high-profile member of the Valley of Little Rock in 1949, and was honored for his many services to Freemasonry with the rank and decoration of KCCH in 1987, and the 33° in 1991. In 1997, he was elected to the Scottish Rite's highest honor, the Grand Cross.

Bibliography:
Archive of the Supreme Council, 33°, S.J.
In Memoriam. *Transactions*. 2005: 262.

Harold Edward Stassen
Grand Cross of the Court of Honour at age 90 years, 5 months, and 20 days
Tenure 3 years, 5 months, and 1 day
Nomination by Saint Paul, Minnesota Scottish Rite Bodies

Born: April 13, 1907 – Died: March 4, 2001
Life span: 93 years, 11 months, and 21 days
Governor of Minnesota

Progress in Scottish Rite Masonry:

4°-14°: March 12, 1940, invested by *Saint Paul* Lodge of Perfection, Saint Paul.

15°-18°: March 13, 1940, invested by *Saint Paul* Chapter of Rose Croix, Saint Paul.

19°-30°: March 13, 1940, invested by *Saint Paul* Council of Kadosh, Saint Paul.

31°-32°: March 14, 1940, invested by *Minnesota* Consistory, Saint Paul.

32°, KCCH: October 16, 1945.

33°, IGH: elected October 19, 1987; coroneted by Ill. Louis K. Thompson, 33°, Sovereign Grand Inspector General for Minnesota December 12, 1987.

Grand Cross of the Court of Honour: October 3, 1997.

Scottish Rite Biography:

Raised a Master Mason on November 29, 1929, in *Shekinah* Lodge, No. 17 in St. Paul, Ill. Stassen was installed as Master on January 14, 1939, just 11 days after being inaugurated as Governor. A member of the Valley of St. Paul while he was Governor, in recognition of his service to mankind and the nation, he was honored with the KCCH in 1945, 33° in 1987, and Grand Cross in 1997. As Ill. Stassen lay in state in the Capitol rotunda in St. Paul, state, civic, international, and fraternal leaders eulogized him as one who "truly gave of himself to make his state, nation, and world a better place."

Bibliography:

Archive of the Supreme Council, 33°, S.J.

In Memoriam. *Transactions.* 2001: 260.

1997

Rex David Thomas
Grand Cross of the Court of Honour at age 63 years, 3 months, and 1 day
Tenure 6 years, 3 months, and 5 days
Nomination by Miami, Florida Scottish Rite Bodies

Born: July 2, 1932 – Died: January 8, 2002
Life span: 69 years, 6 months, and 6 days
President of Wendy's Food

Progress in Scottish Rite Masonry:
4°-32°: November 16, 1961, invested by Ft. Wayne Scottish Rite Bodies, Indiana, Northern Masonic Jurisdiction.
4°-32°: December 18, 1991, affiliated with Miami, Florida Scottish Rite Bodies.
32°, KCCH: October 18, 1993.
33°, IGH: elected October 9, 1995; coroneted by Ill. Robert Goldsmith, 33°, Sovereign Grand Inspector General for Florida November 25, 1995.
Grand Cross of the Court of Honour: October 3, 1997.

Scottish Rite Biography:
Brother Rex David Thomas was raised a Master Mason in Sol. D. Bayless Lodge, No. 359 in Fort Wayne, Indiana, and became a 32° Scottish Rite Mason on November 16, 1961, in the Scottish Rite Bodies of Fort Wayne, Indiana. He affiliated with the Miami, Florida, Scottish Rite Bodies on December 18, 1991, was invested a KCCH on November 13, 1993, in Jacksonville, Florida, and was coroneted a 33° Scottish Rite Mason in 1995, receiving the Grand Cross by unanimous election of the Supreme Council in 1997. Ill. Rex David Thomas, 33°, Grand Cross was an example of the philanthropic endeavor whose life will inspire all Americans and Freemasons for generations to come.

Bibliography:
Archive of the Supreme Council, 33°, S.J.
In Memoriam. *Transactions.* 2003: 211.

1997

Stephen Joel Trachtenberg
Grand Cross of the Court of Honour at age 59 years, 9 months, and 19 days
Tenure – present

Nomination by Washington, District of Columbia Scottish Rite Bodies

Born: December 14, 1937 – present
President of George Washington University

Progress in Scottish Rite Masonry:

4°-14°: October 26, 1990, invested by *Mithras* Lodge of Perfection, Washington, D.C.

15°-18°: October 27, 1990, invested by *Evangelist* Chapter of Rose Croix, Washington, D.C.

19°-30°: October 27, 1990, invested by *Robert de Bruce* Council of Kadosh, Washington, D.C.

31°-32°: October 27, 1990, invested by Albert Pike Consistory, Washington, D.C.

32°, KCCH: October 21, 1991.

33°, IGH: Elected October 18, 1993; coroneted the Supreme Council, 33°, S.J., October 19, 1993.

Grand Cross of the Court of Honour: October 3, 1997.

Scottish Rite Biography:

Brother Stephen Joel Trachtenberg received the first three Degrees of Freemasonry in *Benjamin B. French* Lodge No. 15, Washington, D.C. and the Scottish Rite Degrees in the District of Columbia Scottish Rite Bodies, all in 1990. He received his 32°, KCCH in 1991 and coroneted the 33°, IGH in 1993.

Professionally, Trachetenberg served as the 15th President of George Washington University between 1988 and 2007. He retired, taking on the title of President Emeritus and served as a professor of public service. In 2007, GWU Board of Trustees voted to rename the School of Public Policy and Public Administration after Trachtenberg in recognition for his distinguished service.

Bibliography:

Archive of the Supreme Council, 33°, S.J.

Archives of the Orient of the District of Columbia and Archives of the Grand Lodge of the District of Columbia, F.A.A.M.

1997

James Tracy Tresner, II
Grand Cross of the Court of Honour at age 55 years, 11 months, and 22 days
Tenure 20 years, 8 months, and 9 days
Nomination by Guthrie, Oklahoma Scottish Rite Bodies

Born: November 11, 1941 – Died: July 12, 2018
Life span: 76 years, 8 months, and 1 day

Progress in Scottish Rite Masonry:
4°-14°: January 17, 1964, invested by *Guthrie* Lodge of Perfection, Guthrie.
15°-18°: January 18, 1964, invested by *Guthrie* Chapter of Rose Croix, Guthrie.
19°-30°: January 18, 1964, invested by *Guthrie* Council of Kadosh, Guthrie.
31°-32°: January 18, 1964, invested by *Guthrie* Consistory, Guthrie.
32°, KCCH: October 17, 1977.
33°, IGH: elected October 17, 1983; coroneted by Ill. Frederick A. Daugherty, Sovereign Grand Inspector General for Oklahoma December 10, 1983.
Grand Cross of the Court of Honour: October 3, 1997.

Scottish Rite Biography:
Brother Tresner's Masonic journey began at age twelve when he joined the Order of DeMolay. He was raised to the Sublime Degree of Master Mason in 1963 in *Garfield* Lodge, No. 501, of Enid, OK, and became a 32° Master of the Royal Secret in 1964 in the Valley of Guthrie, OK. He was invested with the rank and decoration of a Knight Commander of the Court of Honour in 1977, was coroneted a 33°, IGH in 1983, and received the Grand Cross of the Court of Honour in 1997.

Ill. Jim's particular passion was the Scottish Rite, and he served for many years as Director of the Work for the Valley of Guthrie. Perhaps his greatest renown came as an author. He was book review editor of the Scottish Rite Journal for twenty-one years, 1996-2017, and the Author of several books including Albert Pike: *The Man Behind the Monuments*; *Vested in Glory*; *The Aprons, Collars, Caps, and Jewels of the Degrees of the Ancient & Accepted Scottish Rite of Freemasonry*.

Bibliography:
Archive of the Supreme Council, 33°, S.J.
In Memoriam. *Transactions*. 2019: 137.

1999

Joe Lewis Allbritton
Grand Cross of the Court of Honour at age 76 years, 9 months, and 2 days
Tenure 13 years, 2 months, and 11 days
Nomination by Houston, Texas Scottish Rite Bodies

Born: December 29, 1923 – Died: December 12, 2012
Life span: 88 years, 11 months, and 12 days
Attorney, Banker, and Philanthropist

Progress in Scottish Rite Masonry:
4°-14°: October 8, 1952, invested by *San Jacinto* Lodge of Perfection, Houston.
15°-18°: October 9, 1952, invested by *Houston* Chapter of Rose Croix, Houston.
19°-30°: October 10, 1952, invested by *Houston* Council of Kadosh, Houston.
31°-32°: October 11, 1952, invested by *Houston* Consistory, Houston.
32°, KCCH: October 20, 1975.
33°, IGH: October 19, 1981; coroneted Ill. John Wilkins Chandler, 33°, Sovereign Grand Inspector
General for Texas November 23, 1981.
Grand Cross of the Court of Honour: October 1, 1999.

Scottish Rite Biography:
Ill. Brother Allbritton's journey in Masonry began October 19, 1949, when he was raised a Master Mason
in *Baylor* Lodge, No. 1235 in Waco Texas. He became a Master of the Royal Secret in the Valley of
Houston on October 11, 1952, was invested a Knight Commander of the Court of Honour in 1975,
coroneted an Inspector General Honrary in 1981, and elected to receive the Grand Cross of the Court of
Honour on October 1, 1999. Brother Allbritton was a member of the Board of Trustees of the Texas
Scottish Rite Hospital for Children from 1982-1985.

Bibliography:
Archive of the Supreme Council, 33°, S.J.
In Memoriam. *Transactions*. 2013: 191.

1999

Eugene Alexander Barham
Grand Cross of the Court of Honour at age 87 years, 9 months, and 10 days
Tenure 1 month and 21 days
Nomination by Monroe, Louisiana Scottish Rite Bodies

Born: December 21, 1911 – Died: November 22, 1999
Life span: 87 years, 11 months, and 1day
U.S. Navy Admiral

Progress in Scottish Rite Masonry:
4°-14°: September 29, 1973, invested by *Monroe* Lodge of Perfection, Monroe.
15°-18°: September 29, 1973, invested by *Monroe* Chapter of Rose Croix, Monroe.
19°-30°: September 29, 1973, invested by *Monroe* Council of Kadosh, Monroe.
31°-32°: September 29, 1973, invested by *Monroe* Consistory, Monroe.
32°, KCCH: October 15, 1979.
33°, IGH: elected October 16, 1989; coroneted by the Supreme Council, 33°, S.J., October 18, 1989.
Grand Cross of the Court of Honour: October 1, 1999.

Scottish Rite Biography:
A Dedicated Freemason, Ill. Barham was a member of *Brookville* Lodge, No. 161, in Oak Ridge, Louisiana. He was invested a 32° Scottish Rite Mason in 1973, Valley of Monroe, and later elected KCCH (1979) and 33° (1989) for his many services to our Order and America. He not only served our nation as a distinguished military leader, but also labored with outstanding service for Masonry throughout his life. The latter service was recognized in formal manner on September 3, 1998, when, with Admiral Barham present, the Orient of Louisiana's third Scottish Rite Childhood Language Disorders Clinic was dedicated in Monroe, Louisiana, and named the Admiral E. A. Barham Speech and Hearing Clinic in his honor. Rear Admiral Barham was unable to attend the 1999 Biennial Session. Had he been present, he would have been saluted as a newly elected Grand Cross, the highest honor the Rite can bestow.

Bibliography:
Archive of the Supreme Council, 33°, S.J.
In Memoriam. *Transactions.* 2001: 255.

1999

Henry Olaf Dormann
Grand Cross of the Court of Honour at age 67 years, 6 months, and 26 days
Tenure 18 years, 7 months, and 10 days
Nomination by Washington, District of Columbia Scottish Rite Bodies

Born: March 5, 1932 – Died: May 11, 2018
Life span: 86 years, 2 months, and 6 days
Publisher

Progress in Scottish Rite Masonry:
4°-14°: December 14, 1967, invested by *Long Island* Lodge of Perfection, Long Island.
15°-18°: December 16, 1967, invested by *Long Island* Chapter of Rose Croix, Long Island.
19°-30°: December 16, 1967, invested by *Long Island* Council of Kadosh, Long Island.
31°-32°: December 16, 1967, invested by *Long Island* Consistory, Long Island.
June 27, 1978, affiliated with Washington, District of Columbia Scottish Rite Bodies.
32°, KCCH: October 15, 1979.
33°, IGH: elected October 17, 1983; coroneted the Supreme Council, 33°, S.J., October 19, 1983.
Grand Cross of the Court of Honour: October 1, 1999.

Scottish Rite Biography:
Having received his Degrees in Long Island, New York, Brother Dormann submitted his petition for affiliation to the Washington, District of Columbia Scottish Rite Bodies in June 1978, and the following year was elected a 32°, KCCH. Four years later he was elected and coroneted a 33°, IGH. Brother Dormann was not an active member in the District of Columbia Scottish Rite Bodies as he still retained his residence in New York City. Professionally, Dormann received notable acclaim for his interviews and relationships with Presidents of the United States and foreign leaders.

Bibliography:
Archive of the Supreme Council, 33°, S.J.
Archives of the Orient of the District of Columbia and Archives of the Grand Lodge of the District of Columbia, F.A.A.M.

1999

Donald Prieto Garrido
Grand Cross of the Court of Honour at age 71 years, 11 months, and 15 days
Tenure 22 years, 1 month, and 21 days
Nomination by Balboa, Panama Canal Scottish Rite Bodies

Born: October 16, 1927 – Died: November 22, 2021
Life span: 94 years, 1 month, and 6 days
Pilot

Progress in Scottish Rite Masonry:
4°-14°: July 15, 1972, invested by *Panama Canal* Lodge of Perfection, Balboa.
15°-18°: August 19, 1972, invested by *Panama Canal* Chapter of Rose Croix, Balboa.
19°-30°: September 16, 1972, invested by *Panama Canal* Council of Kadosh, Balboa.
31°-32°: October 21, 1972, invested by *Panama Canal* Consistory, Balboa.
32°, KCCH: October 15, 1979.
33°, IGH: elected October 17, 1983; coroneted by the Supreme Council, 33°, S.J., October 19, 1983.
Grand Cross of the Court of Honour: October 1, 1999.

Scottish Rite Biography:
Brother Carrido is Master Mason in *Cibola* Lodge, No. 151, at San Antonio. He joined the Scottish Rite Bodies of Panama Canal Valley, Balboa and became a 32° Master of the Royal Secret on October 12, 1972. Brother Carrido was invested as a Knight Commander of the Court of Honour in 1979, coroneted by the Supreme Council an Inspector General Honorary, 33° on October 19, 1983. In 1995 Brother Carrido affiliated with the Scottish Rite Bodies of the Valley of San Antonio. He served the Valley of Panama Canal as a Chairman of the Executive Committee. Ill. Donald, Prieto Carrido, 33°, received the Scottish Rite's highest honor, the Grand Cross of the Court of Honour on October 1, 1999.

Bibliography:
Archive of the Supreme Council, 33°, S.J.

1999

Charles Ernest Grassley
Grand Cross of the Court of Honour at age 66 years, 1 month, and 1 day
Tenure present
Nomination by Des Moines, Iowa Scottish Rite Bodies

Born: September 17, 1933 – present
U.S. Senator

Progress in Scottish Rite Masonry:
4°-14°: February 27, 1965, invested by *Des Moines* Lodge of Perfection, Des Moines.
15°-18°: February 27, 1965, invested by *Des Moines* Chapter of Rose Croix, Des Moines.
19°-30°: February 27, 1965, invested by *Des Moines* Council of Kadosh, Des Moines.
31°-32°: February 27, 1965, invested by *Des Moines* Consistory, Des Moines.
32°, KCCH: October 19, 1987.
33°, IGH: elected October 16, 1989; coroneted by the Supreme Council, 33°, S.J., October 18, 1989
Grand Cross of the Court of Honour: October 1, 1999.

Scottish Rite Biography:
Brother Grassley was raised a Master Mason in 1960 in his townhome *Lodge of Beaver*, No. 472, which consolidated in 1994 with *Black Hawk* Lodge, No. 65, Cedar Falls, Iowa, where Bro. Grassley is a member. A member of the Scottish Rite Bodies of Des Moines since 1965, Ill. Grassley was invested with the KCCH in 1987, coroneted IGH in 1989, and decorated with the Grand Cross at the 1999 Biennial Session – all in recognition of his outstanding services to Iowa, America, and Freemasonry.

Bibliography:
Archive of the Supreme Council, 33°, S.J.
Grassley, Charles E. Freemasonry Solid as a Rock. *The Scottish Rite Journal*, February 2000.

1999

Sam George Kapourales
Grand Cross of the Court of Honour at age 64 years, 5 months, and 22 days
Tenure - present
Nomination by Charleston, West Virginia Scottish Rite Bodies

Born: April 19, 1935 – present
Pharmacist

Progress in Scottish Rite Masonry:
4°-14°: May 17, 1975, invested by *Charleston* Lodge of Perfection, Charleston.
15°-18°: May 17, 1975, invested by *Charleston* Chapter of Rose Croix, Charleston.
19°-30°: May 17, 1975, invested by *Charleston* Council of Kadosh, Charleston.
31°-32°: May 17, 1975, invested by *Charleston* Consistory, Charleston.
32°, KCCH: October 21, 1991.
33°, IGH: elected October 18, 1993; coroneted by the Supreme Council, 33°, S.J., October 19, 1993.
Grand Cross of the Court of Honour: October 1, 1999.

Scottish Rite Biography:
Brother Kapourales was raised to the sublime Degree of Master Mason in *O'Brien* Lodge, No. 101, Williamson, West Virginia. A member of the Scottish Rite since 1975, he received the rank and decoration of the Knight Commander of the Court of Honour in 1991 and was coroneted an Inspector General Honorary in October 1993. He was President of the Lee O. Rockwell Language Disorder Center, and very active in the Center's Endowment Fund campaign. The Grand Cross of the Court of Honour was awarded to Illustrious Sam Kapourales, 33°, October 1, 1999, by the Supreme Council of the Thirty-Third Degree of the Southern Jurisdiction for his dedication to the Scottish Rite and his outstanding support of the Childhood Language Disorders Center, and for his service to the community and to Southern West Virginia.

Bibliography:
Archive of the Supreme Council, 33°, S.J.
Scottish Rite Bulletin of the Valley of Charleston, Orient of West Virginia, November 1999.

1999

James Wilmer Keebaugh
Grand Cross of the Court of Honour at age 84 years, 2 months, and 7 days
Tenure 6 years, 7 months, and 11 days
Nomination by Nebraska Scottish Rite Bodies

Born: July 24, 1915 – Died: May 12, 2006
Life span: 90 years, 7 months, and 16 days
Businessman

Progress in Scottish Rite Masonry:
4°-14°: March 6, 1951, invested by *Alliance* Lodge of Perfection, Alliance.
15°-18°: March 7, 1951, invested by *Alliance* Chapter of Rose Croix, Alliance.
19°-30°: March 8, 1951, invested by *Alliance* Council of Kadosh, Alliance.
31°-32°: November 16, 1951, invested by *Alliance* Consistory, Alliance.
32°, KCCH: October 17, 1961
33°, IGH: elected October 18, 1971; coroneted by Ill. Herbert Alden Ronin, 33°, Sovereign Grand Inspector General for Nebraska December 11, 1971.
Grand Cross of the Court of Honour: October 1, 1999.

Scottish Rite Biography:
Brother Keebaugh became a member of *Alliance* Lodge, No. 183 in 1949. He joined the Alliance Scottish Rite in 1951, received the rank and decoration of Knight Commander of the Court of Honour in 1961, was coroneted a 33° Inspector General Honorary in 1971, and received the Grand Cross in 1999. In 1984, he was elected Secretary of the Alliance Bodies and served in this position until his death.

Bibliography:
Archive of the Supreme Council, 33°, S.J.
In Memoriam. *Transactions.* 2007: 243.

1999

Robert Rodger Lyons
Grand Cross of the Court of Honour at age 52 years, 11 months, and 25 days
Tenure present
Nomination by Alexandria, Virginia Scottish Rite Bodies

Born: November 6, 1946 – present
Certified Public Accountant

Progress in Scottish Rite Masonry:
4°-14°: October 22, 1988, invested by *Alexandria* Lodge of Perfection, Alexandria.
15°-18°: October 22, 1988, invested by *Alexandria* Chapter of Rose Croix, Alexandria.
19°-30°: October 22, 1988, invested by *Alexandria* Council of Kadosh, Alexandria.
31°-32°: October 22, 1988, invested by *Alexandria* Consistory, Alexandria.
32°, KCCH: October 16, 1989.
33°, IGH: elected October 21, 1991; coroneted by the Supreme Council, 33°, S.J., October 22, 1991.
Grand Cross of the Court of Honour: October 1, 1999.

Scottish Rite Biography:
Brother Lyons was raised a Master Mason in *Henry Knox Field* Lodge, No. 349, in Alexandria, VA. He joined the Scottish Rite Bodies of the Valley of Alexandria in 1988, and on the following year was elected a Knight Commander of the Court of Honour. On the Session of the Supreme Council for 1991 Brother Lyons was coroneted a 33°, Inspector General Honorary. On October 1, 1999, Ill. Robert Roger Lyons, 33°, received the Scottish Rite's highest honor, the Grand Cross of the Court of Honour.

Bibliography:
Archive of the Supreme Council, 33°, S.J.

1999

Fred Wylie McPeake
Grand Cross of the Court of Honour at age 79 years, 7 months, and 23 days
Tenure 9 years, 3 months, and 22 days
Nomination by Knoxville, Tennessee Scottish Rite Bodies

Born: February 8, 1920 – Died: January 23, 2009
Life span: 88 years, 11 months, and 15 days
Lawyer

Progress in Scottish Rite Masonry:
4°-14°: April 13, 1943, invested by *John Chester* Lodge of Perfection, Memphis.
15°-18°: April 13, 1943, invested by *Calvary* Chapter of Rose Croix, Memphis.
19°-30°: April 14, 1943, invested by *Cyprus* Council of Kadosh, Memphis.
31°-32°: April 15, 1943, invested by *Tennessee* Consistory, Memphis.
November 9, 1945, affiliated with Knoxville Scottish Rite Bodies.
32°, KCCH: October 20, 1953.
33°, IGH: elected October 22, 1957; coroneted by the Supreme Council, 33°, S.J., October 25, 1957
Grand Cross of the Court of Honour: October 1, 1999.

Scottish Rite Biography:
Brother Fred was a Past Master of *Beaver Ridge* Lodge, No. 366. He became a Master of the Royal Secret in 1943 in the Memphis Scottish Rite Bodies, transferred his membership to Knoxville in 1945, received the rank and decoration of a KCCH in 1953, was coroneted an Inspector General Honorary in 1957, and received the Grand Cross of the Court of Honour in 1999. Ill. McPeake became the Secretary of the Valley of Knoxville in 1956 and held this position for 43 years. During his tenure, Knoxville's "Mercy Fund" grew from providing medical equipment for anyone in need to include the shoe program in each county, an Americanism Program, and a scholarship program providing up to $20,000 in annual scholarships. He secured the participation of the Knoxville Bodies in the Speech and Hearing Centers at the University of Tennessee, Knoxville; Mountain Region Speech and Hearing Center, Kingsport; and the East Tennessee State University Speech and Hearing Center, Johnson City.

Bibliography:
Archive of the Supreme Council, 33°, S.J.
In Memoriam. *Transactions*. 2009: 257.

1999

Stephen Brent Morris
Grand Cross of the Court of Honour at age 49 years, 6 months, and 3 days
Tenure present
Nomination by Baltimore, Maryland Scottish Rite Bodies

Born: March 28, 1950 – present
Ph.D. in Mathematic Sciences
Managing Editor of *The Scottish Rite Journal*

Progress in Scottish Rite Masonry:

4°-14°: April 20, 1974, invested by *Carle A. Woodruff* Lodge of Perfection, Raleigh.

15°-18°: October 14, 1980, invested by *Meredith* Chapter of Rose Croix, Baltimore.

19°-30°: October 22, 1980, invested by *Maryland* Council of Kadosh, Baltimore.

31°-32°: October 25, 1980, invested by *Chesapeake* Consistory, Baltimore.

December 2, 1976, affiliated with Baltimore Scottish Rite Bodies.

32°, KCCH: October 21, 1985.

33°, IGH: elected October 16, 1989; coroneted by the Supreme Council, 33°, S.J., October 18, 1989.

Grand Cross of the Court of Honour: October 1, 1999.

Scottish Rite Biography:

Brother Morris was raised to the Sublime Degree in *Highland Park* Lodge, No. 1150, at Highland Park, Texas, and later affiliated with the *Patmos-Solomon's* Lodge, No. 70, at Ellicott City, Maryland. The Scottish Rite Degrees from 4° to 14° were invested to Brother Morris by *Carle A. Woodruff* Lodge of Perfection at Raleigh, North Carolina on April 20, 1974. But he became a 32°, Master of the Royal Secret six years after on October 25, 1980, when affiliated with the Scottish Rite Bodies of the Valley of Baltimore. Brother Morris received the rank and decoration of Knight Commander of the Court of Honour in 1985, coroneted a 33°, Inspector General Honorary in 1989, and received the Scottish Rite's highest honor, the Grand Cross of the Court of Honour on October 1, 1999. On October 2, 2001, Ill. Morris was appointed by Sovereign Grand Commander C. Fred Kleinknecht, 33°, as Director of Membership Development for the Supreme Council, 33°, S.J. Brother Morris has been studying and writing about the Fraternity and Masonic membership particularly for decades, including his Editor's status of the *Herdom*, an annual publication of the Scottish Rite Research Society, and he was uniquely qualified for this position. However, the scholarly talent of Ill. Morris, who is an internationally recognized Masonic Scholar, leads him to the position of the Managing Editor of *The Scottish Rite Journal*, which he carried on from May–June 2005 to May–June 2021, along with other countless positions and duties. Ill. Stephen Brent Morris, 33°, GC, is always on demand for editing, for writing, and especially for speaking, because he is one of the most effective spokesmen Freemasonry has ever had.

Bibliography:

Archive of the Supreme Council, 33°, S.J.

1999

Lonnie Melvin Tillis
Grand Cross of the Court of Honour at age 67 years, 1 month, and 23 days
Tenure 20 years, 1 month, and 18 days
Nomination by Joplin, Missouri Scottish Rite Bodies

Born: August 8, 1932 – Died: November 19, 2017
Life span: 85 years, 3 months, and 11 days
Country Music Singer

Progress in Scottish Rite Masonry:
4°-14°: July 31, 1993, invested by *Joplin* Lodge of Perfection, Joplin.
15°-18°: July 31, 1993, invested by *Joplin* Chapter of Rose Croix, Joplin.
19°-30°: July 31, 1993, invested by *Joplin* Council of Kadosh, Joplin.
31°-32°: July 31, 1993, invested by *Joplin* Consistory, Joplin.
32°, KCCH: October 9, 1995.
33°, IGH: elected October 6, 1997; coroneted by Ill. Walter S. Downs, 33°, Grand Cross, at the Supreme Council, 33°, Washington, D.C. December 15, 1997.
Grand Cross of the Court of Honour: October 1, 1999.

Scottish Rite Biography:
Brother Lonnie Melvin Tillis was a member of *Branson* Lodge No. 587 in Branson, MO. He received his 4°-14° on July 31, 1993, invested by the *Joplin* Lodge of Perfection, his 15°-18° on July 31, 1993, invested by the *Joplin* Chapter of Rose Croix, his 19°-30° on July 31, 1993, invested by the *Joplin* Council of Kadosh, and his 31°-32° on July 31, 1993, invested by the *Joplin* Consistory. He was elected 32°, KCCH on October 9, 1995. On October 6, 1997, he was elected 33°, IGH and coroneted December 15, 1997, by Ill. Walter S. Downs, 33°, Grand Cross, at the Supreme Council, 33°, in Washington, D.C. A dedicated Scottish Rite Mason, Mel, for the few years in a row has performed an annual benefit show at his theater in Branson, as a memorial tribute to fellow singer, philanthropist, and Scottish Rite Mason, Ill. Burl Ives, 33°, G.C. Half of the proceeds from this shows has gone to benefit the Scottish Rite Childhood Language Disorders Program in the Southern Jurisdiction. In recognition of his outstanding charitable achievements, the Supreme Council, 33°, awarded Illustrious Tillis its highest honor, the Grand Cross, on October 1, 1999.

Bibliography:
Archive of the Supreme Council, 33°, S.J.
About Mel Tillis... *Transactions*. 2001: 289.
In Memoriam. *Transactions*. 2019: 136.

1999

Ned Elvin Wick
Grand Cross of the Court of Honour at age 71 years, 6 months, and 11 days
Tenure 5 years, 11 months, and 18 days
Nomination by Deadwood, South Dakota Scottish Rite Bodies

Born: March 20, 1928 – Died: September 19, 2005
Life span: 77 years, 5 months, and 29 days
Professor

Progress in Scottish Rite Masonry:
4°-14°: October 20, 1956, invested by *Black Hills* Lodge of Perfection, Deadwood.
15°-18°: October 23, 1956, invested by *Black Hills* Chapter of Rose Croix, Deadwood.
19°-30°: October 29, 1956, invested by *Black Hills* Council of Kadosh, Deadwood.
31°-32°: October 30, 1956, invested by *Black Hills* Consistory, Deadwood.
32°, KCCH: October 3, 1967.
33°, IGH: elected October 20, 1975; coroneted by the Supreme Council, 33°, S.J., October 23, 1975.
Grand Cross of the Court of Honour: October 1, 1999.

Scottish Rite Biography:
Brother Ned was raised a Master Mason in *Mt. Rushmore* Lodge, No. 220, at Rapid City. In 1956, he joined the Scottish Rite Bodies of the Valley of Black Hills, and became a 32°, Master of the Royal Secret on October 30, 1956. He was elected to receive the Knight Commander of the Court of Honour in 1967, and coroneted as a 33°, Inspector General Honorary on October 23, 1975. Ill. Ned Elvin Wick, 33°, was awarded the Grand Cross of the Court of Honour on October 1, 1999.

Bibliography:
Archive of the Supreme Council, 33°, S.J.
In Memoriam. Transactions. 2007: 327.

2001

George Robert Baddour
Grand Cross of the Court of Honour at age 74 years, 8 months, and 29 days
Tenure 7 years, 4 months, and 25 days
Nomination by Memphis, Tennessee Scottish Rite Bodies

Born: January 29, 1927 – Died: February 23, 2009
Life span: 82 years and 24 days
Embalmer and Funeral Director

Progress in Scottish Rite Masonry:
4°-14°: April 15, 1952, invested by *John Chester* Lodge of Perfection, Memphis.
15°-18°: April 16, 1952, invested by *John Chester* Chapter of Rose Croix, Memphis.
19°-30°: April 17, 1952, invested by *John Chester* Council of Kadosh, Memphis.
31°-32°: April 18, 1952, invested by *John Chester* Consistory, Memphis.
32°, KCCH: October 3, 1967.
33°, IGH: elected October 20, 1975; coroneted by the Supreme Council, 33°, S.J., October 23, 1975.
Grand Cross of the Court of Honour: September 28, 2001.

Scottish Rite Biography:
Brother Baddour was raised a Master Mason in *Tipton* Lodge, No. 226, Munford, in 1948. Brother Baddour received the 32° in 1952 in the Memphis Bodies and the rank and decoration of KCCH in 1967, was coroneted an Inspector General Honorary in 1975, and received the Grand Cross of the Court of Honour in 2001. He served the Memphis Bodies as Master of Kadosh, 1978-79; Treasurer, 1980-91; Venerable Master, 1992-93; and Personal Representative, 1987-2007.

Bibliography:
Archive of the Supreme Council, 33°, S.J.
In Memoriam. *Transactions.* 2009: 258.

2001

Clyde Manford Brown, Sr.
Grand Cross of the Court of Honour at age 88 years, 7 months, and 13 days
Tenure 10 years, 11 months, and 28 days
Nomination by Portland, Oregon Scottish Rite Bodies

Born: February 15, 1913 – Died: August 26, 2012
Life span: 99 years, 6 months, and 11 days
U.S. Navy Commander

Progress in Scottish Rite Masonry:
4°-14°: May 5, 1993, invested by *Oregon* Lodge of Perfection, Portland.
15°-18°: May 5, 1993, invested by *Ainsworth* Chapter of Rose Croix, Portland.
19°-30°: May 5, 1993, invested by *Multnomah* Council of Kadosh, Portland.
31°-32°: May 5, 1993, invested by *Oregon* Consistory, Portland.
32°, KCCH: October 15, 1979.
33°, IGH: elected October 16, 1989; coroneted by Ill. David O. Johnson, 33°, Sovereign Grand Inspector General for Oregon November 11, 1989.
Grand Cross of the Court of Honour: September 28, 2001.

Scottish Rite Biography:
Brother Brown was raised to the Sublime Degree of a Master Mason in *Robert Burns* Lodge, No. 243 in Lynwood, Washington, on March 15, 1955, became a Master of the Royal Secret in the Valley of Portland on May 1973, receiving the rank and decoration of a Knight Commander of the Court of Honour in 1979, and was coroneted an Inspector General Honorary in 1989, and was elected by the Supreme Council to receive the Grand Cross of the Court of Honour in 2001. In the Scottish Rite, Brother Clyde was a pivotal leader in the ritual work. He served as Director of both the KCCH and 33° Degree Conferrals for the Orient of Oregon. For the Valley of Portland, he was Master of the 27°. Annually he held a seminar at his home for Valley Degree Directors and Masters, and stage crew that the work might be done well.

Bibliography:
Archive of the Supreme Council, 33°, S.J.
In Memoriam. *Transactions*. 2013: 187.

2001

Russel Avery Cloud
Grand Cross of the Court of Honour at age 80 years, 10 months, and 10 days
Tenure 14 years, 3 months, and 8 days
Nomination by Phoenix, Arizona Scottish Rite Bodies

Born: November 18, 1920 – Died: January 6, 2016
Life span: 95 years, 1 month, and 18 days
Microbiologist

Progress in Scottish Rite Masonry:
4°-14°: April 17, 1952, invested by *Phoenix* Lodge of Perfection, Phoenix.
15°-18°: April 18, 1952, invested by *Phoenix* Chapter of Rose Croix, Phoenix.
19°-30°: April 19, 1952, invested by *Phoenix* Council of Kadosh, Phoenix.
31°-32°: April 19, 1952, invested by *Phoenix* Consistory, Phoenix.
32°, KCCH: October 20, 1959.
33°, IGH: elected October 3, 1967; coroneted by Ill. Nelson C. Bledsoe, 33°, Sovereign Grand Inspector General for Arizona December 9, 1967.
Grand Cross of the Court of Honour: September 28, 2001.

Scottish Rite Biography:
Brother Cloud was raised a Master Mason in *Warren* Lodge, No. 15, in Connersville, Indiana, later on affiliated *Oriental* Lodge, No. 20, in Mesa. In April of 1952, he joined the Scottish Rite Bodies of Phoenix. Immediately becoming an active and involved member, he served as presiding officer of the Council of Kadosh in 1959 and Lodge of Perfection in 1962. He was a proficient ritualist and member of the 15° and 26° casts. Beginning October 1981, he commenced a 17-years term of service as Personal Representative in the Valley of Phoenix and retired in January 1998. Having relinquished that office, he continued his contributions to the Rite, assuming the position of President of the Language Clinic program. Brother Cloud was invested as a KCCH in 1959, coroneted as IGH, 33°, in 1967, and elected by the Supreme Council to receive the Grand Cross of the Court of Honour in September 2001.

Bibliography:
Archive of the Supreme Council, 33°, S.J.
In Memoriam. *Transactions*. 2017: 106.

2001

Joseph Angelo Diele
Grand Cross of the Court of Honour at age 83 years, 6 months, and 18 days
Tenure 3 years, 5 months, and 27 days
Nomination by Tokyo, Japan, and Korea Scottish Rite Bodies

Born: March 10, 1918 – Died: March 25, 2005
Life span: 87 years and 14 days
Business Manager

Progress in Scottish Rite Masonry:
4°-14°: April 25, 1968, invested by *Tokyo* Lodge of Perfection, Tokyo.
15°-18°: April 25, 1968, invested by *Tokyo* Chapter of Rose Croix, Tokyo.
19°-30°: April 26, 1968, invested by *Tokyo* Council of Kadosh, Tokyo.
31°-32°: April 26, 1968, invested by *Tokyo* Consistory of Kadosh, Tokyo.
32°, KCCH: October 15, 1973.
33°, IGH: elected October 20, 1975; coroneted November 29, 1975.
Deputy: for the Orient of Japan and Korea September 1, 1976 – retired November 1, 2004.
Grand Cross of the Court of Honour: September 28, 2001.

Scottish Rite Biography:
Brother Diele became a Master Mason in Lodge *Hiogo and Osaka*, No. 498, in Kobe. In 1968 Brother Diele received the 32° and went on to serve as Wise Master, Commander, and Venerable Master of the Tokyo Bodies. In 1973 he was elected a Knight Commander Court of Honour rank, in 1975, an Inspector General Honorary, and in 1976 Ill. Diele was appointed Deputy of the Supreme Council in Japan and Korea, a position he filled with distinction until his retirement in November 2004.

Bibliography:
Archive of the Supreme Council, 33°, S.J.
In Memoriam. *Transactions.* 2005: 265.

2001

Sean David Graystone
Grand Cross of the Court of Honour at age 45 years, 1 month and 21 days
Tenure present
Nomination by Santa Fe, New Mexico Scottish Rite Bodies

Born: August 7, 1956 – present
Construction Industry

Progress in Scottish Rite Masonry:
4°-14°: October 6, 1986, invested by *Santa Fè* Lodge of Perfection, Santa Fè.
15°-18°: October 7, 1986, invested by *Santa Fè* Chapter of Rose Croix, Santa Fè.
19°-30°: October 7, 1986, invested by *Santa Fè* Council of Kadpsh, Santa Fè.
31°-32°: October 8, 1986, invested by *Santa Fè* Consistory, Santa Fè.
32°, KCCH: October 21, 1991.
33°, IGH: elected October 9, 1995; coroneted by the Supreme Council, 33°, S.J., October 10, 1995.
May 16, 1998, plural Member in Las Cruces Scottish Rite Bodies, Las Cruces; demitted December 22, 2009.
August 23, 2007, Dual Membership in Houston Scottish Rite Bodies, Texas.
October 1, 2009, Dual Membership in Washington, D.C. Scottish Rite Bodies, Orient of the District of Columbia.
Grand Cross of the Court of Honour: September 28, 2001.

Scottish Rite Biography:
Brother Graystone was raised a Master Mason in *Cerrillos* Lodge, No. 19, at Santa Fè. In 1986 he joined the Scottish Rite Bodies of the Valley of Santa Fè. In 1991, he was invested as a Knight Commander of the Court of Honour, and in 1995 coroneted an Inspector General Honorary, 33°. Brother Graystone served his Valley as Venerable Master of the Lodge of Perfection, as Wise Master of Chapter of Rose Croix, and as Master of Kadosh of Consistory. On September 28, 2001, Ill. Sean David Graystone, 33°, was awarded the Grand Cross of the Court of Honour. On the Supreme Council level, Ill. Greystone served on the *ad hoc* committee assisting Dr. Rex R. Hutchens, 33°, GC in the revision of the Ritual, and as a Building (House of the Temple) Superintendent, and now serving as a Member of the Board of Directors of the Scottish Rite Research Society.

Bibliography:
Archive of the Supreme Council, 33°, S.J.

2001

Harold Lloyd Gwatney
Grand Cross of the Court of Honour at age 72 years, 1 month, and 11 days
Tenure 20 years, 3 months, and 9 days
Nomination by Little Rock, Arkansas Scottish Rite Bodies

Born: August 17, 1929 – January 7, 2022
Life span: 92 years, 4 months, and 20 days
Salesman

Progress in Scottish Rite Masonry:
4°-14°: May 4, 1953, invested by *Arkansas* Lodge of Perfection, Little Rock.
15°-18°: May 5, 1953, invested by *Arkansas* Chapter of Rose Croix, Little Rock.
19°-30°: May 5, 1953, invested by *Arkansas* Council of Kadosh, Little Rock.
31°-32°: May 6, 1953, invested by *Arkansas* Consistory, Little Rock.
32°, KCCH: October 9, 1995.
33°, IGH: October 4, 1999; coroneted by the Supreme Council, 33°, S.J. October 5, 1999.
Grand Cross of the Court of Honour: September 28, 2001.

Scottish Rite Biography:
Brother Gwatney was raised a Master Mason in *Big Rock* Lodge, No. 633, in North Little Rock and a 32° Master of the Royal Secret on May 6, 1953. He received his first Scottish Rite distinction, the rank and decoration of a Knight Commander of the Court of Honour in 1995, and at the Session of the Supreme Council of 1999 was elected and coroneted a 33° Inspector General Honorary. Ill. Harold Lloyd Gwatney, 33° on September 28, 2001, was elected by the Supreme Council to receive the Grand Cross of the Court of Honour. Brother Gwatney became a major Philanthropist and Investor in the Southern Jurisdiction. During a reception held in honor of Ill Harold Lloyd Gwatney, 33°, Grand Cross, and his wife Syble, at the Albert Pike Scottish Rite Memorial Temple in Little Rock, Arkansas, on November 18, 2002, Ill Gwatney and his wife generously presented a $2 million gift to the Scottish Rite Foundation. It was the largest single charitable trust donation that has been made to the Foundation. On the following year the Supreme Council honored Brother Gwatney as Supreme Temple Architect and displayed his portrait in the Supreme Temple Architects Hall of Honor at the house of the Temple, and Mrs. Gwatney's portrait in the Pillars of Charity portrait Gallery.

Bibliography:
Archive of the Supreme Council, 33°, S.J.
Ill. Harold L. Gwatney, 33°, G.C., Invested in Our Future. *The Scottish Rite Journal*, March 2003.

2001

Ralph Humphrey Head
Grand Cross of the Court of Honour at age 88 years, 6 months, and 7 days
Tenure 1 year and 21 days
Nomination by Los Angeles, California Scottish Rite Bodies

Born: March 21, 1913 – Died: October 19, 2002
Life span: 89 years, 6 months, and 28 days
Businessman

Progress in Scottish Rite Masonry:
4°-14°: December10, 1942, invested be *Los Angeles* Lodge of Perfection, Los Angeles.
15°-18°: December11, 1942, invested be *Los Angeles* Chapter of Rose Croix, Los Angeles.
19°-30°: December12, 1942, invested be *Los Angeles* Council of Kadosh, Los Angeles.
31°-32°: December12, 1942, invested be *Los Angeles* Consistory, Los Angeles.
32°, KCCH: October 19, 1949.
33°, IGH: elected October 18, 1955; coroneted by Ill. Henry C. Clausen, 33°, Sovereign Grand Inspector General for California January 7, 1956.
Grand Cross of the Court of Honour: September 28, 2001.

Scottish Rite Biography:
Brother Head was raised a Mason in *Sunset* Lodge, No. 352. A leader of the Scottish Rite Bodies of Los Angeles since 1942, his imposing stature and rich voice benefited the Ritual of many Degrees. For this and many other services to the Rite, he was invested a KCCH in 1949, coroneted a 33° IGH in 1955, and elected a Grand Cross, the Scottish Rite highest honor, in 2001.

Bibliography:
Archive of the Supreme Council, 33°, S.J.
In Memoriam. *Transactions*. 2003: 209.

2001

Jesse Alexander Helms
Grand Cross of the Court of Honour at age 80 years and 20 days
Tenure 6 years, 9 months, and 6 days
Nomination by Raleigh, North Carolina Scottish Rite Bodies

Born: October 18, 1921 – Died: July 4, 2008
Life span: 86 years, 8 months, and 16 days
U.S. Senator

Progress in Scottish Rite Masonry:
4°-14°: November 14, 1978, invested by *Carle A. Woodruff* Lodge of Perfection, Raleigh.
15°-18°: November 15, 1978, invested by *John C. Drewry* Chapter of Rose Croix, Raleigh.
19°-30°: November 16, 1978, invested by *Raleigh* Council of Kadosh, Raleigh.
31°-32°: November 16, 1978, invested by Raleigh Consistory, Raleigh.
32°, KCCH: October 19, 1981.
33°, IGH: elected October 16, 1989; coroneted by the Supreme Council, 33°, S.J., October 18, 1989.
Grand Cross of the Court of Honour: September 28, 2001.

Scottish Rite Biography:
Brother Helms was a Master Mason in *Raleigh* Lodge, No. 500. He joined the Raleigh, North Carolina, Scottish Rite Bodies in 1978, receiving the rank and decoration of a Knight Commander of the Court of Honour in 1981, was coroneted an Inspector General Honorary in 1989, and received the Grand Cross of the Court of Honour in 2001.

Bibliography:
Archive of the Supreme Council, 33°, S.J.
In Memoriam. *Transactions.* 2009: 253.

2001

William Kenneth Lyons, Jr.
Grand Cross of the Court of Honour at age 55 years, 4 months, and 29 days
Tenure – present
Nomination by Washington, District of Columbia Scottish Rite Bodies

Born: May 30, 1946 – present
Minister

Progress in Scottish Rite Masonry:
4°-14°: November 3, 1973, invested by *Mithras* Lodge of Perfection, Washington, D.C.
15°-18°: November 3, 1973, invested by *Evangelist* Chapter of Rose Croix, Washington, D.C.
19°-30°: November 17, 1973, invested by *Robert de Bruce* Council of Kadosh, Washington, D.C.
31°-32°: November 17, 1973, invested by *Albert Pike* Consistory, Washington, D.C.
32°, KCCH: October 21, 1985.
33°, IGH: elected October 16, 1989; coroneted by the Supreme Council, 33°, S.J., October 18, 1989.
Grand Cross of the Court of Honour: September 28, 2001.

Scottish Rite Biography:
The Revered and Brother William Kenneth Lyons, Jr. received the first three Masonic Degrees in *Potomac* Lodge No. 5, and was raised to Master Mason on May 21, 1973. He received the Scottish Rite Degrees in 1973 through the District of Columbia Scottish Rite Bodies and served with distinction on several committees alongside his father – a fellow Scottish Rite Mason. The Supreme Council elected Ill. Lyons an Assistant Grand Chaplain in 2000 and their Grand Chaplain in 2001, which he currently holds to this day. Brother Lyons has served as a pastor of Etchison-Mt. Tabor for over 50 years and has been recognized in the dozens of fraternal, civil, service, and faith-based institutions for his outstanding service and achievement.

Bibliography:
Archive of the Supreme Council, 33°, S.J.
Archives of the Orient of the District of Columbia and Archives of the Grand Lodge of the District of Columbia, F.A.A.M.

2001

Lee Edwin Schlessman
Grand Cross of the Court of Honour at age 74 years, 9 months, and 30 days
Tenure 17 years, 5 months, and 8 days
Nomination by Denver, Colorado Scottish Rite Bodies

Born: November 29, 1926 – Died: March 6, 2019
Life span: 92 years, 3 months, and 7 days
Businessman

Progress in Scottish Rite Masonry:
4°-14°: November 26, 1951, invested by *Delta* Lodge of Perfection, Denver.
15°-18°: November 27, 1951, invested by *Mackey* Chapter of Rose Croix, Denver.
19°-30°: November 28, 1951, invested by *Denver* Council of Kadosh, Denver.
31°-32°: November 28, 1951, invested by *Colorado* Consistory, Denver.
32°, KCCH: October 22, 1963.
33°, IGH: elected October 18, 1971; coroneted by Ill. Clarence Wheeler Barnes, 33°, Sovereign Grand Inspector General for Colorado November 27, 1971.
Grand Cross Court of Honour: September 28, 2001.

Scottish Rite Biography:
Brother Lee Edwin Schlessman was a Master Mason in *Albert Pike* Lodge, No. 117, Denver, and a member of the Denver, Colorado, Scottish Rite Bodies. On November 26, 1951, Bro. Schlessman received the 4°-14°, which were invested by *Delta* Lodge of Perfection, Denver. On November 27, 1951, he received the 15°-18°, invested by *Mackey* Chapter of Rose Croix, Denver. He then received the 19°-30° on November 28, 1951, invested by the *Denver* Council of Kadosh, Denver, and the 31°-32° on November 28, 1951, invested by *Colorado* Consistory, Denver. He received his KCCH on October 22, 1963. He was elected as a 33°, IGH on October 18, 1971, and was coroneted November 27, 1971, by Ill. Clarence Wheeler Barnes, 33°, Sovereign Grand Inspector General for Colorado. Finally, on September 28, 2001, he was honored with the title of Grand Cross Court of Honour. He was the Potentate of El Jebel Shrine Temple in 1970 and treasurer of the Scottish Rite Foundation until his death.

Bibliography:
Archive of the Supreme Council, 33°, S.J.
In Memoriam. *Transactions*. 2019: 134.

2001

John William Teets
Grand Cross of the Court of Honour at age 68 years and 13 days
Tenure 9 years, 11 months, and 7 days
Nomination by Tucson, Arizona Scottish Rite Bodies

Born: September 15, 1933 – Died: August 5, 2011
Life span: 77 years, 11 months, and 20 days
Businessman

Progress in Scottish Rite Masonry:
4°-14°: October 29, 1990, invested by *Phoenix* Lodge of Perfection, Phoenix.
15°-18°: October 29, 1990, invested by *Phoenix* Chapter of Rose Croix, Phoenix.
19°-30°: October 29, 1990, invested by *Phoenix* Council of Kadosh, Phoenix.
31°-32°: October 29, 1990, invested by *Phoenix* Consistory, Phoenix.
32°, KCCH: October 21, 1991.
33°, IGH: elected October 18, 1993; coroneted by the Supreme Council, 33°, S.J., October 19, 1993.
Grand Cross of the Court of Honour: September 28, 2001.

Scottish Rite Biography:
Brother Teets was Master Mason in *Monitor* Lodge, No. 522, in Elgin, became a 32° Master of the Royal Secret in a special ceremony in the Temple Room of the House of the Temple in 1990, received the rank and decoration of a Knight Commander of the Court of Honour in 1991, was coroneted a 33°, Inspector General Honorary in 1993, and was received the Grand Cross of the Court of Honour in 2001.

Bibliography:
Archive of the Supreme Council, 33°, S.J.
In Memoriam. *Transactions*. 2011: 242.

2001

James Bernard Wilkinson
Grand Cross of the Court of Honour at age 75 years, 6 months, and 6 days
Tenure 9 years, 3 months, and 28 days
Nomination by Richmond, Virginia Scottish Rite Bodies

Born: March 22, 1926 – Died: January 26, 2011
Life span: 84 years, 10 months, and 4 days
Judge

Progress in Scottish Rite Masonry:
4°-14°: November 11, 1947, invested by *Libertas* Lodge of Perfection, Richmond.
15°-18°: November 12, 1947, invested by Chapter of Rose Croix, Richmond.
19°-30°: November 18, 1947, invested by *St. Omar* Council of Kadosh, Richmond.
31°-32°: November 19, 1947, invested by *Dalco* Consistory, Richmond.
32°, KCCH: October 18, 1971.
33°, IGH: elected October 21, 1985; coroneted by Ill. David Kruger, 33°, Sovereign Grand Inspector General for Virginia November 9, 1985.
Grand Cross of the Court of Honour: September 28, 2001.

Scottish Rite Biography:
Brother Wilkinson was raised to the Sublime Degree in the Lodge of *Strict Observance*, No. 207, at Richmond. In November 1947 he joined the Scottish Rite Bodies in Richmond and became a 32°, Master of the Royal Secret. He received the rank and decoration of a Knight Commander of the Court of Honour on October 18, 1971; on the Session of the Supreme Council of 1985 was elected by the Supreme Council a 33°, Inspector General Honorary and coroneted by Ill. David Kruger, 33°, Sovereign Grand Inspector General for Virginia November 9, 1985. Ill. Wilkinson served his Valley as Secretary of the Childhood Language Center in Richmond, and his Orient as Personal Representative for Sovereign Grand Inspector General for Virginia. On September 28, 2001, Ill. James Bernard Wilkinson, 33°, received the highest honor of the Supreme Council, the Grand Cross of the Court of Honour.

Bibliography:
Archive of the Supreme Council, 33°, S.J.

2001

Robert William Woodward
Grand Cross of the Court of Honour at age 71 years, 5 months, and 16 days
Tenure 8 years, 11 months, and 3 days
Nomination by American Military Scottish Rite Bodies

Born: April 12, 1930 – Died: September 11, 2010
Life span: 80 years, 4 months, and 26 days
President of Insurance Company

Progress in Scottish Rite Masonry:
4°-32°: June 26, 1960, invested by Army Branch *Seneca* Consistory, Frankfurt, Germany.
32°, KCCH: October 15, 1979.
33°, IGH: elected October 15, 1979; coroneted by the Supreme Council, 33°, October 18, 1979.
Grand Cross of the Court of Honour: September 28, 2001.
Deputy: May 6, 1986 – laid down his Craft tools while in Office September 11, 2010.

Scottis Rite Biography:
Brother Woodward was a Master Mason of the *Oregon* Military Lodge, No. 223. Brother Woodward was a founding member in 1968 of the American Military Scottish Rite Bodies in Frankfurt, Germany. In 1971, he founded the Brussels Scottish Rite Club. Brother Woodward was invested with the rank and Decoration of the Knight Commander of the Court of Honour in 1973 and was coroneted an Inspector General Honorary in 1979. In 1986, he was appointed Deputy of the Supreme Council for the American Military Scottish Rite Bodies – NATO Bases. In 2001 Illustrious Woodward was invested the Grand Cross of the Court of Honour.

Bibliography:
Archive of the Supreme Council, 33°, S.J.
In Memoriam. *Transactions.* 2011: 240.

2003

Leonilo Trimana Alger
Grand Cross of the Court of Honour at age 70 years, 4 months, and 28 days
Tenure present
Nomination by Agana, Guam Scottish Rite Bodies

Born: May 5, 1933 – present
Optician

Progress in Scottish Rite Masonry:
4°-14°: October 18, 1974, invested by *Guam* Lodge of Perfection, Agana.
15°-18°: October 19, 1974, invested by *Guam* Chapter of Rose Croix, Agana.
19°-30°: October 25, 1974, invested by *Guam* Council of Kadosh, Agana.
31°-32°: October 26, 1974, invested by *Guam* Consistory, Agana.
32°, KCCH: October 9, 1995.
33°, IGH: elected October 6, 1997; coroneted by Supreme Council, 33°, S.J., October 7, 1997.
Grand Cross of the Court of Honour: October 3, 2003.

Scottish Rite Biography:
Brother Alger was raised to the Sublime Degree in *Milton C. Marvin* Lodge, No. 123, in Agana, Guam. He joined the Scottish Rite Bodies of the Valley of Guam in 1974; received the rank and decoration of a Knight Commander of the Court of Honour in 1995; coroneted by Supreme Council, 33°, S.J., a 33°, Inspector General Honorary in 1997; and elected a Grand Cross of the Court of Honour in 2003. Ill. Leonilo Trimana Alger, 33°, GC, was very dynamic in his dedication to the Scottish Rite and was the main source of power to have the Scottish Rite Temple in Agana completed in its repairs. He served a long term as the Secretary of the Valley and Personal Representative to the Sovereign Grand Inspector General for Hawaii and Guam.

Bibliography:
Archive of the Supreme Council, 33°, S.J.
Archive of the Valley of Agana.

2003

Pat Beard
Grand Cross of the Court of Honour at age 77 years, 7 months, and 11 days
Tenure 10 years, 1 month, and 27 days
Nomination by Waco, Texas Scottish Rite Bodies

Born: June 22, 1925 – Died: November 30, 2013
Life span: 88 years, 5 months, and 7 days
Attorney

Progress in Scottish Rite Masonry:
4°-14°: September 28, 1957, invested by *Dallas* Lodge of Perfection, Dallas.
15°-18°: October 5, 1957, invested by *Dallas* Chapter of Rose Croix, Dallas.
19°-30°: October 19, 1957, invested by *Dallas* Council of Kadosh, Dallas.
31°-32°: October 26, 1957, invested by *Dallas* Consistory, Dallas.
April 7, 1958, affiliated with Waco Scottish Rite Bodies.
32°, KCCH: October 19, 1965
33°, IGH: elected October 20, 1968; coroneted by Ill. Robert Lee Lockwood, 33°, Sovereign Grand Inspector General for Texas November 15, 1968.
Grand Cross of the Court of Honour: October 3, 2003.

Scottish Rite Biography:
Brother Beard was a Master Mason in *J. H. Lookwood* Lodge, No. 1343. Ill. Beard was active in the Scottish Rite and attained the 33° degree. He was passionate about the work of the Scottish Rite Children's Hospital of Texas and served many years on the board of the hospital.

Bibliography:
Archive of the Supreme Council, 33°, S.J.
In Memoriam. *Transactions*. 2015: 144.

2003

Michael Bilirakis
Grand Cross of the Court of Honour at age 73 years, 2 months, and 17 days
Tenure present
Nomination by Tampa, Florida Scottish Rite Bodies

Born: July 16, 1930 – present
U. S. Congressman

Progress in Scottish Rite Masonry:
4°- 32°:1952, invested by Corning, New York Scottish Rite Bodies, Northern Masonic Jurisdiction.
March 13, 1967, affiliated with Tampa, Florida, Scottish Rite Bodies, Southern Masonic Jurisdiction.
32°, KCCH: October 16, 1991.
33°, IGH: elected October 21, 1991; coroneted by the Supreme Council, 33°, October 22, 1991.
Grand Cross of the Court of Honour: October 3, 2003.

Scottish Rite Biography:
Brother Bilirakis was initiated, passed, and raised a Master Mason at *Garden City* Lodge, No. 183, in New York. In 1970 he affiliated with *Tarpon* Lodge, No. 112, Tarpon Springs, Florida. Brother Bilirakis received his Scottish Rite Degrees from the Valley of Corring, New York in 1952, became a dual member in Pittsburg, Pennsylvania in 1956, and in 1967 affiliated with the Valley of Tampa. In 1991 Brother Bilirakis received the rank and decoration of a Knight Commander of the Court of Honour, and on the same Session of the Supreme Council, 33°, S.J., was elected and coroneted as 33°, Inspector General Honorary. Ill. Michael Bilirakis, 33°, was awarded the Grand Cross of the Court of Honour on October 3, 2003.

Bibliography:
Archive of the Supreme Council, 33°, S.J.
Scottish Rite Bulletin Valley of Tampa. July–August 2011.

2003

Joseph Daniel Brackin
Grand Cross of the Court of Honour at age 74 years, 1 month, and 14 days
Tenure 1 year, 1 month, and 24 days
Nomination by Dothan, Alabama Scottish Rite Bodies

Born: August 19, 1929 – Died: November 27, 2004
Life span: 75 years, 3 months, and 8 days
Electric Technician

Progress in Scottish Rite Masonry:
4°-14°: March 7, 1964, invested by *Dothan* Lodge of Perfection, Dothan.
15°-18°: March 7, 1964, invested by *Montgomery* Chapter of Rose Croix, Montgomery.
19°-30°: March 8, 1964, invested by *Montgomery* Council of Kadosh, Montgomery.
31°-32°: March 8, 1964, invested by *Montgomery* Consistory, Montgomery.
October 21, 1975, member of the Dothan Scottish Rite Bodies, Dothan.
32°, KCCH: October 18, 1971.
33°, IGH: elected October 20, 1975; coroneted by Ill. James Richard Rogers, 33°, Sovereign Grand
Inspector General for Alabama, December 13, 1975.
Grand Cross of the Court of Honour: October 3, 2003.

Scottish Rite Biography:
Ill. Brackin's distinguished Masonic career includes being a longtime Master of *Pythagoras* Lodge, No.
659, Dothan. A member of the Scottish Rite Bodies of Dothan, he was honored for his outstanding service
by his election to the rank of KCCH in 1971, his election to receive the 33° in 1975, his appointment as
Orient of Alabama Personal Representative in 1999, and his election as a Grand Cross in 2003. He was
only the second Alabama Scottish Rite Mason to receive this highest honor of our Order.

Bibliography:
Archive of the Supreme Council, 33°, S.J.
In Memoriam. *Transactions*. 2005: 264.

2003

George Richard Carr
Grand Cross of the Court of Honour at age 81 years, 2 months, and 2 days
Tenure 4 years, 10 month, and 22 days
Nomination by Des Moines, Iowa Scottish Rite Bodies

Born: August 1, 1922 – Died: August 12, 2008
Life span: 86 years and 11 days
Secretary, Valley of Des Moines

Progress in Scottish Rite Masonry:
4°-14°: October 2, 1948, invested by *Tabernacle* Lodge of Perfection, Des Moines.
15°-18°: October 9, 1948, invested by *Emmanuel* Chapter of Rose Croix, Des Moines.
19°-30°: October 16, 1948, invested by *Cyrus* Council of Kadosh, Des Moines.
31°-32°: October 23, 1948, invested by *Des Moines* Consistory, Des Moines.
32°, KCCH: October 20, 1975.
33°, IGH: elected October 21, 1985; coroneted by Ill Harry S. Barrows, 33°, Sovereign Grand Inspector General for Iowa December 7, 1985.
Grand Cross of the Court of Honour: October 3, 2003.

Scottish Rite Biography:
Brother Carr was a Master Mason of *Capital* Lodge, No. 110, Des Moines. Ill. Carr joined the Scottish Rite in 1948, received the rank and decoration of KCCH in 1975, was coroneted Inspector General Honorary in 1985, and received the Grand Cross of the Court of Honour in 2003. He was a member of the 20° and 32° casts, Secretary-Registrar and Personal Representative of the Des Moines Scottish Rite Bodies, Orient Personal Representative, and Secretary of the Iowa Scottish Rite Masonic Foundation.

Bibliography:
Archive of the Supreme Council, 33°, S.J.
In Memoriam. *Transactions.* 2003: 254.

2003

Robert Glenn Davis
Grand Cross of the Court of Honour at age 55 years, 5 months, and 20 days
Tenure present
Nomination by Guthrie, Oklahoma Scottish Rite Bodies

Born: April 13, 1948 – present
Secretary Emeritus of the Guthrie Scottish Rite Bodies

Progress in Scottish Rite Masonry:
4°-14°: May 24, 1971, invested by *Guthrie* Lodge of Perfection, Guthrie.
15°-18°: May 24, 1971, invested by *Guthrie* Chapter of Rose Croix, Guthrie.
19°-30°: May 25, 1971, invested by *Guthrie* Council of Kadosh, Guthrie.
31°-32°: May 25, 1971, invested by *Guthrie* Consistory, Guthrie.
32°, KCCH: October 19, 1981.
33°, IGH: elected October 16, 1989; coroneted by the Supreme Council, 33°, S.J., October 18, 1989.
Grand Cross of the Court of Honour: October 3, 2003.

Scottish Rite Biography:
Brother Davis was raised a Master Mason in *Corinthian* Lodge, No. 307, in Cherokee, and later affiliated with *Albert Pike* Lodge, No. 162, in Guthrie, and *Garfield* Lodge, No. 501, in Enid. In 1971 Brother Davis joined the Scottish Rite Bodies of the Valley of Guthrie, and ten years after that received his first Scottish Rite honor a Knight Commander of the Court of Honour. On the Session of the Supreme Council for 1989 he was elected and coroneted a 33°, Inspector General Honorary. Ill. Robert Glenn Davis, 33°, having served the Guthrie Scottish Rite Bodies as Secretary for 30 years. At the same time, Ill. Davis carried out many key positions on an Orient and Supreme Council level: served as the editor of *Oklahoma Scottish Rite Mason*, the *Plumbline*, *Heredom*, the Transactions of the Scottish Rite Research Society, and as Vice President of the Scottish Rite Research Society. On October 3, 2003, Ill. Robert Glenn Davis, 33°, was elected by the Supreme Council to receive the Scottish Rite's highest honor, the Grand Cross of the Court of Honour. Currently Ill. Davis serves on a Board of Directors of the Scottish Rite Research Society

Bibliography:
Archive of the Supreme Council, 33°, S.J.

2003

Arnold D. Hermann
Grand Cross of the Court of Honour at age 50 years, 4 months, and 13 days
Tenure present

Nomination by Long Beach, California Scottish Rite Bodies

Born: May 20, 1953 – present
Software Video

Progress in Scottish Rite Masonry:
4°-14°: July 16, 1988, invested by *Long Beach* Lodge of Perfection, Long Beach.
15°-18°: July 16, 1988, invested by *Long Beach* Chapter of Rose Croix, Long Beach.
19°-30°: July 16, 1988, invested by *Long Beach* Council of Kadosh, Long Beach.
31°-32°: July 16, 1988, invested by *Long Beach* Consistory, Long Beach.
32°, KCCH: October 21, 1991.
33°, IGH: elected October 18, 1993; coroneted by the Supreme Council, 33°, S.J., October 19, 1993.
Grand Cross of the Court of Honour: October 3, 2003.

Scottish Rite Biography:
Brother Arnold D. Hermann is a Master Mason in *Lomita* Lodge, No. 644, Lomita, California. He received the Scottish Rite Degrees on July 16, 1988, which were invested by the Long Beach Scottish Rite Bodies. Brother Hermann became a KCCH on October 2, 1991, and on the following Session of the Supreme Council was elected and coroneted a 33°, IGH. Brother Hermann, a native of Romania has greatly assisted the rebirth of Freemasonry and the Scottish Rite particularly throughout much of Eastern Europe. On November 1990, in Prague, Sovereign Grand Commander C. Fred Kleinknecht, 33°, communicated the Fourth through Fourteenth Degrees on eighteen Czechoslovakian Brothers assisted by Ill. H. Douglas Lemons, 33°, SGIG in California, and Arnold Hermann, 32°. In May 1991, along with the Grand Commander and some Members of the Supreme Council, Brother Hermann attended as guest and observer the Thirty-six Conference of European Grand Commanders. On June 8, 1991, Brother Hermann again assisted Grand Commander and SGIG Lemons of conferring Scottish Rite Degrees during a one-day Reunion in Prague on approximately fifty Slavic Brethren. For carrying on the mission of creating a new arena of fraternal harmony and progress, Brother Hermann on October 3, 2003, was elected the Grand Cross of the Court of Honour.

Bibliography:
Archive of the Supreme Council, 33°, S.J.
Allocution. *Transactions*. 1991: 26-27.

2003

Sidney Michael Johnston
Grand Cross of the Court of Honour at age 73 years, 4 months, and 24 days
Tenure 13 years, 7 months, and 10 days
Nomination by Anchorage, Alaska Scottish Rite Bodies

Born: May 9, 1930 – Died: May 13, 2017
Life span: 86 years and 4 days
Accountant

Progress in Scottish Rite Masonry:
4°-14°: October 23, 1965, invested by *Anchorage* Lodge of Perfection, Anchorage.
15°-18°: April 23, 1966, invested by *Anchorage* Chapter of Rose Croix, Anchorage.
19°-30°: May 21, 1966, invested by *Anchorage* Council of Kadosh, Anchorage.
31°-32°: May 22, 1966, invested by *Anchorage* Consistory, Anchorage.
32°, KCCH: October 15, 1973.
33°, IGH: elected October 17, 1977, coroneted November 19, 1977, by Ill. Robert John Rogers, 33°, Deputy for Alaska.
Grand Cross of the Court of Honour: October 3, 2003.

Scottish Rite Biography:
Brother Johnston entered Masonry in May of 1956, being raised in *Oakland* Lodge, No. 16, Oakland, Oregon. Later, moving to Anchorage, Alaska, Brother Johnston received the Scottish Rite Degrees from the Valley of Anchorage, completing the Degree work in May of 1966. Commencing soon thereafter, he served the Valley of Anchorage as Treasurer over two separate periods, spanning more than 25 years. During that time, he was instrumental in establishing the Alaska Scottish Rite Foundation, and Rite Care Clinics in Anchorage, Alaska, and Fairbanks, Alaska.

Bibliography:
In Memoriam. *Transactions.* 2017: 117.

2003

Arthur Joseph Kerr
Grand Cross of the Court of Honour at age 80 years, 2 months, and 25 days
Tenure 12 years, 10 months, and 19 days
Nomination by Balboa, Panama Canal Scottish Rite Bodies

Born: July 8, 1923 – Died: August 22, 2016
Life span: 92 years, 11 months, and 13 days
U.S. Army Programs Officer

Progress in Scottish Rite Masonry:
4°-14°: July 20, 1968, invested by *Panama Canal* Lodge of Perfection, Balboa.
15°-18°: August 17, 1968, invested by *Panama Canal* Chapter of Rose Croix, Balboa.
19°-30°: September 21, 1968, invested by *Panama Canal* Council of Kadosh, Balboa.
31°-32°: October 19, 1968, invested by *Panama Canal* Consistory, Balboa.
32°, KCCH: October 18, 1987.
33°, IGH: elected October 21, 1991; coroneted by the Supreme Council, 33°, S.J., October 22, 1991.
Deputy: January 3, 1996 – retired December 31, 2014.
Grand Cross of the Court of Honour: October 3, 2003.

Scottish Rite Biography:
Brother Kerr was raised a Master Mason in *Army* Lodge in the Canal Zone, which later became *Balboa* Lodge, where he served as Master. In October of 1968, he joined the Scottish Rite Bodies of Balboa, Canal Zone. An active and involved member, he was Secretary of the Balboa Bodies from 1988 to January 1996 and was of key assistance in the reconstitution in 1994 of the Colombia Supreme Council. Appointed in January of 1996, he served as Deputy in the Panama Canal for 19 years, retiring in 2015. Ill∴ Kerr was Invested a Knight Commander of the Court of Honour in 1987, Coronated an Inspector General Honorary 33° in 1991, and elected by the Supreme Council to receive the Grand Cross, Court of Honour on October 3, 2003.

Bibliography:
Archive of the Supreme Council, 33°, S.J.
In Memoriam. Transactions. 2017: 111.

2003

J. C. Alvin Montgomery, Jr.
Grand Cross of the Court of Honour at age 61 years, 1month, and 5 days
Tenure present
Nomination by Dallas, Texas Scottish Rite Bodies

Born: August 28, 1942 – present
Hospital Administration

Progress in Scottish Rite Masonry:
4°-14°: August 23, 1975, invested by *Dallas* Lodge of Perfection, Dallas.
15°-18°: August 23, 1975, invested by *Dallas* Chapter of Rose Croix, Dallas.
19°-30°: August 23, 1975, invested by *Dallas* Council of Kadosh, Dallas.
31°-32°: August 23, 1975, invested by *Dallas* Consistory, Dallas.
32°, KCCH: October 15, 1979.
33°, IGH: elected October 21, 1991; coroneted by Ill. Sam Hilburn, 33°, Sovereign Grand Inspector
General for Texas on November 16, 1991.
Grand Cross of the Court of Honour: October 3, 2003.

Scottish Rite Biography:
Brother Montgomery was raised a Master Mason in *John L. DeGrazier* Lodge, No. 1349, in Dallas. Later
he affiliated with *Knox-Corinthian* Lodge, No. 851. Brother Montgomery joined the Scottish Rite Bodies
of the Valley of Dallas and became a 32° Master of the Royal Secret on August 23, 1975. In 1979, he was
invested as a Knight Commander of the Court of Honour, and during the Session of the Supreme Council
of 1991 was elected a 33°, Inspector General Honorary and coroneted by Ill. Sam Hilburn, 33°, Sovereign
Grand Inspector General for Texas on November 16, 1991. More than two decades Brother Montgomery
served as President at Texas Scottish Rite Hospital for Children. The Texas Office of Prevention of
Developmental Disabilities established an annual award named in honor of J. C. Alvin Montgomery Jr., for
his dedication to the safety and well-being of children in the hospital. On October 3, 2003, Ill. J. C. Alvin
Montgomery Jr., 33°, received the highest honor of the Supreme Council, the Grand Cross of the Court of
Honour. At present Brother Montgomery is a Chairman Emeritus Texas Scottish Rite Hospital.

Bibliography:
Archive of the Supreme Council, 33°, S.J.

Fitzhugh Knox Powell
Grand Cross of the Court of Honour at age 75 years, 8 months, and 6 days
Tenure present
Nomination by Jacksonville, Florida Scottish Rite Bodies

Born: January 27, 1928 – present
Insurance Executive

Progress in Scottish Rite Masonry:
4°-14°: March 26, 1955, invested by *Jacksonville* Lodge of Perfection, Jacksonville.
15°-18°: March 29, 1955, invested by *Jacksonville* Chapter of Rose Croix, Jacksonville.
19°-30°: April 2, 1955, invested by *Jacksonville* Council of Kadosh, Jacksonville.
31°-32°: April 2, 1955, invested by *Jacksonville* Consistory, Jacksonville.
32°, KCCH: October 15, 1979.
33°, IGH: elected October 9, 1995; coroneted by Ill. Robert Goldsmith, 33°, Sovereign Grand Inspector General for Florida November 25, 1995.
Grand Cross of the Court of Honour: October 3, 2003.

Scottish Rite Biography:
Brother Powel is a Master Mason in *Solomon* Lodge, No. 20, in Jacksonville. He joined the Scottish Rite Bodies in Jacksonville and became a Master of the Royal Secret on March 26, 1955. He was elected a Knight Commander of the Court of Honour in 1979, and 33°, Inspector General Honorary on October 9, 1995. Brother Powell was coroneted by Ill. Robert Goldsmith, 33°, Sovereign Grand Inspector General for Florida November 25, 1995, and continues a loyal supporter of his Valley by steady contributions to the Almoner and Building Funds. Ill. Fitzhugh Knox Powell, 33°, received the Scottish Rite's highest honor, the Grand Cross on October 3, 2003.

Bibliography:
Archive of the Supreme Council, 33°, S.J.

2003

Alexander Gus Spanos
Grand Cross of the Court of Honour at age 79 years, 11 months, and 5 days
Tenure 15 years and 6 days
Nomination by Stockton, California Scottish Rite Bodies

Born: September 28, 1923 – Died: October 9, 2018
Life span: 94 years, 11 months, and 11 days
Real Estate Developer

Progress in Scottish Rite Masonry:
4°-14°: November 29, 1951, invested by *Stockton* Lodge of Perfection, Stockton.
15°-18°: November 29, 1951, invested by *Stockton* Chapter of Rose Croix, Stockton.
19°-30°: November 30, 1951, invested by *Stockton* Council of Kadosh, Stockton.
31°-32°: December 1, 1951, invested by *Stockton* Consistory, Stockton.
32°, KCCH: October 19, 1981.
33°, IGH: elected October 9, 1995; coroneted by Ill. Homer Douglas Lemons, 33°, Sovereign Grand Inspector General for California December 2, 1995.
Grand Cross of the Court of Honour: October 3, 2003.

Scottish Rite Biography:
Brother Alexander Gus Spanos was a Master Mason in *San Joaquin* Lodge, No. 19, Stockton. He received his 4°-14° invested by *Stockton* Lodge of Perfection, and 15°-18° invested by *Stockton* Chapter of Rose Croix, on November 29, 1951. He received 19°-30° on November 30, 1951, invested by *Stockton* Council of Kadosh. On December 1, 1951, he received 31°-32°, invested by *Stockton* Consistory. Brother Spanos received his KCCH on October 19, 1981. He was elected 33°, IGH, on October 9, 1995, and was coroneted December 2, 1995, by Ill. Homer Douglas Lemons, 33°, Sovereign Grand Inspector General for California. Ill. Spanos, 33°, was elected the Grand Cross of the Court of Honour on October 3, 2003.

Bibliography:
Archive of the Supreme Council, 33°, S.J.
In Memoriam. *Transactions*. 2019: 135.

2003

Roland Thornton Stayton
Grand Cross of the Court of Honour at age 74 years, 11 months, and 17 days
Tenure present
Nomination by Louisville, Kentucky Scottish Rite Bodies

Born: September 16, 1928 – present
Dispatcher

Progress in Scottish Rite Masonry:
4°-14°: September 25, 1969, invested by *Louisville* Lodge of Perfection, Louisville.
15°-18°: October 9, 1969, invested by *Louisville* Chapter of Rose Croix, Louisville.
19°-30°: October 30, 1969, invested by *Louisville* Council of Kadosh, Louisville.
31°-32°: November 15, 1969, invested by *Louisville* Grand Consistory, Louisville.
32°, KCCH: October 20, 1975.
33°, IGH: elected October 19, 1981; coroneted by Ill. George Richard Effinger, 33°, Sovereign Grand Inspector General for Kentucky November 28, 1981.
Grand Cross of the Court of Honour: October 3, 2003.

Scottish Rite Biography:
Brother Stayton is a Master Mason in *Shively* Lodge, No. 951, in Louisville. He joined the Scottish Rite Bodies of the Valley of Louisville, and on November 15, 1969, became a 32°, Master of the Royal Secret. He received the rank and decoration of a Knight Commander of the Court of Honour in 1975; on a Session of the Supreme Council of 1981 was elected 33°, Inspector General Honorary, and coroneted by Ill. George Richard Effinger, 33°, Sovereign Grand Inspector General for Kentucky on November 28, 1981. Brother Stayton served his Valley as an Almoner. Ill. Ronald Thornton Stayton, 33°, received the Scottish Rite's highest honor, the Grand Cross in 2003.

Bibliography:
Archive of the Supreme Council, 33°, S.J.

2003

Charles Harrington Webber
Grand Cross of the Court of Honour at age 85 years, 3 months, and 21 days
Tenure 4 years, 5 months, and 6 days
Nomination by Portland, Oregon Scottish Rite Bodies

Born: July 12, 1917 – Died: March 9, 2008
Life span: 90 years, 7 months, and 27 days
Accountant

Progress in Scottish Rite Masonry:
4°-14°: May 17, 1949, invested by *Oregon* Lodge of Perfection, Portland.
15°-18°: May 18, 1949, invested by *Ainsworth* Chapter of Rose Croix, Portland.
19°-30°: May 24, 1949, invested by *Multnomah* Council of Kadosh, Portland.
31°-32°: May 31, 1949, invested by *Oregon* Consistory, Portland.
32°, KCCH: October 17, 1961.
33°, IGH: elected October 17, 1983; coroneted by Ill. David O. Johnson, 33°, Sovereign Grand Inspector General for Oregon November 5, 1983.
Grand Cross of the Court of Honour: October 3, 2003.

Scottish Rite Biography:
Brother Webber was raised a Master Mason in *Friendship* Lodge, No. 160, 1944. He joined the Scottish Rite in 1949, received the rank and decoration of KCCH in 1961, was coroneted an Inspector General Honorary in 1983, and was elected a Grand Cross of the Court of Honour in 2003.

Bibliography:
Archive of the Supreme Council, 33°, S. J.
In Memoriam. *Transactions*. 2009: 251.

2005

John Robert Amidon
Grand Cross of the Court of Honour at age 66 years, 3 months, and 12 days
Tenure present
Nomination by Phoenix, Arizona Scottish Rite Bodies

Born: June 18, 1939 – present
Data Processing Manager

Progress in Scottish Rite Masonry:
4°-14°: November 21, 1985, invested by *Phoenix* Lodge of Perfection, Phoenix.
15°-18°: November 21, 1985, invested by *Phoenix* Chapter of Rose Croix, Phoenix.
19°-30°: November 21, 1985, invested by *Phoenix* Council of Kadosh, Phoenix.
31°-32°: November 23, 1985, invested by *Phoenix* Consistory, Phoenix.
32°, KCCH: October 23, 1991.
33°, IGH: elected October 6, 1997; coroneted by Ill. Robert F. Hannon, 33°, Sovereign Grand Inspector General in Arizona December 13, 1997.
Grand Cross of the Court of Honour: September 30, 2005.

Scottish Rite Biography:
Brother Amidon was raised a Master Mason in *Silver Trowel* Lodge, No. 29, in Phoenix, Arizona. He joined the Scottish Rite Bodies in the Valley of Phoenix and became a Master of the Royal Secret on November 23, 1985. He received the rank and decoration of a Knight Commander of the Court of Honour in 1991; elected 33°, Inspector General Honorary and coroneted by Ill. Robert F. Hannon, 33°, Sovereign Grand Inspector General in Arizona December 13, 1997. Brother Amidon served his Valley as Personal Representative for SGIG for a long term. On September 30, 2005, Ill. John Robert Amidon, 33°, received the highest honor of the Supreme Council, 33°, S.J., the Grand Cross of the Court of Honour.

Bibliography:
Archive of the Supreme Council, 33°, S.J.

Frederick William Clarke, Jr.

Grand Cross of the Court of Honour at age 82 years, 8 months, and 3 days
Tenure 7 years, 2 months, and 4 days
Nomination by Mobile, Alabama Scottish Rite Bodies

Born: February 27, 1923 – Died: December 4, 2012
Life span: 89 years, 9 months, and 7 days
Banker

Progress in Scottish Rite Masonry:
4°-14°: April 28, 1953, invested by *Mobile* Lodge of Perfection, Mobile.
15°-18°: April 29, 1953, invested by *Mobile* Chapter of Rose Croix, Mobile.
19°-30°: April 30, 1953, invested by *Mobile* Council of Kadosh, Mobile.
31°-32°: April 30, 1953, invested by *Mobile* Consistory, Mobile.
32°, KCCH: October 22, 1957.
33°, IGH: elected October 19, 1965; coroneted by Ill. Frederic William Clarke, 33°, Sovereign Grand Inspector General December 4, 1965.
Deputy: December 10, 1968 – resigned November 6, 1973.
Grand Cross of the Court of Honour: September 30, 2005.

Scottish Rite Biography:
Brother Clarke was Master Mason in *Mobile* Lodge, No. 40, Mobile. He became a Master of the Royal Secret in 1953, served as Wise Master of *Mobile* Chapter of Rose Croix in 1955, was invested with the rank and decoration of a Knight Commander of the Court of Honour, and was coroneted as Inspector General Honorary in 1965. He served the Valley of Mobile as Assistant Almoner and Treasurer. In 1968, he was appointed Deputy of the Supreme Council of Alabama. Ill. Clarke, 33°, was elected to receive the Grand Cross of the Court of Honour on October 1, 2005.

Bibliography:
Archive of the Supreme Council, 33°, S.J.
In Memoriam. *Transactions.* 2013: 190.

2005

Arthur Robert Datnoff
Grand Cross of the Court of Honour at age 87 years, 8 months, and 22 days
Tenure 2 years 11 months, and 12 days
Nomination by Columbia, South Carolina Scottish Rite Bodies

Born: May 8, 1918 – Died: August 12, 2008
Life span: 90 years, 3 months, and 4 days
U.S. Army Colonel

Progress in Scottish Rite Masonry:
4°-14°: September 26, 1981, invested by *Columbia* Lodge of Perfection, Columbia.
15°-18°: October 10, 1981, invested by *Columbia* Chapter of Rose Croix, Columbia.
19°-30°: October 10, 1981, invested by *Columbia* Council of Kadosh, Columbia.
31°-32°: April 3, 1982, invested by *Columbia* Consistory, Columbia.
32°, KCCH: October 16, 1989.
33°, IGH: elected October 18, 1993; coroneted by Ill. H. Wallace Reid, 33°, Sovereign Grand Inspector General for South Carolina November 20, 1993.
Grand Cross of the Court of Honour: September 30, 2005.

Scottish Rite Biography:
Brother Arthur was raised a Master Mason in *Acacia* Lodge, No. 94, Columbia, South Carolina, in 1981. He became a Master of the Royal Secret in 1983, received the rank and decoration of a KCCH in 1989, was coroneted an Inspector General Honorary in 1993, and received the Grand Cross of the Court of Honour in 2005.

Bibliography:
Archive of the Supreme Council, 33°, S.J.
In Memoriam. *Transactions.* 2009: 255.

241

2005

Earl Elmer Ihle, Jr.
Grand Cross of the Court of Honour at age 52 years, 11 months, and 16 days
Tenure present
Nomination by Baltimore, Maryland Scottish Rite Bodies

Born: October 14, 1952 – present
Director of Development for the Supreme Council, 33°

Progress in Scottish Rite Masonry:
4°-14°: October 16, 1974, invested by *Albert Pike* Lodge of Perfection, Baltimore.
15°-18°: October 23, 1974, invested by *Meredith* Chapter of Rose Croix, Baltimore.
19°-30°: November 16, 1974, invested by *Maryland* Council of Kadosh, Baltimore.
31°-32°: November 16, 1974, invested by *Chesapeake* Consistory, Baltimore.
32°, KCCH: October 21, 1991.
33°, IGH: elected October 6, 1997; coroneted by the Supreme Council, 33°, S.J., October 7, 1997.
Grand Cross of the Court of Honour: September 30, 2005.

Scottish Rite Biography:
Brother Ihle was raised a Master Mason in *Warren* Lodge, No. 51, at Baltimore. In 1974, he joined the Scottish Rite Bodies of the Valley of Baltimore and became a Master of the Royal Secret on November 16, 1974. He was invested as a Knight Commander of the Court of Honour on October 21, 1991, elected and coroneted by the Supreme Council a 33°, Inspector General Honorary on October 7, 1997. On February 2, 1999, Sovereign Grand Commander C. Fred Kleinknecht, 33°, appointed Ill. Earl E. Ihle, 33°, as Director of Major Gifts. Bro. Ihle has been a member of the Fraternity for 25 years and had a strong background in fund-raising. Shortly after, Bro. Ihle was appointed Director of Development for the Supreme Council. He has organized a wide variety of effective fund-rasing initiatives and implemented several new programs for Scottish Rite Members and friends. On September 30, 2005, Ill. Earl Elmer Ihle, 33°, was awarded the Grand Cross of the Court of Honour.

Bibliography:
Archive of the Supreme Council, 33°, S.J.

2005

James Lynn Johnston
Grand Cross of the Court of Honour at age 76 years, 7 months, and 14 days
Tenure 13 years, 4 months, and 8 days
Nomination by Tokyo, Japan and Korea Scottish Rite Bodies

Born: February 16, 1929 – February 8, 2019
Life span: 89 years, 11 months, and 22 days
Dental Technician

Progress in Scottish Rite Masonry:
4°-14°: April 25, 1963, invested by *Tokyo* Lodge of Perfection, Tokyo.
15°-18°: April 25, 1963, invested by *Tokyo* Chapter of Rose Croix, Tokyo.
19°-30°: April 26, 1963, invested by *Tokyo* Council of Kadosh, Tokyo.
31°-32°: April 26, 1963, invested by *Tokyo* Consistory, Tokyo.
32°, KCCH: October 15, 1973.
33°, IGH: elected October 19, 1987; coroneted by Ill. Floren L. Quick, 33°, at Tokyo, Japan November 27, 1987.
Deputy: for Japan and Korea November 1, 2004 – retired, April 1, 2016.
Grand Cross of the Court of Honour: September 30, 2005.

Scottish Rite Biography:
Brother Johnston began his involvement in Masonry with the Order of DeMolay. In 1963, he received the 4°-32° in the Valley of Tokyo, Japan. He was invested with the rank and decoration of a Knight Commander of the Court of Honour in 1983 and coroneted a 33° Inspector General Honorary in 1987. He served as Orient Personal Representative of Japan from 1991 and was a charter member of the Scottish Rite Research Society. In 2004, Grand Commander Ronald A. Seale, 33°, appointed him Deputy of the Supreme Council in the Orient of Japan and Korea, and he retired in 2016. He received the Grand Cross of the Court of Honour on October 4, 2005.

Bibliography:
Archive of the Supreme Council, 33°, S.J.
In Memoriam. *Transactions*. 2019: 129.

2005

John Edward Kelly
Grand Cross of the Court of Honour at age 83 years, 9 months, and 4 days
1 year, 5 months, and 13 days
Nomination by San Antonio, Texas Scottish Rite Bodies

Born: January 26, 1922 – Died: May 13, 2007
Life span: 85 years, 3 months, and 17 days
Office Executive

Progress in Scottish Rite Masonry:
4°-14°: January 27, 1922, invested by *San Antonio* Lodge of Perfection, San Antonio.
15°-18°: February 10, 1922, invested by *San Antonio* Chapter of Rose Croix, San Antonio.
19°-30°: February 10, 1922, invested by *San Antonio* Council of Kadosh, San Antonio.
31°-32°: March 10, 1922, invested by *San Antonio* Consistory, San Antonio.
32°, KCCH: October 15, 1979.
33°, IGH: elected October 17, 1983; coroneted by Ill. John Wilkins Chandler, 33°, Sovereign Grand Inspector General for Texas November 9, 1983.
Grand Cross of the Court of Honour: September 30, 2005.

Scottish Rite Biography:
Brother Kelly joined *Blue Bonnet* Lodge, No. 1219, San Antonio. In 1962 Ill. Kelly joined the San Antonio Scottish Rite. He received the Rank and Decoration of a KCCH in 1979, was coroneted an Inspector General Honorary in 1983, and received the Grand Cross of the Court of Honour in 2005. He was General Secretary of the San Antonio Bodies for nine years, and then served as Personal Representative of the SGIG in Texas for the South Texas area. He also served on the Executive Committee of the Texas Scottish Rite Children's Hospital.

Bibliography:
Archive of the Supreme Council, 33°, S.J.
In Memoriam. *Transactions.* 2007: 246.

2005

James Grubbs Martin
Grand Cross of the Court of Honour at age 69 years, 9 months, and 19 days
Tenure present
Nomination by Charlotte, North Carolina Scottish Rite Bodies

Born: December 11, 1935 – present
U.S. Congressman/Governor

Progress in Scottish Rite Masonry:
4°-14°: October 14, 1975, invested by *Charlotte* Lodge of Perfection, Charlotte.
15°-18°: October 14, 1975, invested by *Mecklenburg* Chapter of Rose Croix, Charlotte.
19°-30°: October 15, 1975, invested by *Charlotte* Council of Kadosh, Charlotte.
31°-32°: October 15, 1975, invested by *Carolina* Consistory, Charlotte.
32°, KCCH: October 19, 1981.
33°, IGH: elected October 21, 1985; coroneted by Ill. Herbert Lloyd Wilkerson, 33°, Sovereign Grand Inspector General for North Carolina November 23, 1985.
Grand Cross of the Court of Honour: September 30, 2005.

Scottish Rite Biography:
Brother Martin is a Member of *Phalanx* Lodge, No. 31, at Charlotte. He became a member of Charlotte Scottish Rite Bodies in 1975. Brother Martin was invested as a Knight Commander of the Court of Honour in 1981, elected 33°, Inspector General Honorary on October 21, 1985, and coroneted by Ill. Herbert Lloyd Wilkerson, 33°, Sovereign Grand Inspector General for North Carolina November 23, 1985. On September 30, 2005, Ill. James Grubbs Martin, 33°, received the highest honor of the Supreme Council, the Grand Cross of the Court of Honour.

Bibliography:
Archive of the Supreme Council, 33°, S.J.

2005

Charles Henry Moore
Grand Cross of the Court of Honour at age 76 years, 11 months, and 3 days
Tenure 13 years, 4 months, and 12 days
Nomination by Cheyenne, Wyoming Scottish Rite Bodies

Born: October 3, 1928 – Died: February 12, 2019
Life span: 90 years, 4 months, and 9 days
Contractor

Progress in Scottish Rite Masonry:
4°-14°: April 22, 1964, invested by *Rocky Mountain* Lodge of Perfection, Cheyenne.
15°-18°: October 22, 1964, invested by *Albert Pike* Chapter of Rose Croix, Cheyenne.
19°-30°: October 29, 1965, invested by *Cheyenne* Council of Kadosh, Cheyenne.
31°-32°: October 30, 1965, invested by *Wyoming* Consistory, Cheyenne.
32°, KCCH: October 20, 1975.
33°, IGH: Elected October 15, 1979; coroneted November 1, 1979, by Ill. John Floyd Holland, 33°,
Sovereign Grand Inspector General for Wyoming.
Grand Cross of the Court of Honour: September 30, 2005.

Scottish Rite Biography:
Brother Charles Henry Moore was a Master Mason in *Rocky Mountain* Lodge, No. 40, Within Scottish
Rite Masonsry, on April 22, 1964, he received 4°-14°, with which he was invested by *Rocky Mountain*
Lodge of Perfection, Cheyenne. On the same day, he received 15°-18°, which were invested by *Albert Pike*
Chapter of Rose Croix, Cheyenne. The following day the *Cheyenne* Council of Kadosh, Cheyenne,
invested him with 19°-30°. Finally, on October 30, 1965, he was invested with 31°-32° by *Wyoming*
Consistory, Cheyenne. On October 20, 1975, he become a KCCH. On October 15, 1979, he was elected to
33°, IGH. He was coroneted November 1, 1979, by Ill. John Floyd Holland, 33°, Sovereign Grand
Inspector General for Wyoming. Brother Moore received his Grand Cross of the Court of Honour on
September 30, 2005.

Bibliography:
Archive of the Supreme Council, 33°, S. J.
In Memoriam. *Transactions*. 2019: 133.

2005

Doyle Wayne Rogers
Grand Cross of the Court of Honour at age 87 years, 11 months, and 20 days
Tenure 7 years, 4 months, and 4 days
Nomination by Little Rock, Arkansas Scottish Rite Bodies

Born: October 20, 1918 – Died: February 4, 2013
Life span: 94 years, 4 months, and 14 days
Businessman

Progress in Scottish Rite Masonry:
4°-14°: November 2, 1953, invested by *Arkansas* Lodge of Perfection, Little Rock.
15°-18°: November 3, 1953, invested by *Arkansas* Chapter of Rose Croix, Little Rock.
19°-30°: November 3, 1953, invested by *Arkansas* Council of Kadosh, Little Rock.
31°-32°: November 4, 1953, invested by *Arkansas* Consistory, Little Rock.
32°, KCCH: October 4, 1999.
33°, IGH: elected October 3, 2001; coroneted by Ill. Dwane F. Treat, 33°, Sovereign Grand Inspector General for Arkansas December 1, 2001.
Grand Cross of the Court of Honour: September 30, 2005.

Scottish Rite Biography:
Ill. Rogers was raised to the Sublime Degree of a Master Mason in *Mt. Zion* Lodge, No. 10 in Batesville, Arkansas, on September 14, 1951. He became a Master of the Royal Secret in the Valley of Little Rock on November 4, 1953, was invested with the rank and decoration of a Knight Commander of the Court of Honour in 1999, was coroneted an Inspector General Honorary in 2001, and was elected by the Supreme Council to receive the Grand Cross of the Court of Honour in 2005.

Bibliography:
Archive of the Supreme Council, 33°, S.J.
In Memoriam. *Transactions*. 2013: 194.

2005

Robert Ned Shupe
Grand Cross of the Court of Honour at age 76 years, 2 months, and 4 days
Tenure present
Nomination by Salt Lake City, Utah Scottish Rite Bodies

Born: July 26, 1929 - present
Life span: present
Printer

Progress in Scottish Rite Masonry:
4°-14°: April 21, 1988, invested by *Salt Lake City* Lodge of Perfection, Salt Lake City.
15°-18°: April 21, 1988, invested by *Salt Lake City* Chapter of Rose Croix, Salt Lake City.
19°-30°: April 22, 1988, invested by *Salt Lake City* Council of Kadosh, Salt Lake City.
31°-32°: April 23, 1988, invested by *Salt Lake City* Consistory, Salt Lake City.
32°, KCCH: October 6, 1997.
33°, IGH: elected October 3, 2001; coroneted by the Supreme Council, 33°, S.J., October 5, 2001.
Grand Cross of the Court of Honour: September 30, 2005.

Scottish Rite Biography:
Brother Shupe was raised a Master Mason in *Salt Lake* Lodge, No. 17, in Salt Lake. In 1988 he joined the Scottish Rite Bodies of the Salt Lake City Valley and became a 32° Master of the Royal Secret on April 22, 1988. Brother Shupe was invested as a Knight Commander of the Court of Honour in 1997; coroneted an Inspector General Honorary, 33° on October 5, 2001, and elected by the Supreme Council to receive the Grand Cross of the Court of Honour on September 30, 2005. Ill. Robert Ned Shupe, 33°, GC, is a Charter member of the Scottish Rite Children's Learning Center.

Bibliography:
Archive of the Supreme Council, 33°, S.J.

2005

Earl Ernst Walker
Grand Cross of the Court of Honour at age 85 years, 7 months, and 18 days
Tenure 5 years, 10 months, and 26 days
Nomination by St. Louis, Missouri Scottish Rite Bodies

Born: February 12, 1920 – Died: August 26, 2011
Life span: 91 years, 6 months, and 14 days
Businessman

Progress in Scottish Rite Masonry:
4°-14°: November 13, 1945, invested by *St. Louis* Lodge of Perfection, St. Louis.
15°-18°: November 14, 1945, invested by *St. Louis* Chapter of Rose Croix, St. Louis.
19°-30°: May 16, 1945, invested by *St. Louis* Council of Kadosh, St. Louis.
31°-32°: May 17, 1945, invested by *St. Louis* Consistory, St. Louis.
32°, KCCH: October 15, 1979.
33°, IGH: elected October 16, 1989; coroneted by Ill. Earl K. Dille, 33°, Sovereign Grand Inspector General for Missouri November 25, 1989.
Grand Cross of the Court of Honour: September 30, 2005.

Scottish Rite Biography:
Ill. Walker began his Masonic journey November 11, 1944, in *Kirkwood* Lodge, No. 484, Kirkwood, Missouri. He became a Master of the Royal Secret in the Valley of St. Louis on May 17, 1946, received the rank and decoration of a Knight Commander of the Court of Honour in 1979, and was coroneted an Inspector General Honorary in 1989. At the Supreme Council Biennial Session of 2005, he was elected to receive the Grand Cross of the Court of Honour. Through the tireless efforts of Bro. Earl and Myrtle, the Walker Scottish Rite Clinic for Childhood Language Disorders was founded in 1988 and had received over 15,000 St. Louis area children.

Bibliography:
Archive of the Supreme Council, 33°, S.J.
In Memoriam. *Transactions*. 2013: 180.
Photo courtesy of Carr Lane CEO Earl Walker Passes Away at 91 (designworldonline.com)

2005

Tommy Fu-Hai Weng
Grand Cross of the Court of Honour at age 72 years, 3 months, and 20 days
Tenure present
Nomination by Taipei, Taiwan Scottish Rite Bodies

Born: June 10, 1933 – present
Engineer

Progress in Scottish Rite Masonry:
4°-14°: September 27, 1974, invested by *Taipei* Lodge of Perfection, Taiwan.
15°-18°: September 27, 1974, invested by *Taipei* Chapter of Rose Croix, Taiwan.
19°-30°: September 27, 1974, invested by *Taipei* Council of Kadosh, Taiwan.
31°-32°: September 27, 1974, invested by *Taipei* Consistory, Taiwan.
32°, KCCH: October 17, 1983.
33°, IGH: elected October 16, 1989; coroneted by Ill. Ian Lin, 33°, Deputy December 1, 1989.
Deputy: for Taiwan and China: November 15, 1993 – June 10, 2013.
Grand Cross of the Court of Honour: September 30, 2005.

Scottish Rite Biography:
Brother Tommy Fu-Hai Weng was raised a Master Mason in *Sun* Lodge, No. 6, Taipei, Taiwan, ROC, on September 4, 1970. He became a Thirty-second Degree Mason in the Taipei Scottish Rite Bodies on September 28, 1974. For many services to Freemasonry and his community, Bro. Weng was invested with the rank and decoration of Knight Commander of the Court of Honour in 1983 and coroneted an Inspector General Honorary in 1989. On November 15, 1953, Ill. Tommy Fu-Hai Weng, 33°, was appointed as a Deputy for Taiwan and China and served in this capacity until June 10, 2013. During his Deputyship, on September 30, 2005, Ill. Tommy Fu-Hai Weng, 33°, received the highest honour of the Supreme Council, the Grand Cross of the Court of Honour.

Bibliography:
Archive of the Supreme Council, 33°, S.J.
Ill. Tommy F. H. Weng Appointed Deputy of Taiwan and China, *The New Age*, February 1994.

2005

Henry Herbert Philips Wilkins
Grand Cross of the Court of Honour at age 77 years and 20 days
Tenure present
Nomination by Pasadena, California Scottish Rite Bodies

Born: September 10, 1928 – present
Banker

Progress in Scottish Rite Masonry:
4°-14°: November 21, 1980, invested by *Pasadena* Lodge of Perfection, Pasadena.
15°-18°: November 22, 1980, invested by *Pasadena* Chapter of Rose Croix, Pasadena.
19°-30°: November 22, 1980, invested by *Pasadena* Council of Kadosh, Pasadena.
31°-32°: November 22, 1980, invested by *Pasadena* Consistory, Pasadena.
32°, KCCH: October 21, 1991.
33°, IGH: elected October 9, 1995; coroneted by Ill. Douglas Lemons, 33°, Sovereign Grand Inspector General for California December 9, 1995.
Grand Cross of the Court of Honour: September 30, 2005.

Scottish Rite Biography:
Brother Wilkins became a Mason in *Arcadia* Lodge, No. 278, in Arcadia and a 32° Master of the Royal Secret in *Pasadena* Consistory on November 22, 1991. He received the rank and decoration of a Knight Commander of the Court of Honour in 1991 and was coronated a 33° Inspector General Honorary by Ill. Douglas Lemons, 33°, Sovereign Grand Inspector General for California on December 9, 1995. Ill. Henry Herbert Philips Wilkins, 33°, served his Valley as a General Secretary from 1998 to 2012, and Personal Representative to Sovereign Grand Inspectors General Ill. Homer Douglas Lemons, 33° and Ill. William Farley Stovall, Jr., 33° from 2002 to 2012. The highest honor of the Supreme Council, the Grand Cross of the Court of Honour Ill. Wilkins, 33°, received on September 30, 2005.

Bibliography:
Archive of the Supreme Council, 33°, S.J.

2007

John Lee Atkinson
Grand Cross of the Court of Honour at age 78 years, 9 months, and 22 days
Tenure 4 years, 9 months, and 7 days
Nomination by Shreveport, Louisiana Scottish Rite Bodies

Born: December 2, 1928 – Died: May 31, 2012
Life span: 83 years, 5 months, and 29 days
U. S. Air Force

Progress in Scottish Rite Masonry:
4°-32°: October 25, 1957, invested by Bay City Scottish Rite Bodies, Michigan Northern Jurisdiction.
June 11, 1974, affiliated with Shreveport Scottish Rite Bodies, Shreveport.
32°, KCCH: October 19, 1981.
33°, IGH: elected October 21, 1985; coroneted by Ill. Dietrich Walter Jessen, 33°, Sovereign Grand Inspector General for Louisiana November 23, 1985.
Grand Cross of the Court of Honour: August 24, 2007.

Scottish Rite Biography:
Ill. Brother John began his life in Masonry, when raised to the Sublime Degrees of a Master Mason on May 22, 1957, in *All Sable* Lodge, No. 243 in Oscoda, Michigan, and became a Master of the Royal Secret in the Valley of Bay City (NMJ), in Bay City, Michigan in 1957. When transferred by the military to Barksdale AFB, in Shreveport, he affiliated with the Valley of Shreveport in 1974. Initially working on the stage crew during reunions, Bro. John was appointed Secretary of the Valley of Shreveport in January 1985, holding that appointment for twenty-four years. During this period, he also served as both Personal Representative and Secretary from 2001 to 2005. Bro. Atkinson was a pivotal and driving force in establishing the Louisiana Scottish Rite Speech and Language Foundation and opening of the first clinic in Shreveport. Ill. Atkinson received the rank and decoration of Knight Commander of the Court of Honour in 1981, was coroneted an Inspector General Honorary in 1985, and on August 24, 2007, was elected to receive the Grand Cross of the Court of Honour.

Bibliography:
Archive of the Supreme Council, 33°, S.J.
In Memoriam. *Transactions.* 2013: 185.

2007

James Orlin Burlingame, Sr.
Grand Cross of the Court of Honour at age 81 years, and 11 days
Tenure present
Nomination by Minneapolis, Minnesota Scottish Rite Bodies

Born: August 13, 1926 – present
Life span: present
Vice President of Sales, Jams & Jellie

Progress in Scottish Rite Masonry:
4°-14°: September 28, 1972, invested by *Minneapolis* Lodge of Perfection, Minneapolis.
15°-18°: October 19, 1972, invested by *Minneapolis* Chapter of Rose Croix, Minneapolis.
19°-30°: December 7, 1972, invested by *Minneapolis* Council of Kadosh, Minneapolis.
31°-32°: December 21, 1972, invested by *Minneapolis* Consistory, Minneapolis.
32°, KCCH: October 17, 1977.
33°, IGH: elected October 16, 1989; coroneted by Ill. Daniel F. Levenduski, 33°, Sovereign Grand Inspector General for Minnesota on December 9, 1989.
Grand Cross of the Court of Honour: August 24, 2007.

Scottish Rite Biography:
Brother Burlingame was raised to the Sublime Degrees on October 12, 1953, in Plymouth Lodge, No. 160, at Crystal Minnesota. In 1972 he joined the Scottish Rite Bodies of the Valley of Minnesota and became a 32° Master of the Royal Secret on December 21, 1972. A few years later on October 17, 1977, he received his first merit the rank and decoration of a Knight Commander of the Court of Honour. On the Session of the Supreme Council for 1989 Brother Burlingame was elected a 33°, Inspector General Honorary and coroneted by Ill. Daniel F. Levenduski, 33°, Sovereign Grand Inspector General for Minnesota on December 9, 1989. The highest honor of the Scottish Rite was invested on Ill. James Orlin Burlingame, Sr., 33°, on August 24, 2007.

Bibliography:
Archive of the Supreme Council, 33°, S.J.
Archive of the Valley of Minneapolis.

2007

Robert Allan Falk
Grand Cross of the Court of Honour at age 72 years, 10 months, and 1 day
Tenure 6 years, 5 months, and 26 days
Nomination by Omaha, Nebraska Scottish Rite Bodies

Born: October 23, 1934 Died: February 20, 2014
Life span: 81 years, 3 months, and 27 days
Banker

Progress in Scottish Rite Masonry:
4°-14°: November 27, 1962, invested by *Omaha* Lodge of Perfection, Omaha.
15°-18°: November 27, 1962, invested by *Omaha* Chapter of Rose Croix, Omaha.
19°-30°: November 28, 1962, invested by *Omaha* Council of Kadosh, Omaha.
31°-32°: November 29, 1962, invested by *Omaha* Consistory, Omaha.
32°, KCCH: October 3, 1967.
33°, IGH: elected October 20, 1975; coroneted by Ill. Herbert Alden Ronin, 33°, Sovereign Grand Inspector General for Nebraska December 6, 1975.
Grand Cross of the Court of Honour: August 24, 2007.

Scottish Rite Biography:
Brother Bob was raised a Master Mason in February 1958 at *Covenant-Welcome* Lodge, No. 526, in Chicago. He demitted to George W. Lininger, No. 268, in November 1962, and joined the Scottish Rite that same month. Illustrious Falk received his KCCH in 1967 and was coroneted an Inspector General Honorary in 2007. Ill. Falk served the Omaha Valley for many years as Personal Representative to the SGIG and was a longtime Financial Adviser for the Orient. He was Past Master of the Lodge of Perfection, member of the 33° Degree Team, and coroneted 33° Inspector General Honorary in 1975. Ill. Falk was only the second 33° Grand Cross in the Omaha Valley and believed to be only the third in the Orient of Nebraska.

Bibliography:
Archive of the Supreme Council, 33°, S.J.
In Memoriam. *Transactions*. 2015: 146.

2007

Douglas Kao
Grand Cross of the Court of Honour at age 72 years, 3 months, and 26 days
Tenure present
Nomination by Taipei, Taiwan, and Agana, Guam Scottish Rite Bodies

Born: April 28, 1935 – present
Photographer

Progress in Scottish Rite Masonry:
4°-14°: April 13, 1985, invested by *Mariana Islands* Lodge of Perfection, Guam.
15°-18°: April 13, 1985, invested by *Mariana Islands* Chapter of Rose Croix, Guam.
19°-30°: April 20, 1985, invested by *Mariana Islands* Council of Kadosh, Guam.
31°-32°: April 20, 1985, invested by *Mariana Islands* Consistory, Guam.
March 25, 1994, dual member in Taipei Scottish Rite Bodies, Taiwan.
32°, KCCH: October 9, 1995.
33°, IGH: elected October 6, 1997; coroneted by Ill. Tommy Fu-Hai Weng, 33°, Deputy for Taiwan and China December 26, 1997.
Grand Cross of the Court of Honour: August 24, 2007.

Scottish Rite Biography:
Brother Kao was raised to the Sublime Degree in *Milton C. Marvin* Lodge, No. 123, at Agana, Guam. He joined the Scottish Rite Bodies of Guam in April 1985 and became a 32° Master of the Royal Secret on April 20, 1985. On March 25, 1994, Brother Kao became a dual member in Taipei Scottish Rite Bodies, Taiwan. He received the rank and decoration of a Knight Commander of the Court of Honour on October 9, 1995. On the following Session of the Supreme Council of 1997 Brother Kao was elected an Inspector General Honorary and coroneted by Ill. Tommy Fu-Hai Weng, 33°, Deputy for Taiwan and China December 26, 1997. On August 24, 2007, Ill. Douglas Kao, 33°, was awarded the Grand Cross of the Court of Honour.

Bibliography:
Archive of the Supreme Council, 33°, S.J.

2007

Clayton James Kicklighter
Grand Cross of the Court of Honour at age 84 years, 5 months, and 18 days
Tenure present
Nomination by Jacksonville, Florida Scottish Rite Bodies

Born: March 6, 1923 – present
Broker

Progress in Scottish Rite Masonry:

4°-14°: March 10, 1962, invested by *Jacksonville* Lodge of Perfection, Jacksonville.

15°-18°: March 17, 1962, invested by *Jacksonville* Chapter of Rose Croix, Jacksonville.

19°-30°: March 24, 1962, invested by *Jacksonville* Council of Kadosh, Jacksonville.

31°-32°: March 24, 1962, invested by *Jacksonville* Consistory, Jacksonville.

32°, KCCH: October 19, 1981.

33°, IGH: elected October 16, 1989; coroneted by the Supreme Council, 33°, S.J., October 18, 1989.

Grand Cross of the Court of Honour: August 24, 2007.

Scottish Rite Biography:

Brother Kicklighter was initiated, passed, and raised a Master Mason in *Orange Park* Lodge, No. 267, Orange Park, Florida. He became a 32° Master of the Royal Secret in the Valley of Jacksonville on March 24, 1962. He was invested as a Knight Commander of the Court of Honour in 1981, elected and coroneted 33°, Inspector General Honorary by the Supreme Council, 33°, S.J., on October 18, 1989. Brother Kicklighter served his Valley as a Personal Representative to Ill. Robert L. Goldsmith, 33°, Sovereign Grand Inspector General for Florida from 1994 to 2000. On August 24, 2007, Ill. Clyton Allan Kicklighter, 33°, received the Scottish Rite's highest honor, the Grand Cross.

Bibliography:

Archive of the Supreme Council, 33°, S.J.

2007

David Bryan Sentelle
Grand Cross of the Court of Honour at age 64 years, 6 months, and 12 days
Tenure present
Nomination by Charlotte, North Carolina Scottish Rite Bodies

Born: February 12, 1943 – present
Life span: present
Senior Judge of the United States Court of Appeals for the District of Columbia Circuit

Progress in Scottish Rite Masonry:
4°-14°: April 25, 1972, invested by *Charlotte* Lodge of Perfection, Charlotte.
15°-18°: April 25, 1972, invested by *Mecklenburg* Chapter of Rose Croix, Charlotte.
19°-30°: April 26, 1972, invested by *Charlotte* Council of Kadosh, Charlotte.
31°-32°: April 27, 1972, invested by *Charlotte* Consistory, Charlotte.
32°, KCCH: October 19, 1987.
33°, IGH: elected October 16, 1989; coroneted by the Supreme Council, 33°, S.J., October 18, 1989.
Grand Cross of the Court of Honour: August 24, 2007.

Scottish Rite Biography:
Brother Sentelle is Master Mason in *Exelsior* Lodge, No. 261. He joined the Scottish Rite Bodies of the Valley of Charlotte in 1972 and became a 32° Master of the Royal Secret on April 27, 1972. He received the rank and decoration of a Knight Commander of the Court of Honour in 1987, and on the following Session of 1989 of the Supreme Council was elected and coroneted a 33°, Inspector General Honorary. Ill. David Bryan Sentelle, 33°, was awarded the Grand Cross of the Court of Honour on August 24, 2007.

Bibliography:
Archive of the Supreme Council, 33°, S.J.

2007

James Manley Tingle
Grand Cross of the Court of Honour at age 76 years and 23 days
Tenure 14 years, 10 months, and 8 days
Nomination by Birmingham, Alabama Scottish Rite Bodies

Born: August 1, 1931 – Died: June 2, 2021
Life span: 89 years, 10 months, and 1 day
Attorney

Progress in Scottish Rite Masonry:
4°-14°: May 3, 1969, invested by *Birmingham* Lodge of Perfection, Birmingham.
15°-18°: May 3, 1969, invested by *Birmingham* Chapter of Rose Croix, Birmingham.
19°-30°: May 10, 1969, invested by *Birmingham* Council of Kadosh, Birmingham.
31°-32°: May 10, 1969, invested by *Birmingham* Consistory, Birmingham.
32°, KCCH: October 20, 1975.
33°, IGH: elected October 15, 1979; coroneted by Ill. James R. Rogers, 33°, Sovereign Grand Inspector General for Alabama December 8, 1979.
Grand Cross of the Court of Honour: August 24, 2007.

Scottish Rite Biography:
Brother Tingle was a Master Mason in *Dolcito* Lodge, No. 596, in Tarrant. He received the Scottish Rite Degrees in May 1969 from the Valley of Birmingham; in May 1969. Six years later Brother Tingle received the rank and decoration of a Knight Commander of the Court of Honour, and on December 9, 1979, was coroneted 33°, Inspector General Honorary by Ill. James R. Rogers, 33°, Sovereign Grand Inspector General for Alabama. On August 24, 2007, the Supreme Council, 33°, SJ, elected Ill. James Manley Tingle, 33°, the Grand Cross of the Court of Honour.

Bibliography:
Archive of the Supreme Council, 33°, S.J.

Duane Erwin Walker
Grand Cross of the Court of Honour at age 66 years, 5 months, and 27 days
Tenure present
Nomination by Santa Fè, New Mexico Scottish Rite Bodies

Born: January 27, 1941 – present
Businessman

Progress in Scottish Rite Masonry:
4°-14°: May 1, 1978, invested by *Santa Fè* Lodge of Perfection, Santa Fè.
15°-18°: May 1, 1978, invested by *Santa Fè* Chapter of Rose Croix, Santa Fè.
19°-30°: May 2, 1978, invested by *Santa Fè* Council of Kadosh, Santa Fè.
31°-32°: May 3, 1978, invested by *Santa Fè* Consistory, Santa Fè.
32°, KCCH: October 18, 1993.
33°, IGH: elected October 4, 1999; coroneted by Ill. Don L. Helberg, 33°, Deputy for New Mexico May 5, 2000.
Grand Cross of the Court of Honour: August 24, 2007.

Scottish Rite Biography:
Brother Walker was raised to the Sublime Degree in *Animas* Lodge, No. 15, at Farmington. He joined the Scottish Rite Bodies of the Valley of Santa Fè and became a 32°, Master of the Royal Secret on May 3, 1978. He received the rank and decoration of a Knight Commander of the Court of Honour in 1993. In 1999 Brother Walker was elected by the Supreme Council, 33°, S.J. an Inspector General Honorary, 33°, and coroneted by Ill. Don L. Helberg, 33°, Deputy for New Mexico on May 5, 2000, at Santa Fè. Ill. Duane Erwin Walker, 33°, received the Scottish Rite's highest honor, the Grand Cross of the Court of Honour on August 24, 2007.

Bibliography:
Archive of the Supreme Council, 33°, S.J.

2007

James McCororry Willson, Jr.
Grand Cross of the Court of Honour at age 85 years, 7 months, and 24 days
Tenure 8 years, 7 months, and 16 days
Nomination by Lubbock, Texas Scottish Rite Bodies

Born: November 30, 1921 – Died: April 10, 2016
Life span: 94 years, 4 months, and 10 days
Businessman
Grand Master of Texas – 1981

Progress in Scottish Rite Masonry:
4°-14°: April 19, 1954, invested by *El Paso* Lodge of Perfection, El Paso.
15°-18°: April 20, 1954, invested by *El Paso* Chapter of Rose Croix, El Paso.
19°-30°: April 21, 1954, invested by *El Paso* Council of Kadosh, El Paso.
31°-32°: April 22, 1954, invested by *El Paso* Consistory, El Paso.
32°, KCCH: October 20, 1959.
33°, IGH: elected October 3, 1967; coroneted by Ill. Robert Lee Lockwood, 33°, Sovereign Grand Inspector General for Texas December 16, 1967.
February 4, 1972, affiliated with Scottish Rite Bodies of Lubbock.
Grand Cross of the Court of Honour: August 24, 2007.

Scottish Rite Biography:
Brother Willson raised a Master Mason in *Floydada* Lodge, No 712 in February 1947. Receiving the Scottish Rite Degree from the Valley of El Paso, Texas, in 1954, he became a Charter Member of the Valley of Lubbok, Texas, when it was organized in 1972. Invested a Knight Commander of the Court of Honour in 1959, and coroneted an Inspector General Honorary in 1967, he was elected by the Supreme Council to receive the Grand Cross of the Court of Honour on August 24, 2007. Ill. Willson served as a Trustee on the Boards of the Texas Scottish Rite Hospital for Children in Dallas, Texas and the Scottish Rite Learning Center of West Texas in Lubbock.

Bibliography:
Archive of the Supreme Council, 33°, S.J.
In Memoriam. *Transactions*. 2017: 108.

2009

George Ralph Adams
Grand Cross of the Court of Honour at age 71 years, 11 months, and 9 days
Tenure present
Nomination by Washington, District of Columbia Scottish Rite Bodies

Born: September 23, 1938 – present
Attorney

Progress in Scottish Rite Masonry:
4°-14°: March 23, 1971, invested by *Mithras* Lodge of Perfection, Washington, D.C.
15°-18°: March 23, 1971, invested by *Evangelist* Chapter of Rose Croix, Washington, D.C.
19°-30°: March 30, 1971, invested by *Robert de Bruce* Council of Kadosh, Washington, D.C.
31°-32°: April 13, 1971, invested by *Albert Pike* Consistory, Washington, D.C.
32°, KCCH: October 17, 1983.
33°, IGH: elected October 21, 1991; coroneted by the Supreme Council, 33°, S.J., October 22, 1991.
Deputy: January 1, 2001 – retired, 2005.
Grand Cross of the Court of Honour: October 2, 2009.

Scottish Rite Biography:
Brother George Ralph Adams was raised a Master Mason in *Benjamin B. French* Lodge, No. 15, Washington, D.C., in 1970. An outstanding ritualist in various Bodies of Freemasonry, Ill. Adams became a Master of the Royal Secret in the Scottish Rite Bodies of the District of Columbia in 1971, 32°, KCCH in 1983, and 33°, Inspector General Honorary in 1991. He performs major roles in 30° and 32° Degrees, served as Venerable Master of *Mithras* Lodge of Perfection in 1999, and is a Trustee at large and member of the Steering Committee of the Scottish Rite Valley of Washington. In addition, he was the author of a financial column in the Scottish Rite Journal and a frequent representative of our Order and Freemasonry to many Capital City communities.

Bibliography:
Archive of the Supreme Council, 33°, S.J.
Archives of the Orient of the District of Columbia and Archives of the Grand Lodge of the District of Columbia, F.A.A.M.

2009

Fred Edwin Allen
Grand Cross of the Court of Honour at age 81 years, 5 months, and 20 days
Tenure 9 years, 3 months, and 29 days
Nomination by Dallas, Texas Scottish Rite Bodies

Born: May 12, 1928 – Died: January 31, 2019
Life span: 90 years, 8 months, and 19 days
Businessman

Progress in Scottish Rite Masonry:
4°-14°: September 29, 1978, invested by *Dallas* Lodge of Perfection, Dallas.
15°-18°: September 30, 1978, invested by *Dallas* Chapter of Rose Croix, Dallas.
19°-30°: September 30, 1978, invested by *Dallas* Council of Kadosh, Dallas.
31°-32°: September 30, 1978, invested by *Dallas* Consistory, Dallas.
32°, KCCH: October 17, 1983.
33°, IGH: elected October 19, 1987; coroneted by Ill. John Wilkins Chandler, 33°, Sovereign Grand Inspector General for Texas November 17, 1987.
Grand Cross of the Court of Honour: October 2, 2009.

Scottish Rite Biography:
Brother Fred Edwin Allen was a member of good standing of *Roy Stanley* Lodge, No. 1367, as well as Dallas Lodge of Perfection, Dallas Chapter of Rose Croix, Dallas Council of Kadosh, and Dallas Consistory located at Dallas, Texas. He was invested with the 32° on September 30, 1978, and was elected KCCH on October 17, 1983. He was a Venerable Master of the Lodge of Perfection, and President of the Four Counties Scottish Rite Club.

Bibliography:
Archive of the Supreme Council, 33°, S.J.
In Memoriam. *Transactions.* 2019: 125.

2009

Ferris Eugene Booker
Grand Cross of the Court of Honour at age 79 years, 1 month, and 23 days
Tenure 13 years and 1 month
Nomination by Pensacola, Florida Scottish Rite Bodies

Born: August 9, 1930 – Died: November 2, 2021
Life span: 92 years, 2 months, and 23 days
Contractor

Progress in Scottish Rite Masonry:
4°-14°: April 15, 1964, invested by *Pensacola* Lodge of Perfection, Pensacola.
15°-18°: April 16, 1964, invested by *Pensacola* Chapter of Rose Croix, Pensacola.
19°-30°: April 29, 1964, invested by *Pensacola* Council of Kadosh, Pensacola.
31°-32°: April 30, 1964, invested by *Pensacola* Consistory, Pensacola.
32°, KCCH: October 6, 1997.
33°, IGH: elected October 6, 2003; coroneted by Ill. Robert L. Goldsmith, 33°, Sovereign Grand Inspector General for Florida November 15, 2003.
Grand Cross of the Court of Honour: October 2, 2009.

Scottish Rite Biography:
Brother Booker is a Master Mason in *Gulf Breeze* Lodge, No. 347, in Gulf Breeze. He joined the Scottish Rite Bodies of Pensacola Valley, receiving the rank and decoration of a Knight Commander of the Court of Honour in 1997. On a Session of the Supreme Council, 33°, S.J., Brother Booker was elected 33°, Inspector General Honorary, and coroneted by Ill. Robert L. Goldsmith, 33°, Sovereign Grand Inspector General for Florida on November 15, 2003. In 2009 Ill. Ferris Eugene Booker, 33°, was elected by the Supreme Council to receive the Grand Cross of the Court of Honour.

Bibliography:
Archive of the Supreme Council, 33º, S.J.

2009

Arturo de Hoyos
Grand Cross of the Court of Honour at age 49 years, 11 months, and 22 days
Tenure present
Nomination by San Antonio, Texas Scottish Rite Bodies

Born: November 10, 1959 – present
Grand Archivist and Grand Historian of the Supreme Council, 33°, SJ, USA

Progress in Scottish Rite Masonry:
4°-14°: November 18, 1988, invested by *San Antonio* Lodge of Perfection, San Antonio.
15°-18°: November 19, 1988, invested by *San Antonio* Chapter of Rose Croix, San Antonio.
19°-30°: November 19, 1988, invested by *San Antonio* Council of Kadosh, San Antonio.
31°-32°: November 19, 1988, invested by *San Antonio* Consistory, San Antonio.
32°, KCCH: October 6, 1997.
33°, IGH: elected October 4, 1999; coroneted by the Supreme Council, 33°, S.J., October 5, 1999.
Grand Cross of the Court of Honour: October 2, 2009.

Scottish Rite Biography:
Brother De Hoyos was raised to the Sublime Degree in *McAllen* Lodge, No. 1110, at McAllen, Texas. He was made a Master of the Royal Secret on November 19, 1988, in the Valley of San Antonio. Brother De Hoyos was elected a Knight Commander of the Court of Honour in 1997, and elected and coroneted 33°, Inspector General Honorary in 1999. On July 7, 1999, Sovereign Grand Commander C. Fred Kleinknecht, 33°, appointed Bro. Art de Hoyos to assume the full-time position of Grand Archivist and Grand Historian of the Supreme Council. At that time Bro. de Hoyos already has an international reputation as an authority on Freemasonry in general and the history of the Scottish Rite, its literature and ritual. This extraordinary knowledge allows Ill. de Hoyos, to serve on the *ad hog* committee assisting Dr. Rex R. Hutchens, 33°, GC in the revision of the Ritual and being a key member of it. From 1995 Ill. De Hoyos shas served on the Board of Directors of the Scottish Research Society. During quarter of the century Ill. De Hoyos has contributed to the *Heredom* and Bonus Book program a countless number of articles and books. He became a dual member of a few Valleys of the Southern Jurisdiction, Honorary Member of a few Supreme Councils, 33°. The fame of Ill. Art de Hoyos, 33°, as the Masonic Scholar has no boundary; some of his books were translated in a few foreign languages. In 2009 Ill. Arturo de Hoyos, 33°, received the highest honor of the Supreme Council, 33°, S.J., the Grand Cross of the Court of Honour.

Bibliography:
Archive of the Supreme Council, 33°, S.J.
Allocution. *Transactions.* 1999: 18-19.

2009

Vernon Brown Ingraham
Grand Cross of the Court of Honour at age 62 years, 8 months, and 9 days
Tenure present
Nomination by Denver, Colorado Scottish Rite Bodies

Born: January 23, 1947 – present
U.S. Air Force

Progress in Scottish Rite Masonry:

4°-14°: February 7, 1970, invested by *San Antonio* Lodge of Perfection, San Antonio.

15°-18°: February 14, 1970, invested by *San Antonio* Chapter of Rose Croix, San Antonio.

19°-30°: February 14, 1970, invested by *San Antonio* Council of Kadosh, San Antonio.

31°-32°: February 28, 1970, invested by *San Antonio* Consistory, San Antonio.

November 4, 1974, affiliated with Denver Scottish Rite Bodies, Colorado.

32°, KCCH: October 9, 1995.

33°, IGH: elected October 1, 1999; coroneted by Ill. Dwight A. Hamilton, 33°, Sovereign Grand Inspector General for Colorado November 27, 1999.

Grand Cross of the Court of Honour: October 2, 2009.

Scottish Rite Biography:

Brother Ingraham was raised a Master Mason in *Prospect Hill* Lodge, No. 1247, in San Antonio, and made a Master of the Royal Secret on February 28, 1970, in the Valley of San Antonio. Later Brother Ingraham affiliated with *Rob Morris* Lodge, No. 92, in Denver, Scottish Rite Bodies of the Valley of Denver, as well, as with the Valley of Grand Junction and Colorado Spring-Pueblo Valley. He received the rank and decoration of a Knight Commander of the Court of Honour in 1995, elected and coroneted a 33°, Inspector General Honorary in 1999. Ill. Vernon Brown Ingraham, 33°, received the highest honor of the Supreme Council, the Grand Cross of the Court of Honour in 2009.

Bibliography:

Archive of the Supreme Council, 33°, S.J.

2009

James Hoyt Kirby
Grand Cross of the Court of Honour at age 81 years, 1 month, and 25 days
Tenure present
Nomination by Lake Worth, Florida Scottish Rite Bodies

Born: August 7, 1928 – present
Druggist

Progress in Scottish Rite Masonry:
4°-14°: November 11, 1950, invested by *Venus* Lodge of Perfection, Lake Worth.
15°-18°: November 12, 1950, invested by *Akairos* Chapter of Rose Croix, Lake Worth.
19°-30°: November 19, 1950, invested by *Menthra* Council of Kadosh, Lake Worth.
31°-32°: November 19, 1950, invested by *Lake Worth* Consistory, Lake Worth.
32°, KCCH: October 29, 1969.
33°, IGH: elected October 17, 1977; coroneted by Ill. William M. Hollis, 33°, Sovereign Grand Inspector General for Florida December 10, 1977.
Grand Cross of the Court of Honour: October 2, 2009.

Scottish Rite Biography:
Brother Kirby is a Master Mason in *Harmonia* Lodge, No. 138, at West Palm Beach. He joined the Scottish Rite of Lake Worth Valley and became a Master of the Royal Secret on November 19, 1950. Brother Kirby was invested as a Knight Commander of the Court of Honour in 1969, elected 33°, Inspector General Honorary on October 17, 1977, and coroneted by Ill. William M. Hollis, 33°, Sovereign Grand Inspector General for Florida on December 10, 1977. Ill. James Hoyt Kirby, 33°, elected by the Supreme Council, 33°, S.J., to receive the Grand Cross of the Court of Honour on October 2, 2009.

Bibliography:
Archive of the Supreme Council, 33°, S.J.

2009

Glenn Howard Liljegren
Grand Cross of the Court of Honour at age 78 years, 3 months, and 8 days
Tenure 6 years, 6 months, and 1 day
Nomination by Duluth, Minnesota Scottish Rite Bodies

Born: June 24, 1931 – Died: April 3, 2016
Life span: 84 years, 9 months, and 9 days
Electronics Technician

Progress in Scottish Rite Masonry:
4°-14°: March 5, 1977, invested by *Duluth* Lodge of Perfection, Duluth.
15°-18°: March 5, 1977, invested by *Duluth* Chapter of Rose Croix, Duluth.
19°-30°: March 19, 1977, invested by *Duluth* Council of Kadosh, Duluth.
31°-32°: March 19, 1977, invested by *Duluth* Consistory, Duluth.
32°, KCCH: October 19, 1987.
33°, IGH: elected October 18, 1993; coroneted by Ill. Daniel F. Levenduski, 33°, Sovereign Grand Inspector General for Minnesota December 11, 1993.
Grand Cross of the Court of Honour: October 2, 2009.

Scottish Rite Biography:
Brother Glenn raised a Master Mason in 1974 in *Euclid* Lodge, No. 198. Initiated a Scottish Rite Mason in 1977 in the Valley of Duluth, Minnesota, he was invested a Knight Commander of the Court of Honour in 1987, and coroneted an Inspector General Honorary in 1983. He was Personal Representative of the Duluth Valley from 1998 to 2004. Most important to Ill. Glen was his work at the Scottish Rite Care Clinic in Duluth. Involved since its inception, he was the Brother who led the work of completely repurposing a building purchased as home for the Clinic. He then led the work again when a Valley-owned building was remodeled for use as an Autistic Treatment facility … he continued to offer his experience and expertise to accomplish major sound and communication system installation upgrades to both the Scottish Rite Center and Duluth Clinic, and he has been the emergency responder for all facilities issues for both.

Bibliography:
Archive of the Supreme Council, 33°, S.J.
In Memoriam. *Transactions*. 2017: 107.

2009

Lester William Miller
Grand Cross of the Court of Honour at age 77 years, 3 months, and 29 days
Tenure 11 years, 4 months, and 13 days
Nomination by Long Beach, California Scottish Rite Bodies

Born: June 3, 1932 – Died: February 15, 2021
Life span: 88 years, 7 months, and 13 days
Attorney

Progress in Scottish Rite Masonry:
4°-32°: date unconfirmed, invested by the Supreme Council, 33°, of Germany.
32°, KCCH: October 18, 1993.
33°, IGH: elected October 6, 1997; coroneted by Ill. H. Douglas Lemons, 33°, Sovereign Grand Inspector General for California December 6, 1997.
Grand Cross of the Court of Honour: October 2, 2009.

Scottish Rite Biography:
Brother Miller was raised to the Sublime Degree in *New Point* Lodge, No. 255, in New Point, Indiana. The Scottish Rite Degrees were invested to him by the Supreme Council, 33°, of Germany. In 1967 Brother Miller affiliated with *Long Beach* Lodge, No. 367, and the Scottish Rite Valley of Long Beach. He received the rank and decoration of a Knight Commander of the Court of Honour on October 18, 1993, was coroneted 33°, by Ill. H. Douglas Lemons, 33°, Sovereign Grand Inspector General for California on December 6, 1997.
Inspector General Honorary and received the Grand Cross of the Court of Honour on October 2, 2009. Ill. Lester William Miller, 33°, GC, was the original Executive Secretary of the Scottish Rite Foundation in 1978 through his retirement in 2008, and a great supporter of the Childhood Language Program.

Bibliography:
Archive of the Supreme Council, 33°, S.J.
Image courtesy of https://www.virginvalleymortuary.com/obituary/Lester-Miller

2011

Alan Wayne Adkins
Grand Cross of the Court of Honour at age 63 years, 6 months, and 20 days
Tenure present
Nomination by Danville, Virginia Scottish Rite Bodies

Born: 1948, January 30 – present
Sovereign Grand Inspector General for Virginia
Grand Master of the Grand Lodge of Virginia – 1997

Progress in Scottish Rite Masonry:

4°-14°: April 3, 1979, invested by *Danville* Lodge of Perfection, Danville.

15°-18°: April 10, 1979, invested by *Danville* Chapter of Rose Croix, Danville.

19°-30°: April 17, 1979, invested by *Danville* Council of Kadosh, Danville.

31°-32°: April 24, 1979, invested by *Danville* Consistory, Danville.

32°, KCCH: October 9, 1995.

33°, IGH: elected October 4, 1999; coroneted by the Supreme Council, 33°, S.J., October 5, 1999.

Grand Cross of the Court of Honour: August 19, 2011.

Deputy: August 17, 2019 – August 21, 2021.

SGIG: elected and crowned August 21, 2021 – present.

Scottish Rite Biography:

Brother Adkins was raised a Master Mason in *Mountain Home* Lodge, No. 263, in Stuart, Virginia. He is a member of the Valleys of Danville and Richmond, A.&A. Scottish Rite and invested a KCCH in 1995, coroneted a 33° in 1999, and awarded the Grand Cross in 2011. Effective August 17, 2019, Ill. Alan W. Adkins, 33°, GC, was appointed as Deputy of the Supreme Council in the Orient of Virginia. On August 21, 2021, Ill. Alan Wayne Adkins, 33°, GC, was elected and crowned as Sovereign Grand Inspector General for Virginia

Bibliography:

Archive of the Supreme Council, 33°, S.J.

Ill. Alan W. Adkins, 33°, GC, Appointed Deputy in Virginia. *The Scottish Rite Journal*, November/December 2019: 16.

2011

James Michael Atchley
Grand Cross of the Court of Honour at age 69 years and 9 days
Tenure 5 years, 5 months, and 8 days
Nomination by Tucson, Arizona Scottish Rite Bodies

Born: August 28, 1942 – Died: January 27, 2017
Life span: 74 years, 4 months, and 29 days
U.S. Postal Service

Progress in Scottish Rite Masonry:
4°-14°: November 6, 1980, invested by *Tucson* Lodge of Perfection, Tucson.
15°-18°: November 6, 1980, invested by *Tucson* Chapter of Rose Croix, Tucson.
19°-30°: November 6, 1980, invested by *Tucson* Council of Kadosh, Tucson.
31°-32°: November 6, 1980, invested by *Tucson* Consistory, Tucson.
32°, KCCH: October 19, 1987.
33°, IGH: elected October 18, 1993; coroneted by Ill. Robert F. Hannon, 33°, Sovereign Grand Inspector General for Arizona November 20, 1993.
Grand Cross of the Court of Honour: August 19, 2011.

Scottish Rite Biography:
Ill. Atchley began his Masonic journey in 1980, when he was raised a Master Mason in *Epes Randolph* Lodge, No. 32. Beginning in 1980, when initiated into the Scottish Rite by the Valley of Tucson, Ill. Michael began 35 years of active and continuous service. He served the Valley as Director of the Work for 20 years beginning in 1985. Coroneted an Inspector General Honorary in 1993, he was appointed Personal Representative of the Tucson Valley in 2008, serving in that position until his passing. For a lifetime of exemplary service, he was elected Grand Cross at the Biennial Session of the Supreme Council in 2011.

Bibliography:
Archive of the Supreme Council, 33°, S.J.
In Memoriam. *Transactions.* 2017: 112.

2011

William Arthur Coffield
Grand Cross of the Court of Honour at age 74 years, 10 months, and 12 days
Tenure present

Nomination by Deadwood, South Dakota Scottish Rite Bodies

Born: October 7, 1936 – present
Teacher

Progress in Scottish Rite Masonry:

4°-14°: September 27, 1958, invested by *Black Hills* Lodge of Perfection, Deadwood.

15°-18°: September 28, 1958, invested by *Black Hills* Chapter of Rose Croix, Deadwood.

19°-30°: October 4, 1958, invested by *Black Hills* Council of Kadosh, Deadwood.

31°-32°: October 5, 1958, invested by *Black Hills* Consistory, Deadwood.

32°, KCCH: October 17, 1977.

33°, IGH: elected October 19, 1987; coroneted by Ill. Marvin K. Bailin, 33°, Sovereign Grand Inspector General for South Dakota December 5, 1987.

Grand Cross of the Court of Honour: August 19, 2011.

Scottish Rite Biography:

Brother Coffield was raised a Master Mason in *Harmony* Lodge, No. 110, in Hot Springs. He became a member of the Scottish Rite Bodies of the Valley of Black Hills on October 5, 1958, and he received his first honor being invested as a Knight Commander of the Court of Honour on October 17, 1977. Ten years later on the Session of the Supreme Council of 1987 Brother Coffield was elected a 33°, Inspector General Honorary and coroneted by Ill. Marvin K. Bailin, 33°, Sovereign Grand Inspector General for South Dakota December 5, 1987. Brother Coffield served his Valley as Venerable Master of the Lodge of Perfection and Personal Representative for the Sovereign Grand Inspector General. On August 19, 2011, Ill. William Arthur Coffield, 33°, received the Scottish Rite's highest honor, the Grand Cross of the Court of Honour.

Bibliography:

Archive of the Supreme Council, 33°, S.J.

2011

Robert Francis Drechsler
Grand Cross of the Court of Honour at age 78 years, 4 months, and 10 days
Tenure 10 years, 2 months, and 1 day
Nomination by Washington, District of Columbia Scottish Rite Bodies

Born: April 9, 1933 – October 20, 2021
Life span: 88 years, 6 months, and 11 days
Agricultural Research Technician

Progress in Scottish Rite Masonry:
4°-14°: March 26, 1968, invested by *Mithras* Lodge of Perfection, Washington, D.C.
15°-18°: March 26, 1968, invested by *Evangelist* Chapter of Rose Croix, Washington, D.C.
19°-30°: March 26, 1968, invested by *Robert de Bruce* Council of Kadosh, Washington, D.C.
31°-32°: March 26, 1968, invested by *Albert Pike* Consistory, Washington, D.C.
32°, KCCH: October 20, 1975.
33°, IGH: elected October 17, 1983; coroneted by Ill. William E. Eccleston, Deputy for the District of Columbia November 12, 1983.
Grand Cross of the Court of Honour: August 19, 2011.

Scottish Rite Biography:
Brother Robert Francis Drechsler received the first three Masonic Degrees in *Anacostia* Lodge No. 21 and served as a Master in 1969. A life member of the Scottish Rite Bodies in Washington, D.C., Drechsler served as the head of *Mithras* Lodge of Perfection in 1977 and *Evangelist* Chapter Rose Croix in 1985. He has chaired the Special Projects Committee and served as Stage Director for 15 years prior to his retirement in 1996. Brother Drechler was invested with the rank of 32°, KCCH in 1975 and 33°, IGH in 1983. Ill. Drechler is the most recent recipient of the Grand Cross of the Court of Honor in the District of Columbia, which he received in 2011.

Bibliography:
Archive of the Supreme Council, 33°, S.J.
Archives of the Orient of the District of Columbia and Archives of the Grand Lodge of the District of Columbia, F.A.A.M.

2011

Jack H. Jones
Grand Cross of the Court of Honour at age 79 years, 7 months, and 11 days
Tenure 5 years, 8 months, and 14 days
Nomination by Tampa, Florida Scottish Rite Bodies

Born: February 8, 1932 – April 27, 2017
Life span: 85 years, 2 months, and 19 days
U.S. Air Force

Progress in Scottish Rite Masonry:
4°-32°: October 18, 1958, invested by *Marquette* Scottish Rite Bodies, Michigan, Northern Jurisdiction.
December 17, 1971, affiliated with *Tampa* Scottish Rite Bodies, Florida, Southern Jurisdiction.
32°, KCCH: October 17, 1977.
33°, IGH: elected October 21, 1985; coroneted by Ill. William M. Hollis, 33°, Sovereign Grand Inspector General for Florida November 30, 1985.
Grand Cross of the Court of Honour: August 19, 2011.

Scottish Rite Biography:
Brother Jack was raised a Master Mason in *Hazel Park* Lodge, No. 570, in Hazel Park, Michigan, in April 1956. Two years later, he became a Master of the Royal Secret in the Valley of Marquette, Michigan (NMJ). Affiliating in 1971 with the Valley of Tampa, Florida, he later affiliated in 1975 with *Hillsborough* Lodge, No. 25, Tampa. Ill. Jones was invested as a Knight Commander of the Court of Honour in 1977; coroneted as Inspector General Honorary, 33°, in 1985; and elected by the Supreme Council to receive the Grand Cross of the Court of Honour on August 23, 2011.

Bibliography:
Archive of the Supreme Council, 33°, S.J.
In Memoriam. *Transactions.* 2017: 114.

2011

Roy James Lewis
Grand Cross of the Court of Honour at age 84 years, 7 months, and 1 day
Tenure 6 months and 13 days
Nomination by Tulsa, Oklahoma Scottish Rite Bodies

Born: January 18, 1927 – Died: March 2, 2012
Life span: 85 years, 1 month, and 14 days
School Director

Progress in Scottish Rite Masonry:
4°-14°: November 8, 1975, invested by *Tulsa* Lodge of Perfection, Tulsa.
15°-18°: November 8, 1975, invested by *Tulsa* Chapter of Rose Croix, Tulsa.
19°-30°: November 9, 1975, invested by *Tulsa* Council of Kadosh, Tulsa.
31°-32°: November 9, 1975, invested by *Tulsa* Consistory, Tulsa.
32°, KCCH: October 21, 1985.
33°, IGH: elected October 18, 1993; coroneted by Ill. Paul Million, Jr., 33°, Sovereign Grand Inspector General for Oklahoma December 5, 1993.
Grand Cross of the Court of Honour: August 19, 2011.

Scottish Rite Biography:
Ill. Lewis began his Masonic journey March 7, 1949, in *Hartford* Lodge, No. 609, Hartford, Arkansas. He became a Master of the Royal Secret in the Valley of Tulsa on November 9, 1975, was invested with the rank and decoration of a Knight Commander of the Court of Honour in 1985 and was coroneted as Inspector General Honorary in 1993. At the Supreme Council Biennial Session of 2011, he was elected to receive the Grand Cross of the Court of Honour.

Bibliography:
Archive of the Supreme Council, 33°, S.J.
In Memoriam. *Transactions.* 2013: 183.

2011

José Rafael López-Rivera
Grand Cross of the Court of Honour at age 62 years and 3 months
Tenure present
Nomination by San Juan, Puerto Rico Scottish Rite Bodies

Born: May 19, 1949 – present
Chemist

Progress in Scottish Rite Masonry:
4°-14°: May 18, 1975, invested by *Arecibo* Lodge of Perfection, Arecibo.
15°-18°: June 10, 1975, invested by *Arecibo* Chapter of Rose Croix, Arecibo.
19°-30°: June 17, 1975, invested by *Arecibo* Council of Kadosh, Arecibo.
31°-32°: June 17, 1975, invested by *San Juan* Consistory, San Juan.
32°, KCCH: October 21, 1991.
33°, IGH: elected October 9, 1995; coroneted by the Supreme Council, 33°, S.J., October 10, 1995.
Deputy: May 14, 2001 – August 20, 2017.
Grand Cross of the Court of Honour: August 19, 2011.
SGIG: elected August 19, 2017; crowned., August 20, 2017 – present.

Scottish Rite Biography:
Brother López was initiated as a Master Mason on March 14, 1974, in Lodge *Faro de Borinquen*, No. 22, in Lares. A member of the Scottish Rite Bodies of Arecibo, since 1975, in recognition of his many services to our Order, Bro. López-Rivera was invested with the KCCH in 1991 and coroneted a 33° Inspector General Honorary in 1995. He has been the Personal Representative of the Deputy in the Valley of Arecibo for eight years and was appointed his Personal Representative by Ill. Martinez for the Orient of Puerto Rico in 2000. Brother López is a member of the Board of Directors of the Scottish Rite Childhood Language Disorders Clinic in San Juan. Effective May 14, 2001, Ill. José R. López-Rivera was appointed as Deputy in the Orient of Puerto Rico, on August 19, 2011, received the highest Scottish Rite honor the Grand Cross of the Court of Honour, and on August 20, 2017, crowned as Sovereign Grand Inspector General in the Orient of Puerto Rico.

Bibliography:
Archive of the Supreme Council, 33°, S.J.
Ill. José R. López, 33°, Appointed Deputy in Puerto Rico," *The Scottish Rite Journal*, August 2001: 38-39.

2011

Lyndon Lowell Olson, Jr.
Grand Cross of the Court of Honour at age 64 years, 5 months, and 12 days
Tenure present
Nomination by Waco, Texas Scottish Rite Bodies

Born: March 7, 1947 – present
U.S. Senator

Progress in Scottish Rite Masonry:
4°-14°: May 27, 1976, invested by *Waco* Lodge of Perfection, Waco.
15°-18°: May 28, 1976, invested by *Waco* Chapter of Rose Croix, Waco.
19°-30°: May 28, 1976, invested by *Waco* Council of Kadosh, Waco.
31°-32°: May 29, 1976, invested by *Waco* Consistory, Waco.
32°, KCCH: October 4, 1999.
33°, IGH: elected October 6, 2003; coroneted by the Supreme Council, 33°, S.J., October 7, 2003.
Grand Cross of the Court of Honour: August 19, 2011.

Scottish Rite Biography:
Brother Olson is a Master Mason in *James H. Lockwood* Lodge, No. 1343, at Waco. He became a member of the Valley of Waco Scottish Rite Bodies in 1976. Brother Olson was elected to receive the Knight Commander of the Court of Honor in 1999; was coroneted as a 33°, Inspector General Honorary on October 7, 2003, and awarded the Grand Cross of the Court of Honour on August 19, 2011.

Bibliography:
Archive of the Supreme Council, 33°, S.J.

2011

Floren Lamont Quick
Grand Cross of the Court of Honour at age 81 years, 2 months, and 6 days
Tenure 3 years, 3 months, and 29 days
Nomination by Tokyo, Japan, Korea, & Okinawa Scottish Rite Bodies

Born: June 13, 1930 – Died: December 18, 2014
Life span: 84 years, 6 months, and 5 days
U.S. Air Force

Progress in Scottish Rite Masonry:
4°-14°: April 22, 1965, invested by *Tokyo* Lodge of Perfection, Tokyo.
15°-18°: April 22, 1965, invested by *Tokyo* Chapter of Rose Croix, Tokyo.
19°-30°: April 23, 1965, invested by *Tokyo* Council of Kadosh, Tokyo.
31°-32°: April 23, 1965, invested by *Tokyo* Consistory, Tokyo.
32°, KCCH: October 20, 1975.
33°, IGH: elected October 15, 1979; coroneted by Ill. Joseph Angelo Diele, 33°, Deputy for Japan November 2, 1980.
December 15, 1998, Dual Member of Alexandria Scottish Rite Bodies, Alexandria, VA.
Grand Cross of the Court of Honour: August 19, 2011.

Scottish Rite Biography:
Brother Quick's Masonic career began on March 27, 1957, when he was initiated in *Moriahyama* Lodge, No. 7, at Asaka, Japan. Ill. Quick received the 32° in Tokyo Consistory in 1964 and the rank and decoration of Knight Commander of the Court of Honour in 1975 and was coroneted as an Inspector General Honorary of the 33° in 1979. He received the Grand Cross for exemplary service to the Rite in 2011.Ill. Quick departed Japan in 1989 and moved to Springfield, VA where he continued serving Freemasonry as a ritualist on the Ill. Walter Downs 33° Degree Conferral team.

Bibliography:
Archive of the Supreme Council, 33°, S.J.
In Memoriam. *Transactions.* 2015: 148.

2011

George Charles Smith
Grand Cross of the Court of Honour at age 77 years, 1 month, and 27 days
Tenure present
Nomination by Cheyenne, Wyoming Scottish Rite Bodies

Born: 1934, June 22 – present
Businessman

Progress in Scottish Rite Masonry:
4°-14°: November 1, 1960, invested by *Alliance* Lodge of Perfection, Alliance.
15°-18°: April 5, 1961, invested by *Alliance* Chapter of Rose Croix, Alliance.
19°-30°: November 2, 1961, invested by *Alliance* Council of Kadosh, Alliance.
31°-32°: November 3, 1961, invested by *Alliance* Consistory, Alliance.
October 6, 1980, affiliated with Cheyenne Scottish Rite Bodies.
32°, KCCH: October 21, 1985.
33°, IGH: elected October 6, 1997; coroneted by the Supreme Council, 33°, S. J., October 25, 1997.
Grand Cross of the Court of Honour: August 19, 2011.

Scottish Rite Biography:
Brother Smith was raised a Master Mason in *Alliance* Lodge, No. 183, at Alliance, Nebraska. In 1961 he joined the Scottish Rite Bodies of the Valley of Nebraska and became a 32° Master of the Royal Secret on November 3, 1961. After moving to Wyoming in 1980, Brother Smith affiliated with *Ashlar* Lodge, No. 10, at Douglas, and the Scottish Rite Bodies of the Valley of Cheyenne. He received the rank and decoration of a Knight Commander of the Court of Honour in 1985 and was coroneted a 33°, Inspector General Honorary in 1997. Brother Smith served his Valley as a Venerable Master of the Lodge of Perfection, Commander of the Council of Kadosh, and personal Representative to the Sovereign Grand Inspector General for Wyoming. On August 19, 2011, Ill. George Charles Smith was awarded the Grand Cross of the Court of Honour.

Bibliography:
Archive of the Supreme Council, 33°, S. J.

2013

Woody Dee Bilyeu
Grand Cross of the Court of Honour at age 59 years, 11 months, and 16 days
Tenure present
Nomination by Monroe, Louisiana Scottish Rite Bodies

Born: September 8, 1953 – present
Businessman

Progress in Scottish Rite Masonry:
4°-14°: May 22, 1982, invested by *Monroe* Lodge of Perfection, Monroe.
15°-18°: May 22, 1982, invested by *Monroe* Chapter of Rose Croix, Monroe.
19°-30°: May 22, 1982, invested by *Monroe* Council of Kadosh, Monroe.
31°-32°: May 22, 1982, invested by *Monroe* Consistory, Monroe.
32°, KCCH: October 9, 1995.
33°, IGH: elected and coroneted by the Supreme Council, 33°, S.J., October 7, 2003.
Grand Cross of the Court of Honour: August 24, 2013.

Scottish Rite Biography:
Brother Bilyeu became a member of the *Eastern Star* Lodge, No. 151, in Winnfield, in early 1982. On May 22, 1982, he joined the Scottish Rite Bodies of the Valley of Monroe. In 1995 he received the rank and decoration of a Knight Commander of the Court of Honour, and on October 7, 2003 he was elected 33°, Inspector General Honorary and on the same date coroneted by the Supreme Council, 33°, S.J. Brother Bilyeu served as Personal Representative of the SGIG in the Valley; as a Venerable Master of the Lodge of Perfection; as Degree Master for 5°, 13°, and 18°; as a Chairman of Membership Committees for the Valley and Orient; as Chairman, of the Scottish Rite Development Committee for the Valley. In addition, Brother Bilyeu is a Member of the Rebuilding the Temple Advisory Panel of the House of the Temple, as well as a Donor for the Rebuilding the Temple Campaign. The Supreme Council, 33°, S.J., elected Ill. Woody Dee Bilyeu, 33°, a Grand Cross of the Court of Honor on August 24, 2013, and displays his portrait in the Pillars of Charity Gallery at the House of the Temple.

Bibliography:
Archive of the Supreme Council, 33°, S.J.
Young, Denise B. Donor Profile: Woody Bilyeu, 33°. *The Scottish Rite Journal*. May/June 2008.

2013

James Gooden Exum, Jr.
Grand Cross of the Court of Honour at age 77 years, 11 months, and 10 days
Tenure present
Nomination by Greensboro, North Carolina Scottish Rite Bodies

Born: September 14, 1935 – present
Chief Justice of the North Carolina Supreme Court

Progress in Scottish Rite Masonry:
4°-14°: October 29, 1968, invested by *James W. Cortland* Lodge of Perfection, Greensboro.
15°-18°: April 24, 1974, invested by *Guilford* Chapter of Rose Croix, Greensboro.
19°-30°: April 25, 1974, invested by *Guilford* Counsil of Kadosh Greensboro.
31°-32°: April 26, 1974, invested by *Guilford* Consistory, Greensboro.
32°, KCCH: October 3, 2001.
33°, IGH: October 20, 2007.
Grand Cross of the Court of Honour: August 24, 2013.

Scottish Rite Biography:
Brother Exum is Master Mason in *Radiance* Lodge, No. 132, at Snow Hills. He was made a Master of the Royal Secret in 1974 in the Valley of Greensboro, elected to receive the Knight Commander of the Court of Honour in 2001, and elected a 33°, Inspector General Honorary in 2007. Brother Exum supported many charities of the Valley. On August 24, 2013, Ill. James Gooden Exum, Jr., 33°, was awarded the Grand Cross of the Court of Honour.

Bibliography:
Archive of the Supreme Council, 33°, S.J.

2013

Reese Lenwood Harrison, Jr.
Grand Cross of the Court of Honour at age 74 years, 8 months, and 19 days
Tenure present
Nomination by San Antonio, Texas Scottish Rite Bodies

Born: January 5, 1938 – present
Attorney

Progress in Scottish Rite Masonry:
4°-14°: May 18, 1959, invested by *San Antonio* Lodge of Perfection, San Antonio.
15°-18°: May 19, 1959, invested by *San Antonio* Chapter of Rose Croix, San Antonio.
19°-30°: May 19, 1959, invested by *San Antonio* Council of Kadosh, San Antonio.
31°-32°: May 21, 1959, invested by *San Antonio* Consistory, San Antonio.
32°, KCCH: October 18, 1971.
33°, IGH: elected October 15, 1979; coroneted by Ill. John Wilkins Chandler, 33°, Sovereign Grand Inspector General for Texas December 11, 1979.
Grand Cross of the Court of Honour: August 24, 2013.

Scottish Rite Biography:
Brother Harrison is a Master Mason in *Albert Pike* Lodge, No. 1169 at San Antonio. In 1959 he joined the Scottish Rite Bodies of the Valley of San Antonio. Brother Harrison was invested as a Knight Commander of the Court of Honour in 1971; elected by the Supreme Council an Inspector General Honorary, 33°, and coroneted by Ill. John Wilkins Chandler, 33°, Sovereign Grand Inspector General for Texas December 11, 1979. Brother Harrison is a Past Venerable Master of the Lodge of Perfection (1978), Past Wise Master of the Chapter of Rose Croix (1981), Past Commander of the Council of Kadosh (1972), and Past Master of Consistory (1981), former Deputy Commander of the Court of Honour and Vice Chairman of the Learning Center. From 2002 to 2014 Ill. Reese Lenwood Harrison, Jr., 33°, GC, served his Valley as a Personal Representative for the Sovereign Grand Inspector General for Texas and now he is a Personal Representative Emeritus, a Chairman of the Executive Committee and now he is a Chairman Emeritus, and a Chairman of the Building Corporation.

Bibliography:
Archive of the Supreme Council, 33°, S.J.

2013

William Edwin Holsomback
Grand Cross of the Court of Honour at age 81 years, 9 months, and 5 days
Tenure present
Nomination by Honolulu, Hawaii Scottish Rite Bodies

Born: November 19, 1932 – present
Manager

Progress in Scottish Rite Masonry:
4°-14°: September 27, 1980, invested by *Honolulu* Lodge of Perfection, Honolulu.
15°-32°: date unconfirmed, invested by Honolulu Scottish Rite Bodies.
32°, KCCH: October 21, 1985.
33°, IGH: elected October 18, 1991; coroneted by Ill. Arthur James Wriston, Jr., 33°, Sovereign Grand Inspector General for Hawaii November 21, 1991.
Grand Cross of the Court of Honour: August 24, 2013.

Scottish Rite Biography:
Brother Holsomback joined the Scottish Rite in the Valley of Honolulu on September 27, 1980, subsequently became a Master of the Royal Secret. He received the rank and decoration of a Knight Commander of the Court of Honour on October 21, 1985, was elected by the Supreme Council, 33°, Inspector General Honorary on October 18, 1991, and coroneted by Ill. Arthur James Wriston, Jr., 33°, Sovereign Grand Inspector General for Hawaii November 21, 1991. Brother Holsomback served his Valley as a Secretary and Personal Representative for the Deputy of Hawaii. On August 24, 2013, Ill. William Edwin Holsomback, 33°, was awarded the Grand Cross of the Court of Honour.

Bibliography:
Archive of the Supreme Council, 33°, S.J.

2013

Daniel Howard Jones
Grand Cross of the Court of Honour at age 66 years, 8 months, and 6 days
Tenure present
Nomination by Nashville, Tennessee Scottish Rite Bodies

Born: January 18, 1947 – present
Life span: present
Secretary of the Valley

Progress in Scottish Rite Masonry:
4°-14°: November 9, 1970, invested by *Moqedah* Lodge of Perfection, Nashville.
15°-18°: November 10, 1970, invested by *Immanuel* Chapter of Rose Croix, Nashville.
19°-30°: November 11, 1970, invested by *St. Michael* Council of Kadosh, Nashville.
31°-32°: November 12, 1970, invested by *Trinity* Consistory, Nashville.
32°, KCCH: October 6, 1997.
33°, IGH: elected August 24, 2007; coroneted by the Supreme Council, 33°, S.J., August 28, 2007.
Grand Cross of the Court of Honor: August 24, 2013.

Scottish Rite Biography:
Brother Daniel Howard Jones is a Master Mason of *John B. Garrett* Lodge, No. 711, Nashville, Tennessee, where he has also served as Secretary and on the Board of Custodians. On becoming a member of the Scottish Rite Brother Jones was elected by his classmates as President of the Class, and immediately started working in the Degrees and later started conferring Degrees. As of this time, he confers the Sixth Degree, The Fourteenth Degree, and the Thirty-Third Degree. Brother Jones was elected Knight Commander of the Court of Honor in 1997 and coroneted an Inspector General Honorary on August 28, 2007. On December 31, 2006, Brother Jones was appointed Executive Secretary of the Nashville Valley of the Ancient and Accepted Scottish Rite of Freemasonry. At the 2013 Biannual Session, he was recognized as one of the Scottish Rite Heroes of the Southern Jurisdiction and received the Grand Cross of the Court of Honour. He is a Life Member of the Scottish Rite Research Society. In 2014, Ill. Jones, 33°, G.C. was honored by Vanderbilt University as the recipient of the Communication Services Award, which he received on behalf of the Nashville Scottish Rite.

Bibliography:
Archive of the Supreme Council, 33°, S.J.
Archive of the Valley of Nashville.

2013

Elmer Ray Leppo, Jr.
Grand Cross of the Court of Honour at age 85 years, 11 months, and 26 days
Tenure present
Nomination by Baltimore, Maryland Scottish Rite Bodies

Born: August 28, 1928 – present
Personal Representative and Secretary of the Valley

Progress in Scottish Rite Masonry:
4°-14°: September 13, 1961, invested by *Albert Pike* Lodge of Perfection, Baltimore.
15°-18°: October 25, 1961, invested by *Meredith* Chapter of Rose Croix, Baltimore.
19°-30°: November 15, 1961, invested by *Maryland* Council of Kadosh, Baltimore.
31°-32°: December 6, 1961, invested by Chesapeake Consistory, Baltimore.
32°, KCCH: October 19, 1965.
33°, IGH: elected October 18, 1971; coroneted by the Supreme Council, 33°, S.J., October 21, 1971.
Grand Cross of the Court of Honour: August 24, 2013.

Scottish Rite Biography:
Brother Leppo was raised a Master Mason in *Pythagoras* Lodge, No. 123, at Cockeysville. In 1961 he joined the Scottish Rite Bodies of the Valley of Baltimore. Brother Leppo was invested as a Knight Commander of the Court of Honour on October 19, 1965; elected and coroneted an Inspector General Honorary, 33°, by the Supreme Council on October 21, 1971. Brother Leppo serves his Valley as a Personal Representative to the Sovereign Grand Inspector General for the Orient of Maryland, as a Secretary of the Valley of Baltimore and as a Vice President of the Scottish Rite Holding Company, as well as supports the charitable Valley Fund. Ill. Elmer Ray Leppo, Jr, 33°, received the highest honor of the Supreme Council, the Grand Cross of the Court of Honour on August 24, 2013.

Bibliography:
Archive of the Supreme Council, 33°, S.J.
Archive of the Orient of Maryland.

2013

Michael Mihai Marsellos
Grand Cross of the Court of Honour at age 81 years, 9 months, and 1 day
Tenure present
Nomination by Los Angeles, California Scottish Rite Bodies

Born: November 23, 1931 – present
Actor

Progress in Scottish Rite Masonry:
4°-14°: October 30, 1981, invested by *Los Angeles* Lodge of Perfection, Los Angeles.
15°-18°: October 30, 1981, invested by *Los Angeles* Chapter of Rose Croix, Los Angeles.
19°-30°: October 30, 1981, invested by *Los Angeles* Council of Kadosh, Los Angeles.
31°-32°: October 30, 1981, invested by *Los Angeles* Consistory, Los Angeles.
32°, KCCH: October 16, 1989.
33°, IGH: elected and coroneted by the Supreme Council, 33°, S.J., October 3, 2001.
Grand Cross of the Court of Honour: August 24, 2013.

Scottish Rite Biography:
Brother Marsellos was raised a Master Mason in *Silver Trowel* Lodge, No. 415, in Los Angeles. In October 1981 he joined the Scottish Rite Bodies of the Valley of Los Angeles. Later, affiliated with *Holliwood-Merlos* Lodge, No. 355, and the Scottish Rite Bodies of the Valley of Long Beach, receiving the rank and decoration of a Knight Commander of the Court of Honour in 1989, and coroneted by the Supreme Council on October 3, 2001, a 33°, Inspector General Honorary. Ill. Michael Mihai Marsellos, 33°, served his Valley as a Venerable Master of the Lodge of Perfection and Personal Representative to the SGIG in California. On August 24, 2013, Brother Marsellos was elected by the Supreme Council, 33°, S.J. to receive the Grand Cross of the Court of Honour.

Bibliography:
Archive of the Supreme Council, 33°, S.J.

2013

Ballard Lee Smith
Grand Cross of the Court of Honour at age 67 years, 9 months, and 24 days
Tenure present
Nomination by Shreveport, Louisiana Scottish Rite Bodies

Born: October 30, 1945 – present
Grand Master of the Grand Lodge of Louisiana – 1999
Certified Public Accountant

Progress in Scottish Rite Masonry:
4°-14°: April 20, 1968, invested by *Lake Charles* Lodge of Perfection, Lake Charles.
15°-18°: April 20, 1968, invested by *Lake Charles* Chapter of Rose Croix, Lake Charles.
19°-30°: April 20, 1968, invested by *Lake Charles* Council of Kadosh, Lake Charles.
31°-32°: April 20, 1968, invested by *Lake Charles* Consistory, Lake Charles.
32°, KCCH: October 19, 1981.
33°, IGH: elected October 19, 1987; coroneted by Ill. Walter Jessen, 33°, Sovereign Grand Inspector General for Louisiana on November 21, 1987.
Grand Cross of the Court of Honour: August 24, 2013.

Scottish Rite Biography:
Brother Smith was raised to the Sublime Degree in *Sulphur* Lodge, No. 424, at Sulphur, Louisiana and later affiliated with *Joppa* Lodge, No. 362, at Shreveport. In 1968, he joined the Scottish Rite Bodies of the Valley of Lake Charles, and soon after affiliated with the Valley of Shreveport, Louisiana and Valley of Little Rock, Arkansas. Brother Smith received the rank and decoration of a Knight Commander of the Court of Honour in 1981; in 1987 was elected by the Supreme Council an Inspector General Honorary, 33°, and coroneted by Ill. Walter Jessen, 33°, Sovereign Grand Inspector General for Louisiana on November 21, 1987. On August 24, 2013, Ill. Ballard Lee Smith, 33°, received the Scottish Rite highest honor, the Grand Cross of the Court of Honour. At that time, he was working upon the most needed historical project for the Orient of Louisiana – Louisiana Scottish Rite Honour Men, which was completed and published on January 6, 2014. Ill. Ballard Lee Smith, 33°, GC, served his Valley as Venerable Master, Wise Master, Commander, Master of Kadosh, Treasurer, and Director of Ritual Work. He also serves as the Director of the 33° team for Louisiana. Currently Ill. Smith, 33°, GC, is a Personal Representative of the Sovereign Grand Inspector General for Louisiana.

Bibliography:
Archive of the Supreme Council, 33°, S.J.
Archive of the Valley of Shreveport.

2015

Virgil Dale Andersen
Grand Cross of the Court of Honour at age 72 years, 11 months, and 22 days
Tenure present
Nomination by Yankton, South Dakota Scottish Rite Bodies

Born: August 29, 1943 – present
Grand Master of Masons of South Dakota 2008
Manager of a Telephone Company

Progress in Scottish Rite Masonry:
4°-14°: May 15, 1965, invested by *Alpha* Lodge of Perfection, Yankton.
15°-18°: May 16, 1965, invested by *Mackey* Chapter of Rose Croix, Yankton.
19°-30°: May 22, 1965, invested by *Robert de Bruce* Council of Kadosh, Yankton.
31°-32°: May 23, 1965, invested by *Oriental* Consistory, Yankton.
32°, KCCH: October 17, 1977.
33°, IGH: elected October 17, 1983; coroneted by Ill. Marvin Klein Bailin, 33°, Sovereign Grand Inspector General for South Dakota December 10, 1983.
Grand Cross of the Court of Honour: August 21, 2015.

Scottish Rite Biography:
Brother Andersen was raised to the Sublime Degree in *St. John's* Lodge, No. 1, in Yankton and later affiliated with *Incense* Lodge, No. 2, in Vermillion. He joined the Scottish Rite Bodies of the Valley of Yankton and was made a Master of the Royal Secret on May 23, 1965. Brother Andersen received the rank and decoration of a Knight Commander of the Court of Honour in 1977; in 1983 was elected by the Supreme Council an Inspector General Honorary, 33°, and coroneted by Ill. Marvin Klein Bailin, 33°, Sovereign Grand Inspector General for South Dakota December 10, 1983. Brother Andersen supports many charities of his Valley, giving a special attention to the Building Fund. On the Session of the Supreme Council of 2015, Ill. Virgil Dale Andersen, 33°, was elected to receive the Grand Cross of the Court of Honour.

Bibliography:
Archive of the Supreme Council, 33°, S.J.

2015

Jan Baker Carnahan
Grand Cross of the Court of Honour at age 78 years and 7 months
Tenure 4 years, 2 months, and 18 days
Nomination by Fairbanks, Alaska Scottish Rite Bodies

Born: January 21, 1937 – Died: November 9, 2019
Life span: 82 years, 9 months, and 18 days
Police officer

Progress in Scottish Rite Masonry:
4°-32°: invested October 14, 1968, by Luzon Scottish Rite Bodies, Philippines.
March 7, 1997, affiliated with Fairbanks Scottish Rite Bodies, Alaska.
32°, KCCH: October 4, 1999.
33°, IGH: elected October 6, 2003; coroneted by the Supreme Council, 33°, S.J. October 7, 2003.
Grand Cross of the Court of Honour: August 21, 2015.

Scottish Rite Biography:
Brother Carnahan was raised a Master Mason in *Fairbanks* Lodge, No. 12, in Fairbanks, Alaska. The Scottish Rite Degrees were invested to him on October 14, 1968, by Luzon Scottish Rite Bodies, Philippines. On March 7, 1997, Brother Carnahan affiliated with Fairbanks Scottish Rite Bodies, Alaska and on October 4, 1999, was invested with the rank and decoration of a Knight Commander of the Court of Honour. During the Session of the Supreme Council of 2003, he was coroneted a 33° Inspector General Honorary. On August 21, 2015, Ill. Jan Baker Carnahan, 33°, received the highest honor of the Supreme Council, the Grand Cross of the Court of Honour.

Bibliography:
Archive of the Supreme Council, 33°, S.J.
Photo courtesy of https://www.legacy.com/us/obituaries/newsminer/name/jan-carnahan-obituary?id=14780412

2015

Thomas Smith Crowl
Grand Cross of the Court of Honour at age 84 years, 11 months, and 11 days
Tenure present
Nomination by McAlester, Oklahoma Scottish Rite Bodies

Born: September 10, 1930 – present
Businessman

Progress in Scottish Rite Masonry:

4°-14°: February 20, 1961, invested by *McAlester* Lodge of Perfection, McAlester.

15°-18°: February 20, 1961, invested by *McAlester* Chapter of Rose Croix, McAlester.

19°-30°: February 21, 1961, invested by *McAlester* Council of Kadosh, McAlester.

31°-32°: February 22, 1961, invested by *McAlester* Consistory, McAlester.

32°, KCCH: October 19, 1987.

33°, IGH: elected October 6, 1997; coroneted by Paul T. Million, Jr., 33°, Sovereign Grand Inspector General for Oklahoma December 7, 1997.

Grand Cross of the Court of Honour: August 21, 2015.

Scottish Rite Biography:

Brother Crowl was raised a Master Mason in in *McAlester* Lodge, No. 96, at McAlester. In February 1961 he joined the Scottish Rite Bodies of the Valley of McAlester. He was invested as a Knight Commander of the Court of Honour on October 19, 1987; elected by the Supreme Council an Inspector General Honorary, 33°, on October 6, 1997, and coroneted by Paul T. Million, Jr., 33°, Sovereign Grand Inspector General for Oklahoma on December 7, 1997. Brother Crowl served his Valley as a Member of many committees, played a part in Degree work, and carry out a short tenure as Personal Representative for the Sovereign Grand Inspector General for Oklahoma. Brother Crowl is a generous contributor to many funds including Temple Restoration, Museum and Library, RiteCare Clinic, and the House of the Temple fundraising program Celebration of the Craft. On August 21, 2015, Ill. Thomas Smith Crowl, 33°, was elected by the Supreme Council to receive the Grand Cross of the Court of Honour.

Bibliography:

Archive of the Supreme Council, 33°, S.J.

2015

Shane Allan Harshbarger
Grand Cross of the Court of Honour at age 44 years, 3 months, and 18 days
Tenure present
Nomination by Des Moines, Iowa Scottish Rite Bodies

Born: May 3, 1971 – present
Life span: present
Secretary, Valley of Des Moines

Progress in Scottish Rite Masonry:
4°-14°: September 30, 1995, invested by *Des Moines* Lodge of Perfection, Des Moines.
15°-18°: November 2, 1996, invested by *Des Moines* Chapter of Rose Croix, Des Moines.
19°-30°: November 9, 1996, invested by *Des Moines* Council of Kadosh, Des Moines.
31°-32°: November 9, 1996, invested by *Des Moines* Consistory, Des Moines.
32°, KCCH: October 6, 2003.
33°, IGH: elected October 2, 2009; coroneted by Ill. Gary L. Sissel, 33°, Sovereign Grand Inspector General for Iowa December 5, 2009.
Grand Cross of the Court of Honour: August 21, 2015.

Scottish Rite Biography:
Brother Harshbarger was raised to the Sublime Degree on June 17, 1991, in *Malta* Lodge, No. 318, in Burlington. In 1995 he joined the Scottish Rite Bodies of the Valley of Des Moines and became a 32° Master of the Royal Secret on November 9, 1996. In 2003 Brother Harshbarger was invested with his first Scottish Rite honor a Knight Commander of the Court of Honour. On the Session of the Supreme Council of 2009, he was elected a 33°, Inspector General Honorary and coroneted by Ill. Gary L. Sissel, 33°, Sovereign Grand Inspector General for Iowa on December 5, 2009. Ill. Harshbarger served his Valley as Venerable Master of the Lodge of Perfection, and Master of Kadosh of the Consistory; 29° Master, member of other Degrees' teams, and member of the several keynote committees. From July 27, 2006, Ill. Harshbarger is the Secretary of the Valley. On August 21, 2015, Ill. Shane Allan Harshbarger, 33°, was elected by the Supreme Council to receive the Grand Cross of the Court of Honour.

Bibliography:
Archive of the Supreme Council, 33°, S.J.
Archive of the Valley of Des Moines.

2015

Gary Max Hinderks
Grand Cross of the Court of Honour at age 74 years, 3 months, and 19 days
Tenure present
Nomination by St. Joseph, Missouri Scottish Rite Bodies

Born: May 2, 1941 – present
Engineer

Progress in Scottish Rite Masonry:

4°-14°: October 26, 1984, invested by *St. Joseph* Lodge of Perfection, St. Joseph.

15°-18°: October 26, 1984, invested by *St. Joseph* Chapter of Rose Croix, St. Joseph.

19°-30°: October 27, 1984, invested by *St. Joseph* Council of Kadosh, St. Joseph.

31°-32°: October 27, 1984, invested by *St. Joseph* Consistory, St. Joseph.

32°, KCCH: October 16, 1989.

33°, IGH: elected October 18, 1993; coroneted by Ill. Earl Kaye Dille, 33°, Sovereign Grand Inspector General for Missouri November 13, 1993.

Grand Cross of the Court of Honour: August 21, 2015.

Scottish Rite Biography:

Brother Hinderks was raised a Master Mason in *Lathrop* Lodge No. 506, Lathrop, Missouri. In 1984 he joined the Scottish Rite Bodies of the Valley of St. Joseph and became a 32° Master of the Royal Secret on October 27, 1993. Afterward Brother Hinderks grew to be a dual member of the Valleys of St. Louis, Kansas City, Columbia, and Joplin, as well, as a great advocate and supporter of his own Valley, and especially the Scottish Rite Preservation Association and Scottish Rite Valley Foundation. In 1989 Brother Hinderks was invested as a Knight Commander of the Court of Honour; in 1993 elected and coroneted a 33°, Inspector General Honorary. Ill. Gary Max Hinderks, 33°, served his Valley as a Personal Representative to the Sovereign Grand Inspector General and on August 21, 2015, was awarded the Grand Cross of the Court of Honour.

Bibliography:

Archive of the Supreme Council, 33°, S.J.

Archive of the Valley of St. Joseph.

2015

John Ralph Marcucci
Grand Cross of the Court of Honour at age 73 years, 11 months, and 20 days
Tenure present
Nomination by Columbia, South Carolina Scottish Rite Bodies

Born: September 1, 1941 – present
Data Processing Manager

Progress in Scottish Rite Masonry:

4°-14°: April 4, 1992, invested by *Kansas City* Lodge of Perfection, Kansas City.

15°-18°: April 4, 1992, invested by *Kansas City* Chapter of Rose Croix, Kansas City.

19°-30°: April 11, 1992, invested by *Kansas City* Council of Kadosh, Kansas City.

31°-32°: April 11, 1992, invested by *Kansas City* Consistory, Kansas City.

September 2, 1992, affiliated with Columbia Scottish Rite Bodies.

32°, KCCH: October 6, 1997.

33°, IGH: elected and coroneted by the Supreme Council, 33°, S.J., October 3, 2001.

Grand Cross of the Court of Honour: August 21, 2015.

Scottish Rite Biography:

Brother Marcucci was raised to the Sublime Degree in *Sempler Fidelis* Lodge, No.680, in Jackson, North Carolina. He joined the Scottish Rite Bodies of the Valley of Kansas City and on April 11, 1992, became a 32° Master of the Royal Secret. On the same year Brother Marcucci affiliated with *Dentsville* Lodge, No. 398, in Columbia and Columbia Scottish Rite Bodies He received the rank and decoration of a Knight Commander of the Court of Honour in 1997 and was elected and coroneted by the Supreme Council a 33°, Inspector General Honorary on October 3, 2001. Brother Marcucci served his Valley as Venerable Master of the Lodge of Perfection, Wise Master of the Chapter of the Rose Croix, Commander of the Council of Kadosh, and Master of Kadosh of the Consistory. On August 21, 2015, Ill. John Ralph Marcucci, 33°, received the highest honor of the Supreme Council, the Grand Cross of the Court of Honour. Currently Ill. John Ralph Marcucci, 33°, GC, serves his Valley as Personal Representative.

Bibliography:

Archive of the Supreme Council, 33°, S.J.

2015

William Donald Patterson
Grand Cross of the Court of Honour at age 70 years and 9 days
Tenure present
Nomination by Tokyo, Japan and Korea Scottish Rite Bodies

Born: August 29, 1945 – present
Grand Master of the Grand Lodge of Japan - 1996
Professor

Progress in Scottish Rite Masonry:
4°-14°: February 22, 1974, invested by *Kansas City* Lodge of Perfection, Kansas City.
15°-18°: February 23, 1974, invested by *Kansas City* Chapter of Rose Croix, Kansas City.
19°-30°: February 23, 1974, invested by *Kansas City* Council of Kadosh, Kansas City.
31°-32°: February 23, 1974, invested by *Kansas City* Consistory, Kansas City.
32°, KCCH: October 9, 1995.
33°, IGH: elected October 6, 1997, coroneted November 28, 1997.
Grand Cross of the Court of Honour: August 21, 2015.

Scottish Rite Biography:
Brother Patterson became a Master Mason in *Old Mission* Lodge, No. 153, in Shawnee Mission, Kansas. In 1974 he became a member of the Scottish Rite Bodies of the Valley of Kansas City. Subsequently Brother Patterson moved to Japan, where he affiliated with *Tokyo Masonic Lodge*, No. 2, and Tokyo Scottish Rite Bodies. On October 9, 1995, he was elected a Knight Commander of the Court of Honour, and on the following Session of 1997, Brother Patterson was elected a 33°, Inspector General Honorary and coroneted November 28, 1997. He served his Valley as Wise Master of the Lodge of Perfection, and about fourteen years as Secretary. On August 21, 2015, Ill. William Donald Patterson, 33°, was selected by the Supreme Council 33°, S.J., to receive the Grand Cross of the Court of Honour.

Bibliography:
Archive of the Supreme Council, 33°, S.J.

2015

William Franklin Perdue
Grand Cross of the Court of Honour at age 80 years and 4 days
Tenure present
Nomination by Newport News, Virginia Scottish Rite Bodies

Born: August 17, 1935 – present
NASA Technician

Progress in Scottish Rite Masonry:
4°-14°: May 10, 1986, invested by *Newport News* Lodge of Perfection, Newport News.
15°-18°: May 10, 1986, invested by *Newport News* Chapter of Rose Croix, Newport News.
19°-30°: May 17, 1986, invested by *Newport News* Council of Kadosh, Newport News.
31°-32°: May 17, 1986, invested by *Newport News* Consistory, Newport News.
32°, KCCH: October 21, 1991.
33°, IGH: elected October 6, 1997; coroneted the Supreme Council, 33°, S.J., October 7, 1997.
Grand Cross of the Court of Honour: August 21, 2015.

Scottish Rite Biography:
Brother Perdue was raised to the Sublime Degree in *Mariner* Lodge, No. 215, in New Port News, later affiliated with *Warwick* Lodge, No. 336, and joined the Scottish Rite Bodies of the Valley of New Port News, becoming a 32°, Master of the Royal Secret on May 17, 1986. He was elected to receive the first Scottish Rite distinction, a Knight Commander of the Court of Honour in 1991, and on the Session of the Supreme Council for 1997 coroneted a 33°, Inspector General Honorary. On August 21, 2015, Ill. William Frank Perdue, 33°, received the highest Scottish Rite honor, the Grand Cross of the Court of Honour.

Bibliography:
Archive of the Supreme Council, 33°, S.J.

2015

Harold Sigfried Stein, Jr.
Grand Cross of the Court of Honour at age 83 years, 11 months, and 4 days
Tenure 6 years, 9 months, and 10 days
Nomination by San Francisco, California Scottish Rite Bodies

Born: September 17, 1931 – Died: May 31, 2022
Life span: 90 years, 8 months, and 4 days
Pharmacist

Progress in Scottish Rite Masonry:
4°-14°: April 9, 1954, invested by *San Francisco* Lodge of Perfection, San Francisco.
15°-18°: April 23, 1954, invested by *San Francisco* Chapter of Rose Croix, San Francisco.
19°-30°: May 14, 1954, invested by *San Francisco* Council of Kadosh, San Francisco.
31°-32°: June 4, 1954, invested by *San Francisco* Consistory, San Francisco.
32°, KCCH: October 22, 1963.
33°, IGH: elected October 20, 1975; coroneted by Ill. Henry C. Clausen, 33°, Sovereign Grand Inspector General for California December 13, 1975.
Grand Cross of the Court of Honour: August 21, 2015.

Scottish Rite Biography:
Brother Stein was raised a Master Mason in *Pacific Star King* Lodge, No. 136. In 1954 he joined the Scottish Rite Bodies of the Valley in San Francisco. Brother Stein was invested as a Knight Commander of the Court of Honour in 1963 and coroneted an Inspector General Honorary, 33°, by Ill. Henry C. Clausen, 33°, Sovereign Grand Inspector General for California on December 13, 1975. Ill. Harold Sigfried Stein, Jr., serves his Valley as Orator, participates in Degree works, and supports the Childhood Language Program. On August 21, 2015, Brother Stein was awarded the Grand Cross of the Court of Honour.

Bibliography:
Archive of the Supreme Council, 33°, S.J.

2015

Ralph Erskine Wayne
Grand Cross of the Court of Honour at age 82 years, 8 months, and 7 days
Tenure present

Nomination by Austin, Texas Scottish Rite Bodies

Born: December 14, 1932 – present
U.S. Congressman

Progress in Scottish Rite Masonry:
4°-14°: November 8, 1965, invested by *Dallas* Lodge of Perfection, Dallas.
15°-18°: November 8, 1965, invested by *Dallas* Chapter of Rose Croix, Dallas.
19°-30°: November 9, 1965, invested by *Dallas* Council of Kadosh, Dallas.
31°-32°: November 9, 1965, invested by *Dallas* Consistory, Dallas.
32°, KCCH: October 20, 1969.
33°, IGH: elected October 6, 2003; coroneted by the Supreme Council, 33°, S.J., October 7, 2003.
Grand Cross of the Court of Honour: August 21, 2015.

Scottish Rite Biography:
Brother Wayne was raised a Mater Mason in *Amarillo* Lodge, No. 731, in Amarillo, and later affiliated with *University* Lodge, No. 1190, in Austin. He joined the Scottish Rite Bodies of the Valley of Dallas in 1969, and on July 3, 1985, affiliated with the Scottish Rite Bodies of the Valley of Austin. Brother Wayne received his first Scottish Rite honor in 1969, being invested as a Knight Commander of the Court of Honour. On the Session of the Supreme Council for 2003, he was elected and coroneted an Inspector General Honorary, 33°. Brother Wayne serves as the President of the Board of Directors for the Scottish Rite Dormitory in Austin and serves on the Board of Directors for the Scottish Rite Children's hospital in Dallas. On August 21, 2015, Ill. Ralph Erskine Wayne, 33°, was awarded the Grand Cross of the Court of Honour.

Bibliography:
Archive of the Supreme Council, 33°, S.J.
Archive of the Valley of Austin.

2017

Theo Justin Bahr
Grand Cross of the Court of Honour at age 61 years, 1 month, and 3 days
Tenure 8 months and 8 days
Nomination by Boise, Idaho Scottish Rite Bodies

Born: July 16, 1956 – Died: April 27, 2018
Life span: 61 years, 9 months, and 11 days
Landscaper

Progress in Scottish Rite Masonry:
4°-14°: April 30, 1988, invested by *Boise* Lodge of Perfection, Boise.
15°-18°: May 1, 1988, invested by *Boise* Chapter of Rose Croix, Boise.
19°-30°: May 1, 1988, invested by *Boise* Council of Kadosh, Boise.
31°-32°: May 7, 1988, invested by *Boise* Consistory, Boise.
32°, KCCH: October 3, 2001.
33°, IGH: elected September 30, 2005; coroneted by Ill. Gary Wade West, 33°, Sovereign Grand Inspector General for Idaho November 5, 2005.
Grand Cross of the Court of Honour: August 19, 2017.

Scottish Rite Biography:
Brother Theo Justin Bahr was Master Mason in *Oriental* Lodge, No. 60, Boise. On April 30, 1988, he was invested with the 4°-14° by the *Boise* Lodge of Perfection. On May 1, 1988, he was invested by the *Boise* Chapter of Rose Croix with the 15°-18°, and on the same date was invested by the *Boise* Council of Kadosh with the 19°-30°. His 31°-32° he received on May 7, 1988, and this was invested by *Boise* Consistory. Brother Bahr became a KCCH on October 3, 2001, and a 33°, IGH, to which he was elected on September 30, 2005, and coroneted November 5, 2005, by Ill. Gary Wade West, 33°, Sovereign Grand Inspector General for Idaho. Brother Bahr served his Valley as a Wise Master of the Chapter of Rose Croix, Commander of the Council of Kadosh, Master of Kadosh of Consistory, and Valley Secretary. Ill. Theo Justin Bahr, 33°, received the Grand Cross of the Court of Honour on August 19, 2017.

Bibliography:
Archive of the Supreme Council, 33°, S.J.
In Memoriam. *Transactions.* 2019: 126.

2017

William Jerald Burfitt, Sr.
Grand Cross of the Court of Honour at age 75 years, 9 months, and 3 days
Tenure present
Nomination by Huntsville, Alabama Scottish Rite Bodies

Born: December 16, 1942 – present
Secretary of the Valley

Progress in Scottish Rite Masonry:
4°-14°: October 11, 1980, invested by *Huntsville* Lodge of Perfection, Huntsville.
15°-18°: October 11, 1980, invested by *Huntsville* Chapter of Rose Croix, Huntsville.
19°-30°: October 18, 1980, invested by *Huntsville* Council of Kadosh, Huntsville.
31°-32°: October 18, 1980, invested by *Huntsville* Consistory, Huntsville.
32°, KCCH: October 16, 1989.
33°, IGH: elected October 18, 1993; coroneted by Ill. Karl Reed, II, 33°, Sovereign Grand Inspector General for Alabama December 11, 1993.
Grand Cross of the Court of Honour: August 19, 2017.

Scottish Rite Biography:
Brother Burfitt was raised a Master Mason in *Apollo* Lodge, No. 921, in Huntsville, Alabama. He joined the Scottish Rite Valley of Huntsville and became a Master of the Royal Secret on October 18, 1980. In October 1989 he was invested with the rank and decoration of a Knight Commander of the Court of Honour, and on December 11, 1993, coroneted a 33° Inspector General Honorary by Ill. Karl Reed, II, 33°, Sovereign Grand Inspector General for Alabama. On August 19, 2007, Ill. William Jerald Burfitt, Sr., 33°, received the highest honor of the Supreme Council, the Grand Cross of the Court of Honour.

Bibliography:
Archive of the Supreme Council, 33°, S.J.

2017

Curtis Manning Edic
Grand Cross of the Court of Honour at age 72 years, 1 month, and 5 days
Tenure present
Nomination by Omaha, Nebraska Scottish Rite Bodies

Born: September 24, 1945 – present
Auctioneer

Progress in Scottish Rite Masonry:
4°-14°: April 14, 1975, invested by *Omaha* Lodge of Perfection, Omaha.
15°-18°: April 24, 1975, invested by *Omaha* Chapter of Rose Croix, Omaha.
19°-30°: April 25, 1975, invested by *Omaha* Council of Kadosh, Omaha.
31°-32°: April 25, 1975, invested by *Omaha* Consistory, Omaha.
32°, KCCH: October 21, 1985.
33°, IGH: elected October 9, 1995; coroneted by Ill. Warren Lichty, 33°, Sovereign Grand Inspector General for Nebraska December 2, 1995.
Grand Cross of the Court of Honour: August 19, 2017.

Scottish Rite Biography:
Brother Edic was raised to the Sublime Degree in *Coral* Lodge, No. 335, at Carson, Iowa. In 1975 he joined the Scottish Rite of the Valley of Omaha and became a 32° Master of the Royal Secret on April 25, 1975, receiving the rank and decoration of a Knight Commander of the Court of Honour in 1985. In 1995 Brother Edic was elected a 33°, Inspector General Honorory and coroneted by Ill. Warren Lichty, 33°, Sovereign Grand Inspector General for Nebraska on December 2, 1995. Brother Edic provides an outstanding service for his Valley. For fourteen years he has served as a Secretary of the Valley; currently serves as a Treasurer of Omaha Foundation, and Secretary/Treasurer for Omaha Cathedral Board. For many decades Brother Edic is a Donor and Supporter of the Century Club, Nebraska Foundation, Omaha Foundation, House of the Temple Fund, and many more. On August 19, 2017, the Supreme Council, 33°, S.J., awarded Ill. Curtis Manning Edic, 33°, the Grand Cross of the Court of Honour.

Bibliography:
Archive of the Supreme Council, 33°, S.J.

2017

Peter Steven Ekholm
Grand Cross of the Court of Honour at age 80 years, 8 months, and 26 days
Tenure present
Nomination by St. Paul, Minnesota Scottish Rite Bodies

Born: November 23, 1937 – present
Attorney

Progress in Scottish Rite Masonry:

4°-14°: September 30, 1959, invested by *St. Paul* Lodge of Perfection, St. Paul.

15°-18°: October 21, 1959, invested by *St. Paul* Chapter of Rose Croix, St. Paul.

19°-30°: December 2, 1959, invested by *St. Paul* Council of Kadosh, St. Paul.

31°-32°: December 16, 1959, invested by *Minnesota* Consistory, St. Paul.

32°, KCCH: October 15, 1979.

33°, IGH: elected October 18, 1993; coroneted by Ill. Daniel Levenduski, 33°, Sovereign Grand Inspector General for Minnesota December 11, 1993.

Grand Cross of the Court of Honour: August 19, 2017.

Scottish Rite Biography:

Brother Ekholm was raised a Master Mason in *MacAlester* Lodge, No. 290, at St. Paul. He became a member of the Scottish Rite Bodies of the Valley of St. Paul in 1959. Brother Ekholm invested as a Knight Commander of the Court of Honour in 1979, elected 33°, Inspector General Honorary by the Supreme Council on October 18, 1993, and coroneted by Daniel Levenduski, 33°, Sovereign Grand Inspector General for Minnesota on December 11, 1993. On August 19, 2017, Ill. Peter Steven Ekholm was awarded the Grand Cross of the Court of Honour.

Bibliography:

Archive of the Supreme Council, 33°, S.J.

Archive of St Paul, Minnesota.

2017

Jerry Lee Fenimore
Grand Cross of the Court of Honour at age 69 years, 3 months, and 1 day
Tenure present
Nomination by Denver, Colorado Scottish Rite Bodies

Born: May 18, 1948 – present
Principal

Progress in Scottish Rite Masonry:

4°-14°: May 8, 1982, invested by *Denver* Lodge of Perfection, Denver.

15°-18°: May 8, 1982, invested by *Denver* Chapter of Rose Croix, Denver.

19°-30°: May 15, 1982, invested by *Denver* Council of Kadosh, Denver.

31°-32°: May 15, 1982, invested by *Denver* Consistory, Denver.

32°, KCCH: October 4, 1999.

33°, IGH: elected October 6, 2003; coroneted by Ill. Dwight A. Hamilton, 33°, Sovereign Grand Inspector General for Colorado November 22, 2003.

Grand Cross of the Court of Honour: August 19, 2017.

Scottish Rite Biography:

Brother Fenimore became a Master Mason in *Black Hawk* Lodge, No. 11, in Denver. He joined the Scottish Rite Bodies in the Valley of Denver in 1982, receiving the rank and decoration of a Knight Commander of the Court of Honour in1999. Brother Fenimore was elected a 33°, Inspector General Honorary on October 6, 2003, and coroneted by Ill. Dwight A. Hamilton, 33°, Sovereign Grand Inspector General for Colorado on November 22, 2003. In 2004 he served his Valley as a Wise Master of the Lodge of Perfection. Ill. Jerry Lee Fenimore, 33°, awarded the Grand Cross of the Court of Honour on August 19, 2017.

Bibliography:

Archive of the Supreme Council, 33°, S.J.

2017

Walter Eugene Johnson, Jr.
Grand Cross of the Court of Honour at age 83 years and 7 days
Tenure present
Nomination by Portland, Oregon Scottish Rite Bodies

Born: August 12, 1934 – present

Manager

Progress in Scottish Rite Masonry:

4°-14°: November 12, 1962, invested by *Oregon* Lodge of Perfection, Portland.

15°-18°: November 12, 1962, invested by *Ainsworth* Chapter of Rose Croix, Portland.

19°-30°: November 14, 1962, invested by *Multnomah* Council of Kadosh, Portland.

31°-32°: November 14, 1962, invested by *Oregon* Consistory, Portland.

32°, KCCH: October 2, 2009.

33°, IGH: elected August 24, 2013; coroneted by the Supreme Council, 33°, S. J., August 27, 2013.

Grand Cross of the Court of Honour: August 19, 2017.

Scottish Rite Biography:

Brother Johnson was raised a Master Mason in *Lents* Lodge, No. 156, in Portland. He joined the Scottish Rite Bodies of the Valley of Portland and became a 32°, Master of the Royal Secret on November 14, 1962. Brother Johnson was elected to receive the Knight Commander of the Court of Honour on October 2, 2009, and was elected and coroneted by the Supreme Council, 33°, S. J., an Inspector General Honorary, 33°, on August 27, 2013. Ill. Walter Eugene Johnson, Jr., 33°, served his Valley as Personal Representative to the Sovereign Grand Inspector General, and received the Scottish Rite's highest honor, the Grand Cross of the Court of Honour on August 19, 2017.

Bibliography:

Archive of the Supreme Council, 33°, S. J.

2017

Bobby Lee Laws
Grand Cross of the Court of Honour at age 79 years, 3 months, and 1 day
Tenure present
Nomination by Guthrie, Oklahoma Scottish Rite Bodies

Born: May 18, 1938 – present
U.S. Air Force Instructor

Progress in Scottish Rite Masonry:

4°-14°: May 16, 1976, invested by *Guthrie* Lodge of Perfection, Guthrie.

15°-18°: May 17, 1976, invested by *Guthrie* Chapter of Rose Croix, Guthrie.

19°-30°: May 17, 1976, invested by *Guthrie* Council of Kadosh, Guthrie.

31°-32°: May 18, 1976, invested by *Guthrie* Consistory, Guthrie.

32°, KCCH: October 17, 1983.

33°, IGH: elected October 21, 1991; coroneted by Ill. Paul Million, 33°, Sovereign Grand Inspector General for Oklahoma December 8, 1991.

Grand Cross of the Court of Honour: August 19, 2017.

Scottish Rite Biography:

Brother Laws was raised a Master Mason in *Altus* Lodge, No. 62, at Altus. He became a member of Guthrie Valley Scottish Rite Bodies in May 1976 and received his first distinction, the Knight Commander of the Court of Honour on October 17, 1983. On the Session of the Supreme Council for 1991, Brother Laws was elected a 33°, Inspector General Honorary and coroneted by Ill. Paul Million, 33°, Sovereign Grand Inspector General for Oklahoma on December 8, 1991. Brother Laws is a loyal supporter of the charities of the Valley, including donations to preserve the House of the Temple. On August 19, 2017, Ill. Bobby Lee Laws, 33°, was awarded the Grand Cross of the Court of Honour.

Bibliography:

Archive of the Supreme Council, 33°, S.J.

2017

John William McNaughton
Grand Cross of the Court of Honour at age 66 years and 7 months
Tenure – present
Nomination by The Supreme Council, 33°, S.J., USA for Northern Jurisdiction, USA

Born: January 19, 1950 – present
Sovereign Grand Commander of The Supreme Council, 33°, A.&A.S.R., N.J., USA

Progress in Scottish Rite Masonry:
4°-14°: April 1, 1975, received from *Fort Wayne* Lodge of Perfection, Fort Wayne.
15°-16°: April 1, 1975, received from *Fort Wayne* Council of Princes of Jerusalem, Fort Wayne.
17°-18°: April 1, 1975, received from *Fort Wayne* Chapter of Rose Croix, Fort Wayne.
19°-32°: April 1, 1975, received from *Fort Wayne* Consistory, Fort Wayne.
33°: conferred September 23, 1997.
Active Member for Indiana: September 29, 1998.
Sovereign Grand Commander: installed August 28, 2006; retired October 1, 2017.
Grand Cross of the Court of Honour: August 19, 2017.

Scottish Rite Biography:
Brother John William McNaughton is a Master Mason in *Maumee* Lodge, No. 725, Fort Wayne. Brother McNaughton joined Fort Wayne Scottish Rite Bodies and rose rapidly through the ranks of the Scottish Rite. He presided as Thrice Potent Master of *Fort Wayne* Lodge of Perfection; received the 33° in 1997; became an Active Member for Indiana in 1998; served on several key Committees within the Supreme Council, became Grand Lieutenant Commander, and on August 28, 2006, Past Sovereign Grand Commander, Illustrious Robert O. Ralston, 33°, installed into office duly elected Sovereign Grand Commander, Illustrious John William McNaughton, 33°. During his tenure, Grand Commander McNaugton displayed his business and managerial acumen by establishing a sound financial footing for the 32°, the Children's Dyslexia Centers, and the Scottish Rite Masonic Museum & Library. He has also streamlined ceremonies; begun work on Degree revisions; insisted that Scottish Rite events be inspirational; focused the charitable endeavors of the Scottish Rite to benefit Brothers in need of assistance.

Bibliography:
https://scottishritenmj.org/about/history/sovereign-grand-commanders

2017

Glen Gordon Pitts
Grand Cross of the Court of Honour at age 74 years, 8 months, and 16 days
Tenure present

Nomination by Memphis, Tennessee Scottish Rite Bodies

Born: January 3, 1943 – present
Supervisor

Progress in Scottish Rite Masonry:
4°-14°: November 12, 1971, invested by *Memphis* Lodge of Perfection, Memphis.
15°-18°: November 13, 1971, invested by *Memphis* Chapter of Rose Croix, Memphis.
19°-30°: November 19, 1971, invested by *Memphis* Council of Kadosh, Memphis.
31°-32°: November 20, 1971, invested by *Memphis* Consistory, Memphis.
32°, KCCH: October 15, 1979.
33°, IGH: elected October 9, 1995; coroneted by Ill. Joseph Martin, 33°, Sovereign Grand Inspector General for Tennessee December 9, 1995.
Grand Cross of the Court of Honour: August 19, 2017.

Scottish Rite Biography:
Brother Pitts was raised to the Sublime Degree in *Unity* Lodge, No. 95, at Memphis. He became a member of the Valley of Memphis Scottish Rite Bodies in November 1971. Brother Pitts received the rank and decoration of a Knight Commander of the Court of Honour on October 15, 1995; was elected a 33°, Inspector General Honorary on October 9, 1995, and coroneted by Ill. Joseph Martin, 33°, Sovereign Grand Inspector General for Tennessee December 9, 1995. Ill. Glen Gordon Pitts, 33°, served his Valley as Secretary, and on August 19, 2017, was elected by the Supreme Council to receive the Grand Cross of the Court of Honour.

Bibliography:
Archive of the Supreme Council, 33°, S.J.

2017

Richard Mahlon Ripley
Grand Cross of the Court of Honour at age 94 years, 11 months, and 26 days
Tenure 3 years, 1 month, and 29 days
Nomination by Raleigh, North Carolina Scottish Rite Bodies

Born: August 23, 1922 – October 18, 2020
Life span: 98 years, 1 month, and 25 days
Colonel

Progress in Scottish Rite Masonry:
4°-14°: October 28, 1994, invested by *Raleigh* Lodge of Perfection, Raleigh.
15°-18°: October 29, 1994, invested by *Raleigh* Chapter of Rose Croix, Raleigh.
19°-30°: October 29, 1994, invested by *Raleigh* Council of Kadosh, Raleigh.
31°-32°: October 29, 1994, invested by *Raleigh* Consistory, Raleigh.
32°, KCCH: October 4, 1999.
33°, IGH: elected September 30, 2005; coroneted by the Supreme Council, 33°, S.J., October 4, 2005.
Grand Cross of the Court of Honour: August 19, 2017.

Scottish Rite Biography:
Brother Ripley was raised a Master Mason in *Doric* Lodge, No. 342, at Grand Rapids, Michigan, later on affiliated with *Raleigh* Lodge, No. 500, at Raleigh, and *Millbrook* Lodge No. 97, at Raleigh. He joined the Scottish Rite Bodies of the Valley of Raleigh and became a 32°, Master of the Royal Secret on October 29, 1994. He received the rank and decoration of a Knight Commander of the Court of Honour in 1999 and was coroneted a 33° Inspector General Honorary in 2006. Brother Ripley served his Valley as Wise Master of the Lodge of Perfection, as Commander of the Council of Kadosh, and as Master of Kadosh of the Consistory. In 2017 Ill. Richard Mahlon Ripley, 33°, received the highest honor of the Supreme Council, the Grand Cross of the Court of Honour.

Bibliography:
Archive of the Supreme Council, 33°, S.J.
Archive of the Valley of Raleigh.

2017

Richard Bruce Smith
Grand Cross of the Court of Honour at age 58 years, 9 months, and 17 days
Tenure present
Nomination by Lake Charles, Louisiana Scottish Rite Bodies

Born: November 1, 1958 – present
Vice President of the Economic Development Alliance

Progress in Scottish Rite Masonry:
4°-14°: October 10, 1981, invested by *Lake Charles* Lodge of Perfection, Lake Charles.
15°-18°: October 11, 1981, invested by *Lake Charles* Chapter of Rose Croix, Lake Charles.
19°-30°: October 24, 1981, invested by *Lake Charles* Council of Kadosh, Lake Charles.
31°-32°: October 25, 1981, invested by *Lake Charles* Consistory, Lake Charles.
32°, KCCH: October 19, 1987.
33°, IGH: elected October 18, 1993, coroneted by the Supreme Council, 33°, S.J. October 19, 1993.
Grand Cross of the Court of Honour: August 19, 2017.
Deputy: January 1, 2019 – August 18, 2019.
SGIG: elected August 17, 2019; crowned August 18, 2019; present.

Scottish Rite Biography:
Brother Smith was raised in 1981 in *Lake Charles* Lodge, No. 165 F&AM. He became a 32° Master of the Royal Secret in the Valley of Lake Charles in 1981 and presided over all four Bodies – Lodge of Perfection, Chapter of Rose Croix, Council of Kadosh and Consistory. In 1993 he was coroneted a 33° Inspector General Honorary, in 1995 he was appointed Personal Representative in Lake Charles, and in 2017 the Supreme Council bestowed on him the Grand Cross of the Court of Honour. On January 1, 2019, Ill. Richard Bruce Smith, 33°, GC, was appointed Deputy for the Orient of Louisiana, and on the Session of the Supreme Council in the same year, on August 17, 2019, the Supreme Council elected Ill. Richard Bruce Smith, 33°, GC, as Sovereign Grand Inspector General for Louisiana and crowned him on August 18, 2019.

Bibliography:
Archive of the Supreme Council, 33°, S.J.
Ill. Richard B. Smith Appointed Deputy in Louisiana, *The Scottish Rite Journal*, January–February 2019: 15.

2017

Frederick Ashley Spicer
Grand Cross of the Court of Honour at age 57 years and 1 month
Tenure present
Nomination by Baltimore, Maryland Scottish Rite Bodies

Born: July 19, 1960 – present
Orient Secretary

Progress in Scottish Rite Masonry:

4°-14°: March 18, 1998, invested by *Baltimore* Lodge of Perfection., Baltimore.

15°-18°: April 1, 1998, invested by *Baltimore* Chapter of Rose Croix, Baltimore.

19°-30°: April 25, 1998, invested by *Baltimore* Council of Kadosh, Baltimore.

31°-32°: April 25, 1998, invested by *Baltimore* Consistory, Baltimore.

32°, KCCH: October 6, 2003.

33°, IGH: elected August 24, 2007; coroneted by the Supreme Council, 33°, S.J., August 28, 2007.

Grand Cross of the Court of Honour: August 19, 2017.

Scottish Rite Biography:

Brother Spicer was raised to the Sublime Degree in *Amicable* Lodge, No. 25, at Hunt Valley. He joined the Scottish Rite Bodies of the Valley of Baltimore in 1998 and became a 32°, Master of the Royal Secret on April 25, 1998, was invested as a Knight Commander of the Court of Honour in 2003, and coroneted a 33°, Inspector General Honorary in 2007. Brother Spicer served his Valley as a Wise Master of the Lodge of Perfection, as a Secretary of the Valley, and as an Acting Personal Representative, along with being a great supporter of the Charitable Fund of the Valley of Baltimore. On August 19, 2017, Ill. Frederick Ashley Spicer, 33°, was elected by the Supreme Council to receive the Grand Cross of the Court of Honour, the highest honor of the Scottish Rite. Now Ill. Frederick Ashley Spicer, 33°, GC, serves the Orient of Maryland as Orient Secretary.

Bibliography:

Archive of the Supreme Council, 33°, S.J.

Archive of the Orient of Maryland.

2019

William Michael Alexander
Grand Cross of the Court of Honour at age 64 years, 2 months, and 5 days
Tenure present
Nomination by Seoul, Japan, and Korea Scottish Rite Bodies

Born: June 12, 1955 – present
U.S. Army Colonel

Progress in Scottish Rite Masonry:
4°-14°: June 8, 1985, invested by *Louisville* Lodge of Perfection, Louisville.
15°-18°: June 8, 1985, invested by *Louisville* Chapter of Rose Croix, Louisville.
19°-30°: June 8, 1985, invested by *Louisville* Council of Kadosh, Louisville.
31°-32°: June 8, 1985, invested by *Louisville* Consistory, Louisville.
32°, KCCH: October 4, 1999.
33°, IGH: elected September 30, 2005; coroneted by the Supreme Council, 33°, S.J., October 4, 2005.
Grand Cross of the Court of Honour: August 17, 2019.

Scottish Rite Biography:
Brother Alexander was raised to the Sublime Degree in *Camp Knox* Lodge, No. 919, in Redcliff, Kentucky. In 1985 he joined the Scottish Rite Bodies of the Valley of Louisville and on June 8, 1985, became a 32° Master of the Royal Secret. In 1998 Brother Alexander was assigned to station in Korea, were he affiliated with *Pusan* Lodge, No. 1675, and the Valley of Seoul. He received his first Scottish Rite distinction, Knight Commander of the Court of Honour on October 4, 1999, and on the Session of 2005, the Supreme Council elected and coroneted him a 33°, Inspector General Honorary. Brother Alexander served his Valley as Commander of the Council of Kadosh, Master of Kadosh of the Consistory, and a long term as Personal Representative. Currently Brother Alexander serves his Valley as Secretary. On August 17, 2019, Ill. William Michael Alexander, 33°, received the highest Scottish Rite honor, Grand Cross of the Court of Honour.

Bibliography:
Archive of the Supreme Council, 33°., S.J.

2019

Larry Don Berry
Grand Cross of the Court of Honour at age 72 years, 11 months, and 18 days
Tenure present
Nomination by Little Rock, Arkansas Scottish Rite Bodies

Born: September 29, 1946 – present
Veterinarian

Progress in Scottish Rite Masonry:
4°-14°: February 13, 1971, invested by *Arkansas* Lodge of Perfection, Little Rock.
15°-18°: February 13, 1971, invested by *Arkansas* Chapter of Rose Croix, Little Rock.
19°-30°: February 20, 1971, invested by *Arkansas* Council of Kadosh, Little Rock.
31°-32°: February 20, 1971, invested by *Arkansas* Consistory, Little Rock.
32°, KCCH: October 15, 1979.
33°, IGH: elected October 21, 1991; coroneted by Ill. Aaron B. Pierce, 33°, Sovereign Grand Inspector General for Arkansas December 7, 1991.
Grand Cross of the Court of Honour: August 17, 2019.

Scottish Rite Biography:
Brother Berry was raised a Master Mason in *Searcy* Lodge, No. 49, at Searcy. In 1971 he joined the Scottish Rite Bodies of the Valley of Arkansas and was made a 32° Master of the Royal Secret on February 20, 1971. In 1979 he received the rank and decoration of a Knight Commander of the Court of Honour; on October 21, 1991, elected by the Supreme Council a 33°, Inspector General Honorary and coroneted by Ill. Aaron B. Pierce, 33°, Sovereign Grand Inspector General for Arkansas on December 7, 1991. Ill. Berry served his Valley as Venerable Master of the Lodge of Perfection, Wise Master of the Chapter of Rose Croix, and Member of the 33° Conferral Cast, along with supporting charities of the Orient and Valley. Ill. Larry Don Berry, 33°, received the highest honor of the Supreme Council, the Grand Cross of the Court of Honour on August 17, 2019. Currently Ill. Larry Don Berry, 33°, GC, serves the Orient as a Personal Representative for the Sovereign Grand Inspector General for Arkansas.

Bibliography:
Archive of the Supreme Council, 33°, S.J.

2019

Leighton Dudley Fowles
Grand Cross of the Court of Honour at age 76 years, 2 months, and 10 days
Tenure present
Nomination by Taipei, Taiwan Scottish Rite Bodies

Born: June 7, 1943 – present
Broker

Progress in Scottish Rite Masonry:
4°-14°: June 29, 1979, invested by *Taipei* Lodge of Perfection, Taiwan.
15°-18°: June 29, 1979, invested by *Taipei* Chapter of Rose Croix, Taiwan..
19°-30°: June 29, 1979, invested by *Taipei* Council of Kadosh, Taiwan.
31°-32°: June 30, 1979, invested by *Taipei* Consistory, Taiwan.
32°, KCCH: October 17, 1983.
33°, IGH: elected October 16, 1989; coroneted by Ill. Ian Lin, 33°, Deputy for Taiwan and China December 1, 1989.
Grand Cross of the Court of Honour: August 17, 2019.

Scottish Rite Biography:
Brother Fowles was raised to the Sublime Degree in *St. John* Lodge, No. 1072, In Bangkok, Thailand. He joined the Scottish Rite Bodies of the Valley of Taipei, and became a 32°, Master of the Royal Secret on June 30, 1979. Brother Fowles received the rank and decoration of a Knight Commander of the Court of Honour in 1983, was elected a 33°, Inspector General Honorary on the Session of the Supreme Council for 1989, and coroneted by Ill. Ian Lin, 33°, Deputy for Taiwan and China December 1, 1989. Ill. Leighton Dudley Fowles, 33°, received the Scottish Rite's highest honor, the Grand Cross of the Court of Honour on August 17, 2019.

Bibliography:
Archive of the Supreme Council, 33°, S.J.

2019

David Hittner
Grand Cross of the Court of Honour at age 80 years, 1 month, and 7 days
Tenure present
Nomination by Houston, Texas Scottish Rite Bodies

Born: July 10, 1939 – present
Judge

Progress in Scottish Rite Masonry:
4°-14°: December 5, 1970, invested by *San. Jacinto* Lodge of Perfection, Houston.
15°-18°: December 5, 1970, invested by *Houston* Chapter of Rose Croix, Houston.
19°-30°: December 5, 1970, invested by *Houston* Council of Kadosh, Houston.
31°-32°: December 5, 1970, invested by *Houston* Consistory, Houston.
32°, KCCH: October 21, 1985.
33°, IGH: elected October 21, 1991; coroneted by Ill. Sam E. Hilburn, 33°, Sovereign Grand Inspector General for Texas on November 15, 1991.
Grand Cross of the Court of Honour: August 17, 2019.

Scottish Rite Biography:
Brother Hittner was raised to the Sublime Degree in *Temple* Lodge, No. 4, in Houston. He joined the Scottish Rite Bodies of the Valley of Houston and received the 32°, Master of the Royal Secret on December 5, 1970. Brother Hittner received the rank and decoration of a Knight Commander of the Court of Honour in 1985, elected by the Supreme Council a 33°, Inspector General Honorary on October 21, 1991, and coroneted by Ill. Sam E. Hilburn, 33°, Sovereign Grand Inspector General for Texas on November 15, 1991.Ill. David Hittner 33°, received the Scottish Rite's highest honor, the Grand Cross of the Court of Honour on August 17, 2019.

Bibliography:
Archive of the Supreme Council, 33°, S.J.

2019

Jerry James Johnson
Grand Cross of the Court of Honour at age 72 years, and 21 days
Tenure present
Nomination by St. Paul, Minnesota Scottish Rite Bodies

Born: July 26, 1947 – present
Educator

Progress in Scottish Rite Masonry:
4°-14°: April 24, 1982, invested by *Minneapolis* Lodge of Perfection, Minneapolis.
15°-18°: April 24, 1982, invested by *Minneapolis* Chapter of Rose Croix, Minneapolis.
19°-30°: April 24, 1982, invested by *Minneapolis* Council of Kadosh, Minneapolis.
31°-32°: April 24, 1982, invested by *Minneapolis* Consistory, Minneapolis.
August 5, 1998, affiliated with St. Paul Scottish Rite Bodies, St. Paul.
32°, KCCH: October 4, 1999.
33°, IGH: elected October 6, 2003; coroneted by Ill. Jerry B. Oliver, 33°, Sovereign Grand Inspector General for Minnesota November 22, 2003.
Grand Cross of the Court of Honour: August 17, 2019.

Scottish Rite Biography:
Brother Johnson was raised to the Sublime Degree in *Ancient Landmark* Lodge, No. 5, at St. Paul. In 1982 he joined the Scottish Rite Bodies of the Valley of Minnesota and made a Master of the Royal Secret on April 24, 1982. He received the rank and decoration of a Knight Commander of the Court of Honour in 1999, elected 33°, Inspector General Honorary on October 6, 2003, and coroneted by Ill. Jerry B. Oliver, 33°, Sovereign Grand Inspector General for Minnesota November 22, 2003. Ill. Jerry James Johnson, 33°, was elected by the Supreme Council to receive the Grand Cross of the Court of Honour in 2019. Brother Johnson served his Valley as a Wise Master of the Lodge of Perfection. Currently Ill. Johnson is an Almoner of the Valley and Orient Personal Representative.

Bibliography:
Archive of the Supreme Council, 33°, S.J.

2019

Robert Mitchel Julian
Grand Cross of the Court of Honour at age 65 years, 1 month, and 20 days
Tenure present
Nomination by Boise, Idaho Scottish Rite Bodies

Born: June 27, 1954 – present
Businessman

Progress in Scottish Rite Masonry:
4°-14°: November 8, 1973, invested by *Boise* Lodge of Perfection, Boise.
15°-18°: November 9, 1973, invested by *Boise* Chapter of Rose Croix, Boise.
19°-30°: November 9, 1973, invested by *Boise* Council of Kadosh, Boise.
31°-32°: November 10, 1973, invested by *Boise* Consistory, Boise.
32°, KCCH: October 17, 1983.
33°, IGH: elected October 21, 1991; coroneted by Ill. Lowell Charles Jensen, 33°, Sovereign Grand Inspector General for Idaho December 7, 1991.
Grand Cross of the Court of Honour: August 17, 2019.

Scottish Rite Biography:
Brother Julian was raised to the Sublime Degree in *Oriental* Lodge, No. 60, in Boise. In 1973 he joined the Scottish Rite Bodies of the Valley of Boise and became a 32° Master of the Royal Secret on November 10, 1973. Later, on November 2, 2012, Brother Julian affiliated with the Scottish Rite Bodies of the Valley of Baker, Orient of Oregon. He received his first Scottish Rite distinction, the rank and decoration of a Knight Commander of the Court of Honour on October 17, 1983. On October 21, 1991, the Supreme Council elected Brother Julian a 33°, Inspector General Honorary, and on December 7, 1991, he was coroneted by Ill. Lowell Charles Jensen, 33°, Sovereign Grand Inspector General for Idaho. On August 17, 2019, Ill. Robert Mitchel Julian, 33°, received the Scottish Rite's highest honour, the Grand Cross of the Court of Honour. At present time Ill. Julian serves his Valley as Acting Secretary.

Bibliography:
Archive of the Supreme Council, 33°, S.J.

2019

James Houston Morgan III
Grand Cross of the Court of Honour at age 72 years, 5 months, and 5 days
Tenure present
Nomination by Baton Rouge, Louisiana Scottish Rite Bodies

Born: March 12, 1947 – present
Attorney

Progress in Scottish Rite Masonry:

4°-14°: October 26, 1974, invested by *Baton Rouge* Lodge of Perfection, Baton Rouge.

15°-18°: October 27, 1974, invested by *Baton Rouge* Chapter of Rose Croix, Baton Rouge.

19°-30°: November 9, 1974, invested by *Baton Rouge* Council of Kadosh, Baton Rouge.

31°-32°: November 10, 1974, invested by *Baton Rouge* Consistory, Baton Rouge.

32°, KCCH: October 15, 1979.

33°, IGH: elected October 4, 1999; coroneted by Ill. Ronald A. Seale, 33°, Sovereign Grand Inspector General for Louisiana on November 13, 1999.

Grand Cross of the Court of Honour: August 17, 2019.

Scottish Rite Biography:

Brother Morgan was raised a Master Mason in *East Gate* Lodge, No. 452, at Baton Rouge on November 20, 1973. In 1974 he joined the Scottish Rite Bodies of the Valley of Baton Rouge, and a few years later, on October 15, 1979, received his first rank and decoration of a Knight Commander of the Court of Honour. On a biennial Session of the Supreme Council in October 1999, Brother Morgan was elected a 33° Inspector General Honorary and coroneted by Ill. Ronald A. Seale, 33°, Sovereign Grand Inspector General for Louisiana on November 13, 1999. Brother Morgan became a beneficial supporter of the Valley and Orient charities of the Louisiana Scottish Rite Foundation, Learning Center, and Almoner Fund and some others. In 2014 Ill. Morgan joined the Development Office of the Supreme Council and became a Major Donor Officer for the Southeast part of the Jurisdiction. On August 17, 2019, Ill. James Houston "Chuck" Morgan, III, 33°, was elected by the Supreme Council to receive the Grand Cross of the Court of Honour.

Bibliography:

Archive of the Supreme Council, 33°, S.J.

2019

Dean Matthew Resch
Grand Cross of the Court of Honour at age 74 years, 9 months, and 18 days
Tenure present
Nomination by Panama City, Florida Scottish Rite Bodies

Born: October 29, 1944 – present
U.S. Army Pilot

Progress in Scottish Rite Masonry:
4°-14°: December 12, 1976, invested by *Dothan* Lodge of Perfection, Dothan.
15°-18°: December 12, 1976, invested by *Dothan* Chapter of Rose Croix, Dothan.
19°-30°: December 12, 1976, invested by *Dothan* Council of Kadosh, Dothan.
31°-32°: December 12, 1976, invested by *Dothan* Consistory, Dothan.
December 30, 1988, affiliated with Guthrie Scottish Rite Bodies, Oklahoma.
June 22, 2001, affiliated with Panama City Scottish Rite Bodies, Florida.
32°, KCCH: September 30, 2005.
33°, IGH: elected August 18, 2011; coroneted by Ill. Dale I. Goering, 33°, Sovereign Grand Inspector General for Florida November 12, 2011.
Grand Cross of the Court of Honour: August 17, 2019.

Scottish Rite Biography:
Brother Resch entered the Masonic Fraternity in 1976 and is a Past Master of *Daleville* Lodge, No. 903, Daleville, AL and *Acacia* Lodge, No. 16, Commonwealth of Virginia. He served as District Deputy Grand Master, Masonic District 6, Virginia for Grand Master James Dean Cole, our Sovereign Grand Commander. Resch is a member of *Pythagoras* Lodge No. 358, Panama City Beach, FL. He became a Scottish Rite mason in 1976 in Dothan, AL. He demitted to the Panama City Valley in 2001 and became very active. He was Coroneted a 33° in 2011 and is currently serving the SGIG as the Personal Representative in the Panama City Valley. He is a continuing personal donor to the Scottish Rite Foundation of Florida as well as being a major fundraiser for the Foundation. Ill. Dean Matthew Resch, 33°, received the Scottish Rite's highest honor, the Grand Cross, on August 17, 2019.

Bibliography:
Archive of the Supreme Council, 33°, S.J.
Blaisdell, Ron. Ill. Dean Resch, 33° of Panama City elected to receive Grand Cross. AASR Orient of Florida, August 2019.

2019

J. Douglas Sorrells
Grand Cross of the Court of Honour at age 82 years, 8 months, and 2 days
Tenure present
Nomination by Montgomery, Alabama Scottish Rite Bodies

Born: December 15, 1937 – present
Technician

Progress in Scottish Rite Masonry:
4°-14°: April 13, 1965, invested by *Pensacola* Lodge of Perfection, Pensacola.
15°-18°: April 14, 1965, invested by *Pensacola* Chapter of Rose Croix, Pensacola.
19°-30°: April 21, 1965, invested by *Pensacola* Council of Kadosh, Pensacola.
31°-32°: April 21, 1965, invested by *Pensacola* Consistory, Pensacola.
March 17, 1999, dual Member in Montgomery Scottish Rite Bodies.
32°, KCCH: October 3, 2001.
33°, IGH: elected September 30, 2005; coroneted by Ill. Karl F. Reed, II, 33°, Sovereign Grand Inspector General for Alabama, December 10, 2005.
Grand Cross of the Court of Honour: August 17, 2019.

Scottish Rite Biography:
Brother Sorrells was raised a Master Mason in *Andalusia* Lodge, No. 434, in Andalusia. He joined the Scottish Rite in Pensacola in 1965, and later, on March 17, 1999, affiliated with the Scottish Rite Bodies of Montgomery Valley. He was elected to the rank and decoration of a Knight Commander of the Court of Honour in 2001, and coroneted a 33° Inspector General Honorary by Ill. Karl Reed, II, 33°, Sovereign Grand Inspector General for Alabama on December 10, 2005. Ill. J. Douglas Sorrells, 33°, received the Grand Cross of the Court of Honour on August 17, 2019.

Bibliography:
Archive of the Supreme Council, 33°, S.J.

2019

Joe Allen Williams
Grand Cross of the Court of Honour at age 83 years, 2 months, and 29 days
Tenure 2 years, 8 months, and 16 days
Nomination by Guthrie, Oklahoma Scottish Rite Bodies

Born: May 16, 1936 – Died: May 2, 2022
Life span: 85 years, 11 months, and 17 days
Judge

Progress in Scottish Rite Masonry:
4°-14°: January 21, 1958, invested by *Guthrie* Lodge of Perfection, Guthrie.
15°-18°: January 21, 1958, invested by *Guthrie* Chapter of Rose Croix, Guthrie.
19°-30°: January 22, 1958, invested by *DeSonnac* Council of Kadosh, Guthrie.
31°-32°: January 22, 1958, invested by *Oklahoma* Consistory, Guthrie.
32°, KCCH: October 19, 1981.
33°, IGH: elected September 30, 2005; coroneted by Ill. Joseph C. Jennings, 33°, Sovereign Grand Inspector General for Oklahoma December 11, 2005.
Grand Cross of the Court of Honour: August 17, 2019.

Scottish Rite Biography:
Brother Williams was raised a Master Mason in *Guymon* Lodge, No. 335, in Guymon, and made a Master of the Royal Secret in 1958 in the Valley of Guthrie. On October 5, 1967, Brother Williams affiliated with the Valley of Tulsa. He was elected a Knight Commander of the Court of Honour on October 19, 1981; on the Session of the Supreme Council of 2005 was elected a 33°, Inspector General Honorary and coroneted by Ill. Joseph C. Jennings, 33°, Sovereign Grand Inspector General for Oklahoma on December 11, 2005. Brother Williams is a generous donor of RiteCare, our Order's main philanthropic outreach to America. On August 17, 2019, Ill. Joe Allen Williams, 33°, received the Scottish Rite's highest honor, the Grand Cross of the Court of Honour.

Bibliography:
Archive of the Supreme Council, 33°, S.J.

2019

Randall Harold Wilson
Grand Cross of the Court of Honour at age 64 years and 15 days
Tenure present
Nomination by St. Louis, Missouri Scottish Rite Bodies

Born: August 2, 1955 – present
Pario Forensic Accounting

Progress in Scottish Rite Masonry:
4°-14°: April 20, 2007, invested by *St. Louis* Lodge of Perfection, St. Louis.
15°-18°: April 20, 2007, invested by *St. Louis* Chapter of Rose Croix, St. Louis.
19°-30°: April 21, 2007, invested by *St. Louis* Council of Kadosh, St. Louis.
31°-32°: April 21, 2007, invested by *St. Louis* Consistory, St. Louis.
32°, KCCH: October 15, 2011.
33°, IGH: elected August 21, 2015; coroneted by the Supreme Council, 33°, S.J., August 25, 2015.
Grand Cross of the Court of Honour: August 17, 2019.

Scottish Rite Biography:
Brother Wilson was raised to the Sublime Degree in *Bridgeton* Lodge, No. 80 at Saint Peters, Missouri and made a Master of the Royal Secret in April 2007 in the Scottish Rite Valley of St. Louis. Brother Wilson was invested as a Knight Commander of the Court of Honour in 2011, and four years later was coroneted a 33°, Inspector General Honorary. Brother Wilson strengthens his Orient and Valley by steady donations to the Missouri Foundation, Preservation Association, and TPAF Society. Ill. Randall Harold Wilson, 33°, on August 17, 2019, received the highest honor of the Supreme Council, 33°, S.J., the Grand Cross of the Court of Honour.

Bibliography:
Archive of the Supreme Council, 33°, S.J.

2019

Charles Danny Wofford
Grand Cross of the Court of Honour at age 72 years, 8 months, and 10 days
Tenure present
Nomination by Atlanta, Georgia Scottish Rite Bodies

Born: November 7, 1946 – present
Draftsmen

Progress in Scottish Rite Masonry:
4°-14°: June 1, 1974, invested by *Atlanta* Lodge of Perfection, Atlanta.
15°-18°: June 1, 1974, invested by *Atlanta* Chapter of Rose Croix, Atlanta.
19°-30°: June 1, 1974, invested by *Atlanta* Council of Kadosh, Atlanta.
31°-32°: June 1, 1974, invested by *Atlanta* Consistory, Atlanta.
32°, KCCH: October 17, 1983.
33°, IGH: elected October 21, 1991; coroneted by Ill. William M. Hutcheson, 33°, Sovereign Grand Inspector General for Georgia November 30, 1991.
Grand Cross of the Court of Honour: August 17, 2019.

Scottish Rite Biography:
Brother Charles Danny Wofford was Raised in *Winder* Lodge No. 333, in 1972. Two years later he petitioned to the Scottish Rite and on June 1, 1974, Brother Wofford received the 4°-32°, which were invested by the Scottish Rite Bodies of Atlanta. On October 17, 1983, he become a Knight Commander of the Court of Honour. On October 21, 1991, Brother Wofford was elected to 33°, Inspector General Honorary, and was coroneted November 30, 1991, by Ill. William M. Hutcheson, 33°, Sovereign Grand Inspector General for Georgia. Ill. Wofford serves as a Member and Degree Master of numerous Degree casts including 14°, 30° and 33°. He serves as a member of the Scottish Rite Hospital Child Care Committee and Georgia House of the Temple Development Committee. Ill. Brother Wofford has served in the highest offices of our Fraternity. He has been a mentor to many and an inspiration to all by his service. For all that, Ill. Charles Danny Wofford received his Grand Cross of the Court of Honour on August 17, 2019.

Bibliography:
Archive of the Supreme Council, 33°, S.J.
Archive of the Valley of Georgia.

2021

Glen Andre Cook, Sr.
Grand Cross of the Court of Honour at age 66 years, 7 months, and 20 days
Tenure present
Nomination by Salt Lake City, Utah Scottish Rite Bodies

Born: December 31, 1954 – present
Attorney

Progress in Scottish Rite Masonry:
4°-14°: April 22, 1994, invested by *Salt Lake City* Lodge of Perfection, Salt Lake City.
15°-18°: April 23, 1994, invested by *Salt Lake City* Chapter of Rose Croix, Salt Lake City.
19°-30°: April 23, 1994, invested by *Salt Lake City* Council of Kadosh, Salt Lake City.
31°-32°: April 23, 1994, invested by *Salt Lake City* Consistory, Salt Lake City.
32°, KCCH: October 4, 1999.
33°, IGH: elected October 6, 2003; coroneted by the Supreme Council, 33°, S.J., October 7, 2003.
Grand Cross of the Court of Honour: August 21, 2021.

Scottish Rite Biography:
Brother Cook was raised to the Sublime Degree in *Acacia* Lodge, No. 17, in Salt Lake City, and made a Master of the Royal Secret in 1994 in the Valley of Salt Lake City. Brother Cook received the rank and decoration of a Knight Commander of the Court of Honour on October 4, 1999, was coroneted a 33°, Inspector General Honorary on October 7, 2003, and received the highest honor of the Scottish Rite, the Grand Cross of the Court of Honour on August 21, 2021. Ill. Glen Andre Cook, Sr., 33°, served his Valley as a Wise Master of the Lodge of Perfection.

Bibliography:
Archive of the Supreme Council, 33°, S.J.
Image courtesy of https://www.avvo.com/attorneys/84121-ut-glen-cook-4459599.html

2021

Robert Oden Hanson

Grand Cross of the Court of Honour at age 72 years, 8 months, and 18 days
Tenure present
Nomination by Billings, Montana Scottish Rite Bodies

Born: December 1, 1948 – present
Businessman

Progress in Scottish Rite Masonry:
4°-14°: November 1, 1984, invested by *Billings* Lodge of Perfection, Billings.
15°-18°: November 2, 1984, invested by *Billings* Chapter of Rose Croix, Billings.
19°-30°: November 3, 1984, invested by *Billings* Council of Kadosh, Billings.
31°-32°: November 3, 1984, invested by *Billings* Consistory, Billings.
32°, KCCH: October 4, 1999.
33°, IGH: elected September 30, 2005; coroneted by the Supreme Council, 33°, S.J., October 4, 2005.
Grand Cross of the Court of Honour: August 21, 2021.

Scottish Rite Biography:
Brother Hanson was raised a Master Mason in *Ashlar* Lodge, No. 29, in Billings, Montana, and made a Master of the Royal Secret on November 3, 1984, in the Valley of Billings. He received the rank and decoration of a Knight Commander of the Court of Honour on October 4, 1994, was elected a 33°, Inspector General Honorary on September 30, 2005, and coroneted by the Supreme Council, 33°, S.J., on October 4, 2005. Brother Hanson served as Personal Representative to the Sovereign Grand Inspector General for the Orient of Montana, and as a Wise Master of the *Billings* Lodge of Perfection. On August 21, 2021, Ill. Robert Oden Hanson, 33°, received the highest honor of the Scottish Rite, the Grand Cross of the Court of Honour.

Bibliography:
Archive of the Supreme Council, 33°, S.J.

2021

James Dee Hardy
Grand Cross of the Court of Honour at age 71 years, 9 months, and 19 days
Tenure present
Nomination by Joplin, Missouri Scottish Rite Bodies

Born: November 2, 1949 – present
Certified Public Accountant

Progress in Scottish Rite Masonry:
4°-14°: April 2, 1993, invested by *Joplin* Lodge of Perfection, Joplin.
15°-18°: April 2, 1993, invested by *Joplin* Chapter of Rose Croix, Joplin.
19°-30°: April 3, 1993, invested by *Joplin* Council of Kadosh, Joplin.
31°-32°: April 3, 1993, invested by *Joplin* Consistory, Joplin.
32°, KCCH: October 4, 1999.
33°, IGH: elected September 30, 2005; coroneted by the Supreme Council, 33°, S.J., on October 4, 2005.
Grand Cross of the Court of Honour: August 21, 2021.

Scottish Rite Biography:
Brother Hardy became a Master Mason in *Fellowship* Lodge, No. 345, in Joplin. He joined the Scottish Rite Bodies of the Valley of Joplin and on April 3, 1993, became a 32° Master of the Royal Secret. On the Session of the Supreme Council for 1999 Brother Hardy was invested as a Knight Commander of the Court of Honour, and on October 4, 2005, coroneted by the Supreme Council, a 33°, Inspector General Honorary. Ill. Hardy served his Valley as Wise Master of the Chapter of Rose Croix, Director and Co-Chair of the Scottish Rite Foundation as well as member of the Audit Committee for this Foundation, also on several Valley committees, a member of Rose Croix Funeral Cast, and Rose Croix Maundy Thursday and Easter Sunday Cast. Brother Hardy twice was a recipient of the Orient Eagle Award. On August 21, 2021, Ill. James Dee Hardy, 33°, received the Scottish Rite's highest distinction the Grand Cross of the Court of Honour Currently Ill. James Dee Hardy, 33°, GC, serves his Valley as Treasurer of the Scottish Rite Foundation from 2017 and Personal Representative from 2012 to the Sovereign Grand Inspector General for Missouri.

Bibliography:
Archive of the Supreme Council, 33°, S.J.

2021

Richard Ross Polk
Grand Cross of the Court of Honour at age 81 years, 8 months, and 18 days
Tenure present
Nomination by Tulsa, Oklahoma Scottish Rite Bodies

Born: December 1, 1939 – present
Physician

Progress in Scottish Rite Masonry:
4°-14°: January 31, 1970, invested by *Tulsa* Lodge of Perfection, Tulsa.
15°-18°: January 31, 1970, invested by *Tulsa* Chapter of Rose Croix, Tulsa.
19°-30°: January 31, 1970, invested by *Tulsa* Council of Kadosh, Tulsa.
31°-32°: January 31, 1970, invested by *Tulsa* Consistory, Tulsa.
32°, KCCH: October 4, 1999.
33°, IGH: elected October 2, 2009; coroneted at Guthrie by Ill. Joseph C. Jennings, 33°, Sovereign Grand Inspector General for Oklahoma on December 13, 2009.
Grand Cross of the Court of Honour: August 21, 2021.

Scottish Rite Biography:
Brother Polk became a Mason in *Broken Arrow* Lodge, No. 243, in Broken Arrow. In 1970 he joined the Scottish Rite Bodies of the Valley of Tulsa and received the rank and decoration of a Knight Commander of the Court of Honour on October 4, 1999, was elected a 33°, Inspector General Honorary on the Session of the Supreme Council of 2009, and coroneted at Guthrie by Ill. Joseph C. Jennings, 33°, Sovereign Grand Inspector General for Oklahoma on December 13, 2009. Brother Polk supports many charities of his Valley among them RiteCare, Almoner Fund and Museum. On August 21, 2021, Ill. Richard Ross Polk, 33°, was elected to receive the Grand Cross of the Court of Honour.

Bibliography:
Archive of the Supreme Council, 33°, S.J.

2021

William G. Sizemore II
Grand Cross of the Court of Honour at age 63 years, 10 months, and 18 days
Tenure present

Nomination by Baltimore, Maryland Scottish Rite Bodies

Born: October 2, 1957 – present
Rear Admiral, U.S. Navy (Retired)
Grand Executive Director of the Supreme Council, 33°, S.J.

Progress in Scottish Rite Masonry:

4°-14°: November 20, 1992, invested by *Mithra* Lodge of Perfection, District of Columbia.

15°-18°: November 21, 1992, invested by *Evangelist* Chapter of Rose Croix, District of Columbia.

19°-30°: November 21, 1992, invested by *Robert de Bruce* Council of Kadosh, District of Columbia.

31°-32°: November 21, 1992, invested by *Albert Pike* Consistory, District of Columbia.

32°, KCCH: October 9, 1995.

33°, IGH: elected October 4, 1999; coroneted October 5, 1999.

Acting/Interim Deputy: for Mississippi: January 1, 2016 – December 31, 2016; for Kentucky: January 7, 2018 - December 31, 2018; for Wyoming: November 2, 2019 – June 19, 2020; for Hawaii and Guam: January 1, 2020 - February 11, 2020; for North Dakota: August 2, 2021 – November 3, 2021.

Grand Cross of the Court of Honour: August 21, 2021.

Scottish Rite Biography:

Brother Sizemore was a member of the Order of DeMolay, Jacksonville, Florida, which met at the Valley of Jacksonville in 1992 and 1993. He became a Master Mason in *Lynnhaven* Lodge, No. 220, Virginia Beach, Virginia, in January 1991, and transferred his membership to *Cherrydale* Lodge No. 42, Arlington, Virginia, in 1994. Brother Sizemore joined the Scottish Rite in 1992 when he became a 32° Master of the Royal Secret in the Valley of Washington, D.C. He is also a member of the Valleys of Corinth, Mississippi, Meridian, Mississippi, Alexandria, Virginia, and Baltimore, Maryland. He received the rank and decoration of a Knight Commander of the Court of Honour in 1995 and was coroneted a 33° Inspector General Honorary in 1999. In 2013 Ill. William G. Sizemore II, 33°, was appointed as the Grand Executive Director of the Supreme Council. One of his first tasks at the Supreme Council was to examine every aspect of the Supreme Council workflow, looking for ways to increase efficiency and effectiveness. During a few years of service Bro. Bill became more than just a manager; he became a leader of the Scottish Rite. For his outstanding accomplishments on August 21, 2021, the Supreme Council awarded Ill. William G. Sizemore II, 33°, the Grand Cross of the Court of Honour.

Bibliography:

Morris, S. Brent, 33°, Grand Cross. ADM Bill Sizemore Joins the Supreme Council Staff, *The Scottish Rite Journal,* 2013, January/February.

2021

Donald Ray Tapia
Grand Cross of the Court of Honour at age 85 years, 8months, and 2days
Tenure present
Nomination by Orange County, California Scottish Rite Bodies

Born: December 1, 1938 – present
Businessman / U.S. Ambassador to Jamaica

Progress in Scottish Rite Masonry:
4°-14°: October 20, 1966, invested by *San Bernardino* Lodge of Perfection, San Bernardino.
15°-18°: October 21, 1966, invested by *San Bernardino* Chapter of Rose Croix, San Bernardino.
19°-30°: November 5, 1966, invested by *San Bernardino* Council of Kadosh, San Bernardino.
31°-32°: November 5, 1966, invested by *San Bernardino* Consistory, San Bernardino.
32°, KCCH: October 6, 1991.
33°, IGH: elected and coroneted by the Supreme Council, 33°, S.J., October 3, 2001.
Grand Cross of the Court of Honour: August 20, 2021.

Scottish Rite Biography:
Brother Tapia was raised a Master Mason in *Havasu* Lodge, No. 64, in Lake Havasu, Arizona. He joined the Scottish Rite Bodies of the Valley San Bernardino in 1966, and became a 32°, Master of the Royal Secret on November 5, 1966. In 1972, Brother Tapia led the creation of the Santa Ana Scottish Rite Club. Serving as President of the nascent Club, he propelled the formation of a full-fledge Valley in Orange County, which received its Charter on October 16, 1979. Under the leadership of Brother Tapia, membership in the Valley rapidly grew to over 2,000 members. In 1991, he received his first Scottish Rite distinction, the Knight Commander of the Court of Honour, and on the Session of the Supreme Council, 33°, S.J., for 2001, he was coronated as a 33°, Inspector General Honorary. In the same, 2001, through considerable personal effort and sizable financial investment from Ill. Tapia, the Santa Ana Childhood Language Center was established. The Center has continued to grow, and Brother Tapia remains a member of the Board of Directors, Emeritus. On
August 20, 2021, Ill. Donald Ray Tapia, 33°, awarded the Grand Cross of the Court of Honour.

Bibliography:
Archive of the Supreme Council, 33°, S.J.
Archive of Orange County Valley.

2021

Donald Samuel Tennyson, Sr.

Grand Cross of the Court of Honour at age 85 years, 4 months, and 3 days
Tenure present
Nomination by Greenville, South Carolina Scottish Rite Bodies

Born: April 17, 1936 – present
Grand Master of the Grand Lodge of South Carolina – 1997-1999
Businessman

Progress in Scottish Rite Masonry:
4°-14°: April 12, 1961, invested by *Piedmont* Lodge of Perfection, Spartanburg.
15°-18°: April 13, 1961, invested by *Spartanburg* Chapter of Rose Croix, Spartanburg.
19°-30°: April 19, 1961, invested by *Bethlehem* Council of Kadosh, Charleston.
31°-32°: April 20, 1961, invested by *Dalcho* Consistory, Charleston.
32°, KCCH: October 18, 1971.
33°, IGH: elected October 17, 1977; coroneted by Ill. John I. Smith, 33°, Sovereign Grand Inspector General for South Carolina on December 3, 1977.
Grand Cross of the Court of Honour: August 21, 2021.

Scottish Rite Biography:
Brother Tennyson was raised to the Sublime Degree of Master Mason in *Drayton* Lodge, No. 360, at Spartanburg on September 27, 1958. On April 12, 1961, Brother Tennyson joined the *Piedmont* Lodge of Perfection at Spartanburg, where he was invested with 4°-14° Scottish Rite Degrees, on the following day he received 15°-18° from the *Spartanburg* Chapter of Rose Croix. The Degrees of the Council of Kadosh and Consistory he received on April 19 and April 20, 1961, from the Scottish Rite Bodies of the Valley of Charleston. On the Session of the Supreme Council for 1971 he was invested as a Knight Commander of the Court of Honour, and coroneted an Inspector General Honorary, 33°, on December 3, 1977. During his Masonic journey Brother Tennyson affiliated with the Valley of Greenville and the Valley of Rock Hill. Ill. Tennyson served his Valley as Venerable Master, worked in 8°, 18°, and 32° Degree Teams, served as Acting Grand Commander in the conferral 33° for North and South Carolina, was the Founder and Charter President of the Tri-County Scottish Rite Club at Rock Hill and the Founder and Charter President of the Pee Dee Scottish Rite Club at Florence. On August 21, 2021, Ill. Donald Samuel Tennyson, Sr., 33°, received the Scottish Rite's highest honor, the Grand Cross of the Court of Honour.

Bibliography:
Archive of the Supreme Council, 33°, S.J.
Image courtesy of https://www.scgrandlodgeafm.org/past-grand-masters.html

2021

Edwin Lowe Vardiman, Sr.
Grand Cross of the Court of Honour at age 93 years, 9 months, and 28 days
Tenure present
Nomination by Covington, Kentucky Scottish Rite Bodies

Born: November 19, 1927 – present
Attorney

Progress in Scottish Rite Masonry:
4°-14°: November 12, 1969, invested by *Louisville* Lodge of Perfection, Louisville.
15°-18°: November 13, 1969, invested by *Louisville* Chapter of Rose Croix, Louisville.
19°-30°: November 14, 1969, invested by *Louisville* Council of Kadosh, Louisville.
31°-32°: November 15, 1969, invested by *Louisville* Consistory, Louisville.
32°, KCCH: October 21, 1991.
33°, IGH: elected October 9, 1995; coroneted by Ill. John Moyers, 33°, Sovereign Grand Inspector General for Kentucky November 25, 1995.
Grand Cross of the Court of Honour: August 21, 2021.

Scottish Rite Biography:
Brother Vardiman was raised to the Sublime Degrees in *Covington* Lodge, No. 109. He joined the Scottish Rite Bodies of the Valley of Louisville and became a Master of the Royal Secret on November 15, 1969. In 1984 Brother Vardiman was affiliated with the Scottish Rite Bodies of the Valley of Covington. In this Valley he was invested as a Knight Commander of the Court of Honour in 1991; elected 33°, Inspector General Honorary on October 9, 1995, and coroneted by Ill. John Moyers, 33°, Sovereign Grand Inspector General for Kentucky on November 25, 1995. Brother Vardiman served his Valley as a Secretary from 2002 to 2010. On December 29, 2020, he was elected Director Emeritus of the Masonic Library and Museum Association of Covington Scottish Rite for his outstanding service to the Library Board. Ill. Edwin Lowe Vardiman, Sr., 33°, was elected by the Supreme Council to receive the Grand Cross of the Court of Honour on August 21, 2021.

Bibliography:
Archive of the Supreme Council, 33°, S.J.
Ed Vardiman, Director Emeritus. *Masonic Home Journal*, March 2021.

2021

Joe Weslie Vawters
Grand Cross of the Court of Honour at age 82 years, 5 months, and 1 day
Tenure present
Nomination by Hattiesburg, Mississippi Scottish Rite Bodies

Born: March 21, 1939 – present
Marine Info Specialist

Progress in Scottish Rite Masonry:

4°-14°: April 9, 2005, invested by *Hattiesburg* Lodge of Perfection, Hattiesburg.

15°-18°: April 9, 2005, invested by *Hattiesburg* Chapter of Rose Croix, Hattiesburg.

19°-30°: April 9, 2005, invested by *Hattiesburg* Council of Kadosh, Hattiesburg.

31°-32°: April 9, 2005, invested by *Hattiesburg* Consistory, Hattiesburg.

32°, KCCH: October 2, 2009.

33°, IGH: elected August 21, 2015; coroneted at Corinth by Ill. J. Keith Lundy, 33°, Deputy for Mississippi November 21, 2015.

Grand Cross of the Court of Honour: August 21, 2021.

Scottish Rite Biography:

Brother Vawters was raised to the sublime degree of Master Mason in *Moses Cook* Lodge No. 111, in Picayune, Mississippi, on June 10, 2004, and is a dual member of *Sherrard Byrd* Lodge, No. 353, Poplarville. In 2005 Brother Vawters joined the Scottish Rite Bodies of the Valley of Hattiesburg and became a 32° Master of the Royal Secret on April 9, 2009. He received the rank and decoration of a Knight Commander of the Court of Honour in 2009, was coroneted a 33°, Inspector General Honorary in 2015, and received the highest honor of the Supreme Council, the Grand Cross of the Court of Honour on August 21, 2021. Ill. Joe Weslie Vawters, 33°, GC, served his Valley as Venerable Master of the Lodge of Perfection, Commander of the Council of Kadosh, Master of Kadosh of Consistory, and as a Mentor for newly invested with the Scottish Rite Degrees Brothers.

Bibliography:

Archive of the Supreme Council, 33°, S.J.

2021

Johnnie Lee Wallace
Grand Cross of the Court of Honour at age 79 years, 7 months, and 18 days
Tenure present
Nomination by Fairbanks, Alaska Scottish Rite Bodies

Born: January 2, 1942 – present
Inspector

Progress in Scottish Rite Masonry:
4°-14°: November 5, 1983, invested by *Fairbanks* Lodge of Perfection, Fairbanks.
15°-18°: November 5, 1983, invested by *Fairbanks* Chapter of Rose Croix, Fairbanks.
19°-30°: November 5, 1983, invested by *Fairbanks* Council of Kadosh, Fairbanks.
31°-32°: November 5, 1983, invested by *Fairbanks* Consistory, Fairbanks.
32°, KCCH: October 16, 1989.
33°, IGH: elected October 6, 1997; coroneted at Ketchikan by Ill. Mitchell R. Miller, 33°, Deputy for Alaska.
Grand Cross of the Court of Honour: August 20, 2021.

Scottish Rite Biography:
Brother Wallace was raised to the sublime Degree in *Fairbanks* Lodge, No. 12, in Fairbanks, Alaska. He joined the Scottish Rite Valley of Fairbanks and became a Master of the Royal Secret on November 5, 1983. On February 4, 1997, Brother Wallace affiliated with Anchorage Valley, was invested with the rank and decoration of the Knight Commander of the Court of Honour in 1989, and coroneted 33° Inspector General Honorary at Ketchikan by Ill. Mitchell R. Miller, 33°, Deputy for Alaska on December 6, 1997. Ill. Jonnie Lee Wallace served as a Personal Representative and as a Secretary of the Valley, and in August 2021 was elected to receive the Grand Cross of the Court of Honour, the highest recognition given by the Supreme Council, 33°, S.J.

Bibliography:
Archive of the Supreme Council, 33°, S.J.
Archive of the Valley of Fairbanks.

2021

Earl Lloyd Wunder
Grand Cross of the Court of Honour at age 79 years, 4 months, and 17 days
Tenure present
Nomination by Tucson, Arizona Scottish Rite Bodies

Born: April 3, 1943 – present
Pharmacist

Progress in Scottish Rite Masonry:
4°-14°: November 18, 1971, invested by *Tucson* Lodge of Perfection, Tucson.
15°-18°: November 19, 1971, invested by *Tucson* Chapter of Rose Croix, Tucson.
19°-30°: November 20, 1971, invested by *Tucson* Council of Kadosh, Tucson.
31°-32°: November 20, 1971, invested by *Tucson* Consistory, Tucson.
32°, KCCH: October 20, 1975.
33°, IGH: elected October 21, 1985; coroneted by Ill. S. Barry Casey, 33°, Sovereign Grand Inspector General for Arizona November 30, 1985.
Grand Cross of the Court of Honour: August 20, 2021.

Scottish Rite Biography:
Brother Wunder was raised to the Sublime Degree in *Winslow* Lodge, No. 13, Winslow, Arizona, and made a Master of the Royal Secret on November 20, 1971, in the Valley of Tucson. He was elected a Knight Commander of the Court of Honour in 1975; on the Session of the Supreme Council, 33°, S.J., of 1985, Brother Wunder was elected a 33°, Inspector General Honorary, and on November 30, 1985, coroneted by Ill. S. Barry Casey, 33°, Sovereign Grand Inspector General for Arizona. On August 21, 2021, Ill. Earl Lloyd Wunder, 33°, received the Scottish Rite's highest honor, a Grand Cross of the Court of Honour.

Bibliography:
Archive of the Supreme Council, 33°, S.J.

Afterword

An aura of greatness and dignity surrounds the images of the Grand Crosses of the Court of Honour – the highest honor bestowed by the Supreme Council, 33°, SJ, USA, on Scottish Rite Brothers. This aura also emanates mystery; a mystery caused, sadly, by a lack of information regarding many of our Grand Crosses. For some, the primary source of information is a brief, "In Memoriam," published in *The New Age*, *The Scottish Rite Journal*, and the *Transactions* of the Supreme Council when the Grand Cross laid down his craft tools and departed for the Celestial Lodge. Regretfully, we must admit the fact that, until the present time, a list of Grand Crosses did not exist. Moreover, we did not know how many of them were elected to this honor from its establishment in 1870.

Yes. I am not mistaken! No attempt was previously made to compile a list and maintain it even for the sake of statistics. This inexcusable omission forced me to start to collect the names and information for the Grand Crosses whenever I came across them while working on different projects. Slowly, the amount of material grew bigger and bigger until it finally allowed me to make a preliminary plan on how I would design the future reference volume about our Grand Crosses.

My reference to the "special aura" around the Grand Crosses in the first paragraph was not in vain. One day, Ill. William Michael Alexander, 33°, G.C., approached my desk, asked for a list of all Grand Crosses, and explained that he dreamed of compiling a book about the recipients of this highest honor. Ill. Alexander did not believe me when I told him that there was no such list, so improbable was my answer. But a glimmer of hope was already there as I described to Ill. Alexander my intention to compile a list. I then invited him to participate in the project.

A few months later, the same word-by-word episode occurred in the library. One day, Ill. Shane Allen Harshbarger, 33°, G.C., approached my desk and asked for the list of the Grand Crosses. Ill. Harshbarger explained that he dreamed of compiling a book about the recipients of this highest honor. Again, so improbable was my answer, he did not believe me when I told him that there was no such list. However, as I had previously explained to Ill. Alexander, a glimmer of hope was already there, and I invited Ill. Harshbarger to participate in the project.

No doubt, I ruined a dream of both these Illustrious Gentlemen to compile their own volumes of the Grand Crosses, but their visits proved to me that this "aura" is calling for action. It was now time to right this historical oversight and convert my Grand Cross project to its active stage. Furthermore, both Ill. Alexander and Ill. Harshbarger agreed to participate in the project and invest in it their inspiration, thoughts, and knowledge. Both their names are on the title of the volume and embellish it by their highest Scottish Rite designation.

This project became a bold attempt to commemorate the 150th anniversary since the election of the first Grand Cross of the Court of Honour and servee as a symbolic groundbreaking ceremony for this collection of Scottish Rite Brothers who were elected by the Supreme Council, 33°, SJ, USA, for this honor. My hope is that the historians of the Orients and Valleys might pick it up, create a Hall of Fame of their Grand Crosses, design a special page on their website devoted to the Grand Crosses, or author a full-size book about the Scottish Rite Brothers from their Orients who were invested with this highest honor.

the Grand Crosses, or author a full-size book about the Scottish Rite Brothers from their Orients who were invested with this highest honor.

Realizing that each Grand Cross deserves a full-size biography to be written, thus resulting in hundreds of volumes, I restricted my task to a true list of the Grand Crosses, applying the cardinal rule of the Brotherhood, "on the level." One page for each Grand Cross became a reference volume consisting of 317 pages – the number of the Grand Crosses that the Supreme Council, 33°, elected on its Sessions, starting from the Session for 1872 to the present time. The primary sources of information for this compilation are archival materials of the Supreme Council, 33°, its data bases, *Transactions*, and Scottish Rite periodicals. In a few rare cases, other sources were used and mentioned in the text.

The most effective way to have a better understanding of this group of Scottish Rite Brothers who were elected to the highest honor of the Grand Cross is to use statistics. Statistics, as a science, provide the most reliable assessment of data on any given study. In our case it will help to view the topic from a few different perspectives that will allow us to be more informed about the status of the Grand Cross of the Court of Honour. Please note, that our statistics are not mathematically pure and have imperfections due to a few missing data points for a small number of Grand Crosses.

Statistics by Number of Grand Crosses Elected during Sessions:
The number of the Grand Crosses elected during the Session is a curious statistic, which might lead to further study of the duty of the Supreme Council to select the Grand Crosses. In 1870, the Committee on Jurisprudence prepared a Statute to establish a Court of Honour and recommended its adoption. The Statute consisted of sixteen paragraphs; paragraph seven stated the following: "The Supreme Council shall at the next, and every subsequent session, select from among the Knights Commanders, three Grand Crosses and no more." Eight years later the biggest revision of the Constitution and Statutes of the Supreme Council, 33°, was made almost with the same provision: "The Supreme Council shall at every regular session, select from among the Knights Commanders, not more than three Grand Crosses of the Court of Honour." The most lengthy and complicated direction on how the Supreme Council shall conduct the election of the Grand Crosses of the Court of Honour was given in the amended Statutes in 1890; however, the provision about the number of elected Grand Crosses in paragraph six is the same, but with some hint of uncertainty: "The Supreme Council may, at every regular session, select from among the Knights Commanders and other Masters of the Royal Secret not more than three Grand Crosses of the Court of Honour." The real statistic of the numbers of the elected Grand Crosses is the following: On the Session for 1872 – 1; on the Session for 1874 – 5; on the Session for 1876 – 24; on the Session for 1878 - only nominations for and no election of the honor of Grand Cross; on the Session for 1880 – 31; on the Session for 1882 – no nominations for and no election; on the Session for 1884 – 2; on the Session for 1886 – no nominations for and no election; on the Session for 1888 – 1; on the Session for 1890 – 1; on the Session for 1892 – 3; on the Session for 1893 - no nominations for and no election; on the Session for 1895 – 3; on the Session for 1897 – 2; on the Session for 1899 – 1; on the Session for 1901 – no nominations for and no election; on the Session for 1903 – no nominations for and no election; on the Session for 1905 – no nominations for and no election; on the Session for 1907 – 2; on the Session for 1909 – 1; on the Session for 1911 – 1; on the Session for 1913 – 1; on the Session for 1915 – no nominations for and no election; on the Session for 1917 – 1; on the Session for 1919 – 1; on the Session for 1921 – 2; on the Session for 1923 – 3; on the Session for 1925 – 3; on the Session for 1927 – 3; on the Session for 1929 – no nominations for and no election: on the Session for 1931 – no

nominations for and no election; on the Session for 1933 – 2; on the Session for 1935 – 2; on the Session for 1937 – 2; on the Session for 1939 – 1; on the Session for 1941 – 2; on the Session for 1943 – no nominations for and no election; on the Session for 1945 – 1; on the Session for 1947 – no nominations for and no election; on the Session for 1949 – no nominations for and no election; on the Session for 1951 – no nominations for and no election; on the Session for 1953 – 1; on the Session for 1955 – 1; on the Session for 1957 – 1; on the Session for 1959 – 1; on the Session for 1961 – 1; on the Session for 1963 – 2; on the Session for 1965 – 2; on the Session for 1967 – 2; on the Session for 1969 – 3; on the Session for 1971 – 3; on the Session for 1973 – 3; on the Session for 1975 – 3; on the Session for 1977 – 3; on the Session for 1979 – 1; on the Session for 1981 – 3; on the Session for 1983 – 3; on the Session for 1985 – 3; on the Session for 1987 – 5; on the Session for 1989 – 5; on the Session for 1991 – 16; on the Session for 1993 – 8; on the Session for 1995 – 5; on the Session for 1997 – 7; on the Session for 1999 – 12; on the Session for 2001 – 13; on the Session for 2003 – 14; on the Session for 2005 – 13; on the Session for 2007 – 9; on the Session for 2009 – 8; on the Session for 2011 – 11; on the Session for 2013 – 8; on the Session for 2015 – 10; on the Session for 2017 – 12; on the Session for 2019 – 12; on the Session for 2021 – 11.

Statistics by Orient:
Each Orient of the Supreme Council, 33°, SJ, USA, have Grand Crosses of the Court of Honour, but the numbers vary as follows: Orient of Alaska – 3; Orient of Alabama – 7; Orient of Arkansas – 6; Orient of Arizona – 7; Orient of California – 29, including Grand Cross Burl Icle Ives, who was nominated by the Orient of California and the Orient of Washington; Supreme Council, 33° for Canada – 1; Orient of Colorado – 7; Orient of the District of Columbia – 23; Orient of Florida – 11, including Grand Cross William Gene Sizemore, who was nominated by the Orient of Florida and the Orient of the District of Columbia; Orient of Georgia – 7; Orient of Guam (Okinawa and Guam) – 1; Orient of Hawaii – 3; Orient of Iowa – 12; Orient of Idaho – 2; Supreme Council, 33° for Ireland – 1; Supreme Council, 33° for Italy – 1; Orient of Japan and Korea – 6; Orient of Kansas – 4; Orient of Kentucky – 9; Orient of Louisiana – 14; Orient of Maryland – 9; Supreme Council, 33° for Mexico – 1; Orient of Minnesota – 10; Orient of Missouri – 13; Orient of Mississippi – 3; Orient of Montana – 2; Orient of NATO – 1; Orient of North Carolina – 9; Orient of North Dakota – 2; Orient of Nebraska – 6; Orient of New Mexico – 3; Supreme Council, 33°, NMJ, USA – 3; Orient of Nevada – 1; Orient of Oklahoma – 9; Orient of Oregon – 12; Orient of Panama Canal -2; Orient of Philippines – 1; Orient of Puerto Rico – 1; Orient of South Carolina – 7; Orient of South Dakota – 5; Orient of Taiwan and China – 3; Orient of Tennessee – 8; Orient of Texas – 20; Orient of Utah – 3; Orient of Virginia – 14; Orient of Washington – 5; Orient of West Virginia – 6; Orient of Wyoming – 3.

Statistics by Age on the Day of Election:
This statistic may be the most curious due to the question, "Does the age of the Scottish Rite Brother restrict him from election to the Grand Cross of the Court of Honour?" Our statistic gives an answer. The youngest Brother who was elected by the Supreme Council to the highest honor was an engineer from the Orient of Washington, Ernest Bertram Hussey. At the day of election, his age was 30 years, 10 months, and 16 days. Twelve more Scottish Rite Brothers received the Grand Cross at their 30th. Thirty-five Scottish Rite Brothers were elected to this Court of Honour at their 40th. Among them were well-known historical figures like King David Kalakaula of Hawaii and John Owen Dominis, Governor of Hawaii. Less known but recognizable by his last name was Luther Hamilton Pike, son of Albert Pike, and two most distinguished contemporary Brothers, Arturo DeHoyos and S. Brent Morris. Forty-six Grand Crosses received the honor at their 50th. Among them, Senator and Governor of West Virginia

Robert Carlyle Byrd; contemporary Scottish Rite Historians Robert Glenn Davis, Rex Richard Hutchens, and James Tracy Tresner, II; two Editors of *The New Age,* John William Boettjer and Aemil Pouler; two Ministers, one of whom is the Grand Chaplain of the Supreme Council, William Kenneth Lyons, Jr. Seventy-four Scottish Rite Brothers elected to receive the honor at their 60th. Among them the 38th President of the United States of America, Gerald Rudolph Ford; the Sovereign Grand Commander of the Supreme Council, 33°, NMJ, USA, John William McNaughton; and Sovereign Grand Commander of the Supreme Council, 33°, for Ireland, John Fitzhenry Townshead; founder of De Molay Frank Sherman Land; and two Rear Admirals, William Gene Sizemore and William G. Sizemore, II. Eighty-six received the honor at their 70th. Among them Bishop Carl Julian Sanders, FBI Director John Edgar Hoover, General Herman Nickerson, and actor Ernest Borgnine. Fifty-one Scottish Rite Brothers elected at their 80th. Among them Minister Norman Vincent Peale, philosopher Manley Palmer Hall, actors Burl Icle Ives and Gene Autry, microbiologist Russell Avery Cloud, pharmacist Harold Sigfried Stein, Jr., and scientist Fowler Marvin Edward. The most senior Brother elected by the Supreme Council to the highest honor was Colonel Richard Mahlon Ripley, who at the day of election was 94 years, 11 months, and 26 days. Six more Scottish Rite Brothers received the Grand Cross at their 90th.

Statistic by Occupation:

The range of the occupations of our Grand Crosses varies from Accountant to Veterinarian. The statistics of this field are approximate because I could not confirm the profession for some Grand Crosses. However, it is still remarkable and clearly exposes the main principal of the Fraternity, 'on the level." Among the most distinguished Scottish Rite Brothers are 9 accountants, 5 actors, 3 admirals, 13 agents from different industries, 5 Air Force servicemen, 3 architects, 1 archivist, 36 attorneys, 9 bankers, 1 barrister, 1 bishop, 2 bookkeepers, 1 bookseller, 3 brokers, 33 businessmen from different fields of industry, 1 cameraman, 1 carpenter, 1 chemist, 5 clerks, 5 colonels, 1 conductor, 12 congressmen, 2 contractors, 1 custom collector, 1 dean, 2 dentists, 2 directors of development, 1 FBI director, 1 dispatcher,1 draftsman 1 druggist, 5 editors, 8 engineers, 1 funeral director, 3 generals, 5 governors, 2 jewelers, 12 judges, 1 king, 1 landscaper, 1 librarian, 1 lieutenant-general, 2 major-generals, 10 managers from varied fields, 1 mathematician, 7 merchants, 1 microbiologist, 1 millwright, 4 ministers, 1 navy commander, 1 newspaper man, 1 obstetrician, 1 operator, 1 optician, 1 organist, 3 pharmacists, 1 philosopher, 1 photographer, 6 physicians, 2 pilots, 1 police officer, 1 postal service man, 1 President of the United States of America, 1 president of a university, 1 priest, 2 principals, 2 printers, 2 professors, 1 programmer, 3 publishers, 1 school director, 1 scientist, 8 secretaries of the Valleys, 9 senators, 4 Sovereign Grand Commanders of the different Supreme Councils, 33°, 1 shipbuilder, 1 school president, 1 singer 1 social worker, 6 surgeons, 2 teachers, 5 technicians, and 1 veterinarian.

Statistics by Tenure:

The length in tenure of possession of the Grand Cross varies widely, but the shortest-lived and longest-lived deserve specific mention in our statistical report. The briefest tenure of the Grand Cross was for U.S. Navy Admiral Eugene Alexander Barham, who held the highest honor one month and 21 days. Nine more Brothers were to hold the highest honor less than 1 year. As a captivating fact, it is interesting to point out here that only one Brother kept the Grand Cross for 33 years, our favorite and most significant number. This 33-year honor was held by an engineer from the Orient of Oregon, Philip S. Malcolm, whose tenure spanned 33 years, 3 months, and 5 days. Twelve more held the highest honor between 30 and 39 years. However, the lengthiest tenure of the Grand Cross goes to John Lonsdale Roper, businessman and Sovereign Grand Inspector General for the Orient of Virginia. Ill. Brother Roper was a Grand Cross for 45 years and 22 days. Four remaining Scottish Rite Brothers held the honor between 40 and 44 years.

Statistics by Date of Birth:
This area of statistics does not relate to any characteristic of the Grand Crosses as a group but gives us a sense of the passage of time. Two of the Grand Crosses were born in the 18th century. The first was Angel Martin, a merchant from Louisiana, who was born on December 24, 1792; and the second was William Leffingwell, a lawyer from Iowa, who was born on January 4, 1799. Born March 26, 1800, Major-General John Lawson Lewis from Louisiana was the first Grand Cross born in the 19th century. Another 109 Grand Crosses were born in the 19th century, and the last was General Lyman Louis Lemnitzer from Japan who was born on August 29, 1899. Louisiana Congressman Otto Ernest Passman, born June 27, 1900, was the first Grand Cross born in the 20th century. Another 198 Grand Crosses were born in the 20th century with the most recent being Ill. Shane Allen Harshbarger, 33°, G.C., born May 3, 1971.

Statistics by Lifespan:
The statistics by lifespan always call us to the spiritual Lodge of Sorrow to lament and pay tribute to the Brothers who laid down their craft tools. At the same time, it is a celebration of life well spent, and in the case of the Grand Crosses, this celebration is especially significant because these Scottish Rite Brothers reached the pinnacle of Scottish Rite achievement. The two longest-living Grand Crosses who passed their 100-year landmark are a principal from the Orient of Oklahoma, Samuel Arch Thompson, who was called by the Grand Architect at the age of 100 years, 8 month, and 22 days; and Senator James Strom Thurmond from South Carolina whose life span was 100 years, 7 months, and 21 days. Forty-four Grand Crosses had a life span ranging from 90 to 99 years. Eighty-six had a life span between 80 and 89 years. Forty-nine had a life span between 70 and 79 years. Twenty-four had a life span between 60 and 69 years. Twelve had a life span between 50 and 59 years. Lastly, one Grand Cross, Nevada Governor Charles Erastus Laughton departed for the Celestial Lodge at age 49 years, 9 months, and 12 days. Today, there are 95 Grand Crosses among us. Let us look upon their faces and see the aura of greatness and dignity.

Acknowledgements:
I could not conclude my short afterword without acknowledging a large group of Scottish Rite Brothers and colleagues who stepped in to help me in compilation of this reference volume. The conception of the "Grand Crosses of the Court of Honor: Concise Scottish Rite Biographical Dictionary" from the very beginning of its development was presented for approval to Ill. Arturo de Hoyos, 33°, G.C., head of the Department of History, Heritage, and Education. Ill. De Hoyos greeted this endeavor with great enthusiasm and appreciation. Moreover, Ill. de Hoyos let me use the images from the special historical archives of the House of the Temple for this project. The pictures of the Grand Crosses are an essential part of the project, but it became the most challenging and unachievable part of it. Despite all efforts to accumulate a full collection of the portraits of the Grand Crosses in their Grand Cross caps, alas, I failed. My hope is that the historians of the Orients will be willing to fill the gaps.

The Grand Executive Director of the Supreme Council, 33°, Ill. William Sizemore, III, 33°, (at the time not yet a Grand Cross) stepped into the project and generously offered his help as needed. Ill. William Michael Alexander, 33°, G.C., Personal Representative and Secretary of the Valley of Seoul, who called from Seoul, Korea, to check on me almost every week. Ill. Alexander, along with Ill. Shane Allen Harshbarger, 33°, G.C., Secretary of the Valley of Des Moines, became two pillars of strength for this project from its very inception to it submission to the publisher.

I had a strong temptation but did not dare ask Ill. S. Brent Morris, 33°, G.C., to assist with this project. Brent was the editor of my first bibliography back in 2002. Yes. For over twenty years, Brent and I worked together in the House of the Temple on projects both large and small. As the years pass by, my first impression of Brent continues to grow. For me, Brent was and still is the intellectual giant of the Holy Empire, and on top of this, for those who are not aware, he is the best magician I have ever met. Knowing how powerful these two combinations are and knowing that because of them Brent is in everlasting high demand, I lamented, but curbed my temptation to invite Ill. Morris to participate in this project.

On August 1, 2022, at 3:45pm, my editor Tammy and I submitted the project to the publisher. At almost the exact time, I received an email from Dr. Paul Rich, President of the Policy Studies Organization, and our publisher at Westphalia Press. Dr. Rich was asking for an update on the status of the manuscript and suggested that perhaps we could include "maybe some words from Brent." To further ensure that we received a response from Brent, Dr. Rich had copied him with the email message. At 5:49pm, Brent knocked at my email address door with this reply:

"Larissa, I would be delighted to make any contribution I can. The brief speech that I sent you was given at the 1999 Gala Banquet as a response on behalf of the new 33rds and the new GCs. The new Grand Crosses present were given their jewels by Fred Kleinknecht at the head table. I was last to be presented my jewel and then was asked to respond on behalf of the new Grand Crosses. The speech that I sent you was what I said. (I had been cautioned to be brutally brief.) It might be amusing to include my words."

Amusing! It truly was. Tammy and I immediately included Brent's words in the manuscript so that every one of you might also enjoy the filigree eloquence of Ill. S. Brent Morris, PhD, 33°, G.C.

Among others who contributed to this project, a lion's portion of the success belongs to Tammy Fannin, Director of Data Management and editor of this dictionary. With unrestricted devotion and professionalism, Tammy meticulously perfected, polished, and shaped the manuscript to the level of publisher requirements. Elizabeth A. W. McCarthy, Director of Strategic Communications and Linda Johnson, former Assistant to the Grand Executive Director, generously offered their collected images of the Grand Crosses, which increased the quality and quantity of the portraits. Ill. Richard L. Fletcher, 33°, former Executive Secretary of the Masonic Services Association and editor of my previous compilation, *The Constellation of the Brotherhood*, assisted by researching the *Transactions* for images of the Grand Crosses missed by me. Ill. Fletcher located one image that would never have been in the dictionary without his insightful intelligence.

I was also fortunate to have the assistance of library intern Maxwell Close. Max brought energy, enthusiasm, and skill to this project. He helped select the files of the Grand Crosses from the historical archives, scanned images, and assisted me as what seemed like an endless cross-referencing of data. It is my hope that in turn, Max gained valuable experience from this wide array of assignments.

For technical support, Jake Dean, Shawn Ortiz, and Jordan Wakefield of Electronic Data Solutions, Inc., expertly managed all technical issues that occurred throughout the project, not least of which was Jake's reformatting of the indexes and certain parts of the manuscript during the final stage.

The following individuals recognized the value of the project and responded to my call for Grand Cross images by putting aside their own business needs: Bret Alan Akers, 33°, Secretary in the Valley of St. Louis; John Robert Amidon, 33°, G.C., Valley of Phoenix; James Luigi Ammons, 33°, former Secretary in the Valley of Raleigh; Gregory Benavente Blas, 33°, Personal Representative and Secretary in the Valley of Agana; William Jerald Burfitt, 33°, G.C., Secretary in the Valley of Huntsville; Timothy Langdon Cable, 33°, Personal Representative in the Valley of Long Beach; Frank Keith Dreier, 33°, Secretary in the Valley of Covington; Donald Leigh Eames, 32°, KCCH, Secretary in the Valley of Austin; James Dee Hardy, 33°, G.C., Secretary in the Valley of Joplin; Reese Lenwood Harrison, Jr., 33°, G.C., Valley of San Antonio; Kenneth Paul Hill, 33°, Secretary for the Valley of Minneapolis; Jamieson Hopkins, 32°, KCCH, Secretary in the Valley of Orange County; Jeffrey Robert Horton, 33°, Secretary in the Valley of Tucson; Rex Richard Hutchens, 33°, G.C., Deputy in the Orient of Arizona; Robert Mitchell Julian, 33°, G.C., Secretary in the Valley of Boise; James Houston Morgan, III, 33°, G.C., Valley of Baton Rouge; Dean Matthew Resch, 33°, G.C., Personal Representative in the Valley of Panama City; Wesley Frederick Revels, 32°, KCCH, Secretary in the Valley of St. Joseph; Ronald Edward Siekert, 33°, Secretary in the Valley of Cheyenne; Ballard Lee Smith, 33°, G.C., Personal Representative in the Valley of Shreveport; Frederick Ashley Spicer, 33°, G.C., Secretary in the Orient of Maryland; Barbara Stein, spouse of the late Harold Sigfried Stein, Jr., 33°, G.C., Valley of San Francisco; Michael Alan Starkey, 33°, Secretary in the Orient of Alaska; William Fredrick Rook, 33°, Secretary in the Valley of Pasadena; Barbara Wunder, wife of Earl Lloyd Wunder, 33°, G.C., Valley of Tucson.

The success of this project belongs to everyone listed above who lent a hand.

Adams, George Ralph, 261	DC	Byrd, Harry Flood, 123	VA
Adkins, Alan Wayne, 269	VA	Byrd, Robert Carlyle, 141	WV
Alexander, William Michael, 309	Japan	Calhoun, Charles Galloway, 122	TX
Alger, Leonilo Trimania, 225	Guam	Camalier, Renah F., 120	DC
Allbritton, Joe Lewis, 200	TX	Carlin, Martin Dale, 160	DC
Allen, Benjamin Bentley, 82	TN	Carlson, Curtis LeRoy, 166	MN
Allen, Fred Edwin, 262	TX	Carnahan, Jan Baker, 288	AK
Amberg, Richard Hiller, 125	MO	Carr, George Richard, 229	IA
Amidon, John Robert, 239	AZ	Carter, James David, 127	TX
Andersen, Virgil Dale, 287	SD	Chadwick, Stephen Fowler, 11	OR
Anderson, Robert Bernerd, 121	TX	Clark, Graham Montague Jr., 138	MO
Ashby, Joseph Knight, 64	TX	Clarke, Bruce Cooper, 132	TX
Atchley, James Michael, 270	AZ	Clarke, Frederick William Jr., 240	AL
Atkinson, John Lee, 252	LA	Clarke, Louis Gaylord, 91	OR
Autry, Gene, 159	CA	Clift, James Monroe, 106	VA
Baddour, George Robert, 212	TN	Cloud, Russell Avery, 214	AZ
Bahr, Theo Justin, 297	ID	Coffield, William Arthur Jr., 271	SD
Baily, Elisha Ingrahamm, 32	OR	Collins, Harry Pryor, 69	IA
Barham, Eugene Alexander, 201	LA	Constine, Donald Ben, 189	CA
Bartholic, Clarence L., 164	CO	Cook, Glen Andre Sr., 321	UT
Beard, Pat, 226	TX	Cook, John William, 6	KY
Beasley. Stephen Henry, 33	AL	Cothran, William, 12	MS
Becker, Quinn Henderson, 180	LA	Craighill, Edward Addison, 35	VA
Bennett, Clement Wells, 7	DC	Cripps, Thomas, 13	LA
Berry, Larry Don, 310	AR	Crosby, Norman Lawrence, 193	CA
Betts, George Charles, 8	NE	Crowl, Thomas Smith, 289	OK
Bilirakis, Michael, 227	FL	Cummings, Daniel Emerson, 70	SD
Bilyeu, Woody Dee, 279	LA	Damon, John Fox, 36	WA
Boettjer, John William, 181	VA	Datnoff, Arthur Robert, 241	SC
Boles, Thomas Miller, 188	CA	Davis, Robert Glenn, 230	OK
Booker, Ferris Eugene, 263	FL	DeHoyos, Arturo, 264	TX
Borgnine, Ernest, 165	CA	Diele, Joseph Angelo, 215	Japan
Bower, Robert Farmer, 9	IA	Dillard, Robert Lionel, 190	TX
Brackin, Joseph Daniel, 228	AL	Dole, Robert Joseph, 182	KS
Brown, Charles T., 34	CA	Dominis, John Owen, 37	HI
Brown, Clyde Manford, 213	OR	Doolittle, James Harold, 161	CA
Brown, Joseph Thomas, 5	DC	Dormann, Henry Olaf, 202	DC
Bubb, Henry A., 152	KS	Downs, Walter Scott, 167	VA
Buist, John Somers, 10	SC	Drechsler, Robert Francis, 272	DC
Burfitt, William Jerald Sr., 298	AL	Earhart, Rockey Preston, 38	OR
Burke, Andrew, 145	CA	Edic, Curtis Manning, 299	NE
Burke, Haslett Platt, 110	CO	Ekholm, Peter Steven, 300	MN
Burlingame, James Orlin Sr., 253	MN	Ervin, Samuel James Jr., 135	NC

Leppo, Elmer Ray, 284	MD	Nunn, Richard Joseph, 22	GA
Levin, Nathaniel, 17	SC	Nunn, Samuel Augustus, 186	GA
Lewis, John Lawson, 18	LA	Olney, Harvey Allen, 23	VA
Lewis, Joseph Sidney, 153	OK	Olson, Lyndon L. Jr., 276	TX
Lewis, Roy James, 274	OK	Page, William Lewis, 24	VA
Liljegren, Glenn Howard, 267	MN	Passman, Otto Ernest, 124	LA
Lobingier, Charles Sumner, 97	PI	Patterson, William Donald, 293	Japan
Loker, William Napoleon, 19	MO	Peale, Norman Vincent, 154	NMJ
Lopez-Rivera, Jose R., 275	PR	Perdue, William Franklin, 294	VA
Lott, Chester Trent, 194	MS	Pike, Luther Hamilton, 52	DC
Lovell, Wood Wilson, 147	GA	Pitts, Glen Gordon, 305	TN
Lyons, Robert R., 207	VA	Polk, Richard Ross, 324	OK
Lyons, William Kenneth Jr., 220	DC	Poore, Benjamin Perley, 25	DC
MacGrotty, Edwin Balridge, 20	DC	Pouler, Aemil, 137	SC
Malcolm, Philip S., 75	OR	Powell, Fitzhugh Knox, 235	FL
Manners, Paul Eddie, 192	GA	Pratt, Irving Washington, 53	OR
Marcucci, John Ralph, 292	SC	Quick, Floren Lamont, 277	Japan
Marsellos, Michael Mihai, 285	CA	Ramos, Tomas E., 99	Mexico
Martin, Angel, 21	LA	Reinecke, William, 54	KY
Martin, James Grubbs, 245	NC	Resch, Dean Matthew, 316	FL
May, Wiley Odell, 144	TN	Reynolds, William Thomas, 55	CA
McCall, Abner Vernon, 169	TX	Rhodes, John Jacob, 142	AZ
McCamant, Wallace, 105	OR	Richey, Charles Robert, 187	DC/OH
McCarty, Chester Earl, 163	OR	Ripley, Richard Mahlon, 306	NC
McCullough, Theodor Wilson, 109	NE	Roberts, William Burchard, 111	MN
McCurdy, Horace Winslow, 128	WA	Rogers, Doyle Wayne, 247	AR
McMath, Sidney Sanders, 195	AR	Roome, William Oscar, 65	DC
McNaughton, John William, 304	NMJ	Roper, John Lonsdale, 30	VA
McPeake, Fred Wylie, 208	TN	Ruppel, Frank Centennial, 114	CA
Miller, Lester William, 268	CA	Ryan, William, 56	KY
Miller, Orville Gilbert, 51	MN	Salomon, Ezekiel, 26	LA
Miller, Raymond Wiley, 136	UT	Sanders, Carl Julian, 172	AL
Miller, Thomas Burchinal, 94	MT	Schaefer, William Donald, 155	MD
Mills, Wilbur Daigh, 133	AR	Schlessman, Lee Edwin, 221	CO
Montgomery, Alvin J. C., 234	TX	Schoonover, George L., 88	IA
Moore, Charles Henry, 246	WY	Schwengel, Frederic Delbert, 173	IA
Moore, William Henson, 170	LA	Sciubba, Elvio, 174	Italy
Morgan, James Houston III, 315	LA	Scott, William Abial, 85	ND
Morris, Brent Stephen, 209	MD	Sentelle, David Bryan, 257	NC
Moses, William Schuyler, 71	CA	Sherman, Buren Robinson, 57	IA
Nesbitt, Charles Alfred, 95	VA	Sherman, Edwin Allen, 78	CA
Newcomb, Charles Bailey, 118	NC	Shivers, Allan, 143	TX
Nickerson, Herman, 171	NC	Shupe, Robert Ned, 248	UT

Simpson, Alan Kooi, 175	WY	Watts, Robert Burnham, 131	CA
Simpson, Robert Edward, 98	NC	Wayne, Ralph Erskine, 296	TX
Singleton, William Reynolds, 58	DC	Webber, Charles Harrington, 238	OR
Sisco, Charles Thomas, 59	MD	Webster, Alfred Frederick, 101	Canada
Sizemore, William G. II, 325	MD	Weng, Tommy Fu-Hai, 250	Taiwan
Sizemore, William Gene, 176	FL/DC	Wick, Ned Elwin, 211	SD
Smith, Ballard Lee, 286	LA	Wilkins, Henry Philips, 251	CA
Smith, George Charles, 278	WY	Wilkinson, James Bernard, 223	VA
Smith, Richard Bruce, 307	LA	Williams, Joe Allen, 318	OK
Smith, Robert Mark, 27	GA	Willson, James McCrorry, 260	TX
Sorrells, Douglas J.,	AL	Wilson, Randall Harold, 319	MO
Spanos, Alexander Gus, 236	CA	Witcover, Hyman Wallace, 84	GA
Spicer, Frederick Ashley, 308	MD	Wofford, Charles Danny, 320	GA
Stafford, William Henry, 156	FL	Woodson, Isaac Thomas, 107	KY
Stanton, Joshua Otis, 28	DC	Woodward, Robert William, 224	NATO
Stassen, Harold Edwards, 196	MN	Wright, Eugene Allen, 179	WA
Stayton, Roland Thornton, 237	KY	Wunder, Earl Lloyd, 331	AZ
Stein, Harold Sigrfied Jr., 295	CA		
Streeper, Charles Schaeffer, 60	IA		
Tapia, Donald Ray, 326	CA		
Teets, John William, 222	AZ		
Tennyson, Donald Samuel, 327	SC		
Thomas, Rex David, 197	FL		
Thompson, Samuel Arch, 177	OK		
Thurmond, James Strom, 157	SC		
Tillis, Lonnie Melvin, 210	MO		
Tingle, James Manley, 258	AL		
Titus, Isaac Sutvene, 29	CA		
Townshead, John Fitzhenry, 61	Ireland		
Trachtenberg, Stephen Joel, 198	DC		
Tresner, James Tracy II, 199	OK		
Trumbo, Graves H., 158	WV		
Tumlin, Emmett Dolphin, 112	WV		
Vallery, George William, 100	CO		
Vardiman, Edwin Lowe Sr., 328	KY		
Vawters, Joe Wesley, 329	MS		
Waddell, Kenneth E., 178	MO		
Waggonner, Joseph David Jr., 134	LA		
Walker, Duane Erwin, 259	NM		
Walker, Earl Ernest, 249	MO		
Walker, Kephart Delwar, 62	WV		
Wallace, Jojunnie Lee, 330	AK		
Wallenstein, Henry, 90	KS		

Orient

Carnahan, Jan Baker, 288	AK	Tapia, Donald Ray, 326	CA
Johnston, Sidney Michael, 232	AK	Titus, Isaac Sutvene, 29	CA
Wallace, Jojunnie Lee, 330	AK	Watts, Robert Burnham, 131	CA
Beasley. Stephen Henry, 33	AL	Wilkins, Henry Philips, 251	CA
Brackin, Joseph Daniel, 228	AL	Brown, Charles T., 34	CA
Burfitt, William Jerald Sr., 298	AL	Hobe, George John, 47	CA
Clarke, Frederick William Jr., 240	AL	Moses, William Schuyler, 71	CA
Sanders, Carl Julian, 172	AL	Reynolds, William Thomas, 55	CA
Sorrells, Douglas J.,	AL	Ives, Burl Icle, 185	CA/WA
Tingle, James Manley, 258	AL	Webster, Alfred Frederick, 101	Canada
Berry, Larry Don, 310	AR	Bartholic, Clarence L., 164	CO
Gwatney, Harold Lloyd, 217	AR	Burke, Haslett Platt, 110	CO
Hammerschmidt, John Paul, 168	AR	Fenimore, Jerry Lee, 301	CO
McMath, Sidney Sanders, 195	AR	Greenleaf Lawrence Nichols	CO
Mills, Wilbur Daigh, 133	AR	Ingraham, Vernon Brown, 265	CO
Rogers, Doyle Wayne, 247	AR	Schlessman, Lee Edwin, 221	CO
Amidon, John Robert, 239	AZ	Vallery, George William, 100	CO
Atchley, James Michael, 270	AZ	Adams, George Ralph, 261	DC
Cloud, Russell Avery, 214	AZ	Bennett, Clement Wells, 7	DC
Hutchens, Rex Richard, 191	AZ	Brown, Joseph Thomas, 5	DC
Rhodes, John Jacob, 142	AZ	Camalier, Renah F., 120	DC
Teets, John William, 222	AZ	Carlin, Martin Dale, 160	DC
Wunder, Earl Lloyd, 331	AZ	Dormann, Henry Olaf, 202	DC
Autry, Gene, 159	CA	Drechsler, Robert Francis, 272	DC
Boles, Thomas Miller, 188	CA	Essex, Josiah, 39	DC
Borgnine, Ernest, 165	CA	Fowler, Marvin Edward, 184	DC
Burke, Andrew, 145	CA	Gibbs, James Bennet, 40	DC
Constine, Donald Ben, 189	CA	Holt, Alexander Hollenbeck, 68	DC
Crosby, Norman Lawrence, 193	CA	Hoover, John Edgar, 126	DC
Doolittle, James Harold, 161	CA	Ireland, William Morton, 3	DC
Hall, Manley Palmer, 151	CA	Kleinknecht, Christian Frederick, 129	DC
Head, Ralph Humphrey, 218	CA	Lyons, William Kenneth Jr., 220	DC
Herman, Arnold, 231	CA	MacGrotty, Edwin Balridge, 20	DC
Hervey, William Rhodes, 106	CA	Pike, Luther Hamilton, 52	DC
Hopkins, Edwin Carmi, 96	CA	Poore, Benjamin Perley, 25	DC
Houser, John Everett, 150	CA	Roome, William Oscar, 65	DC
Ladd, Frank Bacon, 92	CA	Singleton, William Reynolds, 58	DC
Marsellos, Michael Mihai, 285	CA	Stanton, Joshua Otis, 28	DC
Miller, Lester William, 268	CA	Trachtenberg, Stephen Joel, 198	DC
Ruppel, Frank Centennial, 114	CA	Richey, Charles Robert, 187	DC/OH
Sherman, Edwin Allen, 78	CA	Bilirakis, Michael, 227	FL
Spanos, Alexander Gus, 236	CA	Booker, Ferris Eugene, 263	FL
Stein, Harold Sigrfied Jr., 295	CA		

Orient

Hall, John Lewis, 140	FL	Dole, Robert Joseph, 182	KS
Jones, Jack H., 273	FL	Haggard, Forrest DeLoss, 162	KS
Kicklighter, Clayton James, 256	FL	Wallenstein, Henry, 90	KS
Kirby, James Hoyt, 266	FL	Cook, John William, 6	KY
Powell, Fitzhugh Knox, 235	FL	Hall Edwin Gilbert	KY
Resch, Dean Matthew, 316	FL	Head John Frazier	KY
Stafford, William Henry, 156	FL	Kopmeier, George, 86	KY
Thomas, Rex David, 197	FL	Reinecke, William, 54	KY
Sizemore, William Gene, 176	FL/DC	Ryan, William, 56	KY
Lovell, Wood Wilson, 147	GA	Stayton, Roland Thornton, 237	KY
Manners, Paul Eddie, 192	GA	Vardiman, Edwin Lowe Sr., 328	KY
Nunn, Richard Joseph, 22	GA	Woodson, Isaac Thomas, 107	KY
Nunn, Samuel Augustus, 186	GA	Atkinson, John Lee, 252	LA
Smith, Robert Mark, 27	GA	Barham, Eugene Alexander, 201	LA
Witcover, Hyman Wallace, 84	GA	Becker, Quinn Henderson, 180	LA
Wofford, Charles Danny, 320	GA	Bilyeu, Woody Dee, 279	LA
Alger, Leonilo Trimania, 225	Guam	Cripps, Thomas, 13	LA
Dominis, John Owen, 37	HI	Lewis, John Lawson, 18	LA
Holsomback, William Edwin , 282	HI	Martin, Angel, 21	LA
Kalakaula, David, 48	HI	Moore, William Henson, 170	LA
Bower, Robert Farmer, 9	IA	Morgan, James Houston III, 315	LA
Carr, George Richard, 229	IA	Passman, Otto Ernest, 124	LA
Collins, Harry Pryor, 69	IA	Salomon, Ezekiel, 26	LA
Grassley, Charles Ernest, 204	IA	Smith, Ballard Lee, 286	LA
Harshbarger, Shane Allan, 290	IA	Smith, Richard Bruce, 307	LA
Hoberg, Oscar Julian, 89	IA	Waggonner, Joseph David Jr., 134	LA
Leffingwell William, Edward, 1	IA	Gorgas, Ferdinand J. S. , 46	MD
Leffingwell, William , 16	IA	Ihle, Earl E. Jr., 242	MD
Schoonover, George L., 88	IA	Latrobe, John Hazlehurts B., 49	MD
Schwengel, Frederic Delbert, 173	IA	Leppo, Elmer Ray, 284	MD
Sherman, Buren Robinson, 57	IA	Morris, Brent Stephen, 209	MD
Streeper, Charles Schaeffer, 60	IA	Schaefer, William Donald, 155	MD
Bahr, Theo Justin, 297	ID	Sisco, Charles Thomas, 59	MD
Julian, Robert Mitchell, 314	ID	Sizemore, William G. II, 325	MD
Townshead, John Fitzhenry, 61	Ireland	Spicer, Frederick Ashley, 308	MD
Sciubba, Elvio, 174	Italy	Ramos, Tomas E., 99	Mexico
Alexander, William Michael, 309	Japan	Burlingame, James Orlin Sr., 253	MN
Diele, Joseph Angelo, 215	Japan	Carlson, Curtis LeRoy, 166	MN
Johnston, James Lynn, 243	Japan	Ekholm, Peter Steven, 300	MN
Lemnitzer, Lyman Louis, 130	Japan	Hugo, Trevanion W., 73	MN
Patterson, William Donald, 293	Japan	Johnson, Jerry James, 313	MN
Quick, Floren Lamont, 277	Japan	Laird, William Hayes, 83	MN
Bubb, Henry A., 152	KS	Liljegren, Glenn Howard, 267	MN

Orient

Miller, Orville Gilbert, 51	MN	Graham, Robert McCoskry, 4	NMJ
Roberts, William Burchard, 111	MN	McNaughton, John William, 304	NMJ
Stassen, Harold Edwards, 196	MN	Peale, Norman Vincent, 154	NMJ
Amberg, Richard Hiller, 125	MO	Laughton, Charles Erastus, 50	NV
Clark, Graham Montague Jr., 138	MO	Crowl, Thomas Smith, 289	OK
Garrett, Thomas Elwood, 15	MO	Davis, Robert Glenn, 230	OK
Goodman, Thomas Archer, 104	MO	Laws, Bobby Lee, 303	OK
Hall, Melvin Guy, 148	MO	Lewis, Joseph Sidney, 153	OK
Hardy, James Dee, 323	MO	Lewis, Roy James, 274	OK
Hinderks, Gary M., 291	MO	Polk, Richard Ross, 324	OK
Land, Frank Sherman, 119	MO	Thompson, Samuel Arch, 177	OK
Loker, William Napoleon, 19	MO	Tresner, James Tracy II, 199	OK
Tillis, Lonnie Melvin, 210	MO	Williams, Joe Allen, 318	OK
Waddell, Kenneth E., 178	MO	Baily, Elisha Ingrahamm, 32	OR
Walker, Earl Ernest, 249	MO	Brown, Clyde Manford, 213	OR
Wilson, Randall Harold, 319	MO	Chadwick, Stephen Fowler, 11	OR
Cothran, William, 12	MS	Clarke, Louis Gaylord, 91	OR
Lott, Chester Trent, 194	MS	Earhart, Rockey Preston, 38	OR
Vawters, Joe Wesley, 329	MS	Hopp, Carl William, 149	OR
Hanson, Robert Oden, 322	MT	Johnson, Walter Eugene, 302	OR
Miller, Thomas Burchinal, 94	MT	Malcolm, Philip S., 75	OR
Woodward, Robert William, 224	NATO	McCamant, Wallace, 105	OR
Ervin, Samuel James Jr., 135	NC	McCarty, Chester Earl, 163	OR
Exum, James Gooden Jr., 280	NC	Pratt, Irving Washington, 53	OR
Helms, Jesse Alexander, 219	NC	Webber, Charles Harrington , 238	OR
Martin, James Grubbs, 245	NC	Garrido, Donald Prieto, 203	PCanal
Newcomb, Charles Bailey, 118	NC	Kerr, Arthur Joseph, 233	PCanal
Nickerson, Herman, 171	NC	Lobingier, Charles Sumner, 97	PI
Ripley, Richard Mahlon, 306	NC	Lopez-Rivera, Jose R., 275	PR
Sentelle, David Bryan, 257	NC	Buist, John Somers, 10	SC
Simpson, Robert Edward, 98	NC	Datnoff, Arthur Robert, 241	SC
Guptill, Albert Brewer, 76	ND	Levin, Nathaniel, 17	SC
Scott, William Abial, 85	ND	Marcucci, John Ralph, 292	SC
Betts, George Charles, 8	NE	Pouler, Aemil, 137	SC
Edic, Curtis Manning, 299	NE	Tennyson, Donald Samuel, 327	SC
Falk, Robert Allan, 254	NE	Thurmond, James Strom, 157	SC
Furnas, Robert Wilkinson, 14	NE	Andersen, Virgil Dale, 287	SD
Keebaugh, James Wilmer, 206	NE	Coffield, William Arthur Jr., 271	SD
McCullough, Theodor Wilson, 109	NE	Cummings, Daniel Emerson, 70	SD
Graystone, Sean David, 216	NM	Johnson, Harold Keith, 146	SD
Hanna, Richard Henry, 93	NM	Wick, Ned Elwin, 211	SD
Walker, Duane Erwin, 259	NM	Fowles, Leighton Dudley, 311	Taiwan
Ford, Gerald Rudolph, 139	NMJ	Kao, Douglas, 255	Taiwan

Orient

Weng, Tommy Fu-Hai, 250	Taiwan	Perdue, William Franklin, 294	VA
Allen, Benjamin Bentley, 82	TN	Roper, John Lonsdale, 30	VA
Baddour, George Robert, 212	TN	Wilkinson, James Bernard, 223	VA
Frankland, Abraham Ephraim, 2	TN	Damon, John Fox, 36	WA
Jones, Daniel Howard, 283	TN	Hayden James Rudolph	WA
Lang, Elliot, 77	TN	Hussey, Ernest Bertram, 74	WA
May, Wiley Odell, 144	TN	McCurdy, Horace Winslow, 128	WA
McPeake, Fred Wylie, 208	TN	Wright, Eugene Allen, 179	WA
Pitts, Glen Gordon, 305	TN	Byrd, Robert Carlyle, 141	WV
Allbritton, Joe Lewis, 200	TX	Erwin, Willard Holt, 183	WV
Allen, Fred Edwin, 262	TX	Kapourales, Sam George, 205	WV
Anderson, Robert Bernerd, 121	TX	Trumbo, Graves H., 158	WV
Ashby, Joseph Knight, 64	TX	Tumlin, Emmett Dolphin, 112	WV
Beard, Pat, 226	TX	Walker, Kephart Delwar, 62	WV
Calhoun, Charles Galloway, 122	TX	Moore, Charles Henry, 246	WY
Carter, James David, 127	TX	Simpson, Alan Kooi, 175	WY
Clarke, Bruce Cooper, 132	TX	Smith, George Charles, 278	WY
DeHoyos, Arturo, 264	TX		
Dillard, Robert Lionel, 190	TX		
Gunner, Rudolph Edward, 67	TX		
Harrison, Reese Lenwood, 281	TX		
Hittner, David, 312	TX		
Kelly, John Edward, 244	TX		
McCall, Abner Vernon, 169	TX		
Montgomery, Alvin J. C., 234	TX		
Olson, Lyndon L. Jr., 276	TX		
Shivers, Allan, 143	TX		
Wayne, Ralph Erskine, 296	TX		
Willson, James McCrorry, 260	TX		
Cook, Glen Andre Sr., 321	UT		
Miller, Raymond Wiley, 136	UT		
Shupe, Robert Ned, 248	UT		
Adkins, Alan Wayne, 269	VA		
Boettjer, John William, 181	VA		
Byrd, Harry Flood, 123	VA		
Clift, James Monroe, 106	VA		
Craighill, Edward Addison, 35	VA		
Downs, Walter Scott, 167	VA		
Greenwood Frederick	VA		
Lyons, Robert R., 207	VA		
Nesbitt, Charles Alfred, 95	VA		
Olney, Harvey Allen, 23	VA		
Page, William Lewis, 24	VA		

Related Titles from Westphalia Press

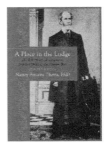

A Place in the Lodge: Dr. Rob Morris, Freemasonry and the Order of the Eastern Star
by Nancy Stearns Theiss, PhD

Ridiculed as "petticoat masonry," critics of the Order of the Eastern Star did not deter Rob Morris' goal to establish a Masonic organization that included women as members. Morris carried the ideals of Freemasonry through a despairing time of American history.

Brought to Light: The Mysterious George Washington Masonic Cave
by Jason Williams MD

The George Washington Masonic Cave near Charles Town, West Virginia, contains a signature carving of George Washington dated 1748. This book painstakingly pieces together the chronicled events and real estate archives related to the cavern in order to sort out fact from fiction.

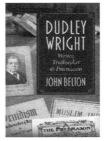

Dudley Wright: Writer, Truthseeker & Freemason
by John Belton

Dudley Wright (1868-1950) was an Englishman and professional journalist who took a universalist approach to the various great Truths of Life. He travelled though many religions in his life and wrote about them all, but was probably most at home with Islam.

History of the Grand Orient of Italy
Emanuela Locci, Editor

No book in Masonic literature upon the history of Italian Freemasonry has been edited in English up to now. This work consists of eight studies, covering a span from the Eighteenth Century to the end of the WWII, tracing through the story, the events and pursuits related to the Grand Orient of Italy.

The Great Transformation: Scottish Freemasonry 1725-1810
by Dr. Mark C. Wallace

This book examines Scottish Freemasonry in its wider British and European contexts between the years 1725 and 1810. The Enlightenment effectively crafted the modern mason and propelled Freemasonry into a new era marked by growing membership and the creation of the Grand Lodge of Scotland.

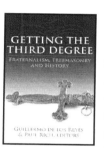

Getting the Third Degree: Fraternalism, Freemasonry and History
Edited by Guillermo De Los Reyes and Paul Rich

As this engaging collection demonstrates, the doors being opened on the subject range from art history to political science to anthropology, as well as gender studies, sociology and more. The organizations discussed may insist on secrecy, but the research into them belies that.

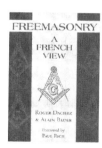

Freemasonry: A French View
by Roger Dachez and Alain Bauer

Perhaps one should speak not of Freemasonry but of Freemasonries in the plural. In each country Masonic historiography has developed uniqueness. Two of the best known French Masonic scholars present their own view of the worldwide evolution and challenging mysteries of the fraternity over the centuries.

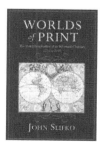

Worlds of Print: The Moral Imagination of an Informed Citizenry, 1734 to 1839
by John Slifko

John Slifko argues that freemasonry was representative and played an important role in a larger cultural transformation of literacy and helped articulate the moral imagination of an informed democratic citizenry via fast emerging worlds of print.

Why Thirty-Three?: Searching for Masonic Origins
by S. Brent Morris, PhD

What "high degrees" were in the United States before 1830? What were the activities of the Order of the Royal Secret, the precursor of the Scottish Rite? A complex organization with a lengthy pedigree like Freemasonry has many basic foundational questions waiting to be answered, and that's what this book does: answers questions.

Made in the USA
Coppell, TX
06 January 2023

10542662R20199